International Law and the Western Sahara Conflict

Juan Soroeta Liceras

International Law and the Western Sahara Conflict

Juan Soroeta Liceras

ISBN: 978-94-6240-137-2 (paperback)
ISBN: 978-94-6240-139-6 (hard back)

Cover image: Juan Soroeta Liceras, Refugee camp in Tinduf, Algeria

Published by:
Wolf Legal Publishers (WLP)
PO Box 313
5060 AH Oisterwijk
The Netherlands
E-Mail: info@wolfpublishers.nl
www.wolfpublishers.com

All rights reserved. No part of this publication may be reproduced, stored in a retrieval system, or transmitted in any form or by any means, electronic, mechanical, photocopying, recording or otherwise, without prior written permission of the publisher. Whilst the authors, editors and publisher have tried to ensure the accuracy of this publication, the publisher, authors and editors cannot accept responsibility for any errors, omissions, misstatements, or mistakes and accept no responsibility for the use of the information presented in this work.

© The author, 2014

"If the power of Morocco ends up subduing the Sahrawi people, that State, admirable for other things, will have obtained the saddest victory, a victory without honor, without shine, built on the lives and dreams of a people who wanted to live in peace on their land with their neighbors, all together, to make the continent a more habitable place" (José Saramago)

"I dream of an Africa which is in peace with itself" (Nelson Mandela)

A mi padre, *veinticinco años más tarde te sigo echando de menos*

A mi madre, *aunque estás detrás de la cortina del Alzheimer sé que sigues ahí*

A Marce, *mi querida e imprescindible compañera de fatigas*

I would like to expressly thank the Basque Government (Human Rights Directorate) for their financial support, without which, this book would not have been possible.

I would also like to thank my colleagues from the Department of Public International Law and International Relations at the University of the Basque Country / Euskal Herriko Unibertsitatea (especially my dear friend and colleague, Professor Francisco Javier López Quel), for the unconditional support they have given me throughout the years as I researched and worked on writing this book. Finally, I would like to thank those, who in one way or another (they know what I mean), have contributed to the final preparation of this book. I mean Arantza Chacón, Leire Elosegi, Timothy F. K. Johnston, Matthew G. Harding and professors Esther Lopez Barrero and Ana Salinas De Frías.

TABLE OF CONTENTS

MOST USED ABBREVIATIONS   V

PRESENTATION   VII

CHAPTER I
THE RIGHT OF PEOPLES TO SELF-DETERMINATION IN
INTERNATIONAL LAW AND THE WESTERN SAHARA CASE   1

1. The right to self-determination as a peremptory norm in International law   1
2. The right to self-determination as a fundamental human right   2
3. The right of self-determination versus territorial integrity   3
4. The right to self-determination and the "uti possidetis iuris" principle   4
5. The right to self-determination in relation to the prohibition to use force in international relations   5

CHAPTER II
THE BACKGROUND OF THE WESTERN SAHARA CONFLICT   9

1. The Spanish colonisation of the territory   9
2. The actions of the organs of the United Nations between Spain's accession (1955) and the Advisory Opinion of the International Court of Justice (1975)   14

CHAPTER III
THE CONSTITUTIVE ELEMENTS OF STATEHOOD AND THEIR
APPLICATION TO WESTERN SAHARA   35

1. Introduction   35
2. The territory: the legislative regulation of "Spanish Sahara"   37
3. The organisation of State power. Difficulties deriving from the existence of the POLISARIO Front-SADR (Sahrawi Arab Democratic Republic) binomial   43
3.1. General aspects   43
3.2. The status of the SADR in the International Community   49
    3.2.1. Scope and consequences of the recognition of the SADR   49
    3.2.2. The admission of the SADR to the Organization for African Unity   54

3.3. The legal status of the POLISARIO Front as a national liberation movement	66
4. The population. The census made by Spain	69
5. Conclusions: the statehood of Western Sahara	70

CHAPTER IV
THE ADVISORY OPINION OF THE INTERNATIONAL COURT OF JUSTICE OF OCTOBER 16, 1975 — 79

1. The formal questions	79
1.1. The question of the *ad hoc* judges	79
1.2. The question of competence	82
2. The core questions	93
2.1. Was Western Sahara *terra nullius* at the time of the Spanish colonization?	93
2.2. The question of the "legal ties" and the "ties of territorial sovereignty"	95
2.2.1. The Advisory Opinion	95
2.2.2. The declarations and opinions of the judges	100
3. Critical analysis of the advisory opinion of the ICJ	105

CHAPTER V
THE FAILURE OF THE DECOLONIZATION PROCESS — 113

1. The Green March	113
1.1. The Green March and the Security Council	113
1.2. The legal classification of the Green March	122
2. The Madrid Agreements	126
2.1. The content of the Agreements	126
2.2. The debate before the Fourth Commission	128
2.3 The Madrid Agreements and the General Assembly	130
2.4. Causes of nullity of the Madrid Agreements	135
2.4.1. The nullity of the agreements due to the subjects involved	138
2.4.2. The nullity of the agreements due to their purpose	145
2.4.3. The nullity of the agreements due their content and effects	150
2.5. The Madrid Agreements and Spanish Law	152
3. The Rabat Agreements of April 14, 1976	155

CHAPTER VI
THE PEACE PLAN (I). THE MISSION OF THE UNITED NATIONS
FOR THE WESTERN SAHARA REFERENDUM (MINURSO)   159

1. The reactivation of the process   159
2. Peacekeeping operations and the intervention of the UN in the electoral process   162
2.1 Main characteristics of the operations carried out by the United Nations and the main requirements that must be complied with for their implementation   164
2.2. Specific characteristics of the operations in which the United Nations have intervened in electoral processes and the principal requirements for their implementation   167
3. The Mission of the United Nations for the Referendum in Western Sahara (MINURSO)   170
3.1. The Pérez de Cuéllar phase: the Peace Plan   171
    3.1.1. Resolution 621 (1988) of the Security Council: the Special Representative of the Secretary General   171
    3.1.2. The report of June 18, 1990: the Peace Plan   172
3.2. The Butros Gali phase: towards the dismantling of the MINURSO   180
    3.2.1. The 1992 reports: the progressive reduction of the MINURSO   181
    3.2.2. The report of January 26, 1993: first suggestion of the dismantling of the MINURSO   182
    3.2.3. The "Commitment Proposal" of the Secretary General (of June 1, 1993). The stoppage of the identification process   185
    3.2.4. The report of 10 March 1994: specific proposals for dismantling the MINURSO   186
    3.2.5. The report of May 8, 1996: the dismantling of the MINURSO   192
3.3 The Kofi Annan Phase: the conclusion of the process of identification and the abandonment of the Peace Plan   194
    3.3.1. The Report of 27 of February 1997: the unblocking of the process   194
    3.3.2. James Baker, Special Envoy of the Secretary General   195
3.3. The Agreements of London, Lisbon and Houston   196
3.4. Lights and shadows of the MINURSO   199

CHAPTER VII
THE PEACE PLAN (II). THE PROBLEM OF CONSULTING THE POPULATION — 205

1. The Waldheim phase. The Report of the Visiting Mission of October 10, 1975 — 205
2. The Pérez de Cuéllar phase — 207
2.1. The Settlement Plan — 207
2.2. The Implementation Plan — 213
2.3. The Report of December 19, 1991. The modification of the identification criteria and the types of evidence admissible — 215
3. The Butros Gali phase — 225
3.1. The "agreement on the interpretation which must be given to criteria 4 and 5" (January 26, 1993) — 226
3.2. "The Compromise put forward to the two parties by the Secretary General" (July 28, 1993) — 228
3.3. Stalling of the process after "the flood of application forms at the last moment" (October 15, 1994). Decisions of the Secretary General (November 24, 1995) and his later disavowal by the Security Council -Resolution 1033 (1995)- — 230
4. The Kofi Annan phase — 235
4.1. The Houston Agreements. The unblocking of the identification process — 235
4.2. Reasons for the abandonment of the Settlement Plan. The "slips" of the Secretary General — 242
4.3. "The Framework Agreement on the Status of Western Sahara" (Baker Plan I) — 244
4.3.1. The powers of the "Sahrawi" organs in the Territory — 244
4.4. "The Peace Plan for the self-determination of the people of Western Sahara" (Baker Plan II) — 246
4.5. Farewell to the Baker Plan: Morocco is left on its own — 250
5. The Ban Ki-moon phase: The Mansahett round of talks, negotiations without a future — 253

CHAPTER VIII
CONSEQUENCES OF THE FAILURE OF THE DECOLONIZATION PROCESS: THE ILLEGAL EXPLOITATION OF NATURAL RESOURCES IN WESTERN SAHARA — 257

CONCLUSIONS — 275

BIBLIOGRAPHY — 285

MOST USED ABBREVIATIONS

A.C.D.I.	Annuaire Canadienne de Droit International
A.D.I.	Anuario de Derecho Internacional
A.F.D.I.	Annuaire Français de Droit International
A.J.I.L.	American Journal of International Law
B.Y.I.L.	British Yearbook of International Law
C.Y.I.L.	Canadian Yearbook of International Law
D.J.I.L	Denver Journal of International Law
E.I.L.R.	Emory International Law Review
G.A..	General Assembly
G.Y.I.L.	German Yearbook of International Law
I.&.C.L.Q.	International and Comparative Law Quarterly
I.L.C.	International Law Commission
I.C.J.	International Court of Justice
I.Y.I.L.	Italian Yearbook of International Law
J.A.L.	Journal of African Law
J.I.S.	Journal of International Studies
N.I.L.R.	Netherland International Law Revue
O.R.G.A..	Official Records of General Assembly
O.R.S.C.	Official Records of Security Council
P.L.O.	Palestine Liberation Organization
P.I	Política Internacional
R.B.D.I.	Revue Belge de Droit International
R.E.D.I.	Revista Española de Derecho Internacional
R.G.D.I.P.	Revue Générale de Droit International Public
R.P.I.	Revista de Política Internacional
S.A.Y.I.L.	South African Yearbook of International Law
S.C.	Security Council
S.G.	Secretary General
S.W.A.P.O.	South West African People's Organization
T.I.L.J.	Texas International Law Journal

PRESENTATION

With the celebration in August 1999 of a referendum for self-determination in the former Portuguese colony of East Timor, Western Sahara reached the unfortunate position of being the last major territory awaiting decolonization. The former territory of "Spanish Sahara", whose colonization by Spain began at the end of the nineteenth century still, well into the twenty-first century, finds itself on the list of Non-Self-Governing Territories and whose decolonization has been on the agenda of the United Nations since its creation, is currently experiencing one of its most critical and crucial moments. After its abandonment by Spain and the immediate occupation by Morocco and Mauritania, sixteen years of war and a peace process of nearly two decades, for the first time since 1975, nothing appears to suggest that the dark cloud hovering over the Territory is on the move, to finally allow it to hold its referendum for self-determination. Serious obstacles systematically put in the way by Morocco to block the successful completion of the decolonization process remain as impenetrable as the wall, which it built to divide the Territory in two. Indeed, in view of the data released by the MINURSO after the last phase of the identification process and upon which the census for the referendum would be based, and faced with the likelihood of a landslide triumph for the option of independence, this State decided to abandon the peace process by accusing none other than the United Nations of bias and thus left the conflict without hope of an end. Further, the French veto prevents the UN from acting within the scope of Chapter VII of its Charter to take responsibility in organising a referendum and imposing its results on the parties involved.

This work aims to help clarify the most important aspects of the conflict from a iusinternationalist perspective and to lay bare the reality of the powerlessness of the International Community when its norms are violated by a permanent member of the Security Council or one of its allies.

CHAPTER I

The Right of Peoples to Self-Determination in International Law and the Western Sahara Case

For over half a century, the right of peoples to self-determination has been one of the most debated and high profile issues in International law. The debate regarding the those peoples who may benefit from self-determination appeared to have been solved by stating that it was applicable to those involved in the decolonisation process, but the breakup of the Soviet Union, Yugoslavia and Czechoslovakia, the German reunification, the Irish conflict and the Quebec or Kosovo process have re-opened this issue and raised new questions regarding its scope. Nevertheless, the purpose of this study is not to consider the right of peoples to self-determination in the light of these situations, but instead to its application to a case which constitutes a classical example of a people subjected to colonial domination and his right to self-determination, namely the Western Sahara case. This concrete case should not therefore give rise to the doubts that might have arisen in recent years outside the strict context of decolonization.

It is necessary first to provide a brief introduction to the main characteristics of the right to self-determination of peoples in order to address the analysis of the Western Sahara conflict. This will enable the reader to better understand the fundamental content of a right that the population of this former Spanish colony have demanded for more than four decades.

1. The right to self-determination as a peremptory norm in International law

Despite not being a definitively answered question, as there is no case law on the matter, today most international doctrine admits that the right of peoples to self-determination enjoys a *ius cogens* status, meaning that it is a peremptory norm and is therefore compulsory for all States[1]. Although international case

---

[1] In this regard, article 19.3 b) of the Draft Articles on State Responsibility, approved at its first reading, stated that "in conformity with the norms of International law in force, an international crime may occur, in particular, (...) from a serious breach of an international obligation of essential importance for the safeguarding of the right of self-determination of

law has not yet ratified this condition, the *erga omnes* nature of the obligations that derive from this right has been expressly stated[2], and the sole logical consequence of this is that of the authority, belonging to all States, to claim that the right of peoples to self-determination has been infringed[3].

Importantly, it was recognised in international legislation in Resolution 1514 (XV) of the United Nations General Assembly, which established that "the subjection of peoples to alien subjugation, domination and exploitation constitutes a denial of fundamental human rights, is contrary to the Charter of the United Nations and is an impediment to the promotion of world peace and co-operation", and was re-affirmed in Resolution 2625 (XXV).

2. The right to self-determination as a fundamental human right

It is undisputed that the right to self-determination is a fundamental human right, since respect for this right of self-determination is considered to be a necessary condition of the existence and exercise of all other fundamental rights of human beings. In this regard, we should point out the well-known tendency of the United Nations to identify colonialism with *apartheid* and the practice of racial discrimination[4]. It is significant in this regard that International Covenant of Civil and Political Rights and the Covenant of Economic, Social and Cultural Rights include this right in its article 1[5]. As we

---

peoples, such as that prohibiting the establishment or maintenance by force of colonial domination" (First part of the Draft, approved by the International Law Commission on its first reading, *YILC, 1980*, Vol. II, Second Part, pages 29 et seq.).

[2] The Judgement of June 30, 1995 on the *East Timor Case* (Portugal versus Australia) expressly states the *erga omnes* effects of the right we are analysing, in the following terms, "In the court's view, Portugal's assertion that the right of peoples to self-determination, as it evolved from the Charter of the United Nations and from United Nations practice, has an *erga omnes* character is irreproachable. The principle of self-determination of peoples has been recognized by the Charter and in the jurisprudence of the Court; it is one of the essential principles of contemporary international law". *Cfr. East Timor (Portugal v. Australia), Judgment, I.C.J. Reports 1995*, par. 29, p. 102).

[3] GONZALEZ CAMPOS, J.D., SANCHEZ RODRIGUEZ, L.I., and ANDRES SAENZ DE SANTA MARIA, M.P., *Curso de Derecho Internacional Público*, 6th ed., Civitas, Madrid (1998): p. 334.

[4] As an example, in its Resolution 2105 (XX), approved on December 20, 1965, the GA declared that, "Fully aware that the continuation of colonial rule and the practice of apartheid as well as all forms of racial discrimination threaten international peace and security and constitute a crime against humanity".

[5] Art. 1.1. "All peoples have the right of self-determination. By virtue of that right they freely determine their political status and freely pursue their economic, social and cultural development".

shall see below, the deprivation of this fundamental right of self-determination is the origin of the human rights violations suffered by the people of Western Sahara.

3. The right of self-determination versus territorial integrity

The main debate concerning the right that we analyse, is not, therefore, focused on its existence and characteristics, but instead on its *scope of application*. United Nations doctrine regarding this question is conclusive when stating that it is only applicable in the context of decolonisation. The repeated references to the principle of territorial integrity of States contained in the principal General Assembly resolutions concerning this matter leave no doubts about this question[6]. Furthermore, when analysing this right, it must always be taken into account that States are the main players in International law so therefore it is not surprising then to limit the scope of the right only to peoples who do not form part of a constituted State, i.e. those peoples submitted to colonial or foreign domination. This thus excludes the possibility that the right to self-determination can be alleged against the territorial integrity of said States. There is thus no conflict between the right of peoples to self-determination and the principle of territorial integrity of States: the first is only applicable when a State has not been constituted in the territory in question.

Doubts about this question may be raised by other conflicts, but none arise from this Western Sahara case since the process is one of decolonization, a typical situation in consonance with the fundamental premises set out by the United Nations in this regard. In fact, the right of peoples to self-determination was promoted by the United Nations in order to provide the peoples subjected to foreign domination with an instrument that might enable them to free themselves from the colonial yoke.

Moreover, since Resolution 1514 (XV) established the international condition of colonial conflicts, the argument put forward by the colonial

---

[6] For example, Resolution 1514 (XV) states that "Any attempt aimed at the partial or total disruption of the national unity and the territorial integrity of a country is incompatible with the purposes and principles of the Charter of the United Nations". Likewise, Resolution 2625 (XXV) stated the following, "Nothing in the foregoing paragraphs shall be construed as authorizing or encouraging any action which would dismember or impair, totally or in part, the territorial integrity or political unity of sovereign and independent States conducting themselves in compliance with the principle of equal rights and self-determination of peoples as described above and thus possessed of a government representing the whole people belonging to the territory without distinction as to race, creed or colour".

powers and States that illegally occupy territories pending decolonisation stating that these are internal conflicts are not admissible. It is commonplace that these States accuse those who help peoples in their struggle for self-determination of meddling in their internal affairs, but as is clearly established in Resolution 2625 (XXV), the self-determination of peoples is not only a right of peoples, but is also a duty of States. They thus do not meddle in internal affairs, but merely comply with their international obligations.

4. The right to self-determination and the "uti possidetis iuris" principle

Closely related to this principle of territorial integrity is the principle of *uti possidetis iuris*, which is especially significant in the case of the former Spanish colony and is related to the principal obstacle that the peace process has repeatedly come up against, the drafting of the census. This is one of the most controversial principles of International law, given the narrow interaction between legal and political questions[7], which come into conflict over this issue. In virtue of the principle of *uti possidetis iuris*, or the intangibility of the frontiers established in the colonial era, border delimitations must be respected and maintained as they had been inherited from the former metropolis (frontiers drawn up in international agreements made by the former colonising owners and those deriving from the simple internal administrative divisions of the colonial powers). This principle, whose objective, in the words of the ICJ was "to preserve the conquests of the peoples who have struggled for their independence, and to avoid the breakup of a balance which would lead to the African continent losing the benefit of so many sacrifices (...) in order to survive, develop and progressively consolidate their independence", constitutes "a principle of general order necessarily linked to decolonisation wherever this might occur"[8]. In fact, it can be stated that the principle of territorial integrity is for States what the *uti possidetis iuris* principle is for peoples subjected to colonial or foreign domination.

As we stated above, when it comes to the Western Sahara conflict, the applicability of this principle is directly related to the question of the drawing up of census. Since the implementation of the Peace Plan, Morocco has intended to include three tribes which live in the south of Morocco into the census because it considered that these were native Western Saharans who

---

[7] YACKEMTCHOUK, R., "Les frontières africaines", *R.G.D.I.P.* (1970): p. 31.
[8] *Frontier Dispute, Judgment, I.C.J., Reports 1986*, p. 566 et seq., paras.25 and 23.

therefore had a right to decide on the future of their territory. However, they refused to accept the possibility that, in the event that the vote for independence won the referendum, the territory inhabited by these tribes could be included in the future Western Saharan State, alleging the necessary application of the *uti possidetis iuris* principle. This is an evident contradiction between the principle and the right of self-determination. We will return to this question below.

5. The right to self-determination in relation to the prohibition to use force in international relations

Another question which must be considered in this brief introduction to the right of peoples to self-determination, which we will return to later, is the question of the *legitimacy of the use of force* by the peoples subjected to colonial domination, which logically includes Western Sahara. There is almost unanimity in International law doctrine as regards the assertion of the compatibility of the prohibition of the use of force set out in article 2.4 of the United Nations Charter[9] with its use by the peoples subjected to colonial domination. Moreover, as mentioned before, in accordance with the aforementioned resolutions 1514 (XV) and 2625 (XXV) of the GA, the conflicts between the colony and the metropolis are no longer considered to be of an internal nature, but instead an international matter. Additional Protocol I to the 1949 Geneva Convention thus considers "armed conflicts in which peoples are fighting against colonial domination"[10].

As stated in the referred two International Covenants of 1966[11], the prohibition of the use of force against peoples subjected to colonial

---

[9] Article 2.4 of the United Nations Charter asserts the principle of the prohibition of the use of force in the following terms, "All Members shall refrain in their international relations from the threat or use of force against the territorial integrity or political independence of any state, or in any other manner inconsistent with the Purposes of the United Nations".

[10] Article 1.4 of the additional Protocol I of the Geneva Conventions of August 12, 1949, concerning the protection of the victims of international armed conflicts, adopted at the Diplomatic Conference on the Reaffirmation and development of International Humanitarian Law applicable to armed conflicts, held in Geneva on June 8, 1977, and which came into force on December 7, 1978.

[11] Article 1.3 of the Covenants on Economic, Social and Cultural Rights and on Civil and Political Rights, approved by the GA through its Resolution 2200 (XXI), of December 16, 1966, stipulates the following, "The States Parties to the present Covenant, including those having responsibility for the administration of Non-Self-Governing and Trust Territories, shall promote the realization of the right of self-determination, and shall respect that right, in conformity with the provisions of the Charter of the United Nations".

domination in their fight to exercise the right to self-determination has two relevant aspects. The first is that of a negative legal duty on States to refrain from taking any measures which might deprive peoples of the exercise of their right to self-determination, while the second is that of a positive legal duty on States to respect, promote and assist peoples in the exercise of this right, which may be provided individually and collectively[12]. It is more important that the United Nations must directly provide assistance to these peoples, as they have done in some cases. The assistance may be material as well as moral, and may include the delivery of war materials in order to allow the peoples to continue an armed fight, any type of political or economic assistance, and any other kind of assistance. Paragraph 2 of Resolution 2621 (XXV) states that "member states shall render all necessary moral and material assistance to the peoples of Colonial territories in their struggle to attain freedom and independence"[13]. As was stated above, the assistance that third party States might give to peoples fighting for their self-determination under no circumstances supposes interference in the internal affairs of the colonial power given that these are conflicts of an international nature.

The main consequence of the prohibition of the use of force when the territory of a people subjected to colonial domination is occupied is that of the negation of any legal effects of this occupation. Thus, Resolution 2625 (XXV) states that, "No territorial acquisition resulting from the threat or use of force shall be recognized as legal", a statement which will have special importance regarding the analysis of the attitude of Morocco in the Western Sahara conflict, and the obligation of the States not to recognise the annexation. In fact, no State has recognized this annexation.

A national liberation movement is the organized expression of the totality or a part of the population of a territory subjected to colonial domination which has the objective of self-determination or the independence of the territory, and has been recognized as such by the international community, conferring on it a privileged international status in order to achieve its objectives[14]. The recognition of the legitimacy of the Movement's fight within the system of the United Nations follows a specific process. In the first place, they are provided with assistance from UN organizations and institutions[15].

---

[12] In this regard, Resolution 2787 (XXVI) of the GA approved on December 6, 1971, points out that, "it is the duty of every State to contribute through joint and independent action to the implementation of the principle of self-determination".

[13] Resolution 2621 (XXV) of the GA, approved on October 12, 1970.

[14] GONZALEZ CAMPOS, J. D., SÁNCHEZ RODRÍGUEZ, L. I., ANDRÉS SAENZ DE SANTA MARIA, M. P., (2008): 913.

[15] BARBERIS, J.A., *Los Sujetos del Derecho Internacional actual*. Ed. Tecnos, Madrid (1984):

Chapter I

Subsequently these are recognized as "authentic" or "legitimate" representatives of their peoples, a recognition which is not related to specifically legal criteria (a consultation put to the population within the territory regarding the representative nature of one or other liberation movement is rather unfeasible), but to "a revolutionary or historical legitimacy and the *de facto* adhesion (or considered to be such) of peoples to its action"[16]. Representatives of the national liberation movements recognized by the UN have been invited to participate in various ways in UN subsidiary organizations, and some representatives have been given the status of observers. Resolution 3280 (XXIX) of the GA[17] invited representatives of national liberation movements recognized by the Organization of African Unity to participate "regularly" and "in their capacity as observers", in the interest of these territories, in the work of the main commissions of the GA and its subsidiary organizations involved in these matters, as well as in the other activities (such as conferences, seminars, etc.), held under the auspices of the United Nations. Among the national liberation movements recognized by the United Nations, two have enjoyed a privileged situation: the *Palestine Liberation Organization (PLO)* and the *South West African People's Organization (SWAPO)*, to which the GA attributed the character of permanent observers through Resolutions 3237 (XXIX)[18] and 31/152[19] respectively[20]. The *SWAPO* lost this condition when Namibia became independent, but the favourable treatment received by the PLO has improved over time, as its capacity to act in the United Nations broadened when it was granted a status practically equal to that of a State, which was without doubt an unprecedented event[21].

---

132 et seq.

[16] In the opinion of Thierry, the *de facto* representative nature of the national liberation movements accepted by the International Organizations may be considered to be an application of the principle of effectiveness. *Cfr.* THIERRY, H., "Cour Général de Droit International Public", *Recueil des Cours*, III, v. 222 (1990): 164.

[17] Resolution 3280 (XXIX) of the GA, approved on December 10, 1974.

[18] Among other things, this resolution points out the following: "1. It invites the PLO to participate in the sessions and work of the GA in the capacity of observer. 2. It invites the PLO to participate in the sessions and the work of all international conferences convened under the auspices of the GA in the capacity of observer. 3. It considers that the PLO is entitled to participate as an observer in the sessions and the work of all international conferences convened under the auspices of other organs of the United Nations".

[19] Resolution 31/152 of the GA, approved on December 20, 1976.

[20] As was pointed out by Suy, this position of the GA concerning the national liberation movements shows the perception of these movements a "future governmental authorities" responsible for the social and economic development of their peoples (SUY, E., "The status of observers in International organizations", *Recueil des Cours*, II, t. 160 (1978): p. 100).

[21] ORGA: *Press Release* GA/9427 and GA/778, both of July 7, 1998.

Turning now to the unique Western Sahara situation where there is the POLISARIO Front, a national liberation movement recognized by the United Nations as the sole and legitimate representative of the Western Saharan people[22] as well as the Saharan Arab Democratic Republic (SADR), a State which has been recognized by more than eighty States and is a full member of the Organization of African Unity, but whose existence has been ignored by the United Nations. Among the consequences of this complicated institutional web, the most surprising is that of the fact that despite Resolution 3280 (XXIX) of the GA granting the national liberation movements recognized by the Organization for African Unity the status of observers, the National Sahara Liberation Movement has not been recognized by the African organization given that it is a Member State itself.

Finally, among the benefits enjoyed by national liberation movements is the fact that their combatants have special protection under Humanitarian Law. As stipulated in Resolution 3103 (XXVIII) of the GA, which establishes the *Basic principles of the legal status of combatants struggling against colonial and alien domination and racist regimes*, considering the international nature of the armed conflicts they intervene in, the members of the national liberation movements have a privileged status as regards the treatment they receive in combat, and the Geneva Conventions of August 12, 1949 are applicable to them[23].

---

[22] Resolution 35/19 of the GA, approved on November 11, 1980.
[23] Paragraph 4 of Resolution 3103 (XXVIII) of the GA, approved on December 12, 1973.

CHAPTER II

THE BACKGROUND OF THE WESTERN SAHARA CONFLICT

1. The Spanish colonisation of the territory

The territory known today as Western Sahara, which until 1975, was known as "Spanish Sahara", has an approximate surface area of 266,000 km², with an Atlantic coast of approximately 1,062 kilometres and land borders amounting to 2,045 kilometres with three neighbouring countries: to the east and south with Mauritania (1,570 km.), to the north with Morocco (445 km.) and to the north east with Algeria (30 km.)[24]. As regards its sea frontiers, these involve Morocco, Mauritania and Spain.

The terrestrial layout of the frontiers was made through three consecutive agreements made by Spain and France between 1900 and 1912[25]: the agreement of June 27, 1900, which established the southern limits of the territory, the agreement of October 3, 1904, which extended the demarcation line to the north[26], and the agreement of November 14, 1912, which finally completed the delimitation. These frontiers, the negotiation of which was conditioned to the share out of territories between these two powers in Equatorial Guinea negotiated at the same time[27], were laid out with rulers[28]

---

[24] This data is included in the Report of the Visiting Mission that travelled through the territory in October 1975 (A/10023/Add.5, para. 117). For a complete analysis of the delimitation of the Western Sahara frontiers, *Cfr.* BROWNLIE, I., *African Boundaries. A Legal and Diplomatic Encyclopaedia*, London (1979): 147-158.
[25] On this question, *cfr.* HODGES, T., *Historical Dictionary of Western Sahara*, London (1982): XXI-XXII; GAUDIO, A., *Le dossier du Sahara Occidental*, Paris (1978): 108-113.
[26] This treaty created Spanish West Africa, which included Ifni and Western Sahara, under the command of a Governor General, in Ifni, and a Sub-Governor in the Sahara.
[27] *Cfr.* In this regard PORTILLO PASQUAL DEL RIQUELME, J., *Historia de los saharauis y crónica de la agresión colonial en el Sahara Occidental*, Doctoral Thesis (unpublished), Madrid (1991): 450 et seq.
[28] VILLAR, F., *El proceso de autodeterminación del Sáhara Occidental*, Fernando Torres, Valencia (1982): 17. As pointed out by this Spanish diplomat, there is one exception to the use of the ruler intended to leave the salt works of Iyil and the control of Galgo Bay. Moreover, as stated Gaudio, these frontiers were the result of a European "necessity" to clearly establish the limits of the territories which were under the jurisdiction of each of the

without taking into account the ethnic make-up of the territory, as happened in the rest of Africa. Thus, the borders did not reflect the social and geographic realities, but instead the relationship between the colonial powers of France and Spain in the region[29].

There was a further administrative division carried out by the Spanish colonial authorities, which established two zones: a northern zone, the "free occupation zone" of *Sakiet El Hamra*, which took in the territories between parallel 27°40' N (south of Cape Juby) and 26° N (south of Cape Bojador), and a southern zone, the colony of *Río de Oro*. The sea frontiers with Morocco, Mauritania and Spain have not yet been drawn as the dispute continues.

Unlike the colonisation carried out by other powers, such as France or Great Britain, the colonial enterprise undertaken by the Spanish Administration in North Africa was launched due to a nationalist desire of recuperation of "colonial grandeur" of the past rather than due to an interest in the wealth of the territory. Undoubtedly, this feeling inspired the Spanish campaign in northern Morocco in 1859 and 1860. However, the reasons were not pretensions to achieve sovereignty, but rather directly related to the colonialist ideas of the epoch, i.e. the attempt to keep the flame of a fading empire alive, and, to a lesser extent, due to the concern of the Spanish authorities for the security of the Canary Islands.

Commercial interest was also a factor in the Government decision to carry out the colonisation but until that time Spanish presence in Western Sahara was due only to private interest. The strong colonising progression of France in the north of Africa at the end of the XIX century led to Spain implementing mechanisms which enabled an successful colonisation of the territory, starting from the few agreements which private Spanish companies had made with the coastal authorities of Western Sahara. Spanish trading interests, previously supported by the Government with little enthusiasm, soon became public and were assumed by the State.

The first steps occurred two years after the Berlin Conference, "The Charter of the Colonization of the African Continent"[30], which was intended to establish the criteria for the colonisation of Africa. The *Canaries-African Fishing Company*, founded in 1876, had obtained the cession of the Dahla peninsula in 1881, through an agreement with the local tribal chiefs, and this would become the starting point for the colonising enterprise in Western

---

States involved in the "share-out", a need which did not exist for the inhabitants of the territory at the time. *Cfr.* GAUDIO, A. (1978): 108.
[29] BARBIER, M., *Le conflit du Sahara occidental*, Ed. L'Harmattan, Paris (1982): 44.
[30] MIAJA DE LA MUELA, A., *La emancipación de los pueblos coloniales y el Derecho Internacional*, 2th ed., Tecnos. Madrid (1968): 35.

Chapter II

Sahara. Shortly afterwards, these commercial interests were joined to the colonial ideology, which was substantially boosted by the Spanish Government. Due to pressure from Spanish companies who were trying to ensure that Spain became strongly involved in controlling fishing on the coast of Western Sahara and the concern of the Government regarding the growing interest of the European powers in this control[31], in November 1883, under the presidency of Cánovas del Castillo, the first Colonial and Commercial Congress was held in Madrid, during which the the *Sociedad Española de Africanistas y Colonialistas* (hereinafter, S.E.A.C.) was set up. Shortly afterwards, this organization requested that the Government occupy the bays of Río de Oro, Cintra and Santa María, with the Government committing to protect Spanish interests in the territory, but discarding the possibility of military intervention.

Due to the passive attitude of the Government, the S.E.A.C. decided to send an expedition to the Sahara led by Emilio Bonelli, who was the Director of the *Sociedad de Africanistas* at the time, aiming to reach an agreement with the Saharans in order to take possession of the territories whose official occupation it had requested. On November 28, de 1884, the S.E.A.C. finalised an agreement on "trade, mutual protection and friendship" in Dahla with the representatives of the population of Western Sahara. This agreement did not entail the transfer of the territories that the Company had requested to be occupied by the military, nor did it create a constitution of a protectorate (forms of colonisation expressly stipulated in the General Act of the Berlin Conference[32]). In fact, it was intended to be a concession of the territories in question to the S.E.A.C. as a rental. Undoubtedly, the reasons why the Saharans negotiated this and subsequent agreements with Spain, and only

---

[31] At the beginning of 1883 the Belgians are in the Canary Islands, attempting to cross to the coast of Sahara; the Germans have overtaken Spain in Cameroon, next to Guinea; the French are in Muni, and an English company, 'The North West African Mineral Concessions Limited, is trying to establish trade relations in Sakiet-al-Hamra. *Cfr.* PORTILLO PASQUAL DEL RIQUELME, J. (1991): 427.

[32] Chapter VI of the Act establishes the following: "Article 34. Any Power which henceforth takes possession of a tract of land on the coasts of the African continent outside of its present possessions, or which, being hitherto without such possessions, shall acquire them, as well as the Power which assumes a Protectorate there, shall accompany the respective act with a notification thereof, addressed to the other Signatory Powers of the present Act, in order to enable them, if need be, to make good any claims of their own. Article 35. The Signatory Powers of the present Act recognize the obligation to insure the establishment of authority in the regions occupied by them on the coasts of the African Continent sufficient to protect existing rights, and, as the case may be, freedom of trade and of transit under the conditions agreed upon".

with Spain, were related to its concern about the colonising progression of France, whose troops were moving north from their colony of Senegal and South West from Algeria. Considering the migratory nature of the Population of Western Sahara, this would have been verified by the inhabitants of the territory. On this point, the literal meaning of the text of the agreement is very significant as it definitively states that the relationship be exclusively between the Western Saharans and the Spanish[33]. The commercial interests of the Saharans are also very relevant. They were involved in an unprecedented commercial crisis due in main to the French advance in the south and the north east and to the reduction of the importance of the internal routes which had practically monopolised trade from the area of Senegal to North Africa.

Faced with the imminent Berlin Conference, the Spanish Government finally decided to take action and notified the other powers that it was assuming the protection of the territories that were the object of the Dahla Agreement. Finally, through the Royal Decree of December 26, 1884, starting from a number of agreements made with the local *Sheikhs*, Spain took the territorial strip between Cape Blanco and Cape Bojador "under its protection", and colonization papers were signed. Therefore, although it was gradual, the Spanish colonisation of the territory of Río de Oro began at the end of 1884[34]. Despite this, the assumption of the agreements made *ad hoc* by the Spanish

---

[33] "We stipulate in this (the reference is to Bonelli) and we will not admit subjects other than those from other Christian nations except for those who belong to the Spanish nation, whose person and goods we will respect and consider with respect and the consideration which corresponds to the religion of Our Lord and Master Mahomet, may blessing and peace be with him. (...) We satisfactorily declare this contract to be voluntary and advantageous for the good and the sincere friendship between Muslims and Spaniards. The Signatory Powers of the present Act recognize the obligation to insure the establishment of authority in the regions occupied by them on the coasts of the African Continent sufficient to protect existing rights, and, as the case may be, freedom of trade and of transit under the conditions agreed upon (...)". Both, the text and other interesting historical data, can be seen in the work of PORTILLO PASQUAL DEL RIQUELME, J. (1991): 432 et seq., and in TOMAS ORTIZ DE LA TORRE, J., "Sahara Occidental: ¿*Terra Nullius*? Algunas bases jurídicas de investigación", *Revista General de Legislación y Jurisprudencia*, June (1975): 563-605. It was then that Bonelli rechristened Río de Oro as Villa Cisneros.

[34] *Cfr.* GAUDIO, A. (1978): 101 et seq. The Decision of the ICJ of October 16, 1975 on Western Sahara pinpointed the commencement of Spanish colonisation in 1884, "the year in which Spain proclaimed its protectorate over the Río de Oro", therefore, it considered that the advisory opinion should analyse the legal status and the legal ties of the territory "as existed in the period which commenced in 1884" (*Western Sahara, Advisory Opinion, I.C.J., Reports* 1975, p. 38, para. 77).

companies when setting up in the territory[35] was slow and tentative. As was pointed out by Portillo, there was a clear reason why successive Spanish Governments were reluctant to assume these agreements: Spain and France were negotiating in Paris the delimitations of their possessions in the Sahara and in Guinea, and both States were bound by the commitment to restrain from undertaking any act which might harm the pending question[36].

As mentioned before, the Spanish colonisation of the territory would take many years before it could be considered fully effective. Wars that Spain was involved in at the end of the XIX century, which entailed the loss of colonial power in Cuba, Puerto Rico and the Philippines, the continual skirmishes occurring in the area with French troops, and the unstable internal situation of the country, aggravated by the assassination of Cánovas del Castillo, meant that this question remained at a secondary level in the priority interests of the Government. Thus, in the first two decades of the colonisation (1884-1904), the Spanish presence in the territory was limited to the establishment of a minimum military detachment whose mission was to provide military protection to the work of the fishing companies installed in the territory; during the fifty years preceding the time Spain joined the United Nations (1905-1955), this presence progressively increased although this took place extremely slowly; finally, once Spain became part of the UN, the Organisation began to put strong pressure on Spain to decolonize the territory. Thus, Spain continued moving counter clockwise from the time clock: while other colonial powers were then beginning to abandon their possessions in Africa, Spain was making its colonisation of the territory really effective, with a progressive exploitation of its natural resources, no longer limiting itself to fishing.

---

[35] This also involves the agreement signed by Bonelli on November 28, 1884, of the Agreement of May 10, 1886, and those signed on July 12, 1886, the last one of which is intended to ensure Spanish sovereignty over the territory.
[36] PORTILLO PASQUAL DEL RIQUELME, J. (1991): 454 et seq.

2. The actions of the organs of the United Nations between Spain's accession (1955) and the Advisory Opinion of the International Court of Justice (1975)

As discussed above, despite the fact that the Spanish colonisation of the territory began in the 1880's this was not effective until 1958[37], and by this time the contrary was taking place in the rest of Africa[38]. Unlike other colonial undertakings carried out by other States, which had had absolute freedom at the time, the Spanish authorities (once it joined the UN on December 14, 1955) faced the head on opposition of the United Nations which put strong pressure on Spain to include the territory among those territories listed in Resolution 66 (I) of the General Assembly[39] as Non-Self-Governing Territory, and to comply with the obligation of transmit information on this in accordance with article 73 e) of the Charter.

In February 1956, the Secretary General of the UN addressed the Spanish Government, requesting it to declare whether it administered any Non-Self-Governing Territories. Unlike to the majority of the new States which joined the UN together with Spain which were asked the same question, the Spanish Government did not give an answer until November 1958, when it converted the Department of Morocco and Colonies into the Department of African Outposts and Provinces, in accordance with the Decree of August 21, 1956[40], and declared that it did not possess any Non-Self-Governing Territories and considered its possessions in Africa as "Spanish provinces"[41].

---

[37] Criado states that, in the period from 1959 to 1975 "*all* the history of Spanish Sahara" took place, since, during this period, the colonisation began, was consumed and extinguished, and the most important events took place: the transformation of the traditional Saharan society, the economic exploitation of the territory and the unavoidable need for the Spanish Government to find a way out of the problem before the international Community. *Cfr.* CRIADO, R., *Sahara: Pasión y muerte de un sueño colonial.* Ruedo Ibérico, Paris (1977): 29. Similarly, DESSENS, P., "Le litige du Sahara Occidental", *Magreb*, vol. 71 (1976): 29.

[38] 1960 was known as "the year of Africa". In this regard, it should be remembered that only during the months of September and October 1960 the following countries became full members of the United Nations: Benin (Dahomey until 1976), Burkina Faso, Cameroon, Chad, the Ivory Coast, Gabon, Madagascar, Mali, Niger, Nigeria, the Central African Republic, Senegal, Somalia, Togo and Zaire.

[39] Resolution 66 (I) of the GA, approved on December 14, 1946.

[40] *Boletín Oficial del Estado (Official State Gazette)* No. 1338, of September 19, 1956.

[41] The Implementation Rules of this Decree date from January 10, 1958 whereby the General government of Spanish West Africa is reorganized, by virtue of which the Spanish possessions were divided into two: the provinces of Ifni and Spanish Sahara. Thus, the Government could state that "Spain don't have colonies, but only provinces. Morality and Law guided the plans of the Government in this regard". *Cfr.* SEVILLANO CASTILLO, R.,

CHAPTER II

Another major difficulty to the Spanish colonising policy in the Sahara was Moroccan independence, which meant that as soon as it became a State it made known its pretensions over the territory. On April 17, 1956 the Hispano-Moroccan Declaration was signed in Madrid. By virtue of this, Spain recognized the independence of Morocco[42] and also started the will of the Spanish Government "to respect the territorial unity of the Empire guaranteed in international treaties". This very unspecific drafting served as a pretext for the Moroccan authorities to extend their claims to the limits which would be called "the Grand Morocco" which, together with those territories which had in fact been broken off from this former colony (Ifni), included the territories of Spanish Sahara and Mauritania[43]. However, the international treaties referred to in the Declaration are those of 1910 and 1912, mentioned above, and by virtue of this, Spanish Sahara remained outside the concept of "territorial integrity of the Empire".

When the Moroccan Government demanded the reintegration of the territory of *Ifni*[44], Spain proposed that the ICJ make a pronouncement on this

---

Los orígenes de la descolonización africana a través de la prensa española (1956-1962), Madrid, Secretaría de Estado para la Cooperación Internacional y para Iberoamérica, Ministerio de Asuntos Exteriores (1986): 50.

[42] The complete text of the Declaration and the additional protocol of Madrid in CORDERO TORRES, J. M., *Textos Básicos de África*, Vol.II (1962): 152-155.

[43] Villar very graphically classifies this policy initiated by Morocco as an "amalgamation operation", and considered that the Spanish Government unwillingly contributed to this policy when it refused to admit that Ifni was Moroccan, a question which both parties linked to the Sahara question, although with opposing pretensions. As regards the question of the "Grand Morocco", at first claimed by the *Istiqlal Party* and subsequently by the Moroccan Government, *cfr.* VILLAR, F. (1982): 47 et seq. This "Grand Morocco" project would have been completely inoperative as from the return of Ifni and the recognition of Mauritania by Morocco, which took place on September 26, 1969, at the Islamic Summit Meeting held in Rabat. Diplomatic relations between both States was established in January 1970.

As pointed out by the Spanish Foreign Minister, Fernando Morán, at a meeting of the Senate Foreign Affairs Commission (February 3, 1983), nationalism is and has been a unifying component in Morocco, an integrating factor concerning Berbers, the inhabitants of the Rif, Arabs, and this nationalism materialises in an institution which is presented with a triple religious legitimacy, that of the Sultan, as the director of prayer, as Imam; a dynastic legitimacy of the Alawite monarchy (…) and a legitimacy operating on the basis of nationalism (…) Operation Sahara was an operation which united the Moroccan nation and which revived Moroccan nationalism". *Cfr. Actividades, Textos y Documentos de la Política Exterior Española*, Ministerio de Asuntos Exteriores, Madrid (1983): 99-100.

[44] As Professor Remiro reminds, the territory of Ifni was "granted in perpetuity to His Catholic Majesty", as payment for damage occurring in the Hispano-Moroccan war of 1860, through the Treaty of Tetuan, on April 26 of that year. *Cfr.* REMIRO BROTONS, A., *Territorio y Constitución de 1978*, Madrid (1978): 50. On the question of Ifni, *cfr.* MATHY, D.,

question. On this occasion, the Moroccan Government opposed the Spanish proposal as it considered that this was not a legal question on which the Court could make a pronouncement, but was a strictly political question. This point cannot be ignored as the positions adopted by both parties, both the Spanish proposal of submittal to the Court and the Moroccan reaction in opposition, would be reproduced almost literally, although in inverse terms, when the need for the Court to make a pronouncement on the Saharan conflict was put forward. This evidences the inconsistencies of the Moroccan Government as regards the future of the territory before and after its occupation.

When the positions of both parties were presented to the United Nations on October 14, 1957, the process took a new direction. On this date, the Moroccan representative before the Fourth Commission expressed the radical opposition of his Government to the proposal that the territories of Mauritania, Spanish Sahara and Ifni were included in the list of Non-Self-Governing Territories as it considered that these "constitute integral parts of Moroccan territory"[45], a position which undoubtedly gave rise to the Moroccan Fundamental Law of June 2, 1960, stating that "it is a national duty to act in order to recuperate territorial integrity and unity"[46].

Added to these Moroccan claims was a question that was proposed before the Fourth Commission by the Soviet, Bulgarian and Ukrainian delegations, and obliged the Spanish Government to seriously reposition the question of the decolonization of Saharan territory. The proposal made by the delegations sought to include the Canary Islands among the Non-Self-Governing Territories together with the territories of Ifni and Spanish Sahara. Undoubtedly, this proposal was determined by the fact that, on November 11, 1960, the representative of the Spanish Delegation at the United Nations, Félix De Lequerica, declared before the Fourth Commission that "the Spanish Government has decided to notify the Secretary General of the territories referred to in Chapter XI of the Charter", which evidently supposed the recognition that Spain administered Non-Self-Governing Territories[47]. Thus,

---

"L'Autodetermination de petits territorires revendiqués par des Etats tiers" (deuxième partie), *R.B.D.I.*, vol. XI, 1, (1975): 129-132.

[45] *ORGA:* A/C.4/SR.670.

[46] Article 13 of the Fundamental Law of the Kingdom of Morocco. Text in CORDERO TORRES, J. M., *Textos Básicos de Africa*, Vol.1 (1962): 197 et seq.

[47] *ORGA:* A/C.4/SR.1047. De Piniés points out that this Declaration did not have the consent of the Spanish Government, which also had to address strong criticism from the Government of Portugal, which saw how Resolution 1542 (XV) included only references to territories under Portuguese administration. These disagreements between the Spanish Delegation before the UNO and the Ministry of the Presidency reached its crucial point with

Chapter II

the Spanish Government finally approved the inclusion of Spanish Sahara and Ifni in the list of those territories to which Resolution 1514 (XV) applied, and, in return, it received the guarantee that the Canary Islands would be excluded from this list[48]. We shall consider later Spain's attitude when transmitting the information referred to in article 73 e) of the Charter[49].

---

the Three Party Madrid Agreements. *Cfr.* DE PINIÉS, J., *La descolonización del Sahara: un tema sin concluir*, Espasa-Calpe, Madrid (1990): 14 et seq.

[48] In May 1961, the Spanish representative before the UNO, De Piniés, mentioned three territories that were administered by Spain: Sahara, Fernando Poo and Río Muni. In November he also provided information on Ifni. *Cfr.* DE PINIÉS, J. (1990): 15.

The "*Canary Island Question*" which, from then on, would not be included in the agenda of the GA, but remained in the agenda of the OAU, returned to the international headlines with special acrimony after the adoption of a resolution by the Committee of the OAU in Tripoli (February 13 to 18, 1978). This resolution considered the Canary Islands to be an "African country to be decolonised", and gave financial and logistic support to the *MPAIAC* (Movimiento para la Autodeterminación e Independencia del Archipiélago Canario), which was recognized as a "Movement for the liberation of the Canary Islands". Although we do not intend to analyse the reasons why the question was again put to the United Nations and the OAU precisely at that time, we should stress the undoubted repercussions of the intransigent position of Algeria in favour of the "decolonization" of the Canary Islands, which might have been due to the irritation of the Algerian Government due to the transfer of the Administration of Western Sahara to Morocco and Mauritania and the ratification of the Hispano-Moroccan fishing treaty. *Cfr.* COLA ALBERICH, J., "Las Islas Canarias y los Acuerdos de la OAU", *Revista de Política Internacional*, n. 156, Marzo/Abril (1978): 65. Algeria had given political asylum to the head of the *MPAIAC*, Antonio Cubillo, in 1964, and gave cover to the broadcasts of the so called *Radio Canarias Libre*, which unsuccessfully called for the "the Guanche population to rise against the Spanish military occupation". The Spanish Congress reacted to these measures by approving a resolution that condemned the interference of the OAU in Spanish internal affairs (text in COLA ALBERICH, J., "Diario de acontecimientos referentes a España", *R.P.I.*, No. 156, Marzo/Abril (1978): 282 et seq.).

As concerns the fundamental issue, undoubtedly if we accept, as Carrillo Salcedo does, the self-determination of peoples and territorial integrity of the State are not antithetical terms and they are different concepts, applicable in today's International law in different cases and situations (*cfr.* CARRILLO SALCEDO, J.A., *Soberanía del Estado y Derecho Internacional*, Tecnos, Madrid (1969; 2nd ed., 1976): 58), the principle applicable in this case is that of territorial integrity, which is admitted by doctrine without discussion. On this point, it is very significant that Gros Espiell bluntly rejects the "right of secession" of the people of the Canary Islands when applying the conclusions of his report on the right of peoples to self-determination in the specific case of the Canary Islands. (GROS ESPIELL, H., "El caso de las Islas Canarias y el derecho a la autodeterminación de los pueblos", *R.E.D.I.*, Vol. XXXI, No. 1-3 (1978-1979): 13-24). In this report Gros never referred to the Canary Islands because "there is no resolution of the United Nations in this regard as it has not been considered to be a case pending (decolonization), and rightly so" (GROS ESPIELL, H., *El Derecho a la Libre Determinación. Aplicación de las Resoluciones de las Naciones Unidas*, Naciones Unidas, Nueva York, 1979, *ORGA: E/CN.4/Sub.2/405/Rev.1*, 15 et seq.). However, when he made a

Regarding a draft resolution, which listed the Non-Self-Governing Territories administered by Spain and Portugal[50], the Spanish Government accepted to transmit the information referred to in article 73 e) of the Charter. The Government of Morocco rejected the inclusion of Spanish Sahara and Ifni among the Non-Self-Governing Territories as it considered both of them to be part of the integral Moroccan territory[51]. The response of the GA to this

---

subsequent approach to the question, he put forward an argument based fundamentally on the following aspects: 1) If we admit that, "there is no foreign and colonial domination when a people lives freely and willingly within a legal state order, whose territorial integrity must be respected on condition that it is real and not a mere legal fiction, and in this case there is no right to secede, in the specific case of the Canary Islands there is no colonial or foreign domination as the Canary Islands, "historically and currently have been administered with no form of discrimination with regard to the rest of Spanish territory" (GROS ESPIELL, H., *ibid.*, p. 40). 2). There is no "Canary Island people", in the sense set out by the ICJ in its advisory opinion on Western Sahara, to which the right could be addressed as "the original population which the Spanish found in the XIV and XV centuries has almost completely disappeared and the population of the islands has been totally Spanish for centuries". 3) The islands form part of the territorial integrity of Spain because "there is no colony, the Canary Islands aren't historically, ethnically or culturally African". As regards the "Canary Island question, besides the works mentioned, *cfr.* DESSENS, A., "Le problème du Sahara Occidental", *Magreb* (1979): 73-86; FERNAUD, P., "La dimensión africana de Canarias", *Cuenta y Razón*, September, n. 24 (1986): 81-91; REMIRO BROTONS, A., *Las Cortes y la Política Exterior Española (1942-1976)*, Valladolid (1976): 42-52; RUIZ MIGUEL, C., *El Sahara Occidental y España: Historia, Política y Derecho. Análisis crítico de la política exterior española*, Dykinson (1995): 169 et seq. Even in 1990, in a complete study of the process that led to the independence of Namibia, Kamto referred to the Canary Islands as one of the African territories pending decolonization. *Cfr.* KAMTO, M., "L'accession de la Namibie à l'indépendance", *R.G.D.I.P.*, v. 94, 3 (1990): 579.

[49] Article 73 states the following, "Members of the United Nations which have or assume responsibilities for the administration of territories whose peoples have not yet attained a full measure of self-government recognize the principle that the interests of the inhabitants of these territories are paramount, and accept as a sacred trust the obligation to promote to the utmost, within the system of international peace and security established by the present Charter, the well-being of the inhabitants of these territories, and, to this end: (...) e) to transmit regularly to the Secretary-General for information purposes, subject to such limitation as security and constitutional considerations may require, statistical and other information of a technical nature relating to economic, social, and educational conditions in the territories for which they are respectively responsible other than those territories to which Chapters XII and XIII apply".

[50] *ORGA: Fifteenth period of sessions*, A/C4/SR.1038 n.27.

[51] *ORGA: Fifteenth period of sessions*, A/C.4/SR.1046, n. 39. In this regard, it should be pointed out that the concept of territorial integrity referred to by Morocco dos not coincide with the concept drafted by the doctrine of the United Nations which, as Miaja de la Muela reminds, is a "concept based on the effectiveness of power and, so, identified with the

question was the adoption of a resolution, which cleared up the situation of the territories under Portuguese administration, and left the situation of those administered by Spain open. Resolution 1542 (XV)[52] listed the territories administered by Portugal and which the Assembly considered to be non-self-governing, but avoided doing this with regard to Spain and restricted itself to pointing out its "satisfaction" at the declaration made by Spain that it was prepared to transmit information to the General Assembly, in accord with what is stipulated in Chapter XI of the Charter.

The approval of the most important decolonising resolutions made by the General Assembly in the course of 1960: Resolutions 1514 (XV) and 1541 (XV), changed the issue and the Moroccan Government took advantage of this to extend its claims to the territories that,

> "Always belonged to Morocco and are under foreign occupation: Mauritania, Sidi Ifni, Sakiet El Hamra, Ceuta and Melilla, (...) which must return to Moroccan sovereignty for political, legal and moral reasons, as well as in the interest of good relations with Spain"[53].

The first resolution of the Committee over the territories of Spanish Sahara and Ifni, approved in 1964[54], which "regretted" the Spanish delay in applying Resolution 1514 (XV), was followed a year later by another GA resolution, 2072 (XX), which, for the first time, asked the Spanish Government "to immediately take the measures for the liberation from colonial domination of the territories". It is surprising that this resolution does not contain the usual reference to the right to self-determination and independence. Despite this point, the most controversial question in the resolution was the request for the Spanish Government "to undertake negotiations on the problems related to

---

integrity of the territories belonging to each State". *Cfr.* MIAJA DE LA MUELA, A. (1968): p. 111.

[52] Resolution 1542 (XV) of the GA, approved on December 16, 1960.

[53] *ORGA:* A/C.4/SR.1005. The intervention of the Moroccan delegate before the Fourth Commission was supported by Saudi Arabia, Syria, Libya, and, very significantly, by Indonesia, which was claiming sovereignty over East Timor at the time. As pointed out by Miaja de la Muela, the Spanish attitude consisting of the denial that it was administering Non-Self-Governing Territories, together with a similar attitude of Portugal, gave rise to the approval of Resolution 1541 (XV). *Cfr.* MIAJA DE LA MUELA, A., "La descolonización en la Organización de las Naciones Unidas", in the collective work *ONU Año XX (1946-1966)*, Madrid (1966): 306.

[54] *ORGA: Nineteenth period of sessions, Annexes,* Annex No. 8, 1st part, (A/5800/Rev. 1), Chapter IX, No. 112.

sovereignty presented by these two Territories"[55], mainly because it does not state who had to be the intermediary with Spain (it should be remembered that not only Morocco had claims on Western Sahara). Furthermore, as it would become evident with the passage of time, the joint treatment of the two matters, Spanish Sahara and Ifni, could only complicate the situation[56].

On the next occasion that the Special Committee dealt with the question, the Government of Morocco made a substantial change to its approach as, although up to that time it had held that the territories of Spanish Sahara and Ifni must purely and simply "be returned", from then on it proposed the independence of both territories, trusting that "when the Moroccan populations" of these territories were masters of their destiny, they would choose unification with the Kingdom of Morocco[57]. However, the Moroccan representation specified to the Committee that, under no circumstances should this pronouncement be interpreted as a renouncement of its rights over Spanish Sahara, a statement that was hardly compatible with the aforementioned proposal of independence[58]. This approach was also shared by Mauritania, which had, likewise, held territorial claims over Spanish Sahara,

---

[55] Resolution 2072 (XX) of the GA, approved on December 16, 1965 with the abstention of Spain and Portugal.

[56] As was pointed out by Bontems, the joint treatment of the two territories "is unfortunate as they have different statutes and historical origins", and "this synthesises all the mistakes made during a decade will overshadow the Western Sahara dossier". *Cfr.* BONTEMS, C., *La guerre du Sahara Occidental*, Presses Universitaires de France, Paris (1984): 88.

[57] The Moroccan representative before the "Committee of 24" stated that "give that their liberation through negotiations and in accord with the formula of pure and simple restitution to Morocco does not seem to be accepted at the present time by the Government of Madrid, the Moroccan Government proposes they (Western Sahara and Ifni) be granted independence as soon as possible" (*ORGA*: A/AC.109/SR.436). As stated by Villar, the main objective of the change of approach by the Moroccan Government would be to increase international pressure on Madrid, which, in the light of this situation, would choose a bilateral problem rather than the independence of the territory. Undoubtedly, the primary objective of the Moroccan Government was to render the question bilateral so that, just as occurred with Ifni, Spain would negotiate the integration of the territory directly with Morocco. This policy which admitted the virtual independence of the territory was risky, but was well directed because at that time the position of the Spanish Ministry of the Presidency could be formulated as follows: "the Sahara for Morocco rather than independent". The failure of this offensive of the Government of Morocco was due to it being premature rather than mistaken. In short, (on June 10, 1966) Morocco expressly proposed the bilateral negotiation of the future of the Sahara, a proposal that was rejected by the Spanish Government (*cfr.* VILLAR, F. (1982): 113 and 115).

[58] *ORGA*: A/AC.109/SR.436.

although its representative specified that the territory should be "completely independent of Spain, but also of Morocco"[59].

As from 1966 the positions of the States involved in the conflict were clearly established. Thus, while Algeria (which intervened before the Special Committee for the first time) and Mauritania demanded that the population of the territory exercise its right to self-determination "under the supervision of international observers", Morocco held that "if the Special Committee preferred the formula of self-determination, Morocco would not object to this"[60], subject to the requirement that Spain complied with three conditions: the withdrawal of its army from the territory under international supervision, the stoppage of organised immigration of Spaniards to the territory, and the authorization for the return of all the refugees. In addition, Morocco demanded to participate in the negotiations for the exercise of the right to self-determination. As we will see below, the passage of time will come to show the Moroccan contradictions since when it negotiated the Peace Plan it opposed the withdrawal of its army, the stoppage of organized Moroccan immigration and the return of Saharan refugees. Moreover, the Spanish Government stated that it was carrying out all the preparations required for the Saharan people to exercise the right of self-determination "with no type of pressure"[61].

Up to this time, following the proposal of the Special Committee[62], the processes of Spanish Sahara and Ifni had progressed in parallel; however, Resolution 2229 (XXI)[63] established a distinction between the procedures to be followed in the decolonization of both territories. As regards Ifni, the rule applicable under this resolution is the one set out in paragraph 6 of Resolution 1514 (XV) as it is not a colony nor is it a protectorate, but an enclave that forms part of the territorial integrity of Morocco[64]. Through this resolution, the GA invited Spain to establish the procedures for the transfer of power with Morocco, "taking into account, however, the aspirations of the indigenous

---

[59] ORGA: Twenty-first period of sessions, Annexes, a.i., 23 (A/6300/Rev. 1), Chapter X, paras. 62 to 116.

[60] As pointed out by Berramdane, a strong supporter of the Moroccan character of Western Sahara, obviously this was only a tactic intended to ensure first the independence of the Sahara and its subsequent integration into Morocco during a second phase (cfr. BERRAMDANE, A., Le Maroc et l'Occident (1800-1974), Ed. Karthala, Paris (1987): 323).

[61] ORGA: Twenty-first period of sessions, Annexes, a.i. 23 (A/6300/Rev.1), Chapter X, annex.

[62] Resolution A/AC.109/214 of the Committee of twenty-four, approved on November 16, 1966 (ORGA: Twenty-first period of sessions, add. a a.i. 23, Annexes, (A/6300/Rev.1), Chapter X, para. 243).

[63] Resolution 2229 (XX) of the GA, approved on December 20, 1966.

[64] Paragraph 6 of Resolution 1514 (XV) prohibits "Any attempt aimed at the partial or total disruption of the national unity and the territorial integrity of a country".

population". On November 29, 1968, the permanent Spanish representative stated to the Fourth Commission that, in a brief period of time, a Spanish delegation would go to Rabat in order "to sign a treaty with the Government of Morocco on the immediate transfer of the territory of Ifni to Morocco"[65]. The GA took note of this and encouraged the administrating Power "to speed up the decolonization of Ifni and (a) taking into account the aspirations of the indigenous population, decide the procedures for the transfer of power with the Government of Morocco, in accordance with Resolution 1514 (XV)"[66]. Finally, the return of Ifni to Morocco took place following the Hispano-Moroccan agreement signed in Fez on January 4, 1969[67].

With regard to Spanish Sahara, Resolution 2229 (XXI) invites Spain "to determine at the earliest possible date, in conformity with the aspirations of the indigenous people (...) and in consultation with the Governments of Mauritania and Morocco and any other interested party" -in clear reference to Algeria-, the procedures for the organisation of a referendum which will be conducted under United Nations auspices, with a view "to enabling the indigenous population of the Territory to exercise freely its right to self-

---

[65] *ORGA*: A/C.4/SR.1799

[66] Resolution 2428 (XXIII) of the GA of the United Nations, approved on December 18, 1968.

[67] Article 8 of this Treaty stated that, "The Spanish State returns to the Kingdom of Morocco the territory which had previously been ceded to Spain in application of article 8 of the Treaty of Tetuan, of April 26, 1860" (*Official Gazette of the City of Ceuta* of February 5, 1970, No. 1041). The Treaty was completed by the Hispano-Moroccan Agreement on Sea Fishing, signed on the same date and in the same place (*Aranzadi*, No. 1054). As is logical, this agreement was "highly beneficial for the Spanish fishermen, who were able to continue their work, which was frequently abusive, in Moroccan waters" (VILLAR, F. (1982): 148), and was denounced by Morocco on December 31, 1972.

The return of Ifni to Morocco, which, although on occasions is considered to have been peaceful, it was a consequence, among other reasons, of warfare, which occurred between 1957 and 1958 (*cfr.* DIEGO AGUIRRE, J.R., "Ifni, la ultima guerra colonial española. Historia del desconocido conflicto de 1957-58 en el Africa Occidental", *Historia 16*, No. 15, 167 (1990) 12-37), and did not receive the unanimous blessing of Spanish doctrine. For example, Cordero classified the ceding of the Jalifiana zone and Tangier (1956), Tarfaya (1958) and Ifni as "Spanish benevolence" (CORDERO TORRES, J.M., "Marruecos y el Sahara Español", *R.P.I.*, No. 122, July/August (1972): 233). For a critical analysis of the procedure followed in the parliamentary proceedings and in the ratification of the treaty for the retrocession of Ifni, *cfr.* REMIRO BROTONS, A. (1978): 78 et seq.; also, VILLAR, F. (1982): 150. Due to "the Spanish blood shed in the territory", the Spanish extreme right wing Deputy Blas Piñar submitted a proposal not ratify the treaty, and despite the fact that a Plenary Session of the Spanish Parliament finally approved it, the result of the ballot was unusual: 69 votes against, 25 abstentions and over one hundred absences (*Boletín Oficial del Estado/Official State Gazette* of June 5, 1970, *Aranzadi*, No. 1053).

determination". Finally, it requests the Secretary General, in consultation with the administering power and with the Special Committee, to appoint a Special Mission "to be sent to Spanish Sahara for the purpose of recommending practical steps" for the indigenous population to exercise its right to self-determination[68]. The importance of this resolution was clear in successive years as the criteria which it sets out would be followed by successive resolutions of the General Assembly on the question until 1974: meaning that the resolutions adopted by the General Assembly in 1967[69], 1968[70] and 1969[71] were limited to repeating its context almost verbatim.

The approval of Resolution 2711 (XXV) of the General Assembly[72] meant a new and important step in the process as it invited Spain to respect the resolutions of the General Assembly concerning the activities of the foreign economic interests operating in Spanish Sahara, and requested that other States abstain from investing in the territory in order to bring forward the implementation of the right to self-determination. This was a key resolution in the process for the decolonization of Western Sahara, as, for the first time, the General Assembly expressly demanded that the natural resources of the territory be safeguarded. This is contrary to the traditional attitude of the United Nations to ignore this question, an attitude that, regrettably, would return after the sharing out of the territory between Morocco and Mauritania in 1975. Thus, Resolution 2711 (XXV) became one of the first specific contributions of the GA in defence of the right of the people of Western Sahara to self-determination, situating it specifically in the geopolitical context of the Maghreb, declaring that, "the continued existence of a colonial situation in the Territory retards stability and harmony in north-west Africa". Finally, it was a pleasant surprise that this resolution recognized "the legitimacy of the

---

[68] Resolution 2229 (XXI) of the GA.

[69] Resolution 2354 (XXII) of the GA, approved on December 19, 1967, by 113 votes in favour (including the vote of Spain), none against and 4 abstentions.

[70] Resolution 2428 (XXIII) of the GA, approved on December 18, 1968, by 114 votes in favour (also including the vote of Spain), none against and 3 abstentions.

[71] Resolution 2591 (XXIV) of the GA, approved on November 16, 1969, by 110 votes in favour, none against and 5 abstentions. Spain abstained. This abstention of Spain after two consecutive years voting in favour of the resolutions adopted by the GA on this question was due to the change which had taken place in the Spanish Government, where Castiella was no longer Foreign Minister, and had been replaced by López Bravo, who gave strict instructions to flatly reject the possibility of sending a visiting mission to the territory. As from that time, the particular dispute between the Presidency Ministry and Foreign Ministry would incline towards the first (*cfr.* VILLAR, F. (1982): 158).

[72] Resolution 2711 (XXV) of the GA, approved on December 14, 1970, by 103 votes in favour, none against and 11 abstentions.

struggle being waged by the colonial peoples for the exercise of their right to self-determination", as this paragraph, included in a resolution with the title "Question of Spanish Sahara", openly indicates the support of the GA for a Saharan liberation movement which was in its very early stages; the embryo of what later would become the POLISARIO Front.

Throughout 1971, the General Assembly remained temporarily apart from the conflict in order not to obstruct the negotiations, which according to declarations of the States involved, were being held in order to find a definitive solution[73]. After a year, the GA again took up the Saharan question and took a further, effective step when it stated for the first time, through Resolution 2983 (XXVII), one of the hardest and clearest resolutions adopted by the GA, "the inalienable right of the people of the Sahara to self-determination and independence in accordance with General Assembly resolution 1514 (XV)", reaffirming "the legitimacy of the struggle of colonial peoples and its solidarity with, and support for the people of the Sahara in the struggle" and asking all States "to give them all necessary moral and material assistance in that struggle"[74]. Morocco quickly reacted to this by enacting new legislation on March 2, 1973 regarding the Moroccan exclusive fishing zone, which was unilaterally extended to seventy nautical miles. This provoked a tense situation between Spain and Morocco, with continual incidents and the seizure of Spanish fishing boats. However, this GA progression took a step back the following year when Resolution 3162 (XXVIII) was approved. Although it reaffirmed the solidarity of the General Assembly with the struggle of the Saharan people, it avoided any reference to the independence of the territory as an objective of this struggle[75].

Parallel to the analysis of the attitude of the UN regarding this question, reference must be made to the attitude adopted by the OAU, an organization on the verge of collapse when it had to address the Saharan problem. Between 1972 and practically up to the Monrovia Summit Meeting of 1979 the Saharan question was taken out of the agenda of the Organization evidently to

---

[73] Undoubtedly, the failed coup d'état against Hassan II on July 10, 1971 at his summer palace in Skhirat was related to the beginning of these negotiations. On August 16 the following year, a second attempt was made to assassinate him and the Alawite monarch escaped unharmed.

[74] Resolution 2983 (XXVII) of the GA was approved on December 14, 1972, by 84 votes in favour, 10 against and 26 abstentions. Spain was among the votes against and this reaffirmed its position still against the self-determination of Western Sahara.

[75] Resolution 3162 (XXVIII) of the GA was approved on December 14, 1973 by 108 votes in favour, none against and 23 abstentions. Spain abstained as, at the last minute, it modified its vote against as a consequence of the insistence of the Spanish delegate, Jaime de Piniés, to Lopez Rodó, the Foreign Minister since June 1973 (*cfr.* DE PINIÉS, J., (1990): 27 et seq.).

avoid confrontations between its members that might put the existence of the OAU at risk. Successive resolutions of the OAU on this matter followed the general lines laid down by the UN. The report submitted by the Secretary General of the Organization at the VIII OAU Summit (Addis Ababa, June 1971) recommended that the OAU put pressure on Spain to accept a Visiting Mission to the territory, as a step prior to holding a referendum on self-determination. The following year, the resolution adopted at the Rabat Summit, which was presided over by Hassan II, declared the solidarity of the OAU with the Saharan people, and affirmed its right to self-determination and independence. Surprisingly this resolution received the favourable vote of Morocco although its Government declared that it would never accept the independence of Spanish Sahara. This *apparent tactical error* of the Moroccan Government was explained by a mistaken calculation of the real strength of the independence movements in the territory. The Moroccan intention was that of a process involving two different phases: in the first place, obtaining the independence of the territory and, secondly, the subsequent integration of the territory in Morocco at the request of MOREHOB (*Mouvement de Résistance des Hommes Bleus*, an organization created on July 21, 1972, which aspired to bring independence to the territory, but with an approach close to the Moroccan thesis). However, the emergence of the POLISARIO Front monopolised the will of the majority of the Saharan population and MOREHOB's possibilities of success suddenly vanished, as also occurred with the P.U.N.S., a party whose creation was promoted by the Spanish Government and which sought the independence of the territory so that, subsequently, it would become a satellite State of the former metropolis.

The adoption of the 1972 resolution by the OAU led the UN, through Resolution 2983 (XXVII)[76] (analysed above) to affirm "the inalienable right of the people of the Sahara to self-determination and independence". The reasons why resolution 3162 (XXVII)[77] (also analysed above), avoided the term "independence" lie in the attitude of the OAU as regards the question; on request from Morocco, this expression had disappeared from the OAU resolutions adopted at the Addis Ababa Summit (1973) and the Mogadiscio Summit (1974).

These resolutions show that in this phase of the conflict both the UN and the OAU were limited to maintaining the difficult balance between demanding the rights of the Saharan people and avoiding confrontation, firstly with the colonising power of the territory and then with Morocco, a significant power

---

[76] Resolution 2983 (XXVII) of the GA, approved on December 14, 1972.
[77] Resolution 3162 (XXVIII) of the GA, approved on December 14, 1973.

in the region, in the hope of concluding an agreement which might put an end to the conflict. While it was generally stated that the Saharan people must exercise the right to self-determination through a referendum to be held under the auspices of the UN -a right, in principle, not questioned by any of the parties-, it avoided establishing the specific characteristics of the referendum (procedure, options, questioned related to the census, etc.).

On August 20, 1974, the Spanish representative before the United Nations, Jaime De Piniés, notified the Secretary General of the UN of the following:

> "The Spanish Government will hold a referendum, under the auspices and guarantee of the United Nations, within the first six months of 1975 on the date which will be established duly in advance; it will adopt the measures required for the indigenous inhabitants of the territory to exercise their right to self-determination in conformity with Resolution 3162 (XXVIII), of December 14, 1973; and will establish the procedure for holding the referendum, through the pertinent consultations, within the period stated"[78].

This new Spanish approach provoked a rapid reaction from Hassan II who, after openly rejecting the possibility of independence, proposed as a basis for the decolonization of the territory the process undertaken in Western Irian, which would entail the "bilateralization" of the conflict between Spain and Morocco[79]. Faced with the new position adopted by Madrid, Morocco decided

---

[78] *ORGA*: A/9714. This same approach was repeated by the Spanish Foreign Minister, Cortina, before the GA (*ORGA*: A/PV.2253, of October 2, 1974, p. 410 et seq.).

[79] In the process which led to Western Irian becoming part of Indonesia, an integration which is still strongly contested by an important sector of the population, the population was not consulted in a referendum, but through consultations made to the tribal councils, and although this was carried out under the supervision of a Special Envoy of the United Nations, there was a reasonable doubt about the representativeness of these tribal councils, especially taking into account the fact that the "consultation" was made under close political control by the Indonesian authorities. As can be seen, the similarity of the "representativeness" of these tribal councils with the Saharan *Yemáa* is evident. In the case of Western Irian the fact that the administration of the territory was transferred to the United Nations during a transitory period of nine months is also especially serious. After this, the administration of the territory was handed over to Indonesia, which would carry out the "consultation" among the tribal councils (approximately 1,000 of the 800,000 inhabitants of the territory were consulted), thus consolidating the integration, which would be approved by the GA through Resolution 2504 (XXIV), of November 19, 1969. As pointed out by Villar, the example of Western Irian is "one of the most regrettable episodes the United Nations has been involved in during a decolonization process" (VILLAR, F. (1982): 258 et

to that its primary objective was to prevent the organisation of the referendum on self-determination[80], which it achieved with approval from the GA after long, bitter discussions between the representatives of the States, in Resolution 3292 (XXIX)[81].

In order to achieve its objectives, Morocco firstly aimed to submit the solution of what was, in its opinion, a conflict between Spain and Morocco, to the ICJ via its contentious jurisdiction, but as Spain refused to resort to litigation (it did not even answer the proposal)[82], Morocco decided to seek a solution through an advisory opinion. To achieve this, in accordance with the requirements of Article 96.1 of the Charter, it was necessary refer the proposal to the GA, which in turn would request the Court for an advisory opinion, which eventually occurred[83]. This Moroccan proposal obtained the support of

---

seq.). Despite this, the case of Western Irian cannot be considered as a precedent, but as "a derogation of the general rule whose legal value continues to be fully valid" (RUCZ, C., "Un référendum au Sahara occidental?", *A.F.D.I.*, vol. XL (1994): 248). Although as Guilhaudis points out, "in the eyes of the United Nations, the integration of a 'colonial' people into a non-colonial power is not surprising (since) fundamentally it constitutes nothing more than a form of independence, of liberty" (GUILHAUDIS, J. F., *Le droit des peuples à disposer d'eux-mêmes*, Presses Universitaires de Grenoble (1976): 86), this integration must be the result of a decision freely adopted by the people in question, which, obviously, did not occur in the case of Western Irian. As regards this question, besides the works mentioned, *cfr.* MORAND, J., "Autodétermination en Irian occidental et à Bahrein", *A.F.D.I.* (1971): 513-540.

[80] As Benjelloun, the Moroccan delegate to the Fourth Commission declared later (November 1977), when Spain stated that it was prepared to organise the referendum, "Morocco had no alternative other than to appeal to the International Court of Justice in order to prevent a fait accompli" as, in its opinion, if the legal ties between Morocco and the populations of Western Sahara were recognized, there would be no need to hold a referendum (*ORGA*: A/C.4/32/SR.14).

[81] Resolution 3292 (XXIX) of the GA was approved on December 13, 1974, with a record number of abstentions. The voting was as follows: 87 in favour, none against and 43 abstentions. With regard to the States involved in the in the Saharan question, Spain was the only one which did not voter in favour of the resolution.

[82] The Spanish Foreign Ministry stated that there was no controversy between the two countries; therefore, he was implicitly denying that Spain would accept submitting the controversy to the ICJ (*ORGA*: A/PV.2253).

[83] The Moroccan request to submit the "case" to the ICJ jointly with Spain, and which was handed over to the Spanish representative on September 23, 1974 and simultaneously sent to the Secretary General of the UNO, is literally as follows, "in order to guide the United Nations towards a definitive solution to the problem of Western Sahara, which is in conformity with the principles of the Charter, and with the higher interests of international peace and security, the Government of His Majesty the King formally presents the proposal to jointly submit this question to the arbitration of the ICJ in conformity with the spirit and the letter of Chapter VI of the United Nations Charter, which deals with the peaceful

Mauritania, without which the initiative would have been unlikely to succeed given the support which this State had in a large part of Black Africa and in the Arab World[84]. The representative of Algeria stated that he only saw advantages in submitting the case to the Court, in what was undoubtedly a crass error of calculation, as time would show. With hindsight, many years on, it is easy to conclude that Spain made a grave mistake in the handling of this issue: there is no doubt that if it had accepted the litigation in order to resolve the conflict, a decision of the ICJ would have ended the colonisation of the territory and the suffering of its population, and it would now be another State in the international community. Instead, to this day it continues to be a territory awaiting decolonization under Moroccan military occupation. However, we must return to 1974, when, for the first time, Spain announced it readiness to send a visiting mission to the territory, which it had firmly opposed up until then[85].

In these circumstances, the Fourth Commission approved a draft resolution[86], which would become Resolution 3292 (XXIX). The debates held

---

settlement of controversies, to the attention of the Spanish Government. Trusting in the good sense of the Spanish Government and its interest in the preservation of the friendship between our two countries, which history and geography predestined for cooperation and understanding, the Government of His Majesty the King is convinced that the Spanish Government will respond positively to its proposal in order to submit this to the ICJ as soon as possible" (*ORGA:* A/9771).

[84] This was such that Villar considered that, on October 1, 1974, the date on which Mauritania accepted the Moroccan proposal, this constituted "a landmark in the history of the decolonization of the Sahara" (VILLAR, F. (1982): 270). Despite the fact that until 1970, the date of its recognition by Morocco, Mauritania had been the subject of the territorial aspirations of the Alawite kingdom ("Grand Morocco"), Morocco had been forced to "share" its claims to the territory of Western Sahara, reserving for itself the "useful triangle, which took in El Aaiún (the capital and most important city in the territory), Smara (the religious capital) and Bu Craa (the phosphate deposits), due to the need to obtain the support of another State in the Maghreb when requesting a ruling from the ICJ. The participation of Mauritania was decisive in the steps previous to achieving the majority of the votes of the GA, such as support for these aspirations, offered by the VII Conference of the Arab League, held in Rabat (from October 26 to 29, 1974), through the approval of a favourable resolution of the request for a ruling from the ICJ.

[85] This declaration was made by Jaime De Piniés before the Fourth Commission, on December 4, 1974 (*ORGA.* A/C.4/SR.2126).

[86] *ORGA:* A/C.4/SR.2131. The original draft, in its English version, mentioned the right of self-determination of "the populations of Spanish Sahara" (*ORGA:* A/C.4/L.1090 and corr.1), however, given that the term "populations" "could be interpreted as a subterfuge in order to damage the unity of the territory", at the request of Spain, this expression was substituted by "population of Spanish Sahara" (*ORGA:* A/C.4/SR.2130).

by this Fourth Commission[87] are of much interest because this analysis of the situation makes it possible to understand the reason for the high number of abstentions when it was approved by the Fourth Commission and later by the GA (forty-three in both cases). As would subsequently be confirmed by the events, this was essentially due to the fear that a postponement of the referendum could dangerously paralyse the process, spoiling the progress, which had without doubt been made up until then[88].

Resolution 3292 (XXIX) fundamentally raises three matters: the request for an advisory opinion from the ICJ, the request for a postponement of the referendum by Spain, and, finally, the sending of a visiting mission to the territory.

As regards the first question, which will be analysed in Chapter IV of this work, Resolution 3292 (XXIX), requests the ICJ,

> "Without prejudice to the application of the principles embodied in General Assembly Resolution 1514 (XV), to give an advisory opinion at an early date on the following questions:
>
> I) Was Western Sahara (Río de Oro and Sakiet El Hamra) at the time of colonisation by Spain a territory belonging to no one (*terra nullius*)?
>
> If the answer to the first question is in the negative,
>
> II) What were the legal ties between this territory and the kingdom of Morocco and the Mauritanian entity?"

---

[87] For further information concerning the debates in the GA and in the Fourth Commission, *cfr. ORGA: Twenty-ninth period of sessions*, A/PV.2249, A/PV.2250, A/PV.2251, A/PV.2252, A/PV.2253, A/PV.2265; *Fourth Commission*, A/C.4/SR.2117, and A/C.4/SR.2125 to 2131.

[88] The States that would later abstain from voting had different approaches to the issue. In the opinion of some of the delegates, the drafting of the resolution would lead to understanding that it was no longer a question of decolonization, but a controversy between certain countries, which was precisely the objective of Morocco. Others expressed their fear that Spain, protected by this resolution, would defer the convening of a referendum indefinitely. Some of the representations stated their inconformity with the text of the resolution as they considered that it was not a legal question that had to be submitted to the Court, but a question of a political nature. Finally, the majority group of States who would subsequently abstain stressed that the Sahara problem was a problem of decolonization that would require the exercise of the right to self-determination through a consultation put to the population (*cfr. ORGA*: A/C.4/SR.2131). In the opinion of Villar, the explanations regarding the voting and the abstentions weighed heavily on the minds of the Judges of The Hague when they pronounced their ruling (VILLAR, F. (1982): 277).

As regards the second question, the resolution calls upon Spain, in its capacity as administering power in the territory, and Morocco and Mauritania, which it considers to be interested parties, "to submit to the International Court of Justice all such information and documents as may be needed to clarify those questions"; urges Spain "to postpone the referendum it contemplated holding in Western Sahara until the General assembly decides on the policy to be followed in order to accelerate the decolonization process in the territory, in accordance with Resolution 1514 (XV), in the best possible conditions, in the light of the advisory opinion to be given by the International Court of Justice"; and, finally, "reiterates its invitation to all the States to observe the resolutions of the General Assembly regarding the activities of foreign economic and financial interests in the territory and to abstain from contributing by their investments or immigration policy to the maintenance of a colonial situation in the territory".

In accordance with the offer made by the Spanish Government, the GA also asked the Special Committee to send a Visiting Mission to the territory in order to provide assistance for this Special Committee, by obtaining first hand information on the prevailing situation there, including information on the political, economic, social, cultural and educational conditions, as well as on the wishes and aspirations of the population. Considering the circumstances, the Visiting Mission was quickly formed, being composed of three members: the permanent representative of the Ivory Coast at the UN, who would preside over the Mission, a representative of Cuba, and another from Iran, assisted by a team of nine UN administrative workers[89].

The Mission carried out its work between May 8 and June 14, 1975, during which time it made as many visits to the territory as to Spain, Algeria and Mauritania, and produced a report which contains exhaustive details of the work done by the Mission and the conclusions it reached after travelling throughout the territory and holding meetings with the Governments of the States mentioned above. Among its conclusions it mentioned that, together with the intrinsic complexity of the problem, "the task of the Mission was especially difficult because Resolution 3292 (XXIX) (...) did not specify its

---

[89] As Bontems pointed out, this composition has a certain international balance as the pro-Western bloc (Iran), the Soviet bloc (Cuba) and the African states (Ivory Coast) are represented (*cfr.* BONTEMS, C. (1984): 115). Despite the fact that the principle of geographical distribution is respected, in the opinion of Villar, who accompanied the Mission during its visit to the territory, from the ideological point of view, the distribution was not balanced as the Iranian representative "had strict instructions to support the cause of the Alawite throne, moreover, "the pro-Moroccan fickleness of Simeón Ake, the President would soon become obvious". *Cfr.* VILLAR, F. (1982): 283.

mandate". The truth is that the lack of content of the mandate became a double-edged sword in the hands of the Mission, and it duly took advantage of this in order to make as broad an interpretation as it wished concerning its true functions in the territory in order to directly obtain important information and an approximate opinion of the real wishes of the population as to its future. Thus, the Mission was able to verify that "within the territory, the population, or at least almost all the persons interviewed by the Mission, were categorically in favour of independence and against the territorial claims of Morocco and Mauritania", and that the POLISARIO Front, "despite having been considered to be a clandestine movement until the arrival of the Mission, seemed to be the dominant force in the territory". The Mission Report also reinforced the need to consult the population "so that it might constitute a lasting solution and make it possible to keep the peace in the region, (...) this must be carried with the agreement and participation of all the parties involved and concerned"[90], and it must take into account "the wishes and aspirations of all the Saharan population in the territory, including those who now live abroad as political exiles or refugees". With this objective in mind, the Mission recommended that the Secretary General designate another Visiting Mission to draft the procedures for the consultation "which must be carried out under the auspices of the United Nations"[91]. Therefore, the report openly defended the rights of the population of Western Sahara and had the unanimous support of its members, despite severe pressure placed on members from their Governments[92].

---

[90] In the context of the problem of Western Sahara, when the SC and the GA use the expression "parties involved" they refer to Morocco and Mauritania, and when they refer to "parties concerned" they refer to Algeria. This is the position held by the UNO from the time that the Visiting Mission used these expressions for the first time (*cfr.* ONU. *La cuestión del Sahara Occidental en las Naciones Unidas*, Publicación del Departamento de Asuntos Políticos, Administración Fiduciaria y Descolonización, No. 17, October, 1980, p. 25, note No. 90).
[91] Villar states that the Iranian representative (Mr Pishva) and the President of the Visiting Mission (Mr Ake) wanted to include a final recommendation which stated that "the final solution proposed may not be placed within the evident traditional framework of the majority of the former colonial territories which have attained autonomy and independence", in an evident attempt to support the Moroccan claim to modify decolonization doctrine as regards the Western Sahara, which had been held by the GA up to that time. This proposal failed due to the opposition of the Cuban, Mrs Jiménez, the third member of the Mission, and the copious and impressive draft report drawn up by the Mission Secretary, Mr Minchin, from the United Kingdom. *Cfr.* VILLAR, F. (1982): 314.
[92] The representatives of Iran and the Ivory Coast had to admit the evidence of the situation in the territory despite having been put under pressure by their respective Governments, which wanted a pronouncement of the Mission more favourable to the Moroccan

The Visiting Mission Report was finally approved by the Special Decolonization Committee (November 7, 1975) although, as we shall see in the following section, the result of the report was to be totally eclipsed by the ruling of the Court.

It is clear that the attitude of the General Assembly during this phase was decidedly negative as regards the Saharan interests, which, theoretically, it was defending. The weakness of the GA, in giving in to the pressure of Morocco at this decisive time, placed the UN in a difficult position. It could however have been worse; the advisory opinion of the ICJ confirmed the UN's approaches from the time that it took charge of the conflict, but if it had adopted a different decision, contrary to the UN's decolonising policy up to then, the UN would have been left with no way out. It can be stated that this attitude of the General Assembly was precisely what caused the stoppage of the process, a process which had it concluded with the organisation of a referendum on self-determination (which Spain was in fact prepared for[93]), it would surely have resulted in the independence of the territory, thus preventing almost twenty years of war following the Green March[94].

Lacking foresight, the General Assembly missed taking the only chance offered by the Spanish authorities at the time, which had become resigned to consider the referendum to be the only way out of the conflict. The apparently exculpatory clarification made by the ICJ to the effect that "the General Assembly took special care to include provisions in the text of Resolution 3292 (XXIX) which specify that the postponement did not affect the right of the populations of Western Sahara to self-determination" is insufficient to justify the suspension of the referendum, as this did not prevent the process being stopped at the time when, for the first time, the end was in sight. Therefore, we must regret this very serious mistake made by the Organisation of the United Nations, which, until then, had been the main guarantor of the

---

aspirations (cfr. FRANCK, T.M., "The Stealing of the Sahara", A.J.I.L., October, vol. 70, n. 4 (1976): 709).

[93] As Cola points out, if there had been no postponement, self-determination would have taken place irreproachably (COLA ALBERICH, J., "España y el Sahara Occidental: antecedentes de una descolonización", R.P.I., No. 154, November-December (1977): 50). In this regard, the Spanish representative at the GA, Jaime De Piniés, had stated the paradox inherent to the text of the resolution that requested a ruling, which it considered to be useless, and, at the same time, it requested the decolonization and a deferral of the referendum that would enable the decolonization.

[94] As stated by the ICJ, it is true that the GA always referred to "postponement of the referendum", "taking care to include provisions in the text of Resolution 3292 (XXIX) which specify that this postponement did not affect the right of the populations of Western Sahara to self-determination " (I.C.J. Recueil 1975, p. 35, para. 66), but its ill timing is evident.

rights of the Saharan people against the intransigence of the administering power of the territory[95].

As was stated above, it is regrettable that the ICJ had to make a pronouncement on the question through an advisory opinion since general consensus suggests that it would have been possible to use litigation to solve the problem, or failing this, that "the parties involved and concerned" would have accepted the binding nature of the decision. Undoubtedly this would have been decisive as regards achieving a definitive solution to the conflict and since Morocco had initially proposed litigation, realistically it would not have been able to oppose it. Spain was the state most reticent to turning to the ICJ. The reason for its withdrawal from the territory was a combination of circumstances, including the very probable celebration of Green March, which made maintenance of control and administration in the territory non feasible. In the light of this situation, it is difficult to understand why Spain did not accept litigation in order to definitively resolve the conflict, especially given that it would have remained exempt from international responsibility as, logically, the ICJ would not have been able to act against the decolonizing policy established over so many years by the GA.

---

[95] The writer Juan Goytisolo maintains that the true reason for the Moroccan request to submit the question to the ICJ was to "frustrate the Franco manoeuvre" which would consist of organizing a referendum in which the independence option would triumph as there were 80,000 Spanish citizens in the territory and the Saharan census made by the Spanish authorities amounted to 74,000 Saharans, and depending on this, the number of possible male voters would not reach the figure of 20,000, "the arithmetic shows us that for each Saharan voter there are four Spaniards in charge of watching over him". *Cfr.* GOYTISOLO, J. *El problema del Sahara*, ed. Anagrama, Barcelona (1979): 40.

CHAPTER III

THE CONSTITUTIVE ELEMENTS OF STATEHOOD AND THEIR APPLICATION TO WESTERN SAHARA

1. Introduction

In this chapter we will analyse whether Western Sahara has the elements required by International law to be considered to be a State. As we will have the opportunity to confirm in the following pages, there are many complex questions to be examined given the very special circumstances in the territory. These include the fact that it is occupied and controlled by Moroccan military forces, and its population is condemned to choosing between suffering the repression of the occupying State in its own land or living as refugees in the inhospitable Algerian *hammada*.

Starting with the consideration that a State is "an entity with a territory, a population and a government, which is sovereign and independent, in the sense that it is not subordinated to any other State"[96], it can be stated that Western Sahara has the requirements needed to be considered to be a State.

However, before addressing the analysis of this problem, we must point out that we will not study the possibility that Western Sahara might be unfeasible as a State, a reasoning usually put forward by the detractors of an independent Sahara State, since international practice clearly shows that this is a question which almost exclusively depends on the willingness of the international community. In this regard, the Nauru case is, perhaps, the most graphic example of this point[97].

---

[96] GONZALEZ CAMPOS, J. D., SÁNCHEZ RODRÍGUEZ, L. I., ANDRÉS SAENZ DE SANTA MARIA, M. P. (2008): 410.

[97] Not even in the cases in which small territories have been declared unfeasible as independent States, due to the limited density of the population and the scarcity of resources, these circumstances were impediments to their existence as States and to their recognition by the United Nations. It is sufficient to remember cases such as Nauru, a State that has hardly any territory. As is logical, those who defend the Moroccan nature of the Sahara usually refer to this question and hold that a Saharan State would not be feasible. In this regard, Colin points out that a Saharan State would have a sparse population, unattractive for capitals, that would cause substantial immigration, and unavoidably it would be destined

As is well known, the requirements which have traditionally been considered necessary for a specific entity to be considered to be a State are the following three[98]: a defined territory, an effective government and a permanent population. Following this classical scheme, in the sections below we will analyse each of these components in order to subsequently argue the statement made above, that Western Sahara fulfils the necessary criteria for statehood.

Firstly, we will examine the legislation on "Spanish Sahara", which went through several phases under Spanish administration, the analysis of which, at least briefly, is essential in order to understand the complicated Spanish colonizing policy.

Secondly, we will examine the creation, consolidation and recognition of the POLISARIO Front and the SADR, and the difficult institutional mesh deriving from the simultaneous existence of a national liberation movement, recognized by the United Nations as the sole and legitimate representative of the Saharan people, and whose legitimate use of force is therefore recognized, and a State recognized by the Organization of African Unity as a member with full rights whose personality is ignored by the UN. Furthermore, although specific references are made in other chapters to certain actions of the OAU concerning the Saharan conflict, mainly as regards the Peace Plan, this chapter contains the analysis of the activity of the African organisation in relation

---

to receive protection from neighbouring Algeria (COLIN, J.P., "Réflexions sur l´avenir du Sahara Occidental", *Revue Française d'études Politiques Africaines*, vol. 13, n° 152-153 (1978): 80 and 90); Grimaud considers that a theoretical Saharan State would be an unfeasible microstate and the defense of this microstate made by some States "leaves the international community perplexed". This author considers that the solution to the conflict entails the concession of "a broad Saharan autonomy within the framework of a Moroccan province" (GRIMAUD, N., "Sahara Occidental: un issue possible?", *Monde Arabe: Maghreb-Machrek*, n. 121, Juillet-Août-Septembre (1988): 93 and 97). Along the same lines, *cfr.* BENNOUNA, M., *Hearing before the Subcommittees on International Organizations and on Africa of the Committee on international elations House of Representatives*, 12 de octubre de 1977, U.S. Government printing Office, Washington (1977): 31 et seq. However, as Gros Espiell points out regarding the right of peoples to free determination, from the legal point of view, as there is no criteria as regards denying the right of free determination depending on the scarcity of population or the smallness of the territory settled by this population; it is not possible to challenge this right even when it ends in independence, with the argument that, if this right is exercised, a microstate might be constituted (GROS ESPIELL, H. (1979): 16).

[98] International Case Law has usually referred to these three elements. Thus, the Mixed German-Polish Arbitration Court in the case of the *Deutsche Continental Gas-Gesellschaft* stated that a State does not exist unless it has territory, a population inhabiting this territory and public power exercised over the population and the territory" (*Recueil T.A.M.*, volume IX, p. 336).

CHAPTER III

the joining of SADR and its recognition by a large number of African States, members themselves of the OAU, and the importance of this situation when assessing the international statehood of Western Sahara.

Finally, we will refer to the third component of statehood: the Saharan population, its main characteristics and the censuses made by the Spanish authorities before they withdrew from the territory.

2. The territory: the legislative regulation of "Spanish Sahara"

Spanish colonial policy was divided into two well-differentiated epochs located in two different continents: America and Africa. As regards the first, as pointed out by Mesa Garrido, the territory of the colony was always considered to be different from the metropolis and, therefore, from the Provinces[99], and its administration always had a well-defined objective: the domination and exploitation to the benefit of the metropolis[100]. As concerns the second, the situation would not vary from the commencement of the colonization (1778 in the case of Guinea, 1884, in the case of the Sahara and 1934 in the case of Ifni) until the time that Spain, under pressure from the United Nations to show whether it was administering a Non-Self-Governing Territory, implemented a policy progressively assimilating the colonial territory to that of the metropolis.

The first significant steps taken by the Spanish administration in this regard, and as regards Western Sahara, were included in the Decree of January 10, 1958, whereby, following the Portuguese policy concerning its African colonial possessions, the territories of Ifni and Western Sahara became "Spanish Overseas Provinces"[101]. This meant that Spain intended to state before the international community that it did not administer any Non-Self-Governing Territory. This also considered by law 8/61, of April 19, 1961, on the Organization of the Legal Regime of the Sahara[102] which, following the

---

[99] As pointed out by Herrero de Miñón, the provincial denomination is often used in Administrative Law and particularly with reference to the African territories in several acceptances, without prejudging their legal condition (HERRERO DE MIÑON, M., "La configuración del territorio nacional en la doctrina reciente del Consejo de Estado español", *Estudios de Derecho Administrativo (Libro jubilar del Consejo de Estado)*, Madrid (1972): 388).

[100] MESA GARRIDO, R., "Algunos problemas coloniales del siglo XIX", *R.E.D.I.*, vol. XLIII, 3 (1965): 380 et seq.

[101] Article 1 of the Decree stated that the territories of Spanish West Africa are made up of the territory of Ifni, and the Northern, Central and Southern areas of Western Sahara (*Aranzadi*, Num. 65). This policy of "provincialisation" also appeared in the Law of the Sea, in the Decree of July 4, 1958 (*Aranzadi*, Num. 1237).

[102] *Aranzadi*, Num. 2218.

same line of argumentation, established a different special legal regime for the Saharan "province"[103].

This last law had the following relevant aspects:
- From then on, once published in the *Boletín Oficial del Estado (Official State Gazette)*, Spanish laws and decrees will be applied in the territory;
- The administration of the territory will correspond to the Presidency of the Government;
- The territory acquires the same right as the "rest of the Spanish provinces" to be represented in the Spanish Parliament and other organs of the Spanish State;
- The territory has municipal organs and other local government organs, including a Local or Provincial Council.

Later this provincialisation policy would be considered by the Spanish Council of State to be "irrelevant as regards modifying the legal classification of these territories and as regards affecting the integrity of the national territory due to the insufficiency of the provincialising norms", to the extent that this simply altered a previous territorial division. In this sense, as pointed out by Herrero de Miñón, "the so-called provincialisation, regardless of its meaning, did not affect the extension of the national territory, since this is regulated by norms which can only be modified by a Law and not by lower level norms, such as a Decree, even less, by a simple *Aviso (Notification)*"[104]. The latter was the channel chosen by the Spanish Government at the time in order to change the denomination of the "Spanish territories of the Gulf of Guinea" to that of the "Province of the Gulf of Guinea"[105]. As stated by this author, the modification of the national territory with the addition of a new province would have required a Law.

The following relevant step concerning the organisation of the territory was the creation of the *Yemáa*, the General Assembly of the Sahara. Despite its short life, it played an important yet very controversial role in the administration of the territory[106]. Decree 1024/67, of May 11, 1967[107],

---

[103] Subsequently, the content of this Law was developed by Decree 2604/61, of December 14, 1961, on the government and administration of the Province of the Sahara (*Aranzadi*, Num. 1837), and by Decree 3249/62, of November 29, 1962, on the legislation of the provincial and local administration of the Province of the Sahara (*Aranzadi*, Num. 2218).

[104] HERRERO DE MIÑON, M. (1972): 393.

[105] *Aviso (Notification)* of January 2, 1957 (*Boletín Oficial del Estado/Official State Gazette* of January 15).

[106] As pointed out by Portillo, the institution of the *Yemáa* (from the Arabic *Yemáa* meaning Community) is previous to the Spanish colonisation. It was made up of the most prestigious and representative men from each tribal group as regards religion, literature, weapons and trade. The matters put forward were decided by consensus and their decisions had to be

attributed to the *Yemáa* the dual functions of "being the superior organ representing the local administration", and of "promoting on its own initiative the matters it considers being of general interest for the territory" (Article 164).

The Saharan General Assembly, which was finally constituted on September 11, 1967, after elections which saw the participation of just 9,056 voters, was made up of a President, a Vice-President, the President of the Council, the mayors of El Aaiún and Villa Cisneros, the *Sheikhs* (heads of tribes or fractions), forty representatives freely elected by the sub-fractions of tribes or fractions, and a Secretary (a government worker, designated by the Governor General) (Article 165).

The main functions attributed to the Assembly by the Decree were the following: to examine and announce decisions regarding all matters of general interest in the territory; to be informed of those provisions, contained in Laws or Decrees, which are in force in the territory and to make necessary suggestions as regards for their adaptation to the peculiarities of the territory; and, finally, on its own initiative, to propose to the Government that it adopt the legal measures and regulations required for compliance with and the development of the Laws of the State (Article 174).

This new step taken by the Spanish Administration was intended to provide the "new Province" with a special status given the peculiarities of the territory, while attempting to set aside the idea of its decolonization. The truly representative nature of the *Yemáa* was called into question throughout the duration of its existence[108]. As pointed out by Rodríguez de Viguri y Gil,

---

obeyed by all the tribal heads over for which the local *Yemáa* were important. These decisions, however, could be appealed against before a superior organism, the *Ait Arbain*, or "Council of the Forty", which had regional competence over the *Yemáa* which were under its jurisdiction, and, in the end, it regulated the differences in legislative matters presented to it (use of wells and pasture land, common offences and violent crimes, disputes between tribes, etc.), and it was responsible for adopting the final decision on whether to declare war (*cfr.* PORTILLO PASQUAL DEL RIQUELME, J. (1991): 187 et seq.).

[107] This Decree (*Boletín Oficial del Estado/Official State Gazette*, of May 20, 1967, Num. 120; *Aranzadi*, Num. 948) modifies the Decree of November 29, 1962. The text of the Decree whereby the *Yemáa* is created can be consulted in LÁZARO MIGUEL, H., *Legislación del Sahara. Años 1965 a 1973*. Dirección General de Promoción de Sahara e Instituto de Estudios Africanos (CSI.C.), Madrid (1974): 167-169.

[108] The polemical representativeness of the *Yemáa* was evident from the time it began to function. For example, on December 30, 1967, a document was approved and sent to the Spanish Head of State and to the UNO. Among other things, this document categorically rejected the need for a United Nations Mission to visit the territory as the Saharan people freely chose that the Spanish nation would assist it until it could attend to its responsibilities

Secretary General of the Spanish Government in the Sahara when the three party agreements were signed in Madrid, the *Yemáa* did not have a full representative character since only 50% of its members were elected by a partial suffrage among the *Sheikhs* or outstanding persons from the tribes[109]. Villar went even further, when he stated that, "the *Yemáa* was in fact the Secretary General of the Government", as the Secretary General was its "adviser"[110].

Although it had no efficacy at all, mention should be made in this section of a project of the Spanish Government at the request of the Ministry of the Presidency. This was known in 1972 as the "project for a written document from the *Yemáa*". By this written document the Saharan Assembly would request the Spanish Government to commence, over a period of five years, a transfer of competences to the *Yemáa*, in order to overcome its operational incapacity. At the end of this period, the territory of Spanish Sahara would have the status of "free association" with Spain. Subsequently, the *Yemáa* could request independence or maintain the associated status, validating this decision through a referendum. However, this document was never submitted to the *Yemáa*.

A special mention must also be made of the proposal of the then Deputy Director General for Africa, Fernando Morán, to the effect that Spanish Sahara would become an independent State in the following terms:

- Spain has the key to the solution, therefore, it must urgently take the initiative;
- Negotiations should begin between the States involved in the conflict (Morocco, Mauritania and Algeria) in order to reach a solution towards which the latter two countries would be favourably inclined, while Morocco would be forced by the difficult situation it was in, and which Spain would compensate with beneficial economic agreements
- Since Resolution 1541 (XV) stipulates for the exercise of self-determination and it is likely that this realistically only includes independence, because integration would not be accepted by the population of the territory and this association would not solve the dispute

---

on its own in the future (*cfr.* MISKÉ, A.B., *Front Polisario: l´âme d´un peuple*, Rupture, Paris (1978): 210).

[109] RODRIGUEZ DE VIGURI GIL, L., Intervención en las Jornadas sobre el 4º aniversario de los acuerdos tripartitos de Madrid, ASOCIACION DE AMIGOS DEL SAHARA, *Madrid, 14 de Noviembre de 1975: la traición*, Ed. Sedersa, Madrid (1980): 65.

[110] VILLAR, F. (1982): 135 and 144.

CHAPTER III

before the International Community, and would thus lead to an increase in tension in the area[111].

Both of these two projects were not effective and they were not the last. On February 20, 1973 the *Yemáa* issued a document for the Spanish Head of State which the Spanish Administration "suggested" should be signed, which requested that the Spanish Government "drive forward the process which would effectively ensure the possibility of a decision on its future" and, until this occurred, "Spain, on behalf of the Saharan people, continues to exercise its international representation and guarantees the integrity of its territory and the defence of its frontiers", considering that this document would constitute the commencement of the "self-determination stage", which would conclude with the referendum[112]. This document, which expressly stated that "the Saharan people are the owners of its natural wealth and resources", managed to save face before the International Community when it stated that "the acceptance by the General Assembly of Sahara does not substitute nor diminish the right of the Saharan population to self-determination regarding its future, and this new stage is one of necessary preparation". However it received strong criticism. Particularly severe were those made by Morocco, which considered the *Yemáa* to be a "colonialist institution", "an assembly of dignitaries at the service of the Spanish authorities" and "lacking any representativeness"[113], accusations it would later forget when, after the Madrid Agreements, it tried to reunite the members of this "assembly of dignitaries" in order to declare "the willingness of the Saharan people to re-join the Kingdom of Morocco"[114]. It should however be remembered that when the Visiting

---

[111] *Ibid.*, p. 196 et seq. In order to prevent the "damage" which Spanish interests might undergo, as from July 19, 1972, and up to September 14, 1974, the information concerning the Sahara was classified as confidential material, as set out in Law 9/68 of April 5, on official secrets, therefore, the information concerning the territory disappeared from the Spanish press.

[112] *ORGA*: A/9176, annex I. This document received the corresponding "acknowledgement" of General Franco, in the following terms, "I ensure you that your statements and your application have been received by me with the attention, and respect which the Saharan people have deserved (...)" (*ORGA*: S/9176, annex II, letter of March 6, 1973). Moreover, in a letter of September 21, 1973, the Spanish Head of State stated, in reference to the application of the *Yemáa*, that "the Spanish State guarantees the territorial integrity of the Sahara (...) it repeats and solemnly guarantees that the population of the Sahara will freely determine its future (...)" (*ORGA*: A/9176, annex IV).

[113] The Government of Morocco denounces before the Visiting Mission what it called "an intended assembly empowered to speak on behalf of the population of Western Sahara and which, in fact, only supported the decisions taken by the colonial authorities" (*ORGA*: A/10023/Add.5, para. 311).

[114] Many other documents testify to the Moroccan position clearly against any type of

Mission which travelled through the territory in 1975 had the opportunity to meet the Permanent Commission of the *Yemáa*, constituted by its President and another fifteen members (there was significant difficulty involved in bringing together all of the members of the *Yemáa*), to find out its opinions concerning the future of the territory, it was clearly told of "its wish that the territory would progress towards self-determination and independence"[115].

A third attempt to solve the conflict, even if much more limited than the previous ones, was the last step of the Spanish Administration as regards the organisation of the territory: this was the failed Statute of Autonomy of the territory of the Sahara which, despite being drafted by the Spanish Government and unanimously approved by the 102 members of the *Yemáa* (July 4, 1974)[116], was not promulgated.

All these attempts were condemned to fail from their very conception due both to Spanish international conduct and internal legal action. It should be remembered that in 1960 Spain began to send the United Nations the information referred to in Article 73 *e)* of the Charter, whereby the condition of its African possessions as Non-Self-Governing Territory was now beyond any doubt[117]. As regards the internal legal acts, the *Ley de Bases* of December 1963, which established the autonomous regime of Equatorial Guinea, had abandoned the idea of assimilation and recognized the right of its population to self-determination.

---

representativeness of the *Yemáa*. For example, on September 30, 1974 the Moroccan Minister Laraki stated before the GA that "Spain has established a so-called Assembly, the *Yemáa*, to speak on behalf of the population" (*ORGA:* A/PV.2251). After the creation of the POLISARIO Front and the self-dissolution of the *Yemáa*, the National Saharan Council would replace this in the Saharan structure.

[115] *ORGA:* A/10023/Add.5, para. 142.

[116] The Spanish Head of State had previously sent a letter to the *Yemáa*, on September 27, 1973, in which he stated the right to self-determination of the Saharan people, and proposed the principles on which the following would be based: "a regime of progressive participation of the Saharan people in the management of its own affairs". This letter was later sent to the UNO as a justification of the decolonizing policy of the Spanish Government. Complete text of the letter in CRIADO, R (1977): 298-300, and in CARRO MARTÍNEZ, A., "La descolonización del Sáhara", *R.P.I.*, 144, Marzo-Abril (1976): 17, in note Num. 2. The complete text of the Statute of the Saharan Territory can be seen in CARRO MARTINEZ, A. (1976): 32-38, and in OLIVER LOPEZ-GUARCH, P., *Sahara, drama de una descolonización (1960-1987)*, Miquel Font, ed., Palma de Mallorca (1988): 265-270.

[117] In 1958 and 1959 Spain addressed the United Nations stating that this information could not be transmitted as there were no self-governing territories (*cfr. ORGA:* A/C.4/385, of November 10, 1958, A/C.4/SR 832, of December 5, 1958 and A/C.4/406, of August 5, 1959)

CHAPTER III

3. The organisation of State power. Difficulties deriving from the existence of the POLISARIO Front-SADR (Sahrawi Arab Democratic Republic) binomial

3.1. General aspects

Having analysed the most important milestones in the organisation of the territory since the effective commencement of its colonisation by Spain, we will now examine the creation of the POLISARIO Front and the SADR. Both entities on occasions have distinct functions within the Saharan power structure, while at other times, primarily within the ambit of international relations, they overlap. This leads, clearly, to a complex institutional framework.

The *Frente Popular para la Liberación de El Saguia el-Hamra y Río de Oro (Frente POLISARIO)* was founded on May 10, 1973 at a clandestine Congress which took place in the border area between Western Sahara and Mauritania. At this Constituent Congress, El Luali Mustafa Sayed was elected Secretary General and the organisation chose armed struggle as the way to the independence of the territory[118], which was first used against Spain, the colonial power, and later against Moroccan and Mauritanian troops in the territory[119]. During the II Congress (July 25-31, 1974), its internal

---

[118] The text of the Constitutive Declaration can be seen in BRIONES, F., *Sahara: Cien años sin libertad*. Friendship Association with the Saharan People of Alicante, Librería Compás, Alicante (1994): 38 et seq.

[119] In this regard, among others, cfr. FRANCISCI, "La controversia per il Sahara Occidentale (1956-1975)", *Politica Internazionale, 9* (1978): 88; HINZ, M.O., *Le Droit a l'autodetermination du Sahara occidental; le chemin difficile du peuple sahraoui. Documents de base avec introduction*, Bonn, Progress Dritte Welt Verlag (1978): 110. The American Lewis states, although with no data to base a statement of this type on, that in 1973 the Government of Morocco provided military and diplomatic aid to the POLISARIO Front in its struggle against Spanish domination (LEWIS, W.H., "Morocco and the Western Sahara", *Current History*, Num. 84, May (1985): 214). The opinion in this respect is not unanimous. Among others, Goytisolo states that the POLISARIO Front "was not created to combat Spanish colonialism, which was then condemned, but to oppose Rabat" (GOYTISOLO, J. (1979): 43). This author stresses the attempt of De Gaulle to create a mini-Saharan State in Algerian territory controlled by France before the independence of Algeria and what the Spanish Government would have done in Western Sahara, taking advantage of the weakness of the recently created State of Morocco (1956), and damaging the territorial integrity of Morocco. Consequently, "the problem of Western Sahara would be a problem that was artificially created by our wizard's apprentices (in reference to the Spanish politicians at the time). Within a few months of 'autonomous' administration closely controlled by France, it would have been very easy to create 'Saharan national awareness', to foster the creation of an

organisation was complemented with two command structures, the Political Committee and the Executive Committee, together with the adoption of a political programme which proposed the creation of a Democratic Arab Republic, based on the principles of non-alignment, the construction of socialism and the recovery of the national wealth.

However, the appearance of the POLISARIO Front on the international scene would not occur until the United Nations Mission visited the territory in 1975. The *P.U.N.S.* (*Partido por la Unidad Nacional Saharaui / Party for National Saharan Unity*), a party which had been sponsored by the Spanish Government in order to achieve the future independence of the territory while maintaining strong economic links with Spain[120], was literally swept from the streets of El

---

independence movement, to promise the share out of dividend from the enormous oil fields among a few hundred thousand inhabitants. In fact, for the former metropolises, creating 'independent' States with wealth that was totally out of proportion with their real necessities and so obtain the support of the native populations. As usual, England set an example with the creation of the Persian Gulf Emirates. However, if the criteria to be followed is the wishes of the native inhabitants as 'conditioned' by colonialism, then we would have to say that the pro-independence English in Gibraltar, the French in Mayotte, the Cabinda Liberation Front, etc. are right" (*ibid.*, pages 32 et seq.). This author and others maintain that the POLISARIO Front was organized and sponsored by Algeria in order to defend its interests in the Maghreb. For example, *cfr.* COLIN, J. P. (1978): 83 et seq. However, apart from the evident interest of Algeria in the Maghreb, those who defend this approach obviously avoid making any reference to the principle of *uti possidetis iuris*, which, as we have already pointed out, states the intangible nature of the frontiers established in the colonial period, therefore, while the frontiers of Western Sahara have well established limits, those of the theoretical Saharan State to be created by France in Algeria would have been invented.

[120] For a detailed description of the circumstances which affected the creation of the P.U.N.S., which would have been "sponsored by the Department for the Promotion of the Sahara (*Dirección General de Promoción del Sahara*)", and which held its foundational Congress on February 16, 1975, *cfr.* DIEGO AGUIRRE, J.R., *Historia del Sahara español*, Madrid, ed. Kaydeda, D.L. (1988): 685-692; VILLAR, F. (1982): 280-283. According to this author, the P.U.N.S. was the personal work of Colonel Rodríguez de Viguri, "his favourite toy" (*ibid.*, pages 280 and 298). The report of the Visiting Mission stated that, "the members of the POLISARIO Front sustain that (the P.U.N.S.) is a creation of the Spanish authorities and accuse it of receiving financial support from them, and that it had been able to increase its members because it gives preferential treatment to those who are affiliated to the party when they apply for a job", and that, "it had not witnessed any public demonstrations" in its support (*ORGA*: supplement Num. 23 (A/10023/Rev.1), vol. III, Chap. XIII, Annex, paragraphs 210 and 211). In any case, there is no doubt that it was the first political party of Franco's Spain, which shows to what an extent it was an "invention" of the Spanish Government. The opinion that the creation of the P.U.N.S. was fostered by the Madrid Government is practically unanimous in the doctrine. For example, *cfr.* MIGUEZ, A. (1978): 73; MISKÉ, A.B. (1978): 164 et seq.; REMIRO BROTONS, A. (1978): 83; SALAS LARRAZABAL, R., "El Sahara. La solución... Mañana", *Anales de la Real Academia de*

Aaiún when the Mission arrived, and the demonstrations organized by Madrid turned out to be totally different from what was planned: the flags of the P.U.N.S. were mostly replaced by flags of the POLISARIO Front. Undoubtedly, the Spanish Government at the time made a serious mistake in its calculations when it failed to measure the real support this party had among the Saharan population[121]. The report made by the Mission stated that, "despite having been considered to be a clandestine movement until the arrival of the Mission, (the POLISARIO Front) seemed to be the dominant political force in the territory".

As regards the *Yemáa*, after the three party agreements of Madrid, Morocco and Mauritania attempted to join it El Aaiún (February 26, 1976), but it was only attended by 27 of a total of 102 members, as the others had joined the refugee's camps of the POLISARIO Front[122]. Despite the fact that some people defended the legitimacy of this call for a meeting[123], the official position of Spain was explained by its permanent representative at the United Nations, who stated that in no case could this meeting be considered to be the exercise of the right to self-determination stipulated in Resolution 3458 B (XXX).

Ciencias Morales y Políticas, n° 42 (67) (1990): 194 et seq.; WEEXSTEEN, R., "La question du Sahara Occidental", *Annuaire de l´Afrique du Nord*, 15 (1976): 257.

In addition, in 1971 as we pointed out above, the Government of Morocco had encouraged the creation of the *Mouvement de Résistance des Hommes Bleus (M.O.R.E.H.O.B.)* in order to defend the idea of the integration of the territory into Morocco. Despite meeting its President, the United Nations Visiting Mission concluded that this movement had hardly any members, and that, with the exception of the aforementioned President, "it did not find any other members or supporters in the territory or beyond its borders" (*ORGA*: supplement Num. 23, A/10023/Rev. 1, vol. III, Chap. XIII, Annex, para. 228).

[121] The very existence of the P.U.N.S. was called into question when three of its main leaders, Jalihenna, Jalil and Hamudi, fled to Morocco in May 1975 in order to swear allegiance to Hassan II. *Cfr.* VILLAR, F. (1982): 282. In 1978 Colonel Rodríguez de Viguri declared before the Foreign Affairs Commission of the Congress of Deputies that the Sahrawi public opinion was deeply hostile to the annexation of the territory by Morocco, that the POLISARIO Front represented this attitude of the people, and that the President of the Mission of the United Nations, which had arrived in the Sahara convinced of the justice of the Moroccan theses, during its stay in the territory became convinced to the contrary (*cfr. Diario de Sesiones del Congreso de los Diputados*, 1978, Num. 30, p. 5).

[122] Although the States occupying the territory had invited observers of the United Nations, the OAU, the Arab League and the Organization of the Islamic Conference, none of these organizations sent representatives to the meeting convened.

[123] A few days after the Spanish withdrawal, Carro wrote that "the colonial situation will last until the Saharans freely decide their future by their vote expressed through the *Yemáa*, as stated in the Declaration of Madrid, just as seems to have been done three days ago (February 26), in the event that this is legally accepted internationally" (CARRO MARTÍNEZ, A. (1976): 31).

Nevertheless, it is impossible to avoid the doubts arising from the literal meaning of the document under which Spain considered its presence in the territory to have ended about what this State understood by "the will of the Saharan people".

The aforementioned document, which acted to dissolve the *Yemáa*, stated that, "the sole and legitimate authority of the Saharan people is the Frente POLISARIO, recognized by the United Nations in accordance with the conclusions of the United Nations investigating mission", and reaffirmed its "unconditional support" to it[124]. Through a letter sent by the Secretary General of the National Saharan Council to the United Nations on December 10, 1975, attention was drawn to the fact that "Morocco and Mauritania, which yesterday denied the representative nature of the Saharan *Yemáa*, today declare that this same Assembly expresses the opinion of our people", and they also state that "it is clear that this *Yemáa* no longer exists" as "the immense majority of its representatives have voluntarily joined our ranks in order to contribute to the war of national liberation"[125]. We can conclude from this that the agreement adopted by the members of the *Yemáa* which Morocco and Mauritania had managed to gather together and which, as mentioned before, unanimously approved the reincorporation of the territory of the Sahara to Morocco and Mauritania, was not valid as the necessary quorum was not met. Consequently, no ballot could be used and this procedure was replaced by a pseudo acclamation[126].

At the same time, the Saharan Arab Democratic Republic (SADR) was proclaimed on February 27 in Bir Lehlu (in the part of the territory not occupied by Morocco), and was approved the Provisional Constitution, which would be in force until its definitive sanction[127], which took place at the III Congress of the POLISARIO Front (August 26-30, 1976). The Congress established the General National Programme, which reaffirmed the fact that it was a national liberation movement whose ultimate objective was the independence of the nation. This document also considered that "the respect of the principle of self-determination is a primordial and determining factor for the preservation of the relations between States and peoples, so that they might coexist in peace, prosperity and stability[128]. Finally, Mohamed

---

[124] *ORGA:* A/10481, S/11902, par. 3 y 5.
[125] *ORGA:* S/11903.
[126] RODRIGUEZ DE VIGURI GIL, L. (1980): 65.
[127] The complete text of the Provisional Constitution can be read in OLIVER LOPEZ-GUARCH, P (1988): 273-276, and in HINZ, M. (1978).
[128] The General National Programme defined in the course of the III Congress can be seen in MISKÉ, A.B. (1978): 360 (Miské was the Ambassador of Mauritania in Paris and at the UNO).

Chapter III

Abdelaziz was appointed as Secretary General, replacing Luali Mustafa Sayed, the first Secretary General of the Saharan liberation movement, who had died in combat on June 9, 1976.

Consequently, this Congress addressed the question of the role corresponding to the POLISARIO Front in the new institutional framework that arose after the constitution of the SADR. In this regard, the Minister of Communications and Energy, Mansour Uld Omar, stated that the POLISARIO Front was a political organ of the SADR, a party which represents all the Saharan people and constitutes the armed organ of the new State, the so-called Army for the Liberation of the Saharan people (E.L.P.S.)[129], a definition which was difficult to understand in legal terms, given the breadth of the concepts used. However, this difficulty can be explained by the peculiar circumstances that the authorities of the territory had to face, as they were forced to proclaim the creation of a new State and its new Constitution when a large part of its population was in refugee camps in Algeria, and a war of national liberation was starting, carried out by the POLISARIO Front. In these circumstances, everyone could see the difficulty involved in the attempt to classify the POLISARIO Front: although the fact that it was a national liberation movement remained beyond any doubt since it had been recognized by the UN as the sole and legitimate representative of the population of Western Sahara, its condition of political party is more questionable as it is clearly not a political party in the traditional sense of the term[130]. Additionally there was the difficulty arising from the coexistence of a national liberation movement, the POLISARIO Front, and a State, the SADR, acting simultaneously. As we will see below, this lead to a big headache for the OAU when the SADR became one of its members.

During the V Congress of the POLISARIO Front (October 12-16, 1982), as a consequence of the SADR joining the OAU, the constitutional text was revised, establishing Western style state structures. Among these was the institutional division between the Head of State and the Prime Minister or Head of Government. The objective was to enable representatives of the SADR to access the structures of the African Organization (Conference of Heads of State, Conference of Prime Ministers, etc.).

---

[129] OLIVER LOPEZ-GUARCH, P., "R.A.S.D.: origen y formación de un Estado", *Cuadernos de Historia Contemporánea*, 11 (1989): 130.

[130] *Cfr.* ZUNES, S., "Participatory democracy in the Sahara: a study of Polisario self-governance", *Scandinavian Journal of Development and Alternatives*, vol. 7 (1988): 146; by the same author, "Nationalism and Non-Alignment: The non-Ideology of the Polisario", *Africa Today*, n° 34, Third Quarter (1987): 38.

Following the first negotiations which ended in the approval of the Settlement Plan (*Plan de Arreglo*), the Congress of the POLISARIO Front on successive occasions became a platform from which the necessity to undertake negotiations with Morocco was repeatedly called for. For example, at the VII Congress (Tinduf, May 2, 1989) the Congress called on Morocco to continue their direct bilateral relations, deemed "the only way to solve the conflict", offering, as proof of their good will and to "encourage dialogue and the search for peace"[131] a unilateral ceasefire during the month of February. The Congress thus insisted the strategy of dialogue and bilateral negotiations.

In the course of the VIII Congress, held at the end of June 1991 and just prior to the entry into force of the ceasefire, which is still in force today, based on the conviction that the proposals of the POLISARIO Front would triumph in the referendum, a Draft Constitution was approved creating the Democratic Social Saharan Republic. This would replace the SADR, and proclaim the values of "democracy, respect for fundamental liberties, multi-parties and a balanced market economy with a strong public sector, principles in accord with the new wind blowing across the international scene"[132]. However, given the stoppage of the peace process, it was necessary to wait until the IX Congress (August 1993) for this modification of the SADR Constitution, in which the name was maintained and no important changes were made in the content of the previous text.

---

[131] This tendency had already appeared during the VI Congress (December 4-9, 1985) where the POLISARIO Front confirmed its decision to undertake negotiations with Morocco in accordance with the Peace Plan approved by the OAU (*ORGA*: A/AC.109/873, para. 7). This ceasefire ended on March 1, the date on which hostilities recommenced (*ibid.*, para. 29). In addition, at the VII Congress there was a declaration of solidarity with the Saharan cause made by the Secretary General of the Algerian National Liberation Front, Abdel Hamid Mehri, who stated that, despite the closer relations of the Governments of Rabat and Algiers, which had been traditionally difficult, Algeria continued with its aid to the SADR. This declaration was obviously received with relief by the leaders of the POLISARIO Front, as the support of Algeria is essential for the struggle being carried out by the Saharan people in order to exercise the right to self-determination. As regards the VII Congress, *Cfr.* SEDDON, D., "Polisario and the struggle for the Western Sahara: recent developments, 1987-1989", *Review of African Political Economy*, n° 45/46, (1989): 132-142; especially, pages 137-140.

[132] SOTILLO LORENZO, J.A., "Sahara: la cuenta atrás", *Tiempo de paz*, n. 21 (1991): 124 et seq.

CHAPTER III

3.2. The status of the SADR in the International Community

3.2.1. Scope and consequences of the recognition of the SADR

In January 2010, the SADR had been recognized by eighty-two States, although there was an absence of European States[133] as only two of these (the

---

[133] It was necessary to wait until the IV Congress of the POLISARIO Front in order to know the position of the Spanish Government. At this Congress there was substantial rapprochement with the Saharan pro-independence movement when the representatives of the political party which governed the country at the time, the Democratic Centre Union (U.C.D.) (Unión del Centro Democrático), participated in this Congress and issued a joint communiqué (October 12, 1978), in which this party recognized the POLISARIO Front and stated that the solution to the conflict necessarily involved the exercise of the legitimate right of the Saharan people to self-determination (*cfr.* ORGA: A/C.4/33/L.22, of November 29, 1978). According to Santos, the governments of the U.C.D of Suárez and Calvo Sotelo made it known that they recognized the SADR (SANTOS, A., "Le basculement vers le sud de la politique de defense de l'Espagne", *Affaires Internationals*, Num. 7, (1985): 30). Despite the official Spanish position not to formally recognize the POLISARIO Front nor the SADR, it has occasionally maintained relations with the first "at the level of subjects of International law". For example, when it jointly adopted the 'Joint Communiqué of the Spanish Government and the POLISARIO Front', of December 17, 1980" (MARIÑO MENÉNDEZ, F.M., "El Derecho Internacional y la actual situación del Sáhara Occidental", *Africa-América Latina, Cuadernos*, n° 6 (1991): 49). The text of this agreement can be seen in the *Revista de Estudios Internacionales*, Vol. 17, p. 249. In 1983 the Spanish Government considered that recognizing the SADR would add "points of confusion" to the conflict (response of the Government to a question asked by the deputy, Mr López Raimundo, concerning Spanish policy as regards the Sahara", *B.O.C.G.*, of September 23, 1983. This can also be seen in *Actividades, textos y Documentos de la Política Exterior Española*, 1983, p. 482 et seq.).
The position of the Socialist Party (P.S.O.E.) concerning the recognition of the POLISARIO Front and the SADR has been changeable depending on its situation as regards the Government. For example, on a visit to the camps in Tinduf on the anniversary of the signing of the Madrid agreements (November 14, 1976), Felipe González proclaimed the following: "we know that your experience is having received many unfulfilled promises. I do not want to promise you anything, but to make a committal with history: our party will be with you until the final victory" (DIEGO AGUIRRE, J. R., "La guerra del Sahara", *Historia 16*, n° 16 (188) (1991): 16. These declarations can be heard on the website of the Television of the SADR: http://www.rasd-tv.com/) The P.S.O.E. issued a joint communiqué with the POLISARIO Front declaring the Madrid agreements null, and, in December 1976, the XXVII Congress of this party adopted a resolution requesting respect for the right of the Saharan to self-determination. On the other hand, during the years following its accession to government, it maintained a difficult balance between its "sympathy" for the struggle of the POLISARIO Front and Spanish fishing interests, which it was negotiating with Morocco. Despite the fact that it has never recognized the Saharan liberation movement, on April 9, 1992, Felipe González, the president of the Spanish Government at the time, received

former Yugoslavia[134] and Albania) recognized it[135].

Mohamed Abdelaziz, in his capacity as "number one" of the POLISARIO Front, although the Spanish authorities were careful to point out that this was a visit "of a private nature".
Under the leadership of José María Aznar, the Government of the Partido Popular (P.P.) came closer to the Saharan positions, highlighted as a consequence of the conflict involving the Island of Perejil in July 2002, although this was probably more a result of the bad relationship of the Spanish President with Mohammed VI rather than a real interest in the cause of the Saharan people. The return of the P.S.O.E to power in 2004 led to the Spanish Government applying a planned policy of "active neutrality" in the conflict, as if there was equidistance between compliance and violation of the Law. On this question, *cfr.* DEZCALLAR MAZARREDO, R., "España y el Sahara Occidental", *Revista Española de Defensa*, abril, (1988): 36 et seq.; ECHEVERRIA JESUS, C., "La profundización de relaciones entre España y los países del Magreb", *Estudios Africanos*, 4 (7) (1989): 20. The return to the Government of the P.P. did not mean any change in this policy. In the same way that all predecessors Governments, President Mariano Rajoy maintains the policy of "active neutrality", supporting the occupying State.

[134] Yugoslavia recognized the SADR on November 28, 1984; however, after its breakup and disappearance, this recognition no longer made sense. However, as shown by the facts, those who foretold the inefficacy of the recognition of the SADR were mistaken. Thus, in 1979, Goytisolo stated that the POLISARIO Front might be recognized by fifteen or twenty small States far from the zone of conflict; nevertheless, this recognition is not sufficient to grant the SADR a minimum of international credibility (GOYTISOLO, J. (1979): 60; COLIN, J. P. (19978): 87). Today, the African States are those who have massively recognized the SADR.

[135] Besides the case of the former Yugoslavia, these are the States which have recognized the SADR, indicating the "withdrawals of recognition" and "freezing" recognition: Afghanistan (1979), Albania (1987), Algeria (1976), Angola (1976), Antigua and Barbuda (1987), Barbados (1988), Belize (1986), Benin (1976, withdrawn in 1997), Bolivia (1982), Botswana (1980), Burkina Faso (1984, "withdrawn" en 1996), Burundi (1976), Cambodia (1979), Cape Verde (1979, "frozen" en 2007), Chad (1980, "withdrawn" en 1997), Colombia (1985, "frozen" en 2000), Congo (1978, "withdrawn" en 1996), Costa Rica (1980), Cuba (1980), Dominica (1979), Ecuador (1983), East Timor (2002), El Salvador (1989, "withdrawn" en 1997), Ethiopia (1979), Equatorial Guinea (1978, "withdrawn" in 1980), Ghana (1979, "frozen" in 2001), Granada (1979), Guatemala (1986, "frozen" in 1998), Guinea- Bissau (1976, "withdrawn" in 1997, and "re-established" in 2000), Guiana (1979), Haiti (2006), Honduras (1989, "frozen" in 2000), India (1985, "withdrawn" in 2000), Iran (1980), Solomon Islands (1981, "withdrawn" in 1989), Jamaica (1979), Kenya (2005, "temporally frozen" in 2006), Kiribati (1981, "withdrawn" in 2000), Laos (1979), Lesotho (1979), Liberia (1985, "withdrawn" in 1997), Libya (1980), Madagascar (1976, "withdrawn" in 2005), Malawi (1994, "withdrawn" in 2001, "re-established" in 2008, and "again withdrawn" that same year), Mali (1980), Mauritania (1984), Mauritius (1982), Mexico (1979), Mozambique (1976), Namibia (1990), Nauru (1981, "withdrawn" in 2000), Nicaragua (1979, "frozen" in 2000, and "re-established" in 2007), Nigeria (1984), North Korea (1976), Panama (1978), Papua New Guinea (1981), Paraguay (2000, "frozen" in 2000, and "re-established" in 2008), Peru (1984, which suspended diplomatic relations in

CHAPTER III

Many surprising case studies have been generated by this question and it is even possible to classify States depending on the steps taken in this regard. Thus, besides the States which have recognized the SADR in traditional terms, it should be pointed out that others have taken up a different position, and have endeavoured to give and withdraw recognition depending on the movements of the powerful and always generous Moroccan diplomacy, occasionally seconded by "illustrious persons" in Spanish politics[136]. A first group of States include those which, after recognizing SADR, endeavoured to withdraw this recognition (Benin, Burkina Faso, Chad, Congo, El Salvador, Equatorial Guinea, India, Kiribati, Liberia, Madagascar, Nauru, Saint Lucia, São Tome and Principe, Solomon Islands, Swaziland, Togo and Tuvalu); a second group includes those who took both these steps of recognition and "withdrawal" of recognition, and then subsequently, "re-established" the initial recognition (Guinea Bissau and Vanuatu); a third group includes those which have culminated this surrealist process with another "de-recognition" (Malawi); a fourth group includes a number of States which have inaugurated a new and surprising *legal concept* of the "freezing" of recognition (Cape Verde, Colombia, the aforementioned Dominican Republic and Guatemala); and finally, a fifth group includes the States which granted recognition, "froze it", and then "re-established" it (Nicaragua and Paraguay).

These incredible cases, which show the enormous power of Moroccan diplomacy, lead us to addressing the question of compatibility with International law of withdrawal, "freezing" or the, even more unusual approach, of conferring recognition, withdrawal of that recognition and a subsequent re-recognition. In the first place, it should be pointed out that recognition is a discretionary act of the States; but this discretion is only restricted to the time it is granted: a State can freely decide whether to recognize another State or not, that is to say, if it considers that the International law's requirements for a State to exist are complied with at the time; however, once granted, it is not possible to reverse the decision. As

---

1996), Dominican Republic (1986, "frozen" in 2002), Ruanda (1976), Saint Lucia (1979, "withdrawn" in 1989), Saint Vincent and the Grenadines (2002), São Tome and Principe (1978, "withdrawn" in 1996), Seychelles (1977), Sierra Leone (1980), South Africa (2004), St. Kitts and Nevis (1987), Surinam (1982), Swaziland (1980, "withdrawn" in 1997), Syria (1980), Tanzania (1978), Togo (1976, "withdrawn" in 1997), Trinidad and Tobago (1986), Tuvalu (1981, "withdrawn" in 2000), Uganda (1979), Uruguay (2005), Vanuatu (1980, "withdrawn" in 2000, and "re-established" in 2008), Venezuela (1982), Vietnam (1979), Yemen (1977), Zambia (1979), and Zimbabwe (1980).

[136] For example, the pressure applied by the former Spanish President, Felipe González, in support of the Moroccan lobby frustrated the recognition of the SADR by Chile on the very day that the Chilean Government publicised the fact that it would do so in 2000.

pointed out by Blumann, although the act of recognition is discretionary in principle, an objective reality must be taken into consideration: if this reality has not changed, the recognizing State is obliged by the rule of *estoppel*[137]. From the legal point of view, what Quel López calls "de-recognition of States" is not possible; such a change of a previous decision cannot have legal effects as, once the legal factors which determine the existence of the State are verified, the recognition of its existence will last until these factors might disappear[138]. As stated by this author, even in the case in which these factors do disappear, "de-recognition" would not be necessary, which is further supported by more recent practice in this regard, such as those States involved in dissolution processes in the last decade of the twentieth century (the USSR, Yugoslavia). The same consequences regarding express recognition are derived from the establishment of diplomatic relations and from the favourable vote for a new State to join an International Organization, which automatically entails the presumption of *iuris et de iure* of recognition which is of an irrevocable nature. In this regard, the supposed "de-recognition" carried out by African States which voted in favour of the SADR joining the OAU (Benin, Cape Verde, Chad, Congo, Ghana, Guinea Bissau, Madagascar, São Tome and Principe, Swaziland and Togo) is even more incomprehensible and obviously incompatible with International law, although in reality it presents few problems in the practice of international relations as, within the area of the African organisation, these States behave as if this "de-recognition" had never occurred.

However, as regards the attitude taken by several International Organisations concerning the question of recognition, practice shows that occasionally "legitimacy" criteria have prevailed over criteria of strict legality[139]. Thus, the admission of Namibia to the ILO, or the acceptance of the United Nations Council for Namibia as the legitimate Government of the proto-State of the former colony of South-West Africa, the "recognition" of the State of Palestine (December 1988)[140] and the Palestine non-Member Observer State status approved by the General Assembly of the UN (November 2012), or Kosovo joining the international Monetary Fund (May

---

[137] BLUMANN, C., "Establissement et rupture des relations diplomatiques", in the collection *Aspects récents du droit des relations diplomatiques*, Pedone, Paris (1989): 27.
[138] QUEL LOPEZ, F.J., "La práctica reciente en materia de reconocimiento de Estados: problemas en presencia", *Cursos de Derecho Internacional de Vitoria-Gasteiz* (1992): 46.
[139] *Ibid.*, p. 53.
[140] Resolution 43/177 of the GA, approved on December 15, 1988, "recognises" the proclamation of a new independent Palestinian State and decides to change the term "P.L.O." to "Palestine".

2009)[141], are good examples of how the institution of recognition is sometimes used in order to highlight the legitimacy of a struggle, which, in the Saharan case, has already been recognized by the UN. These cases of recognition of States do not have a constituent value, but it is evident that it can have the effect of a presumption of the existence of the State and, to a certain extent, of its competence to establish bilateral relations with other States[142].

A sector of international doctrine has criticised the recognitions of the SADR as "premature", based on the fact that the Saharan Government does not effectively control the totality of its territory, which means that it lacks the requirement of the effectiveness traditionally demanded by International law in order to speak of a State in the strict sense. However, besides the evident legitimizing value it has, the context in which the institution of recognition of States arose and the evident changes which have occurred in the international community since then must be taken into account. The recognition of States began at a time when a large number of territories throughout the world had not yet been formed as "definitively constituted States". Just as occurred with the formation of the continents, which make up the world, as we know it, until the twentieth century, military conquest was the rule in international relations and borders fluctuated depending on the military forces of the powers. On the contrary, the basic rule of contemporary International law, which forbids the use of force in international relations, and, consequently, the recognition of the annexation of territories resulting from the use of force, has contributed to the formation of the contemporary map of the world to a great extent. Although no State has recognized the annexation of Western Sahara by Morocco, the non-recognition of the SADR with the excuse that its Government does not effectively control the totality of the territory has a clear consequence: to implicitly promote this annexation. Admitting the premature nature of the recognition of the SADR could lead to the invocation of State Responsibility on the basis of Resolution 2625 (XXV), because despite no explicit acts of recognition of the illegal annexation, they would contribute implicitly to the consolidation of the illegal annexation. This Resolution stated the duty of every States "to promote, through joint and separate action, realization of the principle of equal rights and self-determination of peoples, in accordance with the provisions of the Charter, and to render assistance to the United Nations in carrying out the responsibilities entrusted to it by the Charter regarding the implementation of the principle, in order (…) to bring a speedy end to

---

[141] Of the 185 member States of the IMF, 96 voted in favour of its joining and 10 against, which opened the door to joining the World Bank.
[142] QUEL LOPEZ, F. J. (1992): 53.

colonialism (...)". The recognition of States is an institution dependent on the discretion of the States, but one, as well as others, which can and must contribute to compliance with this obligation.

3.2.2. *The admission of the SADR to the Organization for African Unity*

International organizations inevitably reflect the conflicts that confront their members, and these usually serve as a channel for discussions and debates aimed at resolving these. This happens not only in global organizations but also in regional organizations, including the OAU, which has been a clear example of this rule from its beginnings. As Barbier points out, the conflicts which have taken place within this Organization can be grouped into two different types: conflicts which have led its members towards common, united action, including the movement for the decolonization of the African continent, the struggle against *apartheid* and the problems related to economic and social development, and those other types of conflicts which have resulted in movement in the opposite direction: separation and division. These last include a number of confrontations between the members of the OAU, mainly as a consequence of decolonization, a process whose necessity was met with consensus among the African States although no consensus could be reached over how this was to be carried out. The Western Sahara situation is included in this last type of conflict, and, as we will see, it has placed the organisation on the verge of a complete stoppage on several occasions and has tested its very existence.

Until 1975 the question of "Spanish Sahara" supposed no headaches for the OAU: there was consensus as regards the need to decolonize the territory, just as had slowly taken place in the rest of the African territories. However, since that year, the conflict has affected the OAU with such force that it has nearly sunk the organization on numerous occasions. The decision of the UN to give the OAU the green light to intervene in the process and supported the OAU as the correct platform upon which to resolve the Saharan dispute[143]

---

[143] This was a claim made by Morocco, which repeatedly maintained that the United Nations should leave the decision on the measures to be adopted in order to find a solution to an African problem in the hands of the African Heads of State. As we will see below, when the OAU supported the right of the Saharan people to self-determination, Morocco abandoned its seat in this organisation, and, from then on, it modified the approaches it had defended for so long and so obsessively. Among other documents, which include the attitude of the Moroccan Government regarding this question, *cfr.* ORGA: A/C.4/33/SR.32, para. 31, in which its representative stated that the Fourth Commission must decide *"once and for all"* that the OAU must act on this question. Similarly, the Moroccan representative stated

changed the direction of its evolution[144]. This decision of the UN gave the OAU a leading role in the subsequent development of the conflict although, obviously, this organisation did not need this authorization to intervene. In fact, since 1976, at its summit meetings, the OAU had been examining the situation in Western Sahara. The Liberation Committee of the OAU, which met in Maputo (Mozambique) on January 24, 1976, recommended that the Council of Ministers recognize the POLISARIO Front as a movement for national liberation and the sole representative of the Saharan people.

---

before the "Committee of Twenty-four" in August 1982, that the resolutions and decisions of the OAU concerning this issue (expressly citing Resolution AHG/Res.103 (XVIII) and Decision AHG/IMP.C/WS/Dec.1 (I), which we will refer to below) "are the only ones which will subsequently have authority in the matter as the regional organisation in charge of the matter has given a mandate to a special committee with full powers (...)" (this was a reference to the *Ad hoc Committee*) (*ORGA*: A/AC.109/720, of august 23, 1982).

As we mentioned above, in November 1978, the GA of the OAU sent a letter to the UNO requesting that all the Member States of the Organisation abstain "from any action which might hinder the work" of this Committee, or delay the achievement of a just and peaceful solution to the problem (*ORGA*: A/33/364), which was severely criticised by the POLISARIO Front and Algeria (*ORGA*: A/33/397).

The intervention of the OAU in the conflict goes back to 1966 when its Council of Ministers met in Addis-Ababa, and adopted a resolution on the territories under Spanish domination (*OAU Documents:* CM/Res.82 (VII)). This document called on Spain to commence a process "to grant liberty and independence to all these regions". This resolution was followed by others drafted in similar terms and referring to the Spanish Sahara. Outstanding among these was the one adopted by the Council of Ministers of the OAU in Rabat, in June 1972 (*OAU Document* CM/Res.272 (XIX)), which called on Spain "to create a free, democratic atmosphere in which the people of the territory might exercise their right to self-determination and independence without delay, in conformity with the United Nations Charter".

[144] The action taken by the OAU in the conflict would have decisive importance in its development, as this Organization would give unconditional support to Saharan aspirations. The peculiarities of the Western Sahara case, just as in the case of East Timor, a European colonisation was followed by an occupation by a neighbouring State, led the Government of Morocco (and that of Indonesia with regard to the case of East Timor), to maintain that the right of self-determination corresponded only to the populations of territories administered by foreigners who have evident differences of a racial, cultural or geographical nature, a circumstance, which in the opinion of this State, did not arise in this conflict. Blay calls this, "the right to self-determination against white European domination", which would be based on skin pigmentation, which is totally rejected by the doctrine of the OAU. The right to self-determination is recognized by article 20 of the African Charter on Human and People's Rights ("The Banjul Letter"), which was approved by the 18th assembly of Heads of State and Government of the OAU, which met in Nairobi in June 1981. *Cfr.* BLAY, K.N., "Changing African perspectives on the right of self-determination in the wake on the Banjul Charter on Human and People's rights", *Journal of African Law*, n. 29 (1985): 147-159.

However, this recognition was hindered by a proclamation made one month later (February 27, 1976) by the Saharan Arab Democratic Republic (SADR)[145], which occurred during a session of the Council of Ministers of the OAU[146]: how is it possible to recognize a liberation movement after it has declared itself a State which seeks recognition?[147] Morocco and Mauritania totally rejected this recognition, and threatened to withdraw from the OAU and to support the pro-independence movements in several African countries, as a way to put pressure on States that had favoured recognition. In these circumstances, the question was delayed until further summits of the African Organization[148].

Despite this, the question of the admission of the SADR to the OAU would not be delayed. During the 15th Conference of the Heads of State and Government (Khartoum, July 1978)[149], the OAU decided to create an *Ad hoc*

---

[145] Only some days later, on March 8, 1976, Algeria recognized the SADR, which was furiously attacked by the Mauritanian representative before the GA (*ORGA*: 31st period of sessions, 20th plenary session, October 6, 1976). Previously, on the day of the proclamation, the SADR had been recognized by Burundi and Madagascar (*ORGA*: A/31/59 y S/12002, Annex).

[146] The Council of Ministers of the OAU, which had met in Addis Ababa between February 23 and 29, 1976, affirmed the right of the Saharan people to self-determination (*ORGA*: A/31/59 y S/12002).

[147] At the meeting of the Council of Ministers of the OAU held on February 22, 1976, 17 States voted in favour of the recognition of the POLISARIO Front as a National Liberation Movement, 9 against, and 21 abstained. The reason for the high number of abstentions that prevented this recognition was the proclamation of the SADR as a new independent State, which had been previously agreed to. In this regard, *cfr.* WEEXSTEEN, R. (1978): 225.

[148] During the 27th period of sessions of the Council of Ministers of the OAU (Port Louis, Mauritius, June 24 to July 3, 1976), although no mention was made of the possibility of expressly referring to the possibility of recognizing the SADR, the resolution approved at this meeting, first reaffirmed "the inalienable right of the Western Saharan people to self-determination", which requires "the immediate withdrawal of all the *foreign occupation forces* and respect for the territorial integrity of Western Sahara and the national sovereignty of the Saharan people" (*ORGA*: A/31/136, and S/12141, Annex I – the highlighted part is ours -). However, the most moderate resolution adopted in the course of this session by the Heads of State and Government sowed doubts on the position that the OAU would finally adopt as regards this point. This resolution "invites all the parties concerned and involved, including Western Sahara to cooperate in order to achieve a peaceful solution to the conflict in the interests of peace, justice and good will in the region (...)", and delays the debate on the question until a period of extraordinary sessions are held on the Saharan issue (*ibid.*, Annex II).

[149] At the 15th Conference, Resolution AHG/Res.92 (XV) was approved, and this appears as Annex to the document of the UNO: *ORGA*: A/33/337, of October 31, 1978.
During the 13th Conference (Port Louis, Mauritius, July 2-6, 1976) the Assembly of Heads of State had approved Resolution 81 (XIII), whereby it invited the parties concerned and

Committee, composed of five Heads of State under the Presidency of the Organization, Gaafar Mohamed Nimeiri, entrusted to seek a solution to the conflict compatible with the right to self-determination. This Committee was set in motion by Morocco and Mauritania, while the POLISARIO Front and Algeria did not agree, as they understood that, as many resolutions of the UN had pointed out, this was a question of decolonization and the UN should be aware of it[150]. A subcommittee was immediately constituted to visit the region in order to establish the measures required to restore international peace and security. The parties were also requested to impose an immediate ceasefire that would allow the subcommittee to carry out its functions. The results of this visit to the region materialized in a number of recommendations included in a report that was approved during the 16th Conference of the Heads of State and Government (Monrovia, 1979), through Decision AHG/Dec.114 (XVI), that included among its most relevant aspects a ceasefire and a referendum on self-determination for Western Sahara[151].

However, before the conflict turned back to the United Nations, at the 17th Conference (Freetown, July 1980) one of the most important crises of the OAU took place. This involved the express admission of the SADR as a member with full rights of the Organization (the Saharan-Mauritanian peace

---

involved to cooperate in order to achieve a peaceful and just solution to the conflict (*ORGA*: A/31/136 y S/12141, Annex II, and A/31/138 y S/12143. Text of the resolution, in *ORSC*: S/12141, Annex II, and S/12143). At the 14th Conference (Libreville, July 2-5, 1977) the Assembly decided to hold a n extraordinary Conference on the issue of Lusaka (Zambia), on October 5, 1977, which was not possible due to the situation in the country at the time, (*ORGA*: A/32/310, Annex II, AHG/Dec.110 (XIV), whose delay was repeatedly criticized by the POLISARIO Front, which denounced the delaying tactics of Morocco and its allies in the OAU (*ORGA*: A/32/303, Annex, p. 16).

[150] *ORGA*: A/34/23/Rev.1, p. 106 (suplem. num. 23). The legal basis for the constitution of this Committee is included in article 19 of the Charter of the OAU, which permits the Assembly to create as many commissions as it considers being necessary. As pointed out by Naldi, one outstanding point is that the reference article is 19 and not 20 as this enables the Assembly to establish a Mediation, Conciliation and Arbitration Committee in the case of disputes between member States, a possibility not taken into account in the case of Western Sahara (*cfr.* NALDI, G. J., "The OAU and the Saharan Arab Democratic Republic", *Journal of African Law*, vol. 26, (1982): 159). Probably the reason for the appeal to article 19 lies in the fact that, at that time, the SADR had not yet been recognized as a State by the OAU, when article 20 was intended for "disputes between States".

[151] *Ibid.*, Annex VII. The text of this resolution was included in Resolution 34/37 of the GA of the UNO. It is surprising that, at this time, the conflict referred to two possible solutions through the exercise of the free right to self-determination, but limiting the options to two: "choosing total independence or the maintenance of the *status quo*" (*ORGA*: A/34/483, Annex, Decision AHG/Decl.114 (XVI)).

treaty had already been signed[152]). As regards the report of the *ad hoc Committee* on Western Sahara, which made the formal petition of the SADR to be admitted as a member of the Organization, Morocco rejected that this had the conditions required by International law for the constitution of a new State, and requested an interpretation of articles 4, 27 and 28 of the Charter of the OAU in this respect[153]. The Moroccan representative requested before the Council of Ministers of the OAU (June 24, 1980) that, in application of what is set out in Article 27 of the Charter of the Organization and to the extent that the SADR is attributed the condition of an independent and sovereign State according to Article 4 of the Charter, the two thirds majority of the Heads of State and Government of the members of the Organization which is required for the adoption of a decision concerning the Charter be respected. The States that opposed the recognition of the SADR expressed their intention to abandon the Conference in the event that the interpretation of Article 4 of the Charter in the terms laid down by the Moroccan representative was excluded, which would thus be in violation of the Charter. In such a difficult situation, as the *ad hoc Committee* proposed, the Conference decided to request the Presidency "to deploy all its efforts in order to reconcile the parties in the conflict and to find a peaceful and lasting solution to this question"[154], which supposed that the discussion of the questions were postponed until the *ad hoc Committee* had fulfilled its mission[155]. Faced with such difficult times, the OAU preferred not to make any declarations regarding the question of recognition of the SADR, leaving free reign to possible negotiations, thus, giving a partial victory to the Moroccan theses.

During the 18th Conference of the Heads of State and Government of the OAU (Nairobi, June 1981), as the admission of the SADR seemed inevitable, Hassan II, who attended the Conference personally for the first time, in a last

---

[152] The peace agreement signed in Algiers on August 10, 1979 appears as Annex I of the document of the United Nations (*ORGA*: A/34/427 and S/13503).

[153] The articles of the Charter of the OAU invoked by Morocco state the following: "Article 4. Each independent sovereign African State shall be entitled to become a Member of the Organization. Article 27. Any question which may arise concerning the interpretation of this Charter shall be decided by a vote of two-thirds of the Assembly of Heads of State and Government of the Organization. Art. 28. Any independent sovereign African State may at any time notify the Secretary-General of its intention to adhere or accede to this Charter". As concerns the questions related to this part of the OAU Charter, *cfr.* CASSESE, A., "La Carta dell'Organizzazione dell'Unità Africana", *Rivista* (1964): 430-441.

[154] *Official Documents of the OAU*: Decision AHG/Doc. 118 (XVII).

[155] At the time the Conference was held, the SADR had already been recognized by twenty-six of the fifty States which formed the OAU at the time, therefore, just like Morocco, it did not have the two thirds majority required (article 27).

attempt to impede this admission, decided to accept the organisation of a referendum in the territory for the first time[156]. The adoption of two decisions and a resolution ended the Conference: the first of these decided to organise and coordinate a general, free referendum in Western Sahara, and also proposed the creation of an interim administration in order to ensure the impartiality of the referendum, while the objective of the second decision was "to impose a ceasefire and ensure that it was respected"[157]. Despite the doubts behind his words, doubts which would be corroborated later in a press conference, when the Alawite monarch cynically clarified the acceptance of the referendum on the self-determination of the Saharan people, by stating that, the circumstances may lead to a Head of State saying things which he will not say the following day, or vice versa[158], this decision was a landmark in the process as it constituted the starting point for the negotiations which would conclude with the Settlement Plan years later.

Resolution 103 (XVIII) of the OAU welcomed the "solemn commitment made by His Majesty King Hassan II of Morocco for accepting the organization of a referendum in the territory of Western Sahara", and decided on the creation of a new organ dependent on the Committee, named the *Implementation Committee*, which was responsible for carrying out the referendum and controlling the ceasefire on the basis of the criteria of "one person, one vote"[159]. As Morocco refused to directly negotiate with the POLISARIO Front and withdraw its troops from the territory during the referendum, it was evident that that the committee had been born moribund. However, it has one merit which is beyond doubt: for the first time consideration would be given to questions such as the referendum, the withdrawal of troops from both sides from the territory and the establishment of a transitory period of administration and well as those related to the electoral census, which should be based on the one drawn up by the Spanish authorities in 1974, as well as data provided by the ACNUR; the growth rate

---

[156] On June 26, 1981, Hassan II stated that he admitted the holding of a referendum and declared that he was willing to organise it in three or four months.

[157] *Official Documents of the OAU*: Decision AGH./I.M.P.C./W.S./DEC. 1 (II), Nairobi, 1981.

[158] The text of these declarations is in GRIMAUD, N. (1988): 95. These declarations of Hassan II were intended to placate those who had thought that the attitude of the King was an abandonment of the theoretical Moroccan rights over the territory (for example, the Secretary General of the Socialist Union of Popular Forces, Abderrahim Buabid, dared to criticize this attitude and was condemned to a year in prison for such criticism although he was pardoned in February 1982). In any case, at the Nairobi Conference, he made it clear that he did not intend to negotiate with the POLISARIO Front.

[159] *Official Documents of the OAU*: Resolution AHG/93 (XVI), Report of the Ad Hoc Committee, Annex VII, para. 5.

of the population would also be taken into account. In addition, there was the possibility of establishing an operation for maintaining peace in the territory. Although specific agreements were not reached, the work of the Committee was a first serious attempt to address the questions related to the referendum, which, as we will see below, would have to be taken into account when drafting the 1998 Peace Plan.

Although the positions of the parties were irreconcilable (Morocco even rejected the possibility of establishing a UN/OAU peace operation), it would be necessary to wait for several years to pass before the effects of the efforts made might be appreciated, undoubtedly the contribution of the OAU at this phase of the process was extremely important[160]. In this regard, it is significant that the UN again took up the Saharan question by approving Resolution 39/40 of the General Assembly[161], which totally assumed the content of Resolution 104 (XIX) of the OAU.

Before finalizing the analysis of the Conference of Nairobi, we must also refer to the question of the admission of the SADR as a full member of the OAU mentioned above. This question was put forward by its Secretary General who pointed out that the question of the admission of a new member to the OAU was a purely administrative question, therefore, this was within its exclusive competence. Thus, on the understanding that each Member State was first consulted individually and, once a simple majority of member states had shown they were in favour, the Secretary general notified the State concerned that it had been admitted. The acceptance of a referendum by Morocco opened a door to a general solution of the Saharan conflict and this was a sufficient reason not to put forward the question of the admission of the SADR, at least until the following Conference of the OAU. As Barbier reminds and as time would show, this was "an ambiguous commitment which each party could interpret in its favour", at the same time as it allowed Hassan II to convert the Nairobi Summit, which had been a trial by fire for him, into a personal and diplomatic success[162]. Undoubtedly, for the Alawite monarch it was not a case of calling a referendum in the sense of the resolutions of the UNO and of the OAU, but rather a referendum "confirming" the Moroccan

---

[160] *Cfr.* In this respect, the analysis of the action taken by the OAU during this period made by NALDI, G. J., "Peace-keeping attempts by the Organisation of African Unity", *International and Comparative Law Quarterly*, n° 34 (1985): 593-601.
[161] Resolution approved by the GA on December 5, 1984, by 94 votes in favour, none against and 42 abstentions.
[162] BARBIER, M. (1982): 339.

CHAPTER III

nature of Western Sahara[163]. From that time, the POLISARIO Front demanded direct negotiations with Morocco under the auspices of the OAU.

By February 1982, the SADR had been recognized by twenty-six members of the OAU[164], which was the necessary simple majority of the members States of the Organization, and on February 22 that same year, despite the efforts of the United States to prevent it[165], the Secretary General notified the SADR, "an independent, sovereign African State" (Article 4 of the Charter of the OAU), that it was admitted as new member of the Organization[166] and was invited to attend the Council of Ministers which would take place in Addis-Ababa as a full member[167], which led to the most serious crisis the Organization would suffer. Morocco and another sixteen States withdrew

---

[163] It is very significant that, after the approval of the aforementioned resolution by the OAU, Hassan II declared that the referendum could be organized in three or four months, with the participation of "the population which is in the territory, and the refugees were invited to return in the event that they wanted to participate in the referendum" (*ibid.,* p. 340).

[164] The African States which had expressly recognized the SADR by that date were the following: Algeria, Angola, Benin, Botswana, Burundi, Cape Verde, Chad, Congo, Ethiopia, Ghana, Guinea Bissau, Lesotho, Libya, Madagascar, Mali, Mozambique, Uganda, Ruanda, São Tome and Principe, the Seychelles, Sierra Leone, Swaziland, Tanzania, Togo, Zambia and Zimbabwe. Mauritania had not expressly recognized the SADR although, after it withdrew from the conflict and concluded peace agreements with the POLISARIO Front, it could hardly refuse to give implicit recognition. Equatorial Guinea recognized the SADR on November 3, 1978, and "withdrew" its recognition on May 5, 1980.

[165] The United States considered that the admission of the SADR as a full member of the OAU was a serious error, and requested the pro-Western African States to boycott the summit (*cfr. In this respect,* the U.S. House of Representatives, Committee on Foreign Affairs, Report of a Staff Study Mission to Morocco, Algeria, the Western Sahara, and France, August 25- September, 6, 1982, *U.S. Policy Towards the Conflict in the Western Sahara,* Washington, 1983); also, *cfr.* HODGES, T., *The roots of a desert war,* Westport, Connecticut (1983): 315; ZUNES, S., "The United States in the Saharan War: a case of low-intensity intervention", en la obra colectiva *International dimensions of the Western Sahara conflict,* Edited by Zoubir, Yahia H. & Volman, D., Westport (1993): 422-441).

[166] The SADR was admitted as State number 51 of the OAU. As stated by Bedjaoui, the Secretary General of the OAU has no power to make appreciations as its actions are clearly regulated: once it is verified that the simple majority of the States have recognized a State, admission is automatic (*cfr.* BEDJAOUI, M., "L´admission d´un nouveau membre à l´Organisation de l´Unité Africaine", in *Le Droit des peuples à disposer d´eux-mêmes.Mèthodes d´analyse du Droit International (Mélanges offerts à Charles Chaumont),* Paris (1984): 39).

[167] The 38th session of the Council of Ministers of the OAU was held in Addis-Ababa from the 22nd to the 28th of February 1982, and the SADR was admitted to the OAU on the day the session began, February 22. The reason for this change of approach of the Secretary General of the OAU might have been due to his interest in being re-elected to the post. *Cfr.* VILLAR, F. (1982): 395.

from the Council of Ministers or suspended their participation in the Organization[168], which led to the total freezing of its activity for several months. However, Morocco, which had already threatened to withdraw in order to prevent the admission of the SADR, understood that the best way to combat the agreement on admission was to do so from within the Organization as it had the support of a third of the member States. This is why it did not withdraw, despite the fact that it did not have arguments to prevent the admission of the SADR because the argument that it was not an independent, sovereign State due to the fact that it did not effectively control its territory would require the explanation of the Government of Morocco on this occupation. In addition, this was not the first time that the OAU had admitted the representatives of a national liberation movement as a member State before independence was achieved[169].

---

[168] The generic threat of the Moroccan Government to break off diplomatic relations with the States which recognized the SADR as retaliation had very limited effects as very few States had diplomatic relations with Morocco and the Moroccan Government had different attitudes to each of these States. Thus, in some cases, Morocco broke off diplomatic relations with the states which successively recognized the SADR (Algeria, March, 1976, Ethiopia march 19, 1979, Libya, April 18, 1980), in other cases, after breaking off diplomatic relations and these States had not modified their positions, it re-established relations (among these cases were Angola and Cape Verde). Finally, in other cases Morocco did not break off diplomatic relations (Mali, Nigeria). In the specific case of Algeria, the Moroccan Government re-established diplomatic relations in May 1988. After the Freetown summit meeting, Morocco decided not to sell phosphates to the States that recognized the SADR, but this measure was irrelevant given the facilities that the world phosphate market offered.

[169] This was the case of Guinea Bissau, proclaimed on September 24, 1973 by the representatives of the *P.A.I.G.C.* (Party for the African Independence of the Islands of Guinea and Cape Verde), and admitted as member number 43 of the OAU on November 20, 1973, when the decolonization process had not yet concluded and the effectiveness of the power of the *P.A.I.G.C.* was partial. Furthermore, the independence of Guinea Bissau was not formalised until September 10, 1974, the date on which Portugal, the administering power, and the representatives of this movement concluded the Lisbon Agreements, which opened the way to the independence of the new State. Although the UN GA congratulated itself on the access of the people of Guinea Bissau to independence, "thereby creating created the sovereign State of the Republic of Guinea Bissau" -Resolution 3061 (XXVIII), of November 2, 1973- it was not admitted as new State until September 17, 1974, after the signing of the Lisbon Agreements. In Bennouna's opinion, the explanation of this exceptional attitude of the OAU lies in the fact that it was the only national liberation movement in the territory and there were no claims from neighbouring States (*Cfr.* BENNOUNA, M., "L´admission d´un nouveau membre à l´Organisation de l´Unité Africaine", *A.F.D.I.* l, (1980): 193). As regards this process, besides the work cited, *cfr.* PAZZANITA, A.G., "Legal aspects of membership in the Organization of African Unity: the case of Western Sahara", *Case Western Reserve Journal of International Law*, 17 (1), Winter (1985): 154-156. Barbier considers the situations

Chapter III

Despite the fact that Morocco did not finally fulfil its promise to withdraw from the Organization, the OAU crisis was clearly evidenced by the failed Dakar conference (March 1982), whose objective was the start-up of the P.A.N.A. (Pan-African News Agency). Senegal refused to permit the representatives of the SADR to enter the country, which led to the immediate withdrawal of the Algerian representatives, accompanied by another thirteen delegations meaning that the Conference had to be suspended due to a lack of quorum. This was the first but not the last time in which the Saharan conflict would alter the normal functioning of the OAU as the presence of the SADR representatives led to the withdrawal of representatives to Rabat on several occasions[170]. However, the most difficult time the OAU had to undergo was the failed Tripoli Conference which had been convened for the first week in August 1982 but could not be held due to a lack of quorum when the States opposing the admission of the SADR refused to participate although this was not the main reason for the conflict in the OAU (at this summit a prior question was raised concerning which of the delegations from Chad should occupy the seat corresponding to this country in the Organization[171]). This was the first time since the creation of the OAU that an ordinary summit meeting could not be held. After some months of uncertainty regarding the future of the Organization, an agreement was finally reached whereby the SADR would "voluntarily and provisionally" abstain from participating in the Summit Meeting, which enabled the OAU to function again.

In these circumstances, during the 19th Conference in Addis-Ababa (June 1983), a resolution was approved which would be permanently referred to as

---

of Western Sahara and Guinea Bissau at the time of their admission to the OAU was very similar, and the basic difference lies in the fact that the Saharan population is not in the territory due to the insecurity arising from Moroccan occupation (*cfr.* BARBIER, M., "Le problème du Sahara Occidental et la crise de l'OUA", *Mois en Afrique*, 18, n° 207/208, (1983): 39).

[170] For example, in the course of the meeting of the Council of Ministers held in Salisbury in April that same year, nine delegations withdrew from this for the same reason.

[171] As regards the conflict unleashed in Chad, and its consequences on the functioning of the OAU, *cfr.* BARBIER, M. (1983): 45 et seq. It should be mentioned that the fact that the composition of the two groups of States confronting each other in this conflict was practically the same as that which confronted Moroccans and Saharans was not simple chance as the incipient struggle between France, which was beginning to lose its influence in some States, and the United States, which was making headway there, was looming over the African continent. Concerning the composition of both groups of States and the position adopted by these as regards the voting on resolutions related to the Saharan issue at the OAU and at the UNO during the conflictive decade 1975-1985, *cfr.* The meticulous work of BARBIER, M., "Les pays d'Afrique noire et le problème du Sahara Occidental", *Afrique Contemporaine*, 24, 135 (1985): 10-37.

from then in the resolutions of the OAU and of the UN: this was the aforementioned Resolution AHG/Res.104 (XIX)[172]. The most interesting aspects of this Resolution of the Assembly of the Heads of State and the Heads of Government of the OAU are the following: it mentions the solemn commitment of King Hassan II to accept the holding of a referendum on self-determination in the territory, while "it welcomes the constructive attitude of the Saharan leaders as regards making a 19th ordinary meeting possible by voluntarily and provisionally withdrawing"[173] as this attitude of the Saharans enabled the Conference to be held whereas their presence would have automatically provoked a withdrawal of the Moroccan representatives and those States sharing its approach[174]. Furthermore, this resolution involved the start-up of the mechanisms which would later allow a referendum to be held, so therefore, "the United Nations in conjunction with the OAU to provide a Peace-Keeping Force to be stationed in Western Sahara to ensure peace and security during the organization and conduct of the Referendum". Attention ought to be drawn to another circumstance of the utmost importance: for the first time a resolution of the OAU referred to the POLISARIO Front as one of the parties involved in the conflict[175].

At the 20th Summit Meeting (Addis-Ababa, November 1984) the SADR occupied its seat at the OAU for the first time[176], and this led to the withdrawal

---

[172] The full text of this resolution was included in Resolution 38/40 of the UN GA, approved on December 7, 1983.

[173] *Official Documents of the OAU*: para. 1 of Resolution AHG/Res.104 (XIX) of the Assembly of Heads of State and Government of the OAU.

[174] At a press conference held on June 8, the Minister for Foreign Affairs of the SADR, Ibrahim Hakim, stated the following, "Considering the interests of Africa and, in accord with our wish to contribute to the strengthening of the unity of Africa, which is threatened by the expansionism of Morocco with the collaboration of the United States, the SADR, as a member of the OAU, has voluntarily and temporarily decided not to participate in the 19th summit meeting of the OAU to be held in Addis-Ababa", which was quickly interpreted by Morocco as a victory in the diplomatic field (the text of the declaration is in HODGES, T., "Western Sahara: an obstacle to Maghribi unity", *Africa Contemporary Record*, vol. 16 (1983/84): A 92).

[175] The OAU "urges the parties to the conflict, the Kingdom of Morocco and the POLISARIO Front, to undertake direct negotiations with a view to bringing about a ceasefire to create the necessary condition for a peaceful and fair referendum for self-determination of the people of Western Sahara, a referendum without any administrative or military constraints, under the auspices of the OAU and the UN and calls on the Implementation Committee to ensure the observance of the ceasefire".

[176] Although the admission of the SADR had occurred in 1982, the summit meeting of the Heads of State and Government had to ratify this, and this occurred precisely at the Addis Ababa (1984) Summit Meeting.

of Morocco and the consequent pan-African crisis[177]. The Moroccan representatives stated that although Morocco would respect the commitments acquired up to that time as regards the OAU and the UN concerning the conflict, it would not feel bound by possible resolutions of the African organisation. It was clear that the support of the OAU to the SADR was not only a purely formal question, since in the course of the summit meeting held the following year (21st) in the same place, the President of the SADR, M. Abdelaziz, was elected Vice-President of the OAU[178] thus giving important backing to its pretensions. Subsequently, on the twenty-fifth anniversary of the OAU (held in Addis-Ababa in May 1988), the Assembly of Heads of State approved a Declaration in which it drew attention to the fact that the people of the SADR had not been able to exercise its right to self-determination, and requested the parties involved in the conflict to negotiate in order to find a "rapid and satisfactory" solution[179]. In February 1989, the Council of Ministers of the OAU adopted a resolution in which "it satisfactorily noted" the bilateral conversations begun by Morocco and the POLISARIO Front, and encouraged both parties to find a solution to the conflict[180].

In accordance with the Settlement Plan, which was the fruit of these negotiations, the Western Sahara question, which had started off in the UN and been transferred to the OAU with the hope that progress would be made in the peace process within its scope of action, from then on would be followed by both Organizations, with the UN playing the main role, supported by the presence and cooperation of the OAU.

After this time, the Saharan conflict was not specially dealt with by the OAU, although one decision by the Organisation that did affect the situation

---

[177] As a consequence of the return of the SADR to its seat at the OAU during the 20th ordinary period of sessions, Morocco withdrew from its seat, and Zaire decided to suspend its participation in the activities of the Organization. When the one-year period of notification expired, Morocco officially ceased to be a member of the OAU, with effects as from November 12, 1985 (*ORGA*: A/AC.109/832). Moreover, the Movement of Non-Aligned States, where the POLISARIO Front had the status of guest, again took up the Saharan question in the final draft declaration at the Harare Summit Meeting, held in 1986, and openly supported direct negotiations between the parties involved in the conflict.

[178] Press release NY/OAU/BUR/43 of the OAU, of December 31, 1985. At the 21st period of sessions no decision or resolution would be adopted regarding the Western Sahara question (*ORGA*: A/39/634/Add.1, of November 21, 1984).

[179] *Official Documents of the OAU*: AHG/Decl.(XXIV)/Rev.1 of the Assembly of Heads of State and government of the OAU, approved on May 25, 1988 (text of the declaration in *ORGA*: A/43/398, Annex II).

[180] Resolution CM/Res.1184 (XLIX), which appears as an Annex to the document *ORGA*: A/44/291.

indirectly should be mentioned. This was a decision adopted during the 30th Summit Meeting (Tunis, June 1993) whereby, surprisingly, the Liberation Committee founded at the time of the creation of the OAU was dissolved since it was considered that the decolonization process had ended with the end of *apartheid* in South Africa. This decision, which first seemed contrary to the policy of the OAU until that time, has a clear meaning: the SADR had been admitted as a member State of the Organization, and from then on, the problem of Western Sahara could not be dealt with as a question of pending decolonization, but as one of illegal military occupation of a member State (the SADR) by another (Morocco).

3.3. The legal status of the POLISARIO Front as a national liberation movement

The question of the legal status of the POLISARIO Front gives rise to specific difficulties regarding its characterization. Although its condition as a National Liberation Movement and sole and legitimate representative of the population of Western Sahara has been clearly established by a multitude of resolutions of the organs of the United Nations, this has not occurred as regards its status as an observer. Unlike its attitude as regards other national liberation movements, such as the PLO[181] or SWAPO[182], the United Nations has not expressly attributed this condition to the POLISARIO Front, which gives rise to doubt as to the real willingness of the UN in this regard[183]. Moreover, although Resolution 3280 (XXIX) of the General Assembly granted the status of observer in a generic form "to the movements of national liberation

---

[181] Through Resolution 3210 (XXIX), the GA invited the PLO to participate in its deliberations during plenary sessions, and subsequently, Resolution 3237 (XXIX) extended the invitation to participate as observer in the sessions and work of the GA and in all the International Conferences convened under its auspices, thus acquiring the character of permanent observer, "as its participation is no longer linked to the Palestine question". *Cfr.* BARBERIS, J.A. (1984): 134.

[182] The GA granted the condition of permanent observer to the SWAPO, through Resolution 31/152.

[183] In this context, the GA referred indirectly to the question, through Resolution 34/37 when it recommended "that the POLISARIO Front, the representative of the Western Sahara population, participate fully in any search for a just, lasting and definitive political solution to the question of Western Sahara in conformity with the resolutions and recommendations of the United Nations, the OAU and the non-aligned countries" (Resolution 34/37 of the GA, approved on November 21, 1979) so that Morocco might end the occupation of the territory.

recognized by the OAU", with no reference to specific organizations[184], this approval was given prior to the proposal of recognition of the POLISARIO Front as a National Liberation Movement by the Committee of Liberation of the OAU (1976), a question which would be postponed indefinitely after the Organization appointed the SADR as a full member. However, despite the fact that it has not been expressly recognized, from its role recognized by the United Nations in its daily functioning and from the context in which this resolution was approved, the only interpretation which can be concluded is the confirmation of the status of observer of the POLISARIO Front. It would be absurd that the UN generically recognize the movements of national liberation when this status is recognized by the OAU and did not do so as regards the Saharan movement due to the fact that it has a more privileged status, that of a State, within the African Organization. But this observer status has never been officially declared by the United Nations.

As is clear from the above, the Saharan conflict entails a complex legal and political situation. More than eighty States have recognized the SADR, others which recognized the POLISARIO Front at one time have not changed their position in this regard, and have made no pronouncements concerning the SADR; together with these positions in favour of the recognition of the SADR and the POLISARIO Front (as is well known, the legal consequences of the recognition of a National Liberation Movement and that of an independent sovereign State are very different), there is a substantial group of States which have never recognized either of these. Moreover, as regards the attitude of the international organizations, as pointed out above, the UN has recognized the POLISARIO Front as a National Liberation Movement, and has made no pronouncements concerning the State condition of the SADR, while the OAU has avoided the question of the condition of the POLISARIO Front after it admitted the SADR. Despite these complications, it can be concluded that in fact the POLISARIO Front and the SADR constitute two aspects of the same form of political organisation of the Saharan people, with two objectives: one internal, the exercise of the function of government, and another external, the exercise of the right to self-determination, and they also have a single decision taking mechanism[185].

---

[184] Resolution 3280 (XXIX) decided to invite "the representatives of the movements of national liberation recognized by the Organization for African Unity to participate regularly, and, in conformity with this practice, in their capacity as observers, in the work related to the Principal Commissions of the GA and its subsidiary organisms concerned, as well as at conferences, seminars and other meetings held under the auspices of the United Nations which are of interest for its countries".

[185] MARCELLI, F., "La condizione giuridica internazionale del Fronte Polisario", *Rivista di*

The case of the former colonial power in the territory must be considered separately as it had quasi-official relations with the POLISARIO Front during the years following the Madrid Agreements, allowing it to open an office in the Spanish capital, and then closing it in 1985 as a consequence of a number of incidents related to fishing in waters under Western Sahara jurisdiction (this question will be analysed below). Although due to the agreement of 1988 and the commencement of the Settlement Plan, the Spanish Foreign Minister at the time, Francisco Fernández Ordóñez, declared (on January 25, 1989) that the Government studied the possibility of reopening this office, this never occurred. Since then, Spain has always been extremely careful that its conduct at both international and domestic level be interpreted as recognition of the SADR, even implicitly[186].

Apart from these considerations, and to the extent that the POLISARIO Front has been recognized by the United Nations as the sole and legitimate representative of the Saharan people, all the benefits which International law attributes to the movements of national liberation (application of humanitarian law, etc.) are applicable to it.

Diritto Internazionale, 72, 2 (1989): 295 and 303-305.

[186] Fortunately, although today this only has the value of an anecdote, it should be mentioned at this point as a particular precedent of Spanish Case Law related to this reckless conduct of the administering Power. This was the Sentence of the High Court (Tribunal Supremo) of November 10, 1988, which confirmed the Sentence of the Contentious Courtroom of the Court (Audiencia) of Las Palmas on September 28, 1987 which had annulled an agreement made on October 29, 1986 of Santa Lucía, a municipality of the Canary Islands, concluding the twinning with *Daira de El Guera*, as it was understood that this was not limited to deciding on twinning with another town, but entailed a recognition of sovereignty, thus violating an exclusive competence of the State. The text of the agreement concluded by pointing out that, "twinning entails political support to the cause of the heroic struggle of the Saharan people for its total liberation from the occupation of the Moroccan army, backed by the great international imperialist powers". The decision affirmed that the agreement challenged "entails the recognition of sovereignty (...) of the Saharan Democratic Arab Republic, as well as the institutions and Government of this municipality as belonging to this Republic, when neither the existence nor the sovereignty of this Republic over this municipality have been recognized by Spain, which would mean admitting the existence of a State and of the authorities established by this State in the aforementioned municipality, which is not the will of the Spanish State, the only competent authority to decide on this, as stated in article 149.1.3 of the Spanish Constitution (...)", and expressed its approval of "the correct and brilliant judgement of the issue made by the corresponding Court" (*Aranzadi*, case Law Repertory, Num. 8919). Although we do not agree with its approach, *cfr.* BUSTOS GISBERT, R., *Relaciones Internacionales y Comunidades Autónomas*, C.E.C., Madrid (1996): 359 et seq.

CHAPTER III

4. The population. The census made by Spain

Throughout almost one hundred years of Spanish presence in the territory, the Spanish authorities made several censuses. The first one to deserve our attention was made in 1967 and the data was made public, so its content is not a secret to anyone. By this time, the nomadic nature of the population of the territory had significantly reduced since Spain's arrival in the territory. 50% of the population was located in the most important settlements, while the rest continued to be nomadic. The population included in the census amounted to 26,325 persons, but the estimated total amounted to 46,546[187]. In 1970 the census was updated and amounted to 59,777 persons, which again showed the progressive and unstoppable settling of the population.

According to the 1974 census, the last one made by the Spanish authorities, the population amounted to 95,019 persons; 73,497 of who were "native Saharans", 20,126 were of European origin (mainly natural residents), and 1,396 were from other African countries and resided provisionally in the territory due to their jobs. Of these, 41,207 lived in the main urban centres in the territory: El Aaiún (28,499), Smara (7,295) and Villa Cisneros (5,413)[188]. Thus, the total settled population amounted to 81.9% of the total (40% of the population was located in El Aaiún, the capital of the territory). This data is highly revealing as it is of undoubted interest as a basis for the census of voters with a right to participate in the referendum, and it is a clear indication that something was irreversibly changing in Saharan society. The settlement of the population and the progressive abandonment of a nomadic way of life meant a replacement of the traditional tribal values for national values. This was the beginning of Saharan nationalism[189].

---

[187] The characteristics of this first census that by omission made several mistakes (*cfr* To this regard ALI YARA, O., *La question sahraouie et la mutation strategique du Maghreb*, Tesis Doctoral Thesis, April 1991, Université Paris X-Nanterre, Paris (1997): 145). It can be consulted in AGENZIA IORNALISTICA OLTREMARE, "La Spagna e il Sahara", Quaderni di Documentazione, Roma, vol. X, Num. 20, December 1, 1971, p. 41.

[188] *ORGA*: A/10023/Add.5, par. 122.

[189] As pointed by the Visiting Mission, until 1968, approximately 70% of the population was nomad and lived in tents and moved constantly in search of water and pasture. Nevertheless, the drought that suffered the territory reduced flocks and led the majority to abandon their nomad way of life, establishing themselves in the centres of locations and surroundings so as to find jobs (*cfr. ORGA*: A/10023/Add.5, par. 187). Though many are the works on the characteristics of the traditional Saharan society, the following can be consulted: CARO BAROJA, J., *Estudios Saharianos*, CSIC, Madrid, 1955; DE CHASSEY, F., *L'etrier, la houe et le Livre. "Sociétés traditionnelles" au Sahara et au Sahel occidental*, Ed. Anthropos, Paris, 1977; PORTILLO PASQUAL DEL RIQUELME, J. (1991).

From a broad perspective, Saharan society can be seen as a patriarchal society, where the *Sheikhs* and their *Yemáa* (tribal councils) continue to play an important role. The basic unit in this social structure is the family, which is not considered to be an independent group but as an integral part of a social group (*a fraction of a tribe*) and of a family group (*a sub-fraction of a tribe*)[190]. In this context, attention should be drawn to the fact that, until the time these tribes became sedentary, as nomads they would go beyond the limits established by the colonial powers, which complicated the determination of "those who were native Saharans of the territory". According to data provided by the Spanish authorities to the Visiting Mission, which travelled through the territory in 1975, the number of Saharan natives who lived outside the territory at the time due to political or economic reasons amounted to a maximum of 7,000-9,000. In the opinion of the neighbouring States, these figures amounted to 40,000 to 50,000. In the opinion of this Mission, the "tremendous task" of making a census to cover the native population which lives outside the territory "would have to be based on the demonstrated composition of the family and social groups (fractions and sub-fractions of tribes) which exist in the territory". Thus, the Mission highlighted the need to take into account the specific characteristics of Saharan society when making the census, which had not always occurred in the decolonization processes carried out under the auspices of the United Nations. This would be the basis (fraction and sub-fraction of tribes) for establishing the criteria for the identification of the 1988 Settlement Plan.

5. Conclusions: the statehood of Western Sahara

As we pointed out above, the requirements which have traditionally been considered necessary for an entity to be considered to be a State are basically threefold: a defined territory, effective Government, and a permanent population.

As regards the first of these requirements, and, despite the facts already mentioned, it should not be forgotten that the *limits of the territory* of Western Sahara were established through the international treaties agreed to by France

---

[190] In accord with what is set out in article 1 of the Decree of May 11, 1967 on the Organization of Local administration for the Province of the Sahara, which created the *Yemáa* or General Assembly, "in accordance with Saharan tradition, sub-fraction is understood to be grouping made up of several families; fraction is understood to be a group of several sub-fractions, and a tribe is the socio-political entity which groups together several fractions" (*Boletín Oficial del Estado/Official State Gazette* Num. 120, *cfr.* LÁZARO MIGUEL, H. (1974): 167 et seq.).

and Spain when these were the colonizing powers in the territory (the Paris Agreements of July 27, "Treaty of Muni ", and those of October 2, 1900, and of October 3, 1904[191]); "its frontiers corresponded exactly with those of the former Spanish colony"[192]. Since 1963 when the United Nations took charge of the decolonization of the territory, this was identified as a Non-Self-Governing Territory with an approximate surface area of 266,000 km^2, 1,062 km. of coastline and 2,045 km. of land frontiers, of which 1,570 km. correspond to the frontier with Mauritania, and 475 km. to the frontiers with Morocco and Algeria. In this regard, the reports annually submitted to the General Assembly by the Special Committee, a body in charge of examining the situation concerning the application of the Declaration on the concession of independence to the colonial countries and peoples, delimit the situation and dimensions of the territory in these same terms.

Although there is no doubt that these frontiers "do not reflect the social and geographical realities", but instead show the correlation of forces between the colonial powers, France and Spain, in the region[193], in application of the *uti possidetis iuris* principle, proclaimed in the OAU Charter as one of the principles which must guide the relations between the States in the African continent[194], it must be admitted that the Saharan frontiers are perfectly defined[195]. It was not a chance reference to this principle made by the

---

[191] By virtue of the 1904 Treaty, the annexation of the territory of Rio de Oro by Spain was confirmed, and this included the territories located between Cape Blanco and Cape Bojador -as far as parallel 26°-. Besides this, which had been the subject of the 1900 Treaty, Spain incorporated the territory of Saguia el Hamra, between parallels 26° and 27°40', to its African possessions.

[192] PAZZANITA, A. G. (1985): 141.

[193] BARBIER, M. (1982): 44.

[194] On this question, *cfr*. BROWNLIE, I., *Basic Documents on African Affairs*, The Clarendon Press, Oxford, (1971): 360 et seq.

[195] As mentioned by Sánchez Rodríguez, "the main principle of *uti possidetis iuris*, the only one with intrinsic value, is the existence of legal ownership which clearly expresses the will of the colonial power as regards its internal limits (...) In the event that the international limits were established by an international treaty, made by the colonizing State and a third party State, the text of the treaty would become an essential legal certificate in order to specify the effects of the succession of States" (SÁNCHEZ RODRIGUEZ, L.I., "Uti possidetis: la reactualización jurisprudencial de un viejo principio (a propósito de la Sentencia del TIJ (Sala) en el asunto Burkina Fasso/República de Mali)", *R.E.D.I.*, vol. XL, 2 (1988): 316). Despite the fact that the applicability of this statement as regards the case of Western Sahara is clear, the reservations made by Morocco concerning this principle and the OAU Charter as its territorial claims over Western Sahara and over the territory of other States in the region go back to the time it became independent. As concerns this last question, this refers more specifically to the Algerian-Moroccan borders, *cfr*. MESA GARRIDO, R., "Las

representative of the POLISARIO Front before the Fourth Commission, in the following terms, "Does the principle of intangibility of frontiers in the OAU Charter and Resolution 1514 (XV) of the UN General Assembly refer only to the white, Christian, European colonizer?"[196]. Furthermore, the ICJ established that there was no controversy regarding the limits to the territory. Finally, in relation to this question, it must not be forgotten that that the Lisbon Agreements (August 29, 1997), subscribed to by both parties expressly agree that these "will in no way change, affect or alter the frontiers of Western Sahara internationally recognized, and will not serve as a precedent to allege that there have been changes or alterations made to these".

Thus, it seems to be clear that not even Morocco calls the limits of the territory into question[197], although it should not be forgotten that this acceptance by Morocco is explained in the argument put forward by the POLISARIO Front that, if the controversial tribal groups which live exclusively in the south of Morocco, that is to say outside the former Spanish Sahara (H41, H61 and J51/52), were included in the referendum census, the map of Western Sahara would have to be modified and this geographical zone would have to be included in its territory. Other than this, waiting for the day that Morocco, Mauritania and Spain negotiate with SADR their common sea frontiers, the Parliament (National Saharan Council) approved on January 21,

---

fronteras de la descolonización: reflexiones en torno al conflicto argelino-marroquí", *R.E.D.I.*, 2 (1966): 51-76, especially pages 72 et seq.

Although this is an extremely minority approach, Ruiloba defended that, if there were any ownership rights over Spanish Sahara "worthy of being taken into account at the time of the decolonization, these must be attributed to Mauritania. The *uti possidetis iuris*, whose validity in Africa cannot recently be admitted without reservations, cannot oppose this" (RUILOBA SANTANA, E., "Notas sobre un caso de descolonización: El Sahara Español", *A.D.I.*, vol. I (1974): 346).

[196] Intervention of the representative of the POLISARIO Front before the Fourth Commission, on October 7, 1996. In the opinion of Marcelli, one of the reasons which had moved a large number of African States to recognize the SADR derived precisely from the concern these States had regarding the possibility the principle of the intangibility of the frontiers inherited from colonialism in their own territories might be called into question. *Cfr.* MARCELLI, F. (1989): 299.

[197] Moroccan domestic policy concerning the territory of Western Sahara as regards "legitimising" its presence there must not be ignored. Thus, the reform of the Moroccan Constitution was the result of a "referendum" held on September 4, 1992, which supposedly included the participation of the Saharan population (the referendum was approved by 99% affirmative votes!). The successive elections (municipal, legislative, etc.) were also held in occupied territory. These were acts of domestic law, but with evident consequences at international level, which were reproved by the United Nations, which did not prevent them being carried out, nor that Spain provided financial backing for these.

CHAPTER III

2009 Law 03/2009 that sets the water zones of the SADR, through which it proclaims its internal waters, Territorial waters, Contiguous zone, Exclusive Economic Zone and Continental shelf. Setting rights and duties in each of the mentioned areas of water is in conformity with the international norms established in the United Nations Convention on the Law of the Sea (UNCLOS) in 1982[198].

As regards the *organisation of state power*, as pointed out by Naldi, *prima facie* it can be stated that the SADR does not comply with this last requirement, to the extent that it does not exercise its authority exclusively in the territory[199]. On this point, the lack of control over part of the territory is not the responsibility of the SADR, but of the power occupying it illegally. The fact that part of the territory under the control of the POLISARIO Front has been reduced during the conflict does not condition its ownership at all[200]. Western Sahara has had a Government and political institutions since the time of the declaration of independence of the SADR (February 27, 1976). This is structured in an organized way and has a cabinet led by a Prime Minister, a legislative organ (the National Saharan Council), half of whose members are elected by the population, and a President, who is also the Secretary General of the POLISARIO Front. The fact that, on referring to the proclamation of the SADR, its President, Mohamed Abdelaziz, appearing before the Fourth Commission (November 11, 1976), stressed that the declaration of independence had occurred in Bir Lehlu, "liberated territories", clearly shows the concern the Saharan leaders had to effectively control at least a part of the territory, knowing that a Government needs to exercise effective power over a territory in order to proclaim the existence of a new State[201].

---

[198] On this question, *cfr.* SOROETA LICERAS, J., "La délimitation et l'exploitation des espaces maritimes du Sahara Occidental, un caillou (de plus) dans la chaussure des relations Espagnole-Marocain", in the collection *Protection maritime et violence dans la mer* (Dir. Sobrino Heredia, J. M.), Bruylant, Bruxelles (2011): 131–145.

[199] NALDI, G. J. (1982): 156.

[200] Thus, although the POLISARIO Front managed to control an important part of the territory -approximately 90% according to some authors (*cfr.* NALDI, G. J. 1982): 154), or 75%, according to others (*cfr.* PAZZANITA, A. G. (1985): 141)- after the construction of successive walls by Morocco, this was considerably reduced to approximately 30% in 1987- (*cfr. Jeune Afrique*, Num. 1368, of March 25, 1987).

[201] ORGA: A/C.4/31/SR.22, para. 31. In this respect, Zunes considers that the SADR "is not a government in exile", as its population is in Algeria for reasons of security. In the opinion of this author, the situation of Western Sahara precisely the contrary of that of other territories which are or have been under foreign occupation (Palestine, East Timor) as in the Saharan case, "although most of the population is in exile, the government is not" (*cfr.* ZUNES, S. (1988): 141). In any case, as stated by the Permanent People's Court, "when it was

The importance of this question for both parties was highlighted during the XII Congress of the POLISARIO Front (December 2007). This congress took place ignoring Moroccan government's protest, in Tifariti (Saharan territories controlled by the POLISARIO Front). This point was decided precisely to intensify the effectiveness of the Saharan Government over territories under their control, empowering the growth of this location. This led Moroccan government to the point of threatening (threats that were reported by the Secretary General of the UN), to "use adequate means, including air strikes (...) to prevent further construction in the area of Tifariti". In an extremely cynical way, Morocco, who had already violated openly the Settlement Plan, claimed that through this decision, and given the celebration of the Congress in that location, the POLISARIO Front had violated the 1991 agreements[202].

In addition, the SADR has diplomatic representations in a large number of States, some of which are embassies, while others are "offices" or "missions", similar in some cases to diplomatic representations.

As regards the third requisite, as the current situation of the conflict has shown, Western Sahara has a *permanent and certain population*. The most relevant questions put forward at the time the census was drawn up refer to the difficulty involved in determining which citizens were Saharans and, depending on this, who then had the right to participate in the referendum on self-determination, but in no case was doubt cast upon the existence of an original Western Sahara population. The ICJ referred to this question when it referred to cases such as Gibraltar or the Islas Malvinas (Falkland Islands) and pointed out that consulting the population was the fundamental factor concerning the self-determination of peoples, but in some cases the exercise of this right does not correspond with reality as there are no people in the territory seeking self-determination. Evidently, this is not the case of Western

---

constituted as a State in the part of the territory which it had managed to liberate, (...) faced with the impotence of the UNO to achieve respect for the resolutions of the General Assembly and of the CS, as well as the pronouncement of the ICJ, the qualified representatives of the Saharan people were had only one option left: the constitution of a new State, within the limits stipulated by the aforementioned consultative decision" (*Avis sur le Sahara* Occidental, para. 51, in JOUVE, E., (Dir.) *Un Tribunal pour les Peuples*, Serie Points Chauds, Paris (1983): 67). As Tiedrebeogo points out, the institution of the "State in exile" (mentioned among others by BONTEMS, C. (1984): 159), is not included in International law, but does entail the reality of a people on the way to perfecting a State, therefore, despite not having the totality of the requirements and points needed for statehood, undoubtedly, it has a type of international subjectivity (*cfr.* TIEDREBEOGO, P.R., *Le Droit des peuples à l'autodetermination et son aplication au Sahara Occidental*, Institut Universitaire de Hautes Etudes Internationales, Genève (1988): 102 et seq.).

[202] ORSC: S/2008/251, of 14 April 2008.

CHAPTER III

Sahara as the right of its population to self-determination has been recognized on countless occasions by organs of the United Nations. As stated by Pazzanita in this regard, the determination of the exact number of persons that make up its population is a secondary question[203]. Finally, it should be remembered that, for these purposes, the ICJ has emphatically stated "the right of the people of Western Sahara to self-determination" and the non-existence of sovereignty links between Western Sahara and Morocco and the Mauritanian group, an evident reference to a group of well-defined persons.

Furthermore, as mentioned by the Secretary General of the UN, neither the resolutions which have affirmed the right of the Saharan people to self-determination, nor those which have specified the right of peoples to self-determination have given "a definition of 'people' in order to exercise this right"[204]. Although the concept of "people" referred to in these resolutions cannot absolutely ignore the ethnic question, it is more closely linked to the territorial component. In this way, the "Saharan people" referred to in the General Assembly resolutions is constituted by "the population of the territory", regardless of the fact that the links of an ethnic nature which this population might have with populations which inhabit the neighbouring territories are relatively close. Undoubtedly, this is the concept of "territorial people", which despite not having been expressly mentioned has always been present in the philosophy of these resolutions, confirmed by the general nature of the *uti possidetis iuris* principle which is always linked to the decolonization process and which has reiterated the fact that the frontiers established during the colonial period remain in force, even though their artificial nature is not ignored.

Article 1 of the Montevideo Convention on the Rights and Duties of States, signed on December 22, 1933, incorporated a fourth requisite to the three requisites mentioned in order to attribute statehood to a determined entity: the *capacity to relate to other subjects of International law*. As regards Western Sahara, it should be stated that it has complied with this requisite since the POLISARIO Front was recognized as having the status of a national liberation movement and the SADR became a full member of the OAU, where

---

[203] PAZZANITA, A. G. (1985): 143. Likewise, Tiedrebeogo has pointed out that, although the number of persons with a right to participate in the referendum is a question of great importance, however, "this is totally irrelevant as a constituent component of the State" (TIEDREBEOGO, P. R. (1988): 106); also, *cfr.* NALDI, G.J., "The Statehood of the Saharan Arab Democratic Republic", *Indian Journal of International Law*, vol. 25, 1985, p. 455; BROWNLIE, I., *Principles of Public International Law*, 4th ed., Clarendon Press, Oxford (1990): 75; CRAWFORD, J., *The creation of States in International Law*, Oxford (1979): 40 et seq.

[204] Report of the Secretary General of November 24, 1993 (*ORGA*: S/26797, p. 7).

its President even became Vice-Secretary of this Organization[205]. This international subjectivity of the SADR is without doubt not derived from the recognition granted by several States since, as accepted by most doctrine, this is merely declarative or strictly political. However, although the recognition of other States is not a necessary condition for the existence of a new State, evidently this surely consolidates its international legal personality and its insertion in the International Community, even as regards the States which do not recognize it[206], especially when a large number of States which grant it recognition are members of an International Organization which the recognized State intended to join, which is the case of the OAU as regards the SADR[207].

Despite what is referred to in the preceding paragraphs, if we come to the conclusion that the reference to Western Sahara as a State may not be quite appropriate from the strictly legal point of view[208], at least, it can be stated that this involves a "proto-state", in the sense that, if it is not at present a State entity, it does have the conditions to acquire the status of State if it can make its powers over the territory effective. This is what Remiro Brotons has called "virtual sovereignty"[209]. As in the case of Eastern Timor, Judge Weeramantry

---

[205] In Joffe's opinion, the population of Western Sahara has demonstrated its resistance to Moroccan occupation, that it is a "people" in the sense attributed to the term by the United Nations (*cfr.* JOFFE, G., "The conflict in the Western Sahara", in the collection *Conflict in Africa*, ed. OLIVER FURLEY, Tauris Publishers, London/New York (1995): 127). In this same regard, the Permanent People's Tribunal made a declaration (Avis sur la Sahara Occidental, para. 35, in JOUVE, E. (1983): 59). The concept of people referred to by Joffe is defined by Smith as "a distinct ethnic group which constitutes a homogeneous community, not only culturally homogeneous but culturally different from other communities" (SMITH, A.D., *Nationalism in the Twentieth Century*, Martin Robertson ed., Oxford (1979): 2-4).

[206] CARRILLO SALCEDO, J.A., *Curso de Derecho Internacional Público*, Tecnos, Madrid (1992): 47 et seq. Along the same lines, PAZZANITA, A. G. (1985): 139.

[207] In this regard, Vance points out that, "the recognition of the Government of the SADR in exile may (...) serve to sanction Morocco's non-acceptance of an international norm of *jus cogens*, such as the right of peoples to self-determination" (VANCE, R.T., "Recognition as an Affirmative step in the Decolonization process: The Case of Western Sahara", *Yale Journal of World Public Order*, 7, Num. 1, Fall 1980, p. 63). Pazzanita also declared in a similar fashion, stressing the effect of recognition at the level of diplomatic action (PAZZANITA, A. G. (1985): 148 et seq.).

[208] Marcelli points out that if a Saharan State had been created in the brief period between the Spanish withdrawal from the territory until its occupation by Morocco and Mauritania, and this State had established its own governmental power over the territory, it would have been possible to speak of an authentic Saharan State, but this did not occur (*cfr.* MARCELLI, F. (1989: 303).

[209] REMIRO BROTONS, A., *Derecho Internacional*, McGraw-Hill, Madrid (1997): 112.

stated that, "The Charter was so structured that the interests of territories not able to speak for themselves in international forums were to be looked after by a Member of the United Nations entrusted with their welfare, who would have the necessary authority for this purpose. In other words, its underlying philosophy in regard to dependent territories was to *avoid leaving them defenceless and voiceless in a world order which had not yet accorded them an independent status*"[210]. In this regard, as pointed out by Barbier, "it is clear that the SADR cannot be reduced to a simple legal fiction. It is not a fully finished State... it is not only a State in formation, but a State struggling for existence"[211].

---

[210] *East Timor (Portugal v. Australia), Judgment I.C.J. Reports 1995*, p. 179 (highlighted by the author).
[211] BARBIER, M., "La formation de la RASD", *Actes du colloque International de juristes tenu à l'Assemblée Nationale. Paris, le 20 et 21 octobre 1984*, Paris (1984): 58.

CHAPTER IV

THE ADVISORY OPINION OF THE INTERNATIONAL COURT OF JUSTICE OF OCTOBER 16, 1975

As was pointed out above, GA Resolution 3292 (XXIX) requested the ICJ to issue an advisory opinion which would establish whether the territory was *terra nullius* at the time when Spain began its colonisation (1884) and, if it was not-, what type of legal ties existed between the territory and the Kingdom of Morocco and the Mauritanian Entity. However, before analysing the substantive issue, the Court was obliged to pronounce on formal questions, which were, of course, of maximum importance in conditioning its position as regards the core of the matter to a great extent: these were the questions of the *ad hoc* judges and the competence of the Court itself.

1.   The formal questions

1.1. *The question of the ad hoc judges*

The Court began its work listening to "the parties concerned and involved"[212] in the conflict in order to determine the possible inclusion of *ad hoc* judges in its composition and concluded, through an Order of May 22, 1975, that an *ad hoc* judge would be designated by Morocco, although the one proposed by

---

[212] As pointed out by Tomás Ortiz de la Torre, and even if is obvious, it should be mentioned that, as a advisory opinion, it is not correct to use the term "parties", as this condition is reserved for those who intervene in a litigious process before a Court. It should be interpreted as "appearing States". This circumstance stresses even more the contention appearance of the process before the Court, question that we will analyse below. *Cfr.* TOMÁS ORTIZ DE LA TORRE, J. (1975): 566.

[212] The judge *ad hoc* put forward by Morocco was Alphons Boni, President of the Supreme Court of the Ivory Coast. The acceptance of the Moroccan right to design a judge *ad hoc* was backed by 10 votes in favour and 5 votes against. The decision to deny the right of designing an *ad hoc* judge to Mauritania was approved by 8 votes in favour and 7 against (*Western Sahara, Order of 22 Mayo 1975, I.C.J.*, p. 8).

Mauritania was rejected[213] as it was considered that the advisory opinion requested related to a legal controversy pending at the time between two States, Spain and Morocco, excluding Mauritania.

The decision of the Court was based on the consideration that "there seems to be a legal controversy" between Spain and Morocco. This decision would be of a provisional nature and would not prejudge the intentions of the parties in the case submitted to the advisory opinion. However, it is clear that the Court was here adopting a very clear option, affecting the totality of the conflict[214], when it stated that this was a legal controversy between two states, as had been the intention of Morocco for a long time, ignoring the policy clearly established by the resolutions of the General Assembly, which analyse the conflict in the context of decolonization. As pointed out by Judge Gros, from the documentation provided by the Secretary General of the UN, it is not possible to deduce, any "trace of any specific legal question between Morocco and Spain, which however the present Advisory Opinion has described as a 'legal dispute... regarding the Territory'"[215]. In his opinion, the General Assembly did put forward a legal question, but this does not confront Spain and Morocco, however, affecting solely the latter, and can be summed up in the following question: "is Morocco entitled to claim reintegration of the Territory into the national territory of the Kingdom of Morocco, to which it belonged, according to Morocco, at the time of colonization by Spain?"[216].

---

[214] Likewise, the judge Petrén stated that this type of decisions "is definitive and can be used during the whole process", because "to accept such designation on the supposition that there is a legal difference, leaving in suspense other decisions as to the existence of that difference, leads to serious risks", as "in this position is finally negative (...) it would imply that no *ad hoc* judge at all should have been designed" (*Western Sahara, Advisory Opinion, I.C.J., Reports 1975*, p. 107). This judge states that by the approach of using the correct questions to the three concerned States, the Court "could have obtained the necessary information to verify or not if there were legal differences between the States on the question of Western Sahara, so the answer should not have been differed to this question until the end of the process on the core of the matter". Likewise, *cfr.* VALLÉE, Ch. (1976): 48.

[215] Cortina pointed in the same sense before the GA: "Spain has no dispute or controversy with any country in particular, as all resolutions that defend the self-determination as a proper way of decolonizing a territory reach all member States of this Organisation", underlining that "different from the Sahara question (...), the Gibraltar matter has always been considered by the pertinent resolutions of this Organisation as a conflict between States -Spain and United Kingdom- that must solve the question of sovereignty and Spanish territorial integrity implicit in the decolonizing process of the Rock" (*ORGA*: A/PV.2253, pages 410-411).

[216] *Western Sahara, Advisory Opinion, I.C.J., Reports 1975*, p. p. 70, par. 1. As stated in this sense by Judge Petrén, statements of Spanish and Moroccan representation from the beginning of

CHAPTER IV

This would be the only legal question that the Court should have pronounced on, since the judge considers that the rest of the questions analysed by the opinion "are unrelated to the object of the request"[217].

In addition, if we maintain that there is no legal dispute between Morocco and Spain, for the same reason we must reject that this situation exists between Spain and Mauritania; if the Court decided to grant Morocco the right to have an *ad hoc* judge in the proceedings, it does not seem reasonable to deny this possibility to Mauritania[218] with the argument that there was no legal dispute between Mauritania and Spain when, on one hand, the opinion could have concluded the existence of historical rights of Mauritania over the territory of Western Sahara, and, on the other, throughout the proceedings, Morocco and Mauritania are treated at the same level[219].

In conclusion, in this first phase of its work the Court used very weak arguments, which, at the time, gave rise to reasonable doubts regarding the future of the proceedings. It should not be forgotten that the decision of the Court was based on such weak grounds as the "appearance" of a legal dispute between Morocco and Spain, and the absence of such appearance between Mauritania and Spain. It is certain that, despite the fact that the Court denied it, this decision on a preliminary question prejudged the core of the matter[220]. The Court had to expressly and definitively pronounce on the existence of a legal controversy before granting or denying the possibility of the appointment of *ad hoc* judges, especially since it did not return to this question in the opinion, avoiding any pronouncements in this regard.

---

the process before the Court "made it clear that there is no legal question in this matter between these States referring Western Sahara. Morocco does not deny the actual Spanish sovereignty in the territory; both Morocco and Spain accept the application of the General Assembly resolution on decolonization. In other words, the Court is not before a legal claim formulated by Morocco against Spain and contested by the mentioned (...). The fact that States that take part in the General Assembly debates express differences about debated questions cannot be considered as constitutive of a legal difference between them" (*Western Sahara, Advisory Opinion, I.C.J., Reports 1975*, p. 109).

[217] Gros agrees, by saying that it is not enough that two States maintain different thesis, or even opposed ones as to an event or situation, to suppose litigation between them (*cfr. ibidem*).

[218] Judge Morozov expressed a different opinion, justifying his vote against the matter, understanding that the arguments that supported the acceptance of an *ad hoc* judge for Morocco were valid for the designation of a judge *ad hoc* on the Mauritanian side (*Western Sahara, Advisory Opinion, I.C.J., Reports 1975*, p. 10).

[219] Likewise, *cfr.* the individual opinion of Judge Petrén (*Western Sahara, Advisory Opinion, I.C.J., Reports 1975*, p. 109).

[220] Similarly, *cfr.* BARBIER, M., "L´avis consultatif de la Cour de la Haye sur le Sahara Occidental", *Revue Juridique et Politique Independence et Cooperation*, 30 (1976): 75.

1.2. The question of competence

Once the decision concerning the *ad hoc* judges was adopted, the Court addressed the question of their competence, but in our opinion failed to give this point the attention it deserved. We share the position taken by the Spanish representative in this phase of the proceedings, who defended the question put to the Court by the GA: "does not constitute a real and existing legal question, but instead a simple question of an academic nature"[221], meaning therefore the

---

[221] The Spanish representation sustained that the appropriate exercise of the Court should lead to examine not only the Territory statute in the past and the eventual rights that other States could have exerted before, but also and before pronouncement, to the *rights and duties existent nowadays that have been established in the course of the decolonization process carried out by the United Nations* (highlighted by the author) (I.C.J., Pleadings, Western Sahara, Vol. I, p. 222, par. 387). In our opinion, Spain raised the question quite rightly, as in the petition of the Advisory Opinion there is no legal question to solve. In effect, a legal question must be resolved by the application of legal techniques (ROSENNE, S., *The Law and Practice of the International Court*, 2th ed., Martinus Nijhoff Publishers, Dordrecht/ Boston/ Lancaster, 1985, p. 702), and in the case that we are dealing with, the used techniques are mainly of an historical character. Furthermore, as pointed by Hinojo, the fact that the question is of a legal nature does not necessarily mean that the Court should pronounce a ruling, though to do so, the aforementioned condition must be present. This author celebrates the attitude of the Court: "firm and brave" to give its opinion exerting its jurisdictional function each time it has been asked to pronounce itself, answering to the challenges posed by political organs and committing to its duty in contemporary International law and international society (HINOJO ROJAS, M. (1997): 85 and 91). We don't agree with this statement, because the fact that the Court accepted to pronounce its advisory opinion (promoted by Morocco with the only objective of postponing and even blocking the celebration of the referendum that Spanish authorities were preparing) was one of the main reasons for which the process entered a dead end. There is no doubt that, if the advisory opinion had been rejected, the referendum would have resolved the conflict definitely.

Judge De Castro adopted in his dissenting opinion a less radical approach, considering that at least "There are reasons for doubting the competence of the Court. The Court really does not seem to be the appropriate advisory opinion, questions of fact or questions of which the historical aspect is predominant. However the Court's spirit of collaboration in relation to the other organs of the United Nations, together with the very special nature of a case, may be justification for the Court not applying Article 65 of its Statute strictly" (*Western Sahara, Advisory Opinion, I.C.J., Reports* 1975, p. 142). The judge continues pointing that "Even on the hypothesis of the Court concluding that it had no competence to reply to a *quaestio facti*, such as that of the existence of legal ties at the time of colonization by Spain, it would not have followed that the Court had no competence to reply to the request for an advisory opinion. And it did not seem to me that the right approach was to adopt a restrictive or negative interpretation that would lead to the conclusion that the request for an advisory opinion was without object. The Court should rather do its best to assist the General Assembly in the task of decolonization" *(ibid.,* p. 166).

CHAPTER IV

Court must refuse to comply with the request made by the General Assembly, invoking Article 65.1 of its Statutes[222] since this involves a "displacement of the true problem towards questions of territorial sovereignty (which), necessarily, require a cross examination of the facts, which is impossible to

---

Nevertheless, some of the opinions are not unanimously shared by doctrine. In this sense, Ruiloba states that it cannot be pleaded that that petition of ruling to the ICJ were inadmissible due to its political nature, because what was being debated was the reciprocal relations between the self-determination right and the territory integrity right, and the previous question of the validity of the titles claimed by both parties. These two questions are with no doubt of a legal nature. In this author's opinion, the need of free expression of the will of peoples, which is the essential element of the right of self-determination, must always be the priority, and this, independent of the nature of the links that could have existed between peoples and the neighbouring authorities. Ruiloba seems to be near to these approaches when clarifying the previous statements by adding that it is difficult to maintain that the existence of an eventual historical title of territorial sovereignty may put aside or annul the right of self-determination (RUILOBA SANTANA, E. (1974): 341 et seq.).

[222] Article 65.1 of the Statue of the ICJ states: "The Court *may* give an advisory opinion on *any* legal question at the request of whatever body may be authorized by or in accordance with the Charter of the United Nations" (emphasized by author). The judge Petrén points also that this article leaves to the Court the freedom to refuse to deliver a advisory opinion "if it is not considered inopportune", as the judge himself maintains regarding the Western Sahara matter (*Western Sahara, Advisory Opinion, I.C.J., Reports 1975*, p. 113). Similar positions are defended by judge De Castro, that, however, reminds that up to the present time the Court has not used such optional power, refusing to deliver a advisory opinion (*Western Sahara, Advisory Opinion, I.C.J., Reports 1975*, p. 137). Again in this sense, *cfr.* BLAYDES, L.E. Jr., "International Law. International Court of Justice does not find ´legal ties´ of such a nature to affect self-determination in the decolonization process of Western Sahara. Advisory opinion on Western Sahara, (1975) I.C.J., *T.I.L.J.*, 11, (1976): 361.
Even if judge Petrén insists on the freedom of the Court on this question, the truth is that the Court established that "it cannot deliver a advisory opinion on a non-legal question. If a matter is not legal, the Court has no optional power on the matter: it must refuse to deliver ruling that may have been requested" (*Certain Phosphate Lands in Nauru (Nauru v. Australia), Preliminary Objections, Judgement, I.C.J., Reports 1992*, p. 156). Without any doubt, the freedom that the judge is referring to is the one that belongs to the Court in the case that, even being a legal matter, and it is competent on, it may refuse to deliver ruling, according to the circumstances that occur in the case (*Interpretation of Peace Treaties, Advisory Opinion: I.C.J. Reports 1950*, p. 72).
Judge Dillard stated that the Court should have declared itself non-competent: "First it was immediately apparent that the two questions were exclusively confined to an historical period and second they raised no issue whatever as to the legitimacy of Spain's original occupation of the territory or its present authority over it. It appeared, therefore, that the two questions invited an enquiry which, while no doubt historically fascinating, was far removed from any contemporary problem whatever" (*Western Sahara, Advisory Opinion, I.C.J., Reports 1975*, p. 116).

carry out within the advisory jurisdiction" of the Court[223]. As pointed out by Daillier, the Court must contribute to the proper functioning of the Organization but, although Article 65 gives a discretionary character to its advisory competence, only 'decisive reasons' can justify the rejection of a request of this nature[224]; in our opinion and as time would unfortunately show, this was one of the situations where the opinion would negatively contribute to the correct functioning of the UN as regards decolonization. The Court should not have pronounced on the nature of the ties that might have existed at the time of the Spanish colonisation unless it had previously considered whether the finding of this would have some type of repercussion on the decolonization process in the territory[225]. On this point, the second factor which the Court

---

[223] *I.C.J., Pleadings, Western Sahara*, Vol. I, p. 223, par. 389. In this same regard, judge Ignacio-Pinto declared to by only partially in agreement with the Court conclusions, finding that, though it should have declared itself competent regarding the form, it should not have done the same regarding the core of the matter, because even the composition of the questions, pursue a "hidden" objective: "the recognition of sovereignty rights in favour of Morocco on the one hand, and of Mauritania, on the other hand, over this or that part of Western Sahara". This judge, as would do so judge Petrén, refuses from paragraph 162 all that does not refer to the relations of sovereignty over the territory by Morocco and Mauritania, assuming, however, the rest of the considerations within the advisory opinion (*Western Sahara, Advisory Opinion, I.C.J., Reports 1975*, p. 78, 104 et seq.). As even the ICJ established in 1962 "according to the article 65 of the Statute, the Court can only deliver a advisory opinion if the matter is of a legal nature. If the question is not legal, the Court lacks of optional characteristics to do so; refusing the request of delivery" (*Certain expenses of the United Nations (Article 17, paragraph 2, of the Charter), Advisory Opinion of 20 July 1962: I.C.J. Reports 1962*, p. 155).
Similarly López Martín, points out that, in view of the literal content of the questions forwarded by the GA, its answer contains the solution of a territorial problem of attribution of sovereignty over Western Sahara, as to establish that sovereign relations existed, as pleaded both States (Morocco and Mauritania), on the basis of the continuous and peaceful exercise of authority of the State in favour of one or the other, it would have meant the recognition as sovereign of the mentioned territory, this is, the attribution of territorial sovereignty. In this case, the consent of Spain would have been necessary (*cfr.* LÓPEZ MARTIN, A.G., *El ejercicio continuo y pacífico de funciones de Estado como modo de adquisición del título territorial en la jurisprudencia internacional: el problema de su prueba*, Universidad Complutense de Madrid, Servicio de Publicaciones Madrid (1995): 274 et seq.). Similarly, *cfr.* BARBIER, M. (1976): 82.
[224] DAILLIER, P., "Commentaire à l'article 96", in *La Charte des Nations Unies*, (Dir. COT, J-P. y PELLET, A.), Ed. Economica / Bruylant, Paris / Bruxelles (1985): 1288.
[225] The Spanish representation insisted, with a similar position to the one held before the Court, that the previous and repeated acceptance, of all "concerned and involved" parts, thus, Morocco, Mauritania, Algeria and even Spain, on the Saharan people's self-determination right. For this reason "resolutions of the General Assembly about Western Sahara, due to the fact that those resolutions were accepted by the administering Power and the

must take into account when using the discretionary power attributed to it by the Charter must not be forgotten, but this was ignored in this case: the Court must provide a useful response[226], a usefulness which we cannot quite imagine in this case.

Furthermore, it must be remembered that Morocco has previously requested of Spain that the same questions put forward by Resolution 3292 (XXIX) be submitted by both States, by common agreement, to the contentious jurisdiction of the Court[227], and that the silence of the Spanish authorities regarding this request led to Morocco taking the case to the General Assembly, the results of which are already known.

The decision concerning the determination of the legal or purely academic nature of the question submitted by the General Assembly to the ICJ was not insignificant as it was to mark the course of the debates: the doubts concerning this question would have repercussions on the proceedings themselves because, as we pointed out above, in spite of the advisory nature of the opinion,

---

neighbouring States, "concerned parties" of the decolonization, *has created an objective situation related to the actual statute in Western Sahara*. From this situation comes out the attribution of rights of the population of this territory and the establishment of duties of the administering Power. This situation also entitles the "concerned parties" to be consulted about the modes to observe the referendum under the auspices of United Nations. (...) Therefore, the determination of the Court on the actual situation of Western Sahara implies a preliminary character and a certain conditioning in relation to the answers to the questions formulated by the General Assembly (...)" (stressed characters by author) (*I.C.J., Pleadings, Western Sahara*, Vol. I, p. 221, par. 382 et seq.)

[226] DAILLIER, P. (1985): 1288.

[227] Petition of September 17, 1974, in the following terms: "You claim Sahara was '*terra nullius*. That it is a disinherited land or good, with no established power of administration; Morocco claims the contrary. We ask for arbitration of the International Court of Justice of The Hague (...)" (*Western Sahara, Advisory Opinion, I.C.J., Reports 1975*, p. 14, par. 26). This statement is also collected on the individual opinion of judge De Castro (*ibid.*, p. 129). Furthermore, the Visiting Mission Report of October 1975 can be consulted on this question (*ORGA*: A/10023/Add.5, par. 100, y A/9771, annex).

Judge De Castro's opinion is that, even if Spain would have accepted to forward both question in litigation before the Court, the possibility would not have been feasible, as "Spain did not have at that moment, nor has it nowadays, the quality to be party in this matter with Morocco o any other State concerning the actual or past sovereign titles referred to a territory with the status of Non-Self-Governing Territory, and of which Spain remains the administering Power. Spain did not have what is called in procedure the passive legitimacy" (*Western Sahara, Advisory Opinion, I.C.J., Reports 1975*, p. 145). We agree only partially with these approaches, because, though Spain did not aspire to be sovereign of the territory, according to its administering Power condition of the territory, Spain not only had legitimacy to defend the interests of the population, but also was compelled to do so.

it "has not managed to offload its contentious premises", in particular as regards the composition of the Court and its conclusions[228].

The Spanish delegation maintained that, if the Court began to analyse the questions submitted by the General Assembly through advisory proceedings, when Spain had previously rejected contentious proceedings, it would be converting advisory jurisdiction into "a means to get round the consent of the States in contentious jurisdiction"[229] as "this approach could result in the introduction of obligatory jurisdiction through a majority vote within a political organ"[230], thus ignoring the philosophy of the Statute of the Court[231]. After analysing the position of the Spanish representative in the course of the debates in the General Assembly and in the phases of the process carried out before it, the Court concluded that it could not be deduced from this analysis that Spain had given its consent that the questions put forward by 3292 (XXIX) be directed to the Court. Thus, Spain continued to submit objections to these, and

> "the fact that it abstained and did not vote against the resolution cannot be interpreted as implying its consent to the adjudication of those questions by the Court. Moreover, its

---

[228] FLORY, M., "L´Avis de la Cour Internationale de Justice sur le Sahara Occidental", *A.F.D.I.*, XXI (1975): 253-277.

[229] *I.C.J., Pleadings, Western Sahara*, Vol. I, p. 222, par. 389.

[230] *Western Sahara, Advisory Opinion, I.C.J., Reports 1975*, p. 14, par. 27

[231] Even if Judge Petrén did not completely agree with the approaches of the Spanish representation on this point, he pointed out that the quasi exclusive use of the Court of documentation presented by Spain, Morocco, Mauritania and Algeria (which corresponds more to litigation procedures than to advisory ones, as in consultative procedures it is the proper Court that provides the necessary documents, whenever States do not provide so), "has provided the process with a much more litigious aspect than a consultative one", so the participation of these States "had conferred (...) a wholly unusual character tending to obscure the difference in principle between contentious and advisory proceedings" (*ibid.*, p. 112). Likewise, judge De Castro describes the procedure as "hybrid" and "quasi-litigious", due to the fact that "the way in which those parties proceeded was not that of amici curiae. Throughout the proceedings, the attitude of the interested parties was that of parties in contentious proceeding" (*ibid.*, pages 136, 137 and 142,). In the same sense, *cfr.* SHAW, M., "The Western Sahara case", *B.Y.I.L.*, 49 (1978): 124 et seq.; and VALLÉE, Ch. (1976): 48. Even if ZICCARDI considers that the procedure had a quasi-litigious character, he considers that the Court acted always in conformity with the purpose and provisions that regulate the consultative function, referring to the various precedents in which the Court had exercised the consultative function in relation to international controversy (*cfr.* ZICCARDI CAPALDO, G., "Il parere consultivo della Corte Internazionale di giustizia sul Sahara Occidentale: Un occasione per un riesame della natura e degli effetti della funzione consultiva", *Comunicazioni e Studi*, 15 (1978): 535-544, especially 544-545).

participation in the Court's proceedings cannot be understood as implying that it has consented to the adjudication of the questions posed in Resolution 3292 (XXIX), for it has persistently maintained its objections throughout"[232].

The fact that, in the debates held in the General Assembly, the Spanish delegation even declared that it was prepared to adhere with the claim, "on condition that another question intended to achieve a satisfactory balance between the historical and legal explanation of the problem and the current situation, considered in the light of the United Nations Charter and the relevant resolutions of the General Assembly concerning the decolonization of the territory was added to the questions put forward", led the Court to consider that "Spain did not oppose the reference of the Western Sahara question as such to the Court's advisory jurisdiction: it objected rather to the restriction of that reference to the historical aspects of that question"[233]. So, in the Court's opinion, Spain has not really opposed the questions raised before the Court, but the terms by which these questions were finally posed.

However, as was expected, the Court rejected the Spanish pretensions, mainly for two reasons, both of which related to the characteristics of the advisory opinions: on one hand, because its effects are not binding on the States, unlike those of contentious proceedings, and, on the other hand, because as the Court had established in the case of the *interpretation of the peace treaties concluded with Bulgaria, Hungary and Romania, first phase,*

> " The Court's Opinion is given *not to the States, but to the organ which is entitled to request it*; the reply of the Court, itself an 'organ of the United Nations', represents its participation in the activities of the organization, and, in principle, should not be refused"[234].

However, it understands that, in certain circumstances that in its opinion do not affect this case, the lack of consent of an interested State may render the giving of an advisory opinion incompatible with the Court's judicial character. This circumstance would arise "when the circumstances disclose that to give a reply would have the effect of circumventing the principle that a State is not obliged to allow its disputes to be submitted to judicial settlement without its consent". The Court understands that the consent of a State concerned is

---

[232] *Western Sahara, Advisory Opinion, I.C.J., Reports 1975*, p. 15, par. 29.
[233] *Ibid.*, p. 16, par. 30.
[234] *Interpretation of Peace Treaties, Advisory Opinion: I.C.J. Reports 1950*, p. 71 (emphasized by author).

important, not from the point of view of its competence, but "for the appreciation of the propriety of giving an opinion"[235]. In the case in question, there is a legal controversy, but one "which arose during the proceedings of the General Assembly and in relation to matters with which it was dealing. It did not arise independently in bilateral relations". When the Spanish Government stated that possesses no "Non-Self-Governing Territories, but provinces", Morocco expressly stated its reservations to this affirmation as regards, among others, the territory of "Spanish Sahara". This legal dispute remained unchanged within the Organization in the period from 1966-1974, during which Morocco accepted the right to self-determination of the population of "Spanish Sahara". Mauritania was in the same situation as from the time that it became a member of the UN (1960) as it then declared that "Spanish Sahara" was part of its territory.

The Court insisted on the object of the Advisory Opinion requested, which coincides with the request of the General Assembly to enlighten the United Nations in its actions[236], as,

> "The legitimate interest of the General Assembly in obtaining an opinion from the Court in respect of its own future action cannot be affected or prejudiced by the fact that Morocco made a proposal, not accepted by pain, to submit for adjudication by the Court a dispute raising issues related to those contained in the request. It is difficult to see on what basis the sending of the Note would make Spain's consent necessary for the reference of the questions to the Court, if that consent would not otherwise be needed"[237].

In our opinion, and not only in this case but in any work of the Court, advisory proceedings may and must be a valid component to overcome the excessively horizontal nature of the contemporary international community[238]. If this

---

[235] *Western Sahara, Advisory Opinion, I.C.J., Reports 1975*, p. 17, par. 32.

[236] Likewise pronouncement of judge Nagendra Singh, when pointing out that among the functions of the Court are those of determining the effects of relations that would have existed between Morocco, Mauritania and the Western Sahara population at the moment of the Spanish colonization, "this is a vital aspect which has to be stated fully and in clear and unambiguous terms to enlighten the General Assembly" (*Ibid.*, p. 79).

[237] *Ibid.*, p. 19, par. 41.

[238] Similarly, *cfr.* GROSS, L., "The International Court of Justice: Consideration of Requirements for Enhancing its Role in the International Legal Order", *A.J.I.L.* (1971): 253, and HINOJO ROJAS, M., *A propósito de la jurisdicción consultiva de la Corte Internacional de Justicia*, Cuadernos de Derecho Internacional, n° 8, Servicio de Publicaciones de la Universidad de Córdoba, Córdoba (1997).

CHAPTER IV

analysis were guaranteed by a more progressive interpretation of its legal function and more committed opinions than those currently produced by the Court[239], this would mark progress, an evolution towards overcoming the relativity of contemporary International law and an expression of the collaborator role which the Court must play as another important part of the structure of the United Nations, in which, it must not be forgotten, it is one of the principal organs[240].

As concerns the second reason, the Court considered that "the reference in those questions to a historical period cannot be understood to fetter or hamper the Court in the discharge of its judicial functions", which necessarily must take into account "existing rules of International law which are directly connected with the terms of the request and indispensable for the proper interpretation and understanding of its Opinion"[241]. The Court finds that is competent to entertain the request by which the General Assembly has referred to it questions "embodying such concepts of law as *terra nullius* and legal ties, regardless of the fact that the Assembly has not requested the determination of existing rights and obligations"[242].

This pronouncement of the Court did not have the unanimous backing of its members. In the opinion of Judge Petrén, an opinion we fully subscribe to,

"The question of the extent to wich, an under what conditions, past legal ties may influence the decolonization of a territory

---

[239] In this respect, it must be reminded the deceiving advisory opinion of the International Court of Justice of June 8, 1996 about the *Legality of the use of nuclear weapons by State in an armed conflict*. On this occasion, as stated by Carrillo Salcedo, the Court had been invited to make pronouncement on a legal problem of high importance, essential for international relations of the fifties on the existence of the UNO. As highlighted by this author, the ambiguous nature, and even the contradictory explanations of this advisory opinion are important and have their explanation in outstanding and notorious political factors (*cfr.* CARRILLO SALCEDO, J.A., prólogo a la obra de HINOJO ROJAS, M., *A propósito de la jurisdicción consultiva de la Corte Internacional de Justicia*, Cuadernos de Derecho Internacional, nº 8, Córdoba, 1997. On the other hand, it is alarming to confirm the progressive tendency to limit the use of consultative procedures in the last times, as since the Court pronounced the ruling on the Western Sahara question they have opted for a consultative option in only eleven times (1975-2014). Hinojo corroborates that the ICJ has underused the resource of consultative jurisdiction (*ibid.*, p. 142).

[240] Likewise, *cfr.* ZICCARDI CAPALDO, G. (1978): 535-545. Also, Chaumont states that "consultative opinions contribute to the formation of real organic International law, mainly of the United Nations" (CHAUMONT, Ch., *L'Organisation des Nations Unies*, ed. Puf, Paris (1994): 110).

[241] *Western Sahara, Advisory Opinion, I.C.J., Reports 1975*, p. 22, par. 52.

[242] *Ibid.*, p. 12, par. 20.

seems to me to fall within an as yet inadequately explored area of contemporary International law. That is why I find that the Court should not have approached those questions without first examining both their theoretical and their practical aspects"[243].

Furthermore, as pointed out by Judge Dillard,

"Nor is it apparent that an exclusively historical question could be automatically converted into a legal one merely because of the use of a legal term such as *terra nullius* or because the question itself baptized the term *ties* with a legal label by referring to them as *legal ties* a device which also appeared to be question-begging"[244].

For the same reasons, we disagree with the approach taken by the Court when it states that

"The issue between Morocco and Spain regarding Western Sahara is not one as to the legal status of the territory today, but one as to the rights of Morocco over it at the time of colonization. The settlement of this issue *will not affect the rights of Spain today as the administering Power, but will assist the General Assembly in deciding on the policy to be followed* in order to accelerate the decolonization process in the territory. It follows that *the legal position of the State which has refused its consent to the present proceedings is not in any way compromised by the answers that the Court may give to the questions put to it*"[245].

What the Court means by this statement is very difficult to understand. How is the opinion of the Court going to influence the right of the people of Western Sahara to self-determination? What would have been the consequences if the opinion had it established ties of sovereignty between Morocco and/or the Mauritanian Entity over Western Sahara? Would it have proclaimed the legality of the annexation of a territory which, in this way, "would return it to

---

[243] *Ibid.*, p. 112 (emphasized by author). Maintaining such opinion, the judge states that the wide range of geographic and other circumstances that must be taken into account in the decolonization process "have not allowed yet the constitution of a sufficiently elaborated set of rules and practices to cope with all the situations that may give problems", what, in other words, means that "the decolonization right does not constitute a finished body of doctrine and practice" (*Ibidem,* p. 110).
[244] *Ibid.*, p. 109.
[245] *Ibid.*, p. 19, par. 42 (emphasized by author).

the mother country", thus stealing the possibility of the population to freely express its will? As stated in the opinion, if the legal position of Spain is not to be changed as a consequence of the advisory opinion, what sense does the fact that the opinion might evaluate the legal or territorial nature of the ties that might have existed in 1884 when Spain commenced the colonisation have?[246] In what way could the opinion of the General Assembly influence "the policy to be followed in order to accelerate the process of self-determination", when this was well defined in the resolutions on decolonization of the territory? These questions were unanswered and, since the opinion did not find links of sovereignty over the territory (it tacitly persevered the policy established by the General Assembly as regards decolonization?), more questions were not put forward as regards this matter. In our opinion, this is the most neglected aspect of the opinion of the Court and, in which the opinions given by the judges in this matter, which we shall see below, are most deceptive.

Furthermore, the Court had already pronounced on the value of the legal ties in accordance with inter-temporal law meaning that a reference to this subject would not have been in any way complicated. In the case of *Minquiers et des Ecréhous*, the analysis of useless historical controversies was considered to be unnecessary, and it was concluded that the original entitlement loses its value if new events occur and these must be considered in the light of new law:

> "a legal fact must be appreciated in the light of contemporary law. (...) When the legal system under which the entitlement was validly created disappears, this right cannot be maintained

---

[246] The same question is raised by the Algerian representative, M. Bedjaoui, before the Fourth Commission in the following terms: "(...) the aforementioned asks about the *value and authority of the historical titles regarding a territory in the case they should exist*. If the nations had to support his claims on the territories of other peoples according to historical titles derived from more or less lasting conquers, all peaceful live on earth would be impossible. If this were the case, why not reconstruct the Persian Empire from actual Iran, or the Phoenician domains from Lebanon of our days or the Napoleon Empire from contemporary France or the Alexander Magnum from Modern Greece or the vast territory conquered by the Romans from the Italy we now know or even add Andalusia to an Arab country, for example Morocco? The decolonization does not consist of mere substitution of the territory competence of the administering power by another competence that historically has been there before without the consent of the population in question. (...) After a long evolution, the contemporary world has emerged as a principle that *peoples must decide on the destiny of their territory, and not the other way*, as the dignity of the people is in game, and this cannot be treated as a mere accessory question of the portion of land. The logical consequence is that *historical rights can only prevail when supported by the acquiescence of the people of the territory in question*" (ORGA: A/C.4/32/SR.13, par. 25 et seq., November 2, 1977) (emphasized by author).

under the new legal system it complies with the conditions set out in the new system"[247].

In the case of Western Sahara, the changes in the circumstances of the territory are evident: if the colonisation was carried out in accordance with the law at the time, since the seventies the maintenance of colonialism was considered to be contrary to the United Nations Charter, therefore the territory was included among the Non-Self-Governing Territories, about which the administering powers have the duty to provide information as referred to in Article 73e) of the Charter[248], thus establishing Spain's obligation to put an end to colonial domination. As a culmination to this process, at the time the Court was requested to issue an advisory opinion, the right of the population of Western Sahara to self-determination had already been established by several resolutions[249].

As stated by Judge De Castro,

"whatever the existing legal ties with the territory may have been at the time of colonization by Spain, legally those ties remain subject to intertemporal law and that, as a consequence, they cannot stand in the way of the application of the principle of self-determination"[250].

The 1975 Visiting Mission seemed to ask this same question when it asked the Algerian President if, in his opinion, in the event that the Court pronounced in favour of the existence of ties of sovereignty of Morocco or Mauritania over Western Sahara territory, "should the principle of self-determination be obligatorily applied". In even blunter terms, the President of the mission asked the President of Algeria the following questions,

"Would it be necessary to consult the population on the transfer of powers?" or, "Could this transfer be made simply through

---

[247] *The Minquiers and Ecrehos case, Juzgement of November 17th, 1953: I.C.J. Reports,* vol. II, p. 375.

[248] Spain started to transmit to the Secretary General of the United Nations the information referring article 73 e) of the Charter on Mayo 18, 1961 (*ORGA*: A/4785, supl. No. 15).

[249] Resolutions 2229 (XXI), December 20, 1966, 2354 (XXII), December 19, 1967, 2428 (XXIII), December 18, 1968, 2591 (XXIV), December 196, 1969, 2711 (XXV), December 14, 1970, 3162 (XXVII), December 14, 1973 and 3292 (XXIX), December 13, 1974.

[250] *Western Sahara, Advisory Opinion, I.C.J., Reports 1975,* p. 171. In this sense, *cfr.* SALCEDO, J. A., "Libre determinación de los pueblos e integridad territorial de los Estados en el dictamen del T.I.J. sobre el Sáhara Occidental", *R.E.D.I.,* Vol. XXIX, n°1 (1976): 48 et seq.

negotiations between Spain and the country designated by the Court?"[251]

Undoubtedly, the President of the Mission was "speaking aloud", when he expressed his doubts on the potential consequences of a decision of the Court in favour of the pretensions of annexation of the States neighbouring on Western Sahara. The answer given by the Algerian President could not have been more sensible and more in accord with international legality, "it is not logical that the United Nations should contravene its own decisions on decolonization. The fear that some seem to have regarding consulting the population is incomprehensible". In his opinion, it is not possible to ignore the will of the people, "no matter how small this is"[252] which, in our opinion, would make a pronouncement of the Court on this question unnecessary[253].

2. The core questions

2.1. *Was Western Sahara terra nullius at the time of the Spanish colonization?*

After resolving the preliminary question regarding its competence, the Court began to analyse the two core questions presented by Resolution 3292 (XXIX). As regards the first question, which was aimed at determining whether the territory was *terra nullius* or not[254] at the time it was colonized by

---

[251] *ORGA*: A/10023/Add.5, Appendix II, par. 51.

[252] *Ibid.*, par. 52 and 54.

[253] This approach is also defended by the Permanent People's Court, in its ruling on the Western Sahara, maintaining that if the right of self-determination should enter in conflict with legal ties, or even, in the case these did not exist, with a sovereign relation former to the colonization, it would be convenient to verify at the moment of the decolonization if the reintegration of the territory in an existing State would satisfy the free and true will of the majority of the inhabitants of this territory (JOUVE, E. (1983): 69).

[254] Regarding the first questions put forward by the GA to the ICJ, Moreno maintains that such an approach nowadays has no sense, as, states Moreno, we lack of criteria to judge whether a territory is *'terra nullius'* or not, because the evolution of International law, especially the existence within the Law of the principle of equal rights of peoples has made disappear the concept of *'terra nullius'*: peoples that are inhabitant of a territory are always a valid owner of it and, unless it is demonstrated that it belongs to a certain State, peoples are the only ones to decide their destiny according to the right of self-determination. The problem now is not to judge whether it is a "terra nullius" or not, but to determine who is its legitimate owner. In a case of decolonization this will condition the principle according to which the decolonization must take place: self-determination of peoples or territorial integrity of States (MORENO LÓPEZ, M.A., "Sahara Español: una descolonización controvertida", *R.P.I.*, 139, Mayo-Junio (1975): 90). Furthermore, Vallée states that it would

Spain[255], the conclusion reached by the Court was negative, and was based on the law in force at the time of the colonisation. According to this law, *terra nullius* was all the territory which could be occupied as it did not have an owner; in other words, because it was not inhabited by socially and politically organized populations.

The decision was mainly supported by two arguments. On one hand, because "at the time of colonization Western Sahara was inhabited by peoples which, if nomadic, were socially and politically organized in tribes and under chiefs competent to represent them"; and on the other hand, because in colonizing Western Sahara, "Spain did not proceed on the basis that it was establishing its sovereignty over *terrae nullius*". In its Royal Order of 26 December 1884, far from treating the case as one of occupation of *terra nullius*, Spain proclaimed that the King was taking the Rio de Oro under his protection on the basis of agreements that had been entered into with the chiefs of the local tribes[256]. Likewise, in negotiating with France concerning the limits of Spanish territory to the north of the Rio de Oro, that is, in the Sakiet El Hamra area, Spain did not rely upon any claim to the acquisition of sovereignty over a *terra nullius*[257].

The decision of the Court concerning this first question put forward by the General Assembly was, therefore, quite clear when it pointed out that, at the time of the Spanish colonisation, the territory was not *terra nullius*, and it is also significant that the decision was unanimously adopted by its members although some of these stated that their vote in favour had been forced as it was impossible to abstain[258]. In our opinion, the Court should not have

---

have been a moment for the Court to condemn the notion of de *terra nullius*, always invoked in the course of centuries to justify conquers and colonization (VALLÉE, Ch. (1976): 48), though, in our opinion, to a certain amount, the Court condemned the notion really.

[255] About this concept of "*terra nullius*" in International law, *cfr.* BEDJAOUI, M., *Terra nullius, "droits" historiques et autodétermination*, Oral expositions before ICJ on the Western Sahara matter, on May 14, and 14, 15,16 and 29 July 1975, ed. United Nations, The Hague (1975); TOMAS ORTIZ DE LA TORRE, J. (1975): 592-604.

[256] The Order referred expressly to "the documents which the independent tribes of this part of the coast" had "signed with the representative of the Sociedad Española de Africanistas", and announced that the King had confirmed "the deeds of adherence" to Spain (*Western Sahara, Advisory Opinion, I.C.J., Reports 1975*, p. 39, par. 81)

[257] *Ibidem*.

[258] I.C.J., *Pleadings, Western Sahara*, Vol. I, p. 134, par. 163. Likewise, judge Gros stated that, even if he had no doubt of the nature of the territory, that in no case was *terra nullius*, "the question was not a legal one (…) it was purely academic and served no useful purpose", and therefore has a "loaded nature", because the concept of *terra nullius* was never relied on by any of the States interested in the status of the Territory at the time of colonization; no treaty or diplomatic document has been produced relying on this concept in connection with

CHAPTER IV

pronounced on this question as we do not see to what extent the response to this question enlightened the General Assembly in its decolonizing policy, especially when the condition of *terra nullius* of the territory had not been questioned by any of the States involved in the conflict[259]. If the Court had only pronounced on the second question posed by the General Assembly, the response to the first question would have been given in the event that it was stated that there were ties of the sovereignty of Morocco and/or Mauritania over the territory, because obviously the territory would not be *terra nullius* and in the event that such ties were denied, the response to the first question would be without purpose.

2.2. The question of the "legal ties" and the "ties of territorial sovereignty"

2.2.1. The Advisory Opinion

On analysing the second question posed by the General Assembly, as a prior question, the Court considered that it should clarify the sense in which it interpreted the expression "*legal ties* between the territory and the Kingdom of Morocco and the Mauritanian entity", used in Resolution 3292 (XXIX), understanding this as referring to such "to such legal ties as may affect the policy to be followed in the decolonization of Western Sahara"[260].

Western Sahara, and States at the time spoke only of zones of influence (…) It is not for a court to enquire into what would have happened in 1884 if States had relied on this concept, but into what did happen" (*ibid., par. 9*).
Same approach defended by judge Dillard (*Western Sahara, Advisory Opinion, I.C.J., Reports 1975*, p. 124) and judge Petrén: the notion of *terra nullius*, used by doctrine and by case law to define the legality of certain ways of acquiring territories, is not applicable in the case of Western Sahara, as in no case the legitimacy of the acquisition of the territory by Spain is questioned. Spain on the other hand, never claimed before the Court its sovereignty over it. In his opinion, "the question of whether the territory was *terra nullius* at the time of colonization is thus without object in the context of the present case". In view of the foregoing, the judge find it pointless and consequently inappropriate for the Court to answer the first of the two questions put" (*ibid.*, pages 104, 113 et seq.). Also on this matter: GILBERT, K., "Aboriginal sovereign position: summary and definitions", Extract from Gilbert, K., Aboriginal Sovereignty: Justice, the Law and Land (1987), *Social Alternatives*, vol.13, no.1, April (1994): 13-15, that makes a comparative study of the cases of Western Sahara and the Maori population of Australia, to conclude that in none of the cases can we talk about *"terra nullius"*.
[259] Likewise, *cfr.* BLAYDES, L.E. Jr. (1976): 362.
[260] *Western Sahara, Advisory Opinion, I.C.J., Reports 1975*, p. 40 et seq., par. 85 (emphasized by author).

Once this point was clarified, it went on to analyse the core of the second question, by first referring to the relations between the territory and Morocco and, then to the relations between the territory and the Mauritanian entity.

A) The ties between Western Sahara and Morocco

The Court first established the premises to support its argumentation in this question, pointing out that it would give priority to evidence directly related to the effective exercise of authority in the territory at the time of the Spanish colonisation and during the period prior to this colonisation, rather than "indirect inferences drawn from events in past history"[261]. In this regard, despite admitting that the Sherifien State had a particular nature as "its special character consisted in the fact that it was founded on the common religious bond of Islam existing among the peoples and on the allegiance of various tribes to the Sultan (...) rather on the notion of territory", it denies relevance to this question as "common religious links have, of course, existed in many parts of the world without signifying a legal tie of sovereignty or subordination to a ruler"[262]. In the opinion of the Court, these ties do not necessarily suppose the authentic exercise of state authority.

The Court made a separate study of two different areas of action of Morocco: the domestic and the international. As concerns the first of these, it understands that the evidence submitted by Morocco, which, in the opinion of the authorities of this State must justify "its internal deployment of authority in the territory",

> "the material so far examined does not establish any tie of territorial sovereignty between Western Sahara and that State. It does not show that Morocco displayed effective and exclusive State activity in Western Sahara. It does however provide indications that a legal tie of allegiance had existed at the relevant period between the Sultan and some, but only some, of the nomadic peoples of the territory"[263].

---

[261] *Ibid.*, par. 93. Ruling mentions specifically that this criterion had been established by its own case law, in the case *The Minquiers and Ecrehos case, Juzgement of November 17th, 1953: I.C.J. Reports,* p. 57.

[262] *Western Sahara, Advisory Opinion, I.C.J., Reports 1975,* p. 44 , par. 95.

[263] *Ibid.*, par. 107. The same reasoning would be repeated in the final paragraphs of the advisory opinion (*ibid*, par. 162). The then President of Algeria, Boumediene, pointed out to this respect that "the spiritual authority of religious leaders did not coincide, geographically, with administrative divisions" (*ORGA*: A/10023/Add.5, appendix II, par. 47)

Chapter IV

This moderation or prudence of the Court would later serve as an excuse for Morocco to justify the Green March, alleging that the ties of allegiance referred to in the opinion were a form peculiar to the Arab world of effectively exercising power over a territory, an interpretation which is openly distant from what the Court actually stated[264].

As concerns the international acts which took place between 1767 and 1911, and which, according to Morocco, justify the recognition by other States of its sovereignty over all or part of the territory, the conclusion reached by the Court did not differ much from what we have just mentioned about the internal area. Fundamentally, the Moroccan representatives alleged the following international acts, from whose analysis would derive recognition in favour of Moroccan sovereignty over the territory[265]:

a) The Hispano-Moroccan Treaty of Marrakech (1767)[266], and treaties made with the United States of America (1836), Great Britain (1856) and Spain (1861) referring to the rescue of shipwrecked persons in the coasts adjacent to those of Noun or in its proximity[267]. After analysing the specific content of each of these treaties and the controversy regarding interpretation arising in the first of these due to the different content of the texts drafted in Spanish and Arabic, the Court concluded that it cannot be considered that these international acts entail the international recognition of territorial sovereignty of the Sultan over Western Sahara, but they constitute "the display of the Sultan's authority or influence in Western Sahara only in terms of ties of allegiance or of personal influence in respect of some of the nomadic tribes of the territory"[268].

---

[264] Amongst those who think this statement of the Court means recognition of the right of Morocco on the territory, approach that we do not obviously agree with, *cfr.* ISOART, P., "Réflexions sur les liens juridiques unissant le Royaume du Maroc et le Sahara Occidental", *Revue Juridique Politique et Economique du Maroc* (1978): 11-47. Dupuy thinks this attitude is due to a traditional eurocentred vision of the Court. (DUPUY, R.J., "L'Avis Consultatif de la Cour Internationale de Justice", in *Hassan II presénte la Marche Verte* (dir. by Bardonnet, Basri, Dupuy, J.R., Laroui and vVdel, Paris (1990): 119 et seq.)

[265] *Western Sahara, Advisory Opinion, I.C.J., Reports 1975*, p. 41, par. 108.

[266] This treaty was concluded between the Sultán Sidi Mohamed Ben Abdellah Ben Ismaïl and the King of Spain, Carlos III.

[267] On the nature of Hispano-Moroccan agreements, *cfr.* TOMAS ORTIZ DE LA TORRE, J. (1975): 572-592.

[268] *Western Sahara, Advisory Opinion, I.C.J., Reports 1975*, p. 45, par. 118. In this way, for example, article 18 of the Treaty of Marrakech of 1767, states the following: "S.M. Imperial se aparta de deliberar sobre el establecimiento que S.M. Católica quiere fundar al sur del Río Noun, pues no puede hacerse responsable de los accidentes y desgracias que sucedieran a causa de no llegar allí sus dominios". In this way, it was acknowledging that it was not exercising control over the territory situated to the south of the Noun river.

b) Anglo-Moroccan Treaty of 1895, whereby Great Britain would have recognized Moroccan sovereignty over the territories located south of Cape Bojador. As regards this treaty, the ICJ stated that "what those provisions yielded to the Sultan was acceptance by Great Britain not of his existing sovereignty but of his interest in that área"[269].

c) Hispano-Moroccan diplomatic correspondence concerning the execution of the provisions of Article 8 of the Treaty of Tetuan of 1860, and of a subsequent agreement made with Spain in 1900, in which Spain had recognized Moroccan sovereignty south of Cape Bojador. The ICJ concluded that Morocco did not sufficiently prove the existence of these protocols, which was also denied by Spain and Mauritania, meaning that they were in fact not taken into account[270].

d) An exchange of Franco-German letters in 1911, where it was agreed that "Morocco includes all the territory in the North of Africa between Algeria, French West Africa and the Spanish colony of Río de Oro". In the opinion of the Court, this correspondence was intended to delimit the zones of political interest of France as regards Germany; therefore, they cannot be considered to be evidence of recognition of the limits of Morocco[271].

> In conclusion, and as regards Moroccan pretensions, the Court understands that
>
> "Examination of the various elements adduced by Morocco in the present proceedings does not, therefore, appear to the Court to establish the international recognition by other States of Moroccan territorial sovereignty in Western Sahara at the time of the Spanish colonization. Some elements, however, more especially the material relating to the recovery of shipwrecked sailors, do provide indications of international recognition at the time of colonization of authority or influence of the Sultan, displayed through Tekna caids of the Noun, over some nomads in Western Sahara"[272].

B) *The ties between Western Sahara and Mauritania*

Since the State of Mauritania did not yet exist at the time the colonisation of the territory was carried out, the Court chose the denomination "Mauritanian

---

[269] *Ibid*, p. 46, par. 120..
[270] *Ibid.*, p. 47, par. 123.
[271] *Ibid.*, p. 48, par. 127.
[272] *Ibid.*, p. 48, par. 128.

entity", an expression used for the first time in 1974 in the course of the debates of the General Assembly which would conclude with the approval of Resolution 3292 (XXIX), showing the lack of a distinct collective personality at the time of the colonisation of the territory with respect to the emirates and tribes which composed it. In this regard, and, although it recognises that the nomadic character of a large part of the population of the territory logically resulted in the establishment of determined ties of a legal nature among the tribes of Western Sahara and those who lived in the territories which today form part of the Islamic Republic of Mauritania, it rejects "at the time of the colonisation by Spain there existed between the territory of Western Sahara and the Mauritanian entity any tie of sovereignty, or of allegiance of tribes, or of 'simple inclusion' in the same legal entity"[273].

This second question was resolved by the Court through an express referral to paragraph 162 of the Advisory Opinion, in the following terms,

> "The materials and information presented to the Court show the existence, at the time of Spanish colonisation, of legal ties of allegiance between the Sultan of Morocco and some of the Tribes living in the territory of Western Sahara. They equally show the existence of rights, including some rights relating to the land, which constituted legal ties between the Mauritanian entity, as understood by the Court, and the territory of Western Sahara. However, the Court's conclusion is that the materials and information presented to it do not establish any tie of territorial sovereignty between the territory of Western Sahara and the kingdom of Morocco or the Mauritanian entity. Thus, the Court has not found legal ties of such a nature as might affect the application of Resolution 1514 (XV) in the decolonization of Western Sahara and, in particular, of the principle of self-determination through the free and genuine expression of the will of the peoples of the Territory (*cfr.* paragraphs 54-59 above)".

As can be appreciated from the literal meaning of the paragraph cited, the Court reached three conclusions:

---

[273] *Ibid.*, p. 64, par. 150. Judge De Castro states his disagreement regarding this conclusion of the Court, in the same way he had regarding the theoretical legal relation of Morocco over Western Sahara (*ibid.*, p. 164). Likewise, *cfr.* SHAW, M. N., *International Law*, 3th ed., Cambridge (1991): 153.

1) The existence of legal ties of allegiance between the Sultan of Morocco and certain tribes that inhabited Western Sahara.
2) The non-existence of ties of territorial sovereignty over Western Sahara by Morocco and Mauritania.
3) The non-existence of ties that might modify the application of Resolution 1514 (XV) of the General Assembly.

2.2.2. The declarations and opinions of the judges

The criticism and dissidence of the members of the Court against the conclusions contained in this paragraph are multiple and of different types. Thus, some of these wanted to show their disagreement with the reference made in the Opinion to the question of the existence of legal ties, considering that the Court should have specified "precisely the implications of those ties in terms of decolonization which is the very object and the main theme of the exercise pending before the General Assembly"[274]. Despite this, they considered that the statement that there were no sovereignty ties over the territory was "a correct, clear and conclusive reply to the real questions put to the Court"[275]. In opposition to this majority position, a limited number of judges stated that the legal ties referred to by the opinion are also ties of sovereignty[276].

A) Opinions of the judges who deny the existence of "legal ties", or, if these exist, they have no relevance

The most radical opinion against the pronouncement of the Court is that of the Argentinian Judge Ruda, who maintained the only dissenting opinion made by the members, stating that the ties existing between the Sultan of Morocco and certain populations of Western Sahara, "legal ties of allegiance and authority" in the words of the Court, do not have the legal character attributed to them because they are exclusively "personal ties". In his opinion, if these types of legal ties of allegiance and authority had actually existed, they would have created a territorial right, since "the normal legal inference of such a finding would have been that the Sultan of Morocco was the sovereign of the territories where these tribes live; but this is a proposition which the Court has

---

[274] *Western Sahara, Advisory Opinion, I.C.J., Reports 1975*, p. 79 (Decl. judge Nagendra Singh).
[275] *Ibid.*, p. 127. The judge Nagendra Singh understands, however, that even if relations existed between Sahara and Morocco, the natures of these relations were of a "transitory and non-legal or political significance" (*Ibid.*, p. 147).
[276] *Ibid.*, p. 173 (Separate opinion of judge Boni).

not accepted". Thus, he concluded that there have not been any types of legal ties between Morocco and Western Sahara. However, this judge stated that such ties did exist between the Mauritanian entity and Western Sahara, ties which, in his opinion, had a territorial character. The basis of his argumentation is focused on the traditional freedom of the nomadic populations to cross frontiers, which would provide the Mauritanian entity with characteristics of political unity legally capable in itself to be the holder of territorial rights, political unity which the tribes of Western Sahara would have been part of and in a way no different from the others in the territory denominated "Mauritanian entity"[277].

From a less radical position, Judge Gros criticizes the complexity of the process chosen by the Court in order to respond to the second of the questions put forward by the General Assembly, a response which he considers to be "enigmatic", as

> "*A positive finding* of what are said to be legal ties of allegiance between certain nomadic tribes of the territory and the Emperor of Morocco at the time of the colonisation, and also other ties which are said to be legal, this time between the Mauritanian entity and the Territory, *is combined with a negative decision* as to the existence of any tie of sovereignty over the territory on the part of the Emperor of Morocco or the Mauritanian entity, the conclusion being that no legal tie exists which could influence the principle of self-determination through the free and genuine expression of the will of the people of the Territory (with a fresh cross-reference to paras. 54 to 59 of the Opinion)"[278].

Going even further, Gros points out that, if he did not vote against paragraph 162, this was because it had not been divided into two parts, thus preventing him from expressing his opinion on the question. Thus, although he shares the position of the Court as regards the second part of the paragraph ("no legal tie exists which could influence the principle of self-determination"), he does not share the position as concerns the first part as the intrinsic contradiction which, in his opinion, involves the identification of "legal ties" with "ties of territorial sovereignty" as the latter are not of a legal nature, but instead of ethnic, religious or cultural nature. In the opinion of Judge De Castro, the expression "legal ties" cannot have any other meaning in the context of the

---

[277] *Ibid.,* p. 176 (Dissenting opinion of judge Ruda).
[278] *Ibid.,* p. 75, par. 10 (emphasized by author) (Declaration of Judge Gros).

Western Saharan conflict than that of "State ties relating to the territory and capable of having the value of a legal title to lay claim to the territory, that is to say, a right of sovereignty over the territory"[279].

In the opinion of Judge Gros, it is not right to attempt to assimilate institutions of a "separate world" to those institutions of Europe and from another epoch:

> "It is the duty of a Court to establish facts, that is to say, to make findings as to their existence (...) a Court may neither suppose the existence of facts nor deduce them from hypotheses unsupported by evidence. How can one speak of a legal tie of allegiance, a concept of feudal law in an extremely hierarchical society, in which allegiance was an obligation which was assumed formally and publicly, which was known to all (...)"[280].

In his opinion, the Court exceeds the powers conferred on it by Article 65 of its Statute when it attributes a legal character to facts that do not have this character:

> "a court does not create the law, it establishes it; (...) the ties which it describes as legal would only be so if, after having established their existence, the Court could (...) produce an effect on the decolonization of the Territory"[281].

---

[279] Judge De Castro points out that, even if the legal ties can be of diverse nature (taking origin from neighbourhood, a treaty, a war, can be territorial, personal, of sovereignty, of vassalage; they can also be international, of public or private law, of canonical law or Muslim law, etc.), the truth is that in the Saharan conflict, and in the light of the literal content of the questions forwarded to the GA, no other meaning is acceptable than that of sovereignty relations (*Western Sahara, Advisory Opinion, I.C.J., Reports 1975*, p. 135). On the other hand, he also underlined his disagreement with the advisory opinion, understanding that "There is no legal foundation for regarding as ties with the force of *ob-ligare* (*vinculatio*) the personal and sporadic ties of the Sultan with certain unclearly defined tribes" (*ibid.*, p. 164). Of course, the first question on the nature of *terra nullius* of the territory is deeply related to the second, as the answer to this is a direct consequence of the answer given to the first: was the territory *terra nullius* at the moment of Spanish colonization? In the case it were not, who was the sovereign of the territory?: Morocco? The Mauritanian entity? The question is to determine if the existing relations in the territory regarding the neighbour States are of territorial sovereignty. It is patently obvious that relations have existed, as these are frequent and inevitable between any kinds of neighbouring human communities, even more if populations are of a nomad nature. The question of the GA cannot have, in our opinion, another sense.

[280] *Ibid.*, p. 77, par. 11.

[281] *Ibid.*, par. 12).

He thus repeats, although within a more limited scope, the arguments stated by Spain when he affirms the non-competence of the Court in this case. In fact, Spain considered that the Court should not examine a question of a purely historical nature, a "simple question of academic interest" which in no case could condition the exercise of the right of the people of Western Sahara to self-determination, confirmed "in the light of the current rights and obligations established by the decolonization process substantiated by the United Nations", while Judge Gros considers that "it is not an abstract or academic question"[282] and although it is possible that the Court might appreciate the existence of the facts, this does not grant it the power to attribute a legal character to such facts which they do not in reality possess. In his opinion, it is the application of this theory to the provisions of the opinion that makes it abusive[283].

The other members of the Court expressed their doubts as to the content of the first of the points included in the paragraph we are analysing as they considered that the affirmation that there are ties of a legal nature does not rest on sufficient evidence[284], and, despite this, in our opinion, such an affirmation is not really important because of the content of the following two paragraphs and the "limited interest" which can be attributed to the legal condition of ties which existed in 1884, "in the contemporary setting of the decolonization process"[285]. In our opinion, the only ties which can be classified as legal in the context of the Western Sahara conflict, that is to say, in the law on decolonization, would be those capable of affecting the process of self-determination[286]. For the purposes of the General Assembly, the other ties could be of a historical but not of a legal nature, and would be unimportant in the context of the exercise of the right to self-determination.

---

[282] *Ibid.*, par. 6.
[283] *Ibidem*. Defending this thesis, in a very expressive way, judge Petrén states that "The Court is the principal judicial organ of the United Nations; it is not an historical research institute" (*ibid.*, p. 108). Judge Dillard maintains similar approaches (*ibid.*, p. 116 et seq.)
[284] *Ibid.*, p. 119. Judge De Castro, that maintains the same approach, attracts the attention on a key moment of the procedure before the Court: if in its written statements Morocco and Mauritania maintained individual claims on the whole of the territory, in the oral statements, surprisingly, they modified their initial approaches, limiting them from then on to the North and South, respectively, and what is more serious, without referring in any way to the reasons of such change in their attitude nor to the value of the documents presented to that point to justify the claim on the whole of the territory (*ibid.*, p. 132).
[285] *Ibid.*, p. 126.
[286] In this regard, *cfr.* VALLÉE, Ch. (1976): 52.

B) *Opinions of the judges who maintain the existence of "legal ties" and their identification with "sovereignty ties"*

Counter to these approaches, and following the literal meaning of paragraph 162, after celebrating that the Court had assumed a progressive conception of *terra nullius*, according to which today it is no longer possible to any inhabited territory as *terra nullius*, nor to justify conquest and colonisation based on this concept[287], Judge Ammoun made a detailed analysis of the treaties and documents where sovereignty over the territory was questioned, and concluded that, although he shared the opinion of the Court that there were ties of a legal nature between the populations of Western Sahara and Morocco and Mauritania, he did not share the value attributed to these. In his opinion, the legal ties which unite the territory Western Sahara to Morocco and to the Mauritanian entity referred to in paragraph 162 are of a political nature, and refer not to the population which inhabits the territory but to the territory itself[288]. This judge criticizes the fact that the advisory opinion sometimes refers to territory, and sometimes to the population, as if these were separate questions. As pointed out by López de la Torre, Judge Ammoun, a Lebanese lawyer with knowledge of Koranic Law, made an interpretation based on this law, according to which the willingness to render allegiance to the Sultan would be identified with obedience to the State he reigned over and, since the willingness to render allegiance was proclaimed by a sufficient majority of the tribes which inhabited the territory, there would be a real tie between the populations of the territory and Morocco, which was only partially recognized although it was never ignored in the definitive text of the opinion[289].

---

[287] *Western Sahara, Advisory Opinion, I.C.J., Reports 1975*, p. 86 et seq.

[288] Judge Forster maintains practically the same point of view than that of judge Ammoun, considering that the legal ties to which the advisory opinion "indicate the existence of State power and the exercise of political administration analogous to a tie of sovereignty exercised in the Sahara, a territory to which access was difficult, and over tribes some of which were nomadic and others settled" (*ibid.*, p. 95). Likewise stresses the "euro centrist" nature of the ruling (*cfr*. NDIAYE, B., "Avis de la C.I.J. sur le Sahara Occidental 16 octobre 1975", *Revue Sénégalaise de Droit*, 10 (1976): 50 et seq.).

[289] LOPEZ DE LA TORRE, S., "Referéndum en el Sahara Occidental", *Cuenta y Razón*, n° 56-57 (1991): 119. On the Arab concept of nation, in which the central question would turn around the idea of a Human community whose unique effecctive relation is the Muslim religio", *cfr*. FLORY, M., "La notion du territoire Arabe et son application au problème du Sahara", *A.F.D.I.*, 3, (1957): 76 et seq.; MESA GARRIDO, R. (1966): 51-76; DE BURLET, J., *Nationalité des personnes physiques et décolonisation. Essai de contribution à la théorie de la succession d'Etats*, Ed. Bruylant, Bruxelles (1975): especially, pages 54-57.

Judge Boni fully shared these approaches, considering that the error of the ICJ had consisted in failing,

> "to take sufficient account of the local context (...) As regards Morocco, insufficient emphasis has been placed on the religious ties linking the Sultan and certain tribes of the Sakiet El Hamra (...): the legal ties between them were thus not only religious, - which no one denies- but also political, and had the character of territorial sovereignty"[290].

3. Critical analysis of the advisory opinion of the ICJ

The evaluation of the advisory opinion in international doctrine has not been especially positive. From a generic point of view, as pointed out by Carrillo, it is regrettable that the Court allowed the possibilities offered by the request for an opinion to escape, since "it could have been an excellent occasion, which had not been fully taken advantage of, for the ICJ to specify certain unclear aspects of the Law on decolonization"[291], when, at least in theory, this was the objective intended by the request from the General Assembly. From a more specific point of view and, although we have mentioned this issue above, it should be asked to what extent the General Assembly would have been able to oppose its own policy, established through an interminable series of resolutions, in response to an opinion of the ICJ which it had requested. In fact, if, after twenty years of action by the General Assembly in defence of the rights of the population of Western Sahara, the opinion had contradicted the doctrine of the General Assembly, the Assembly would have found itself in a very difficult position, especially taking into account the fact that, although the advisory opinions of the Court are not of a compulsory nature, if the decisions of the Court establish the existence and the content of the international rule

---

[290] *Western Sahara, Advisory Opinion, I.C.J., Reports 1975*, p. 173.
[291] CARRILLO SALCEDO, J.A., *"Libre determinación..."* (1976): 49. Also in the same sense, Vallée sets that "its construction lies on too many uncertainties (VALLÉE, Ch. (1976): 54). Also in the same sense, *cfr.* CHAPPEZ, J., "L´avis consultatif de la C.I.J. du 16/10/1975 dans l´affaire du Sahara Occidental", *R.G.D.I.P.*, n. 4 (1976): 1176; DUTHEIL DE LA ROCHERE, J., "Les procédures de règlement des différends frontaliers", Societé Française pour la Droit International, Colloque de Poitiers, *La Frontière*, Ed. Pedone, Paris (1980): 115; FLORY, M. (1975): 273; LEVY, G.J., "Advisory opinion on the Western Sahara", *Brooklyn Journal of International Law*, vol. 2 (1976): 306 et seq.; RIEDEL, E.H., "Confrontation in Western Sahara in the Light of the Advisory Opinion of the International Court of Justice of 16 October 1975. A Critical Appraisal", *G.Y.I.L.*, vol. 19 (1976): 439; SHAW, M. (1978): 153; ZICCARDI CAPALDO, G. (1978): 539.

with authority, its seems only logical that the requesting organ must adapt its conduct to the legal decision unless it wants to disrespect this rule [292].

Neither is the reference made by the Court to this question very reassuring when it states that

> "In any event, to what extent or degree its opinion will have an impact on the action of the General Assembly is not for the Court to decide", since "for instance with regard to consultations between the interested States, and the procedures and guarantees required for ensuring a free and genuine expression of the will of the people"[293].

Carrillo criticizes this attitude of the Court because, although he states that it is true that the opinion is clear as regards the procedures and guarantees required to ensure the free and genuine expression of the will of the people of Western Sahara, *it is not so clear with regard to the consultations between the States concerned*. He is right when he asks about the meaning of this ambiguous expression, what prevails: the principle of free determination or the territorial claims of the States concerned?[294].

As has been mentioned above, the Court addressed this question in the final paragraph of the opinion, in which, as a conclusion concerning the second question posed by Resolution 3292 (XXIX), it affirmed the existence of "ties of allegiance between the Sultan of Morocco and some of the tribes living in the territory of Western Sahara (...); legal ties between the Mauritanian entity (...) and the territory of Western Sahara", but the non-existence of "any tie of territorial sovereignty between the territory of Western Sahara and the Kingdom of Morocco or the Mauritanian entity", therefore, in no case can

---

[292] PUENTE EGIDO, J., "Consideraciones sobre la naturaleza y efectos de las Opiniones Consultivas", *Zeitschrift für Ausländisches Offentliches Recht und Völkerrecht, 1971, Band* 31, p. 806.

[293] *Western Sahara, Advisory Opinion, I.C.J. Reports 1975*, p. 37, par. 73 y 72.

[294] CARRILLO SALCEDO, J.A., *"Libre determinación..."* (1976): 38 (emphasized by author). Some authors have branded the advisory opinion of the Court as ambiguous in this sense, which we cannot deny, but the use of such ambiguity is very different. Some use it to support similar approaches of those used by King Hassan II to call population to the "Green March" (*Cfr.* GOYTISOLO, J. (1979): 45; LEWIS, W. H. (1985): 214; LÓPEZ GARCIA, B., "Los comunistas marroquíes ante la cuestión del Sahara. Entrevista con Ali Yata, Secretario General del P.P.S. (P.C.N.)", *Materiales*, n° 8 (1978): 147-160). Others have denied such ambiguity to corroborate the non-existence of any kind of right of Morocco or Mauritania over the territory of Western Sahara; to this end, for example, *cfr.* BLAY, K. N., "Changing African perspectives..." (1985): 156. Also in this sense the Court of Peoples pronounced itself, *Avis sur le Sahara Occidental,* par. 4 of the ruling (in JOUVE, E. (1983).

these ties affect "the principle of self-determination through the free and genuine expression of the will of the peoples of the Territory"[295]. The "solomonic judgment"[296] to the two questions put forward by the General Assembly was reflected in the impossibility to achieve the unanimity of its members regarding the legal ties existing at the time of the colonisation between Morocco and the territory (adopted by fourteen votes in favour and two against) and as regards the Mauritanian entity (fifteen votes in favour and one against)[297]. The first doubt which arises concerning paragraph 162 under debate is whether the decision would have been the same in the event that Morocco or Mauritania, or both, had proved the existence of ties of sovereignty over the populations of Western Sahara at the time it was colonized. The declaration by the Court that, at the time of the colonisation, there were legal ties between the Sultan of Morocco and some Western Saharan tribes and between Western Saharan territory and the Mauritanian entity[298], but despite this in neither of the cases "were there ties of territorial sovereignty", a declaration that, as we pointed out above, would serve as an argument for Hassan II to call for the "Green March"[299], gave rise to some of its members expressing their personal points of view concerning "the enigmatic reply"[300] which the Court gave to the question.

---

[295] The importance of these statements of the Court has been underlined, by, among others, Carrillo Salcedo, as the International Court of Justice has reaffirmed the right of self-determination of peoples, and has done so in a categorical way that can be hardly denied from here on that the mentioned right belongs to contemporary positive International Law (CARRILLO SALCEDO, J.A., *"Libre determinación..."* (1976): 33).

[296] RIEDEL, E. H. (1976): 439.

[297] *Western Sahara, Advisory Opinion, I.C.J., Reports 1975*, p. 68, par. 163.

[298] Doubts on the real existence of legal ties between Morocco and Mauritania or between both over Western Sahara have been underlined by different doctrine writings on the matter. In this sense, *cfr.* SHAW, M. (1978): 140.

[299] The permanent representation of Morocco before the United Nations stated on November 1975 that the International Court of Justice "had formally recognized the historical relations of loyalty" (*ORGA*: S/11863 -Secretary General Report -). Also, the King Hassan II insisted on the fact that the International Court of The Hague had passed advisory opinion estimating that the Sahara had always had a loyalty relation to Morocco (LAURENT, E., *Hassan II. La memoria de un Rey*, Ed. B, Grupo ZETA, Barcelona (1994): 189). The monarch affirmed that the Court had pronounced in favour of Moroccan rights over the territory because, for the Islamic Law, the vassalage relations constitute authority (*vid.* The text of these statements in WILSON, C., ZOUBIR, Y., "Western Sahara: a foreign policy success waiting to happen", *Transafrica Forum*, n° 6 (3/4) Spring/Summer (1989): 32).

[300] CARRILLO SALCEDO, J.A., *"Libre determinación..."* (1976): 39. The same expression is used by the judge Gros (Western Sahara, Advisory Opinion, I.C.J., Reports 1975, p. 75).

In our opinion, if some passages of the opinion can be criticized, the ambiguous attitude[301] adopted by some members of the Court in their respective individual declarations and opinions are no less important, and some of these are very close to truly dissenting opinions. As we have seen, some criticized that the opinion had not specified more exactly the effects of these "legal ties" on the decolonization of the territory[302], while others even pointed out the incorrect nature of a pronouncement on the existence of ties beyond those which are strictly legal[303], but the proposals of the judges were in fact not a perfect model of compromise either because they did not even mention the effects which a pronouncement stating the existence of ties of sovereignty might have on the process for the decolonization of Western Sahara.

In any case, it is evident that the conclusions of the Court are incompatible with the tenor of the interpretations made by Morocco or Mauritania[304]. The Court can be criticized for its lack of forcefulness in some of the passages of the opinion, but it is not true that the opinion declared that all the parties were right, as those who pretended the legality of the Moroccan occupation of the territory maintained. Chapez stated that it was feared that, "in these cases with no victor, there is only one loser: the International Court of Justice"[305], while Vallée considered that it was evident and regrettable that, due to certain "mistaken and unusual" aspects, the opinion had reinforced the particular opinion of each of the parties that right was on their side[306]. Although it is

---

[301] As pointed by Sur, the vote of some magistrates in favour of the decision can be explained by tactical reasons than by legal rigor, as this decision represents to their eyes a lesser evil (SUR, S., "Les affaires des essais nucléaires", *R.G.D.I.P.*, n° 4 (1975): 1016). This is precisely the reason for which Vellas attributes to the ruling a "transactional character", though it has not contented any of the parties, which, was an impossible task in this case (VELLAS, P., "La diplomatie marocaine dans l'affaire du Sahara", *Politique Étrangère*, 1 (1978): 54).

[302] Judges Ammoun, Forster and Boni.

[303] Judges De Castro, Dillard, Gros, Ignacio-Pinto, Petrén and Ruda. The opinion of the doctrine on this matter is not unanimous. So, for example, Chappez thinks that maybe the Court could have silenced the existence of these types of relations (CHAPPEZ, J. (1976): 1176).

[304] Likewise, *cfr. ibid.*, p. 1133 et seq.; TOMAS ORTIZ DE LA TORRE, J., "Recientes aspectos jurídico-internacionales del conflicto del Sahara", *Revista General de Legislación y Jurisprudencia*, n. 126 (1977): 558.

[305] CHAPPEZ, J. (1976): 1133.

[306] In this same sense Le Borgne points out, very graphically, that "even if (the advisory opinion) was very wise, it allowed at least Morocco and Mauritania to support their claims, it allowed the POLISARIO Front to justify their fight, and it allowed the UNO, following the Court recommendations, to forward the self-determination principle" (LE BORGNE, C., "Sahara Occidental: miracle ou mirage?", *L'Afrique eta l'Asie modernes*, n°159, Hiver

certain that the lack of proportionality between the enormous amounts of documentation analysed by the Court, the subtle arguments maintained by the parties and the time used in the debates as regards the limited effect of the Opinion, the literal nature of the second part of the aforementioned paragraph 162 does not admit such approaches. Specifically, as pointed out by Flory, the main reason why the opinion expressly referred to the right of self-determination in its final and principal paragraph to highlight that the ties of a legal nature which existed at the time of the Spanish colonisation did not affect the exercise of this right, lay in the uncertainty created by the mountain of documentation, arguments and counter-arguments used by the parties before the Court[307].

The lack of definition of the Court as regards the possibility that the ties of sovereignty existing in the past might result in the inapplicability of the right to self-determination at the present time is unfortunate[308]. When it denies the existence of "rights of sovereignty", although it affirms the existence of "legal rights", it seems to suggest that the existence of the first would have justified a pronouncement other than the applicability of the right to self-determination[309], which, from our point of view, is unacceptable[310].

(1988-1989): 25). Likewise, Shaw considers that the Court's recognition of the existence of legal character relations "provides a legal pretext" to Morocco and Mauritania to defend the success of their aims, claiming the non-capacity of the Court to determine the real reach of the relations established in the past, because the Arabic culture was unknown to the quasi total of their members (cfr. SHAW, M. (1978): 140). In the same sense, cfr. DESSENS, P. (1976): 43.

From pro-Moroccan points of view, Vellas points out that the ruling implies "a big satisfaction for Morocco", as it declares, on the one hand that the territory was not *terra nullius*, and on the other hand, it admits the existence of legal ties, existence of rights, including certain rights related to the land (cfr. VELLAS, P. (1978): 421). In a very strict way the French diplomat Fougerouse describes Morocco as "the big winner" of the Court's ruling, after which "Moroccans just have to "go back home" to reunite with their countrymen" (FOUGEROUSE, M., *Le Maroc: vocations et realites*, Fondation Singer-Polignac, Paris (1987): 86 et seq.).

[307] FLORY, M. (1975): 276.
[308] Also in this sense, cfr. LEVY, G. J. (1976): 289-307.
[309] Likewise, cfr. BLAYDES, L. E. (1975): 367; CARRILLO SALCEDO, J.A., "Libre determinación..." (1976): 46; NDIAYE, B. (1976): 53.
[310] As Remiro points out in a very appropriate way, "an historical sovereignty title of a third party, supposing it existed, would not prevail over the right of self-determination of the genuine colonial population" (REMIRO BROTONS, A., *Derecho Internacional* (1997): 121).

Otherwise, the consultation put to the population, the main component of the right to self-determination[311], could be subject to the verification of situations remote in time which should never be able to affect the current rights of the population. Moreover, it is not by chance that the resolution of the General Assembly pointed out a *proviso* that the reply to the questions put forward did not prejudge the applicability of the right to self-determination[312].

Carrillo Salcedo is correct when he states that the decision of the Court as regards the necessary application of the right to self-determination in the Western Sahara case is coherent with the thesis sustained by the Court itself in its opinion of June 21, 1971 and with the progressive development of International law entailed by Resolution 2625 (XXV) in this matter. In fact, he states that "except for the colonial enclaves, the international legal status of all Non-Self-Governing Territories must be respected just as by the administering Powers as by third party States, even in the situation that there had been alleged legal ties between the Non-Self-Governing Territory and a third party State before the appearance of the colonial power. (...) The historical entitlements, except for the cases of colonial enclaves, cannot hinder the application of the principle of self-determination"[313].

The doctrine which has involved the analysis of the advisory opinions of the Court has coincided in pointing out the fact that, despite the non-binding value of these, in practice, there is a tendency to attribute to these "a value which is close to, but not identical to rulings"[314], and they have an "indubitable

---

[311] As clearly established by the Court "The validity of the principle of self-determination, defined as the need to pay regard to the freely expressed will of peoples, is not affected by the fact that in certain cases the General Assembly has dispensed with the requirement of consulting the inhabitants of a given territory. Those instances were based either on the consideration that a certain population did not constitute a "people" entitled to self-determination or on the conviction that a consultation was totally unnecessary, in view of special circumstances" (*Western Sahara, Advisory Opinion, I.C.J., Reports 1975*, p. 33, par. 59), so the exception to the general rule of the need to consult the population in the exercise of the right of self-determination does not affect, obviously, the case of Western Sahara.

[312] RIEDEL, E. H. (1976): 439. Resolution 3292 (XXIX) "asks the International Court of Justice, *without prejudice of the application of the principles contained in Resolution 1514 (XV) of the General Assembly*, to deliver a advisory opinion (...)" (emphasized by author).

[313] CARRILLO SALCEDO, J.A., *"Libre determinación..."* (1976): 48 et seq.

[314] HINOJO ROJAS, M. (1997): 129. In the same sense, *cfr.* AGO, R., "Les Avis consultatifs 'obligatoires' de la Cour Internationale de Justice: problemes d'hier et d'aujourd'hui", in *Mélanges Michel Virally, Le Droit International au service de la Paix, la Justice et du Développement*, ed. Pédone, Paris (1990): 9-24, especially 10-11; BACOT, G., "Réflexions sur les clauses qui rendent obligatoires les avis consultatifs de la C.P.J.I. et de la C.I.J.", *R.G.D.I.P.* (1980): 1027 et seq., though this last author analyses the question from a more concrete point of view. The one offered by certain clauses of conventional instruments,

legal, political and moral value"[315]. However, the opinion which we analyse was in reality legally useless; it did not contribute to the solution to the conflict nor did it cast light on the future action of the General Assembly, which is obvious in the light of the null effects of the opinion on the solution to the conflict, and, more seriously: the uselessness of the opinion was foreseeable. As opportunely stated by Cassese, "the political interests involved prevent the International Court of Justice from providing the desired effects"[316], and this placed its credibility in question[317]. In addition it is feared that the advisory channel might continue to have little effect on international society. The opinion of the Court concerning the legality of the construction of the wall in the occupied Palestinian territories is a powerful confirmation of this fear as, if for once, the ICJ does not give an inch to those who illegally occupy a territory, as does Morocco in Western Sahara, there are no indications that Israel will comply with the content of the opinion, not even as regards its most *achievable* points[318]. Despite all of this, there is no doubt that, if, instead of an opinion, the ICJ had given a Sentence, the Western Saharan conflict would have ceased to be a conflict some decades ago as, despite all the criticisms against the Court, the fundamental remained extremely clear: the solution to the conflict necessarily involves the exercise of the right to self-determination through the free and genuine expression of the will of the populations of the territory.

---

according to which certain rulings have compulsory force that can be or should be claimed to the Court.

[315] HINOJO ROJAS, M. (1997): 138.

[316] CASSESE, A., "*Commentaire à l'article 1.2*", in *La Charte des Nations Unies*, (Dir. by COT, J-P. et PELLET, A., Ed. Economica/Bruylant, Paris/Bruxelles (1985): 51. In his intervention before the Congress in The United States in 1977, M. Bennouna, the representative of Morocco, accused the Court of being more a political organ than a legal one. To this question Franck replied, in an interesting forum of debate (*cfr. Hearing before the Subcommittees on International Organizations and on Africa of the Committee on international Relations House of Representatives,* October 12 of 1977, U.S. Government printing Office, Washington, 1977, pages 33-34). Likewise, Bennouna, *cfr.* GAUDIO, A. (1978): 265.

[317] To this respect, the Court itself has stated the importance if its contribution to the proper working of the UNO, even if it pointed out that the risk of compromising or discrediting the legal role of the Court would have been a decision taking reason not to give course to the petition (*Application for Review of Judgement No. 273 of the United Nations Administrative Tribunal, Advisory Opinion, I.C.J., Reports 1982*, p. 347), circumstance that should have been taken into account in the petition of the GA about Western Sahara.

[318] Concerning this advisory opinion and the Palestinian conflict, *cfr.* SOROETA LICERAS, J., "Una visión del conflicto palestino: bloqueo histórico, colapso jurídico y fracaso político", *Cursos de Derecho Internacional y Relaciones Internacionales de Vitoria-Gasteiz*, Servicio de Publicaciones de la UPV/EHU (2006): 261-332.

CHAPTER V

THE FAILURE OF THE DECOLONIZATION PROCESS

1. The Green March

1.1. The Green March and the Security Council

The Security Council intervened in the Western Sahara conflict for the first time in October 1975 when, on the day following the publication of the Opinion of the ICJ, the King of Morocco called for a march of "unarmed civilians" ("with no weapons other than the Koran") into the territory: the so called *Green March*[319].

Although officially the Spanish authorities did not know that the *Green March* was being prepared[320] and that its "secret" nature was subsequently

---

[319] More than 524,000 Moroccans had answered to the calling of the Alawite monarch (*cfr*. JOFFE, G. (1995): 122), from which finally 350,000 took part in the Green March. This number would later correspond to the births in a year in Morocco ("the harvest of a year") at the moment of the mentioned march took place. The march was called "green" because this is the sacred colour of Islam (*cfr*. DELANEY, T.A. "Article 2.7 of the UN Charter: hindrance to the self- determination of Western Sahara and Eritrea?", *E.I.L.R.*, vol. 4, 2 (1990): 432). In the call to take part in the March the King mentioned the ICJ ruling in the following terms: Our right has been recognized, and the International Court of Justice has answered that Sahara has never been *terra nullius* before Spanish occupation. Then, what do we need to do, dear peoples? The doors of the Sahara are legally open; the whole world has recognized that Sahara belongs to us from the beginning of times. So, let's occupy the territory (text in GAUDIO, A. (1978): 272 et seq.) As pointed out by Ali Yara, the Green March meant the last example of tactical innovation, as the Moroccan objective was not to find a political answer to the conflict, but to impose itself as a regional power before diplomatic channels should find a different way out (*cfr*. ALI YARA, O. (1997): 58).
I On the impact of the Green March, not only in the territory of the Western Sahara but also the Moroccan domestic policy, *cfr*. WEINER, J.B., "The Green March in Historical Perspective [factors leading up to the march of 350,000 Moroccans into disputed areas of the Western Sahara, Nov. 1, 1975; based on conference paper]", *Middle East Journal*, n° 33, winter (1979): 20-33.
[320] In this sense, Carro, Spanish Minister of the Presidency, that came on as a substitute on January 3, 1974 after the murdered Carrero Blanco, surprisingly described the Green March as a "master move of risk and imagination" (CARRO MARTÍNEZ, A. (1976): 27).

stated by Hassan II[321], it is certain that the intentions of the Alawite monarch were known by the Spanish Government which, in June 1974, had publicly denounced declarations of the Alawite monarch threatening to invade the territory[322]. In a way, the attitude of the Spanish executive showed the divergences within it between the Ministers of the Presidency, reticent from the beginning as regards the "loss" of the African colony, and the Foreign Ministry, the defender of compliance with the international commitments imposed on Spain by the UNO, which would imply the commencement of the decolonization process in the territory[323].

---

[321] Likewise even King Hassan II stated that "a leak would have been mortal and its consequences considerable in an international order" (cfr. LAURENT, E. (1994): 187-189)

[322] So, for example, the Spanish representation before the United Nations had reported before the Secretary General King Hassan II's statements of April 28, in a radio programme of *France Inter*, during which he referred to the march as "the inexorable march that will make the Moroccan peoples, with their king at the head, if bitter or light spirits started the self-determination process in Sahara (A/10082). De Piniés also reported the King's position (letter to the Secretary General August 25) after the statements done by the King on August 20, in which he stated that "in October or November, at the latest, we shall know if we will enter in Sahara by pacific or armed means" (S/11857, Annex III). This diplomatic correspondence was published and distributed to Spanish instances by the General Secretary of the Organization, being the documents mentioned a simple example of the more than imminent march (document S/11857 shows a collection of statements and press releases of the Moroccan Government in the same sense. To this end, cfr. Statements of the Spanish ambassador in Morocco, Martín Gamero, before the Foreign Affair Commission of Chamber of Deputies (*Diario de Sesiones*, num. 31, March, 1978).

In this regard, González Campos asserted that the march took place knowing the Spanish Government that if the march was done in a limited area and also in a limited time, it would not produce an armed answer from the Spanish forces regarding the penetration in the territory (GONZALEZ CAMPOS, J., "Los acuerdos nulos de Madrid", *El País*, September 18, 1977). Even the Government President, Arias Navarro, pointed out to the Visiting Mission that covered the territory in October, 1975 that "it seemed that the Saharan population were threatened by the danger of their annexation against their will and by force" (*ORGA*: A/10023/Add.5, Appendix II, par. 7).

[323] *ORGA*: A/10023/Add.5, Appendix II, par. 7). The different approaches, progressively more different, that were in the origin of the first frictions in 1966 between the approach of the Foreign Affair Minister (Castiella), that defended the need to follow the acquired Spanish international commitments before the United Nations since its entry in this Organization, and the approach of the Presidency (represented at the time, 1966, by Carrero Blanco) who defended that the territory was part of Spanish territorial integrity ("Sahara is as Spanish as is the province of Cuenca", had asserted Carrero Blanco when occupying the post of Under-Secretary Minister of the Government Presidency, in a letter he sent to the General Governor of Sahara, on March 21, 1957, cfr. *Servicio Histórico Militar*, bundle 3, folder 4), would suppose permanently the development of the conflict, regarding the attitude of the Spanish Government. In this sense, the criticism of the Almirant Nieto Antúnez must

CHAPTER V

In these circumstances, Spain's reaction to the *Green March* consisted of asking for an urgent meeting of the Council, "under Article 35 of the Charter"[324] "so that appropiate decisions may be adopted and the Moroccan Government may be dissuaded from carrying out the announced invasion wich, in addition to jeopardizing international peace and security, disregards the right of the Saharan people to self-determination and is contrary to the purposes and principles of the United Nations Charter"[325]. This received a reply from the

---

be recalled, spokesman of the Government of Franco in 1965, to the attitude of the Spanish Delegation before the United Nations, when not taking into account the IV Principle of the National Movement on the "Unity of the Country" (MARTÍNEZ MILLAN, J.M., "Las pesquerías canario-africanas en el engranaje del africanismo español (1860-1910), *A.W.R.A.Q.*, n.11 (1990): 194). These differences are recognized by most of those who took part in the conflict. So, for example, *cfr.* the point of view of Fernando Morán, in VILLAR, F. (1982): prologue, p. 14; in the same sense, even VILLAR, F. (1982): 58. Regarding the constant problems existing between both Ministries and their consequences in the international area that would culminate with the signing of the Madrid Agreements, *cfr.* DIEGO AGUIRRE, J.R., "Los orígenes del Frente POLISARIO. Incidentes en El Aaiún en June de 1970", *Historia 16*, num. 137 (1987): 73-82.

On the other hand, the position of the Ministry of Presidency, in favour of handing the territory to Morocco after the celebration fo the Green March, would have had also domestic political reasons, as an independent Sahara governed by the POLISARIO Front and with the support of Algeria could have been a for the breeding ground for the accentuation of the influence of the MPAIAC (*Movimiento Popular por la Autodeterminación e Independencia del Archipiélago Canario*) of Antonio Cubillo in the Canary Islands, creating in this way a new conflict within Spanish frontiers (*cfr.* DIEGO AGUIRRE, J.R., "La verdad sobre la entrega del Sahara", *Historia 16*, n° 15 (177) (1991): 21).

It is interesting to recall in this section some of the proposals of the epoch to confront the expansionist claims of Morocco, and that were forwarded by Jaime De Piniés, Spanish delegate before the UN, to his own Government. In this sense, he proposed a two-sided negotiation, with Morocco and Algeria in the following terms: 1) Giving back rocks and islets to Morocco; transfer of Melilla sovereignty in a period of twenty years, with a previous statute for the Spanish population, and the linking of the Ceuta question with the Gibraltar one, so that, until Spain regained the sovereignty over the British possession, the Ceuta sovereignty would not be negotiated. 2) Regarding Western Sahara, he proposed a negotiation with Algeria, with the aim to create an independent Sahara, by a way-leave to give Tinduf a way out to the sea, so as to avoid that Morocco could extend to a region that had never belonged to it historically, where the population were totally different to the Moroccan (DE PINIÉS, J., *(1990):* 55 et seq.).

[324] Article 35 of the Charter points in its second paragraph: "A state which is not a Member of the United Nations may bring to the attention of the Security Council or of the General Assembly any dispute to which it is a party if it accepts in advance, for the purposes of the dispute, the obligations of pacific settlement provided in the present Charter".

[325] Letter, October 18, 1975 by the representation of the Spanish Government to the Security Council (*ORSC:* S/11851).

Moroccan Government, protesting to the Security Council because of the use of the term "invasion", which Spain had given to the march, a term they considered to be "a distortion of the facts intended to distort the nature of the Moroccan claims and of the peaceful means wich morocco has always preferred to employ in order to gain recognition of its right to national unity and territorial integrity"[326]. At an emergency meeting, the Security Council approved Resolution 377 (1975)[327]. This was the first resolution of the Security Council on the Western Saharan question. It first pointed out that the Council acted within the framework established by article 34 of the United Nations Charter[328], that is to say, in conformity with Chapter VI of the Charter[329], concerning the peaceful settlement of controversies,

> "without prejudice to any measures which the General Assembly might adopt in virtue of the provisions of its Resolution 3292 (XXIX) and to the negotiations which the parties concerned and interested might undertake in accordance with Article 33 of the Charter"[330].

and

> "the Secretary General is requested to begin immediate consultations with the parties concerned and interested and to inform the Security Council as soon as possible of the results of these consultations so that the Council might adopt the appropriate measures (...)".

---

[326] Letter written to the Secretary General by the Moroccan Permanent representation before the United Nation, October 19, 1975 (*ORSC*: the Secretary General S/11852).

[327] *ORSC*: Resolution 377 (1975) of the SC, approved on October 22, 1975 unanimously.

[328] Article 34 of the Charter of United Nations states: "The Security Council may investigate any dispute, or any situation which might lead to international friction or give rise to a dispute, in order to determine whether the continuance of the dispute or situation is likely to endanger the maintenance of international peace and security".

[329] Cassese thinks that, because of the difficulties due to political interests in question, the Security Council chose, both in the Sahara and Timor conflict, the way of wisdom and moderation, decision that on the other hand has shown as very non-operative (CASSESE, A., "*Commentaire à l'article* 1.2" (1985): 51). Obviously, even respecting the opinion of the great Italian jurist, we cannot support the statement, as, more than of wisdom and moderation, we should talk of fear, ineffectiveness in front of the arrogant attitude of the regional powers of the area (Morocco and Indonesia).

[330] The reference to Article 33 of the Charter was included in the Resolution by France, firm in the defence of Moroccan approaches, to justify what later would be the Madrid Agreements.

At first sight, it is surprising that the Spanish delegation chose Article 35 of the Charter since, as Daoudi pointed out, this constitutes one of the rare occasions on which a State has based its request to present the dispute before the Security Council on this legal precept[331], which could be justified by a wide range of possibilities provided to States by this article when presenting a dispute before the Organization. Thus, in the words of Article 35 itself, Spain "may bring any dispute to the attention of the Security Council" which, as we mentioned above, stated that it was acting precisely within the framework presented in Article 34 in interpreting that the situation provoked by the *Green March* "might lead to international friction or give rise to a dispute".

A result of the consultations made by the Secretary General, in compliance with the aforementioned resolution, is his report of October 31 that same year[332], in which he explained the positions of "the parties concerned and interested ", and these are in general:

- Morocco understood that the *Green March* could not be separated from the question of the decolonization of Western Sahara, a question that it linked to its territorial integrity, and made known its disagreement with the conclusions of the advisory opinion of the ICJ as regards the non-existence of ties of territorial sovereignty of Western Sahara. Conversations had recently begun between the Governments of Morocco and Spain in order to achieve a solution "on a bilateral basis, with the participation of Mauritania".
- Mauritania's position was "basically similar to that of Morocco";
- Algeria "categorically rejected the position adopted by Morocco and Mauritania that Western Sahara belonged to them due to historical ties", and insisted on the need for the Western Saharan people to freely express their decision through a referendum, which should be organized by the UN.
- Spain, which had maintained direct contacts with the Moroccan and Mauritanian Governments, did not commit itself to finding a negotiated solution that would entail bilateral or trilateral agreements. Spain wanted "to reach an agreement which might be acceptable to all the parties in the region". In order to achieve this aim Spain was "ready to co-operate fully with the United Nations which could be called upon to play an appropriate role that might include temporary administration of the Territory by the

---

[331] DAOUDI, R., "*Commentaire à l'article* 35", in *La Charte des Nations Unies*, (Dir. COT, J-P. et PELLET, A.), Ed. Economica / Bruylant, Paris / Bruxelles (1985): 593.
[332] *ORSC: S/11863*, October 31, 1975.

United Nations until such time as the wishes of the population could be ascertained. Various aspects of such an approach were discusse.

In his report, the Secretary General reaches the conclusion that all parties "would be prepared to recognize the United Nations as a fundamental component in the search for an acceptable solution ".

Based on these opinions of the States, the Secretary General drafted what would be called the "Waldheim Plan", whose main aspects were the following: the withdrawal of Spain from the territory; the establishment of a provisional international administration in the territory; and, finally, a consultation of the population which would be carried out within an approximate period of six months. This solution would allow the UN to take over the supervision of an authentic self-determination process, however, as the facts unfortunately corroborated a short time afterwards, the optimism of the Secretary General was unjustified mainly because of the intransigent position of Morocco, which had abandoned the, until then accepted idea, of self-determination, arguing that the events had acted to overtake this approach.

On the day following the publication of this report, Morocco refused to detain the *Green March*, convened for November 4, and Spain again requested an emergency meeting of the Security Council so that it would consider "the appropriate measures, in accordance with the Charter, in order to make the Government of Morocco desist from the announced march"[333]. At this meeting, the Security Council[334] adopted Resolution 379 (1975), which did not mention the *Green March*[335], but basically repeated the requests that were already included in its Resolution 377 (1975). It urges "all the parties concerned and interested to avoid any unilateral or other action which might further escalate the tension in the area", and again requested the Secretary

---

[333] *ORSC:* S/11864.

[334] On this occasion, as occurred in the Security Council that treated the matter, in compliance with what established article 31 of the Charter of the UN and to article 37 of the Security Council Resolution, the Moroccan and Spanish delegations took part with no vote in the debates (Mauritania was member of the Security Council).

[335] The absence of express references in the text to the direct cause of the tense situation in the Western Sahara in those moments -the Green March- was the reason of criticism in the debates after Resolution 379 (1975) by two members of the Council, justifying their vote in favour of the approval of the mentioned due to the need to reach consensus in such a serious matter. So, the Costa Rica delegation pointed that mentioning as clearly as possible the true cause of the problem should not be disregarded, that was nothing else but "the march of 350,000 persons would be undertaken for the purpose of taking over the Territory of Western Sahara (*ORSC:* S/PV.1852, par. 35), being identical the approaches defended by the Swedish representation (*ibid.*, par. 93.)

CHAPTER V

General to continue and intensify the consultations with the parties and to inform the Council so that it could act in consequence[336].

A procedural ploy[337] prevented the delegations from intervening before the approval of the Resolution 379 (1975) meaning that the text does not particularly differ from that of Resolution 377 (1975). Although Spain stated that, in the event that Morocco did not detain the march, it was prepared to use armed force to repel it, the frontier of Western Sahara was "violated by large contingents of Moroccan nationals, including elements of the armed forces and official authorities"[338], without the threat made by the Spanish Government being carried out.

In the course of the 1853rd session, in which Resolution 380 (1975)[339] was approved, several delegations openly pointed out the real importance of the *Green March*. The Swedish delegation asked the Moroccan delegation in the following terms, "Is this a symbolic march?" In the event that it is, "Will there not be a quasi-occupation of the territory of Western Sahara?". Finally, "once the claim has been made through the march, will those participating return to Moroccan territory?". The Moroccan representatives avoided this question, and restricted themselves to pointing out that the march "is not of an aggressive nature", meaning that "a relaxed atmosphere" would prevail in the territory. Despite the lack of interest of the Moroccan response, the question of the Swedish delegation (and another in similar terms made by Tanzania) made it possible to debate the true reasons for the deterioration of the situation in the region, whose turning point was the bluntly stated declaration of the Algerian representative that "regardless of the name given to this initiative (a symbolic march, a pilgrimage or an invasion), the problem is the crossing of a frontier and the invasion of a territory". As the Spanish representatives stated that "a frontier had been violated", the President of the Security Council asked the Moroccan representative "if he considered that it was normal" that the Security Council, "as an organ with the principal responsibility for maintaining international peace and security, could sanction the violating of a frontier", and

---

[336] Resolution 379 (1975) of the Security Council, approved el 2 de November unanimously. The same date, the then Prince of Spain, Juan Carlos, acting Chief of the State since October 30, 1975, stated in El Aaiún that Spain would fulfil its commitments and protect the legitimate rights of the Saharan civil population (*cfr.* DIEGO AGUIRRE, J. R., "La verdad sobre la entrega del Sahara" (1991): 25; also, HODGES, T., *Historical Dictionary of Western Sahara* (1982): 194).

[337] ORSC: S/PV.1852, par. 8 (session 1852 of Security Council, November 2, 1975).

[338] ORSC: S/11867.

[339] Differing to what happened in the approval of Resolution 379 (1975), the different delegations intervened before the voting of Resolution 380 (1975) took place.

Morocco replied that it was not possible to speak of a violation of frontiers "when the movement takes place in the interior of the same territory".

As a previous step to the approval of Resolution 380 (1975), at the same session, the Security Council approved that its President forward a letter to the Moroccan Government expressly requesting it "to put an end forthwith to the declared march into Western Sahara"[340]. This letter obtained a reply from Morocco with the declaration that it was a march of a "peaceful character". The Security Council then approved by consensus Resolution 380 (1975)[341], in which for the first time and very bluntly it "noted with regret" and "deplored" the carrying out of the *Green March*[342] and urged Morocco "to withdraw immediately" all of the participants in the march from Western Sahara, and also asked all of those parties concerned and interested to cooperate with the Secretary General in compliance with the mandate entrusted to him by the Security Council, reproducing the paragraph which had already appeared in Resolution 377 (1975), in the sense that this would all be done,

> "without prejudice to any action which the General Assembly might take under the terms of its Resolution 3292 (XXIX) of 13 December 1974 or any negotiations which the parties concerned and interested might undertake under Article 33 of the Charter of the United Nations".

Although there is no doubt that the pronouncement of the Security Council concerning the march was forceful, the content of this resolution was harshly criticized by Spain as it understood that, although the march was deplored, a fundamental element had been ignored; "the unlawful act that has been commited, namely the violation of a frontier and the trespass against the territorial integrity of the Sahara"[343].

---

[340] *ORSC*: S/11868.

[341] *ORSC*: Resolution 380 (1975) of the Security Council, approved November 6, 1975, unanimously.

[342] What Morocco called *Green March* was later renamed by the POLISARIO Front as "Black March", because of the disastrous consequences for the Saharan (*cfr.* CESSOU, S., PRAZ, H., "Sahara occidental: l'interminable conflit", *Jeune Afrique Economique*, n° 206, 6 noviembre (1995): 106. As asserted by Balta, the parallel march of the Western Sahara population in their escape towards Tinduf suffered attacks by Moroccan aviation, not only with traditional armaments but also with napalm (*cfr.* BALTA, P., *Le Gran Maghreb, des indépendances à l'an 2000*, Ed. La Découverte, Paris, 1990).

[343] The Spanish delegation deplored not having been able to speak before the Council before the approval of the resolution. The same complaint was forwarded by the Algerian delegate (*ORGA*: S/PV.1854).

Chapter V

This was the last resolution that the Security Council adopted concerning Western Sahara until thirteen years later when, through Resolution 621 (1988), the question of the referendum was again taken up. Regrettably, this was another demonstration of the double standards by which the Security Council measures the conflicts submitted to it, depending on the position of its permanent members. We must vindicate the need, pointed out by Cassese, that the affirmation that the use of force in order to prevent the exercise of the right to self-determination constitutes an international crime must be accompanied by "collective counter-measures against those States which flagrantly and systematically breach the right to self-determination", which, in the case of Western Sahara, obviously did not occur[344].

Subsequently, the second report presented by the Secretary General to the Security Council in compliance with Resolution 379 (1975)[345] would finally confirm the termination of the *Green March* as a consequence of the decision of Hassan II that those participating volunteers "return to their departure points", together with the commencement of negotiations in Madrid between Morocco, Mauritania and Spain[346].

---

[344] CASSESE, A., "Le Droit international et la question de l'assistance aux mouvements de libération nationale", *R.B.D.I.*, vol. XIX, 2 (1986): 326.

[345] *ORSC*: S/11876, November 12, 1975. Regarding reports presented by the Secretary General to the Security Council in compliance with the mentioned resolutions, the second (S/11874, November 8, 1975), presented in compliance with paragraph 2 of Resolution 379 (1975) two days after the approval of Resolution 380 (1975), did not bring any novelty as to the question exposed in the first (S/11863). The report pointed out the confronted positions of Morocco and Mauritania, in favour of a tripartite negotiation that would include Spain, and of the Algerian and Spanish position -always taking into account the official position of the Ministry for Foreign Affairs-, in favour of a possible withdrawal of Spain from the territory, that would be administered temporarily by the United Nations. The Secretary General also underlined in this report the increasing tension in the area due to the Green March, pointing out that if the situation continued to worsen, "the chances for a satisfactory sttlement would be increasingly jeopardized".

[346] In a letter of November 8, 1975 the Minister of Presidency, Antonio Carro, asked the end of the Green March to the Alawite Monarch assuring, in the name of my Government, that Spain would restart immediately tripartite negotiations (Spain-Morocco-Mauritania) for the definitive resolution of the Sahara problem. From this letter it is clear the surrender of Spain before the Green March; such is the case, that Carro himself asked Hassan II earnestly that all publicity of this letter should be consulted and negotiated .The text of the letter was published by Carro himself in April, 1976 (*cfr.* CARRO MARTÍNEZ, A. (1976): 28).

1.2. The legal classification of the Green March

A) *Resolution 3314 (XXIX) of the General Assembly*

Despite the fact that there is no doubt that the *Green March* was a violation of the frontiers of a Non-Self-Governing Territory, that fact, that it was carried out by "unarmed civilians", raises a question as to its possible classification as aggression, considering the meaning of aggression contained in Resolution 3314 (XXIX) of the General Assembly (*"Definition of aggression"*). The repeated reference in the text of this Resolution to the armed nature of aggression (Articles 1, 2 and 3[347]) seems to exclude the unprecedented idea of "peaceful aggression"[348] from this concept. The references to the armed nature of aggression seem to imply that "only the most serious form of coercion is covered by the definition"[349]. Despite the doubts concerning the peculiar form in which it was convened and organized, more similar perhaps to the call made by Ayatollah Khomeini to the Iranian people to take the US Embassy in Tehran[350] the fact that the Moroccan civilians had substantial military cover and infrastructure and the fact that its ultimate consequence and first objective was to prevent the exercise of the right to self-determination of the people of Western Sahara[351], the *Green March* cannot be considered a case of aggression in the strict sense. A broad interpretation of Resolution 3314 (XXIX) of the General Assembly could lead to including those actions which, like the Green

---

[347] Article 1 of Resolution 3314 (XXIX) of GA, approved December 14, 1974, describes aggression as "Aggression is the use of armed force by a State against the sovereignty, territorial integrity or political independence of another State, or in any other manner inconsistent with the Charter of the United Nations, as set out in this Definition". Article 2 starts pointing out that "The First use of armed force by a State in contravention of the Charter (...), and Article 3 continues in the same sense, considering as aggression "any of the following acts (a) The invasion or attack by the armed forces of a State of the territory of another State, or any military occupation, however temporary, resulting from such invasion or attack, or any annexation by the use of force of the territory of another State or part of it".
[348] FRANCK, T., M. (1976): 714.
[349] BYMAN, A., "The march on the Spanish Sahara: A test of International Law", *Denver Journal of International Law and Policy*, 6 (1976): 107.
[350] *United States Diplomatic and Consular Staff in Tehran (United States of America v. Iran)*, *Judgement, I.C.J. Reports 1980*, pages 28-31.
[351] Article 7 of the Resolution states that "Nothing in this Definition, and in particular article 3, could in any way prejudice the right to self-determination, freedom and independence, as derived from the Charter, of peoples the right of these peoples to struggle to that end and to seek and receive support, in accordance with the principles of the Charter and in conformity with the above-mentioned Declaration".

March, under an "unarmed disguise"[352] coerce and obtain exactly the same results as would armed force among the actions which must be considered as aggression. However, neither the literal meaning nor its case law interpretation makes it possible to consider this differently today.

Although there are many authors who have said that the use of the term "armed" constitutes an indicator of the level of aggression rather than an explicit requirement[353], meaning that the *Green March* could be included among the cases of aggression, the extremely imprecise nature of some of the main aspects of Resolution 3314 (XXIX) should be borne in mind, which means that, from the legal point of view, this affirmation is at least rather daring. As pointed out by Márquez, the concept of what must be understood by "armed aggression" is extremely difficult to specify as, although the classification of different types of force by its gravity as made by the aforementioned Resolution and by the International Court of Justice in the *Case of military and paramilitary activities in and against Nicaragua* (Nicaragua v. USA)[354] is characterised by its flexibility, "at the same time, adhering to a difference of degree carries certain indeterminacy". In her efforts to achieve specification, this author stresses that the ICJ equates the most serious violation of the prohibition with armed aggression, but it does not specify the "minor uses of force"[355], which gives the Security Council certain leeway when interpreting an action like that of the *Green March*, especially if one takes into account the fact that this is effectively unprecedented in modern history. In fact, "the definition of aggression does not deprive the Security Council of the freedom to appreciate the core of a particular situation"[356]. Furthermore, as stated in Article 4 of Resolution 3314 (XXIX), "the acts enumerated above are not exhaustive", meaning therefore that the Security Council "may determine that other acts constitute aggression under the provisions of the Charter". However, it is true that up to now the Council has not done so, because when

---

[352] Likewise, *cfr.* BYMAN, A. (1976): 121 et seq. In words of Permanent People's Court, the March was " a supposedly peaceful operation" (*Avis sur la Sahara Occidental*, par. 8, in JOUVE, E. (1983): p. 44).

[353] BYMAN, A. (1976): 108.

[354] Regarding the armed groups that intervened in Nicaragua, the International Court of Justice stated that "The Court does not believe that the concept of 'armed attack' includes assistance to rebels in the form of the provision of weapons or logistical or other support " (*Military and Paramilitary Activities in and against Nicaragua (Nicaragua v. United States of America). Merits, Judgement.I.C.J. Reports 1986*, p. 93, par. 195), statement that seems reasonable to apply in the present case.

[355] MÁRQUEZ CARRASCO, M.C., *Problemas actuales sobre la prohibición del recurso a la fuerza en Derecho Internacional*, Tecnos, Madrid (1998): 264.

[356] *Ibid.,* p. 120.

classifying the actions carried out by States it has suffered from a substantial lack of coherence in the texts of its resolutions on too many occasions. This was opportunely highlighted by Virally, who pointed out with good judgment that "the term aggression has been avoided, even on occasions when it seemed to impose itself, in favour of expressions with no legal implications (...)"[357].

Despite these considerations, as pointed out by González Vega, it is clear that Morocco intended to avoid the action being considered a violation of the prohibition of the use of force to resolve a controversy of a territorial nature[358] which, as can be verified in the following section, although was not achieved, did give rise to the reasonable doubt that the action be classified as "aggression". It is clear that, as Western Sahara was a territory under Spanish administration at the time of the invasion and consequently there was no Western Saharan army able to address the "peaceful invasion", the "unarmed" nature of the march is upheld due to the lack of resistance by the Spanish army, meaning that this would suffice for the occupation of the territory, as did occur. In our opinion, this circumstance was definitive as regards excluding Moroccan action from the cases of aggression. However, Morocco's violation of the use of force in international relations is beyond doubt.

B) Article 2 of the Charter of the United Nations

The *Green March* entailed a violation by Morocco of the content of several paragraphs of Article 2 of the Charter. It violates what is set out on paragraph 2 of this precept as the execution in good faith of the obligations assumed in the terms of the Charter prohibited the Government of Morocco from occupying the territory "after the International Court of Justice had rejected any direct territorial pretensions" of this State[359], especially when this was at the request of this State when it applied to the ICJ for a advisory opinion whose consequence was a stoppage of the decolonization process of the territory.

The violation of Article 2.2 of the Charter is even more evident when Morocco occupied the territory that Mauritania would abandon after the signing of the peace agreements with the POLISARIO Front. In this regard, it should be pointed out that Morocco had expressly given up any claim to the part of the territory which "would be adjudicated" to Mauritania, as the legal

---

[357] VIRALLY, M., "*Commentaire à l'article 2.4*", in *La Charte des Nations Unies*, (Dir. COT, J-P. et PELLET, A.), Ed. Economica / Bruylant, Paris / Bruxelles (1985): 119.
[358] GONZÁLEZ VEGA, J.A., *Conflictos territoriales y uso de la fuerza (un estudio de la práctica internacional a la luz del conflicto Irán-Irak)*, ed. Beramar, Madrid (1994): 239.
[359] *Avis sur la Sahara Occidental*, par. 46 (in JOUVE, E. (1983): 64 and 69).

ties previous to the colonisation of this part of the territory did not exist[360]. Therefore, the occupation by Morocco of the part of the territory abandoned by Mauritania is especially serious, and very clearly shows the violation of Article 2.2 of the Charter by this State. In addition, the surprising reference to a theoretical *"derecho de retracto"* (right of first refusal) for Morocco as regards this part of the territory, defended by the Moroccan monarchy, merits no commentary at all[361].

Morocco also violated paragraphs 3 and 4 of Article 2 of the Charter, instead of resorting to peaceful means and respecting the resolutions of the Security Council, it violently occupied a territory in process of decolonization and had turned to the use of force, clearly incompatible with the objectives of the United Nations. If the violation of the content of 4 is obvious as Morocco made recourse to the use of force to occupy the territory, the violation of the content of paragraph 3 is even clearer since, as pointed out by Charpentier, the materialization of the obligation of the States to resolve their differences by peaceful means in paragraph 3 is no more than a "logical corollary" of the prohibition to use force, established in paragraph 4; the obligation established by article 2.3 is one of conduct, while the obligation regulated by 2.4 imposes a result. By carrying out the *Green March*, Morocco violated the content of both paragraphs since, as regards both, "the States must abstain (...) not only from having recourse to force but from aggravating the situation"[362], circumstances that are sadly present in this case.

Moreover, the argument put forward by Morocco in the sense that it was not an international conflict but an internal one, as the territory in dispute was

---

[360] The Court state that "When Morocco refers to Cabo Blanco and Villa Cisneros in stating arguments of a general character, it is not intending thereby to maintain that its sovereignty extended over those regions at the time of the Spanish colonization; for at the period under consideration those regions were an integral part of the Mauritanian entity, to which the Islamic Republic of Mauritania is the sole successor" (*Western Sahara, Advisory Opinion, I.C.J. Reports* 1975, p. 66, par. 155).

[361] Indeed, the Alawite Monarch himself asserted this right of "first refusal" (*"droit de préemption"*). The occupation by Morocco of the territory abandoned by Mauritania after the Peace Treaty signing has been described by Del Pino as an exercise of a supposed right of repurchase, that, obviously, lacks of all sense according to International law (DEL PINO, D., "España y el Sahara", *Leviatán. Revista de hechos e ideas,* 1985, num. 21, p. 52). About this matter, *cfr.* BERRAMDANE, A., *Le Sahara Occidental: enjeu maghrèbin,* Paris (1987): 75 et seq. As states Abellán Honrubia, the notion itself of right of repurchase, related to the Madrid Agreements, would imply that the mentioned would have constituted a "sale" (*cfr. Avis sur le Sahara Occidental,* par. 48 in JOUVE, E. (1983): 65.

[362] CHARPENTIER, J., *"Commentaire à l'article* 2.3" (1985): 104 and 106. In the same sense, *cfr.* VIRALLY, M., *"Commentaire à l'article 2.4", ibid.,* p. 114.

part of its territorial integrity, lacks consistency since, as UN practice clearly shows, dealing with a Non-Self-Governing Territory means that the international nature of the conflict is indisputable. Thus, the allusion in this conflict to paragraph 7 of Article 2, by virtue of which we are confronted with a case that is "essentially within the internal jurisdiction of a State", has no basis in contemporary International law in force.

2. The Madrid Agreements

2.1. *The content of the Agreements*

On November 19, 1975 the Secretary General submitted his third report to the Security Council on the question of Western Sahara[363], where it reported the finalisation of the negotiations between Spain, Morocco and Mauritania, which resulted in the "Declaration of Principles of Madrid", on November 14, 1975[364]. On that same day, the Spanish Ministry of Information and Tourism revealed the conclusion of the agreements with a short "joint communiqué"[365], containing an affirmation, whose importance must be stressed, which intends to justify the Spanish Government for having signed these agreements, as it points out that these "are the fruit of the recommendations of the Security Council" and that they are concluded with "respect to the principles of the United Nations Charter". This communication did not contain the text of the agreements, which would not become public until four days later when the Spanish representation in the United Nations rewarded it to the Secretary General[366].

The Declaration of Principles has the following six sections:

1) Spain decides to terminate its presence in Western Sahara, "terminating the responsibilities and powers wich it possesses over that territory as the administrating Power";

---

[363] ORSC: S/11880, November 19, 1975, Third report presented by the Secretary General to the Security Council in compliance with Resolution 379 (1975).

[364] The Secretary General refers to the Declaration in terms of *"Comunicado Conjunto" (joint communiqué), y "Declaración de Principios (Declaration of Principles)"*.

[365] The opinion of the always surprising Cola Alberich, was that "the only feasible solution to the passivity and inhibition shown by the United Nations". *Cfr.* COLA ALBERICH, J. (1977): 49.

[366] ORSC: S/11880, Annexes I y II, November 18, 1975. Even the members of the Parliament did not know the text of the Declaration when, on November 18, 1975, the Commission in charge of informing about the Draft of Law started to give pertinent explanations... four days after the signing of the agreements. *Cfr.* VILLAR, F. (1982): 352.

2) Spain undertakes "to institute a temporary administration in the territory, in which Morocco and Mauritania will participate, in collaboration with the Yemáa", and will transmit these responsibilities and powers to this Administration. Consequently, "it is accordingly agreed that two Deputy Governors nominated by Morocco and Mauritania shall be appointed to assist the Governor- General of the Territory in the performance of his functions". The termination of the Spanish presence in the Territory was fixed as February 28, 1976.
3) The three states undertook to respect the opinion of the Western Saharan population, which will be "expressed through the Yemáa";
4) The signatory States also undertake to inform the Secretary General of the content of the document, "as a result of the negotiations entered into in accordance with Article 33 of the Charter of the United Nations".
5) The three States repeated that the conclusion of the agreement was reached "in the highest spirit of understanding and brotherhood, with due respect for the principles of the Charte of the United Nations Charter, and as the best possible contribution to the maintenance of international peace and security".
6) Finally, the date of the entry into force of this agreement was set for the same day on which the Law on the Decolonisation of the Sahara would be published in the *Boletín Oficial del Estado* (*Official State Gazette*), "authorizing the Spanish Government to assume the commitments conditionally set forth in this instrument".

Moreover, as a "compensation" for the handover of the territory by Spain, besides recovering its part of the amount invested in the phosphate mines of Bu Craa, and obtaining 35% from the subsequent operation of the deposits by the Moroccan Government[367], Morocco renounced the claim on the other African territories administered by Spain (Ceuta, Melilla, etc.) until the time that Spain might recover Gibraltar[368], which surprisingly linked the resolution

---

[367] Regarding this question, *cfr*. HODGES, T. (1983): 224; NAYLOR, P.C., "Spain and France and the Decolonization of Western Sahara: Parity and Paradox, 1975-87", *Africa Today*, n° 34, Third Quarter (1987): 7-8.

[368] *Cfr*. OLIVER LOPEZ-GUARCH, P (1988): 160. In the same sense, HARRELL-BOND, B., "The struggle for the Western Sahara: Prelude" (part I), "Contemporary politics" (parte II), "The Sahrawi people" (part III), *American Universities Field Staff* (1981): 5; MERCER, J., "The Sahrawis of Western Sahara", *Minority Rights Group*, Report n° 40, London Fevruary (1979): 10. This last author asserts also that among the agreements that never saw the light was the possibility that Spain establishes future military bases in Western Sahara. On the other hand, Morocco had already asked the Special Committee of 24 (January 27, 1975) to include Ceuta, Melilla, Alhucemas Rock, Velez Rock and the Chafarinas Islands in the list of Non-Self-Governing Territories, petition that was not attended (*ORGA*: A/AC.109/475).

of both questions, which had been unconnected at international level until then. However, the real value of the "compensation" is very doubtful. The 35% participation reserved for the INI in the capital of FOSBUCRAA, S. A. resulted in Spain participating in the losses of the company to this extent after operations were stopped due to the war, while the fishing agreement was never ratified by Morocco. In addition, it seems very improbable that an agreement will be reached on Ceuta and Melilla. At least, there is no record of any documents that might justify such an agreement.

The Madrid agreement was radically opposed by a single "concerned or interested" party, the Government of Algeria, which pointed out the following in a document sent to the Secretary General[369]:

1) Spain, as the aadministering Power of the territory, "must give an account of its responsibilities before the United Nations", thus, it cannot transfer its administrative responsibilities over the territory other than to the people of this territory, or, in any other case, to the United Nations;
2) As the Declaration of Principles stated that the agreement was reached within the framework of what was established by Article 33 of the Charter, "the negotiations should have involved 'the parties to the controversy'; that is to say, at least, Spain, the Western Saharan people and the United Nations", although considering that Resolutions 377 (1975), 379 (1975) and 380 (1975) always refer to the parties "concerned and interested", the opinion of Algeria should also have been taken into account[370].
3) Consequently, the "Declaration of Principles" of Madrid is "null and void".

2.2. *The debate before the Fourth Commission*

After the signing of the Madrid Agreements, the annual debate of the Fourth Commission began, during which hard, intense verbal confrontations took place between the delegations[371].

- The Spanish delegate stated that, since the Security Council had been incapable of stopping and acting against the *Green March*, Spain "had had no alternative" than to negotiate, in spite of which it continued to consider

---

[369] *ORGA*: A/AC.109/475, Annex IV.
[370] *ORSC*: S/11880, Annex IV, section I, par. 1. Also A/10373.
[371] For a detailed analysis of debates and different interventions, among which the first intervention of the POLISARIO Front before this Commission (Amin Bachir), *cfr.* VILLAR, F. (1982): 355-363. Official documents of the Fourth Commission of the GA can also be consulted (*ORGA*: A/C.4/SR.2168, 2170, 2171, 2173, 2174, 2175, 2176, 2177, 2178, 2181, 2182).

Chapter V

the resolutions of the General Assembly on decolonization applicable[372]. Furthermore, it quoted declarations made by the Spanish Minister of the Presidency, Antonio Carro, before the Spanish Parliament, to the effect that "the negotiating efforts were subject to the distension of the situation, but these did not compromise the destiny of the territory in any way"[373]. In addition, he stated that, as regards the provisional administration set up in the territory depending on the agreements in force, the legal status of the territory continued to be that of a Non-Self-Governing Territory and Spain continued to be responsible for it during this period[374].

- Morocco made an interpretation adapted to its wishes, but far from reality, arguing that it had worked in accordance with the wishes of the Security Council since the Council had not condemned the *Green March*, but obliged Morocco to recognize the peaceful nature of the march, and had recommended that Morocco negotiate "in order to find a definitive solution to the problem of the decolonization of the Sahara".
- Mauritania shared the Moroccan approach, and like Morocco it stressed the necessary complementary nature of the principles of self-determination of peoples and the territorial integrity of States. Moreover, it expressly denied the applicability of the *uti possidetis iuris* principle, or the intangibility of frontiers established the colonial era, to the Saharan case based on an argument, which was as strange as it was incomprehensible, that this is a principle applicable to the frontiers between States which have already achieved independence, therefore, not applicable to the "reconstruction" of frontiers before independence is achieved. As is evident, the *uti possidetis iuris* principle is fully applicable to Western Sahara as the limits of its frontiers were clearly defined as a consequence of the Franco-Spanish agreements referred to in Chapter II, a question we consider not necessary to return to[375].
- As regards Algeria it stressed the same aspects as those insisted on by its representative before the Security Council and it again highlighted that the negotiations referred to in the resolutions of the General Assembly should include both the "parties concerned" and "the interested parties" and that Algeria, in the latter position had not participated in the negotiations.

---

[372] *ORGA*: A/C.4/SR.2170.
[373] *ORGA*: A/C.4/SR.2171.
[374] *ORGA*: A/C.4/SR.2177.
[375] The POLISARIO Front would have opted for that denomination (Popular Front for the Liberation of Saguia el-Hamra and Río Oro), even if artificial, with the double aim to delimit precisely the frontiers of the struggle and to underline the necessary applicability of the *uti possidetis iuris* principle (MISKÉ, A.B. (1978): 15).

Moreover, it drew attention to the fact that the purpose of the negotiations was not to resolve the problem of decolonization, but the problem arising from the *Green March*.

- Finally, it should be stressed that representatives of Western Saharan political movements intervened in these debates, in their capacity as petitioners. Thus, the representatives of the PUNS and the President of the *Yemáa* declared in defence of the validity of the Agreements while the POLISARIO Front announced its intention to carry out an armed struggle for the independence of the territory[376].

After the presentations, an intense debate was carried out in the Fourth Commission, in the course of which an immense majority of States stated that they were against the Madrid Agreements, and stressed that the principle of territorial integrity was applicable in this case given the numerous resolutions of the General Assembly and the opinion of the ICJ, which never placed the classification of Western Sahara as a Non-Self-Governing Territory in doubt.

2.3 The Madrid Agreements and the General Assembly

On December 10, 1975, the General Assembly approved resolutions 3458 A (XXX) and 3458 B (XXX) that, although they contained components that are clearly contradictory with each other, coincided in pointing out the right of the Western Saharan people to self-determination[377]. The military interventions

---

[376] ORGA: A/C.4/SR.2170, 2173 and 2178.

[377] Resolutions 3458 A (XXX) and 3458 B (XXX) of the GA, approved on December 10, 1975. The first was approved by 43 votes in favour, none against and 41 abstentions. The second was approved by 56 votes in favour, 42 votes against and 34 abstentions. It is not a coincidence the attitude shown in this resolution by States like Indonesia, Argentina, Guatemala or Somalia about the Sahara matter, voting together with Morocco and Mauritania.

In the case of Indonesia it seems unnecessary to explain the reason of their attitude in the Saharan conflict: the same month of the same year, when Spain was preparing the referendum in Western Sahara, Portugal did the same in the territory of East Timor. Also in approximate dates, as Morocco seized Western Sahara with the Green March el Sahara Occidental, Indonesia occupied East Timor.

In the other cases it is also easy to guess the reasons that took the Governments of these States to pronounce themselves close to Morocco in the ballot: Argentina defended its territorial integrity in the Islas Malvinas (Falkland Islands), Guatemala in Belize, and Somalia regarding Djibouti. As to Argentina, the United Nation resolutions have always referred to the territorial integrity principle, not mentioning the self-determining right of the "peoples" of the Islas Malvinas (Falkland Islands). The attitude of Guatemala has a similar explanation, collected also in the Guatemalan Constitution (article 14 of Guatemala Constitution, text in PEASLEE, I., *Constitutions of Nations* (1970): 564-623) though in this case, resolutions of the

of Morocco in Western Sahara and of Indonesia in East Timor broke the decolonizing policy which the United Nations had been recommending and applying since the end of the nineteen sixties. As a consequence of these interventions, from this time, the United Nations was involved in a double-sided policy, which was intended to keep those who supported both absolutely irreconcilable and antagonistic positions content[378].

Resolution 3458 A (XXX) incorporated the Algerian approach to the letter, which is the approach the General Assembly itself had been defending since it took charge of the conflict. Thus, after again reaffirming "the inalienable right of the people of Spanish Sahara to self-determination", it requests the Government of Spain "as the administering Power, in accordance with the observations and conclusions of the Visiting Mission and *in accordance with the advisory opinion of the International Court of Justice* to immediately take all necessary measures, in consultation with all the parties concerned and interested, so that all Saharans originating in the territory may exercise fully and freely, under United Nations supervision, their inalienable right to self-determination". In short, the ultimate objective of this resolution consists in inviting Spain to postpone the referendum until the General Assembly pronounces on the decolonization policy to be followed.

However, Resolution 3458 B (XXX) carried out a Copernican transformation of these approaches, and surprisingly came close to the approaches that inspired the Madrid Agreements. In this regard, as pointed out

---

United Nations recognized specifically the self-determination right of the population of Belize (*ORGA*: Resolution 3432 (XXX) GA of United Nations) that, on the other hand, is full member of the United Nations since September 25, 1981. Finally, as to Somalia, the resolutions of the GA had recognized in various occasions the self-determination right of the population of Djibouti, so it may be justified for the same reasons. Somalia defends in this case "its" territorial integrity (article 6.4 of the Somalian Constitution reinforces the Somalian territorial unity, including the territory that was colonized by France -text in PEASLEE, I., *op. cit.*, pages 776-778-) against the results of two referendums organized in the territory by the former colonial power, France, from which the until then "French Somalia" was now Djibouti, full member of the United Nation since September 20, 1977. Somalia manteined that the territory of the former French colony had always been a part of its territorial integrity, and only accepted the self-determination right in order to keep controlled this territory. As we can see, these approaches correspond closely to Moroccan and former Mauritanian claims, also about the ties that could have existed between the population of these States and the territory object of dispute.

[378] AMANKWAH, H.A. "Self-determination in the Spanish Sahara: a credibility gap in the UN practice and procedure in the decolonisation process", *The Comparative and International Law Journal of Southern Africa*, 14 (1981): 52. For this reason, from then onward, it will be relatively normal to find among the GA resolutions with the same number but with a different letter, A or B, where contradictions of the Organization are clear in this matter.

by some authors[379], this resolution would somehow legitimate these agreements to a certain extent, when it asked *the interim administration,* created by the same, "to take all necessary steps to ensure that all the Saharan populations originating in the territory will be able to exercise their inalienable right to self-determination through free consultations organized with the assistance of a representative of the United Nations appointed by the Secretary General", and would also legitimate the occupation of the territory, which is not done at all in Resolution 3458 A (XXX).

The contradiction in several aspects of these two resolutions of the General Assembly is evident, and it is very significant that, while Resolution 3458 A (XXX) had a broad consensus when it was approved, Resolution 3458 B (XXX) was approved with a narrow margin of votes[380]. The approval of the latter Resolution entailed a worrying change of position in the attitude of the General Assembly which ceded to the Moroccan pretensions and abandoned the firmness with which until then it had defended the rights of the Saharan population to self-determination to take a dangerous new turn in the dispute, full of ambiguities, which would mark the future of the process from that time on. Both resolutions show the dual policy carried out by the Spanish Ministry of the Presidency and the Foreign Ministry, which we referred to above, and they confirm the limitations of the Secretary General, Kurt Waldheim, when imposing his criteria concerning the question[381].

Both resolutions were clearly contradictory as, if the first one maintained the approaches of the General Assembly, the second made it practically impossible to put these into practice. As Franck graphically pointed out, to affirm the right of the Saharans to self-determination on the one hand, and, on the other, place the materialization of this right of the population in the hands of the States that have shared out the territory is "like inviting the cat to consult the canaries"[382].

On February 26, 1976 the Spanish Government contacted the Secretary General in order to communicate that "the persistence of circumstances

---

[379] In the same sense, Franck points out that this resolution "recognized the *fait accompli* of the agreement" (FRANCK, T.M. (1976): 717). In the same sense, *cfr.* BARBIER, M. (1976): 103.

[380] Resolution 3458 A (XXX) was approved by 44 votes in favour, 41 abstentions and no votes against, but Resolution 3458 B (XXX), was approved by 56 votes in favour, 34 abstentions and 42 against.

[381] After the approval of these resolutions, the Secretary General, Kurt Waldheim, declared the following: "I regret its approval; (...) it is something negative. No clearer answer can I give". About the *"Waldheim Plan", cfr.* HODGES, T., *Historical Dictionary of Western Sahara* (1982): 356.

[382] FRANCK, T.M. (1976): 717.

beyond its control" had prevented, until then, the organization of the consultation of the population stipulated in the Madrid Agreements and in accordance with paragraph 2 of these agreements "it definitively terminates its presence in the territory of the Sahara", considering itself "henceforth exempt from any responsibility of an international nature in connection with the administration of the said Territory, in view of the cessation of its participation in the temporary administration established for the Territory"[383].

In its last paragraph, the document posed a question of the maximum importance, when the Spanish Government considered that, "the decolonization of the Western Sahara will be reached when the opinion of the Saharawi population was validly expressed"[384]. However, the drafting of this paragraph did not clarify what this "valid expression of the opinion of the Saharan people" meant for the Spanish government at the time; that is to say, if it referred to the referendum to be organized under the auspices of the United Nations or the decision of the "Saharan General Assembly", the *Yemáa* which had "unanimously approved the reincorporation of the Saharan territory to Morocco and Mauritania" on February 26.

The representative nature of the *Yemáa* had been questioned both by Algeria and by the document known as the "The Historic Document of El Guelta (Western Sahara)"[385], signed by 67 members of the Saharan General Assembly, three Saharan Members of the Cortes (Spanish Parliament), the representatives of the other members of the *Yemáa* and more than 60 Sheikhs and notables of the Saharan tribes. This document denounced the inoperability of the *Yemáa*, which it considered to have been a "puppet institution" from the time of its constitution, and a "colonialist institution (...) which has no real authority and no attributes other than its name of *Assembly*", adding that it was devoid of all representative nature since it was not "democratically elected by the Saharan people", which means that it "cannot decide upon the self-determination of the Saharan people". The document ended by stating that "the General Assembly decides, by unanimous vote its definitive dissolution by the unanimous vote of its members present", attributing "the sole and legitimate representative of the Saharan people" to the POLISARIO Front and requesting that a Saharan Provisional National Council be constituted.

In these circumstances, the UN decided to transfer the dossier on Western Sahara to the OAU, where an analysis of the conflict from a new perspective

---

[383] ORSC: S/11997.
[384] ORGA: A/31/56, S/11997, p. 2 et seq.
[385] ORGA: A/10481, S/11902.

offered by the *Green March* was begun. Thus, in 1976 and in 1977 the action of the General Assembly was limited "to taking note" of the decision of the OAU to organise an extraordinary summit meeting on the issue, and refrained from occupying itself with the problem until the results of the summit meeting were known[386]. After these two years pause in the action of the General Assembly and, despite the reticence of the OAU[387], this organ re-examined the dossier and, as in December 1975, it adopted two resolutions which contradicted with each other in some aspects: these were Resolutions 33/31 A and 33/31 B[388]. The former showed the position of the POLISARIO Front and Algeria and, after affirming the right of the Western Saharan people to self-determination and independence, for the first time the General Assembly made an express allusion to the POLISARIO Front although not in order to recognize its condition as the sole representative of the Western Saharan people, but to congratulate itself on its decision to unilaterally declare a ceasefire (July 1978). Finally, this resolution reaffirmed the responsibility of the UN in the conflict.

Resolution 33/31 B was closer to the positions defended by Morocco and Mauritania, and stated that it "expresses its confidence that the *ad hoc* committee (constituted in the OAU for the Saharan question) will consider all the data on the question of Western Sahara with a view to convening an extraordinary summit meeting".

After some years of vacillation by the General Assembly (1975-1979), Resolution 34/37[389] was a decisive step in the attitude of the UN as regards the Western Sahara question. The General Assembly took note of the decisions of the Assembly of Heads of State and of Government of the OAU adopted at the Monrovia summit[390], which urged that the Western Saharan people exercise the right to self-determination through a referendum, while also taking note of the Peace Agreement agreed to in Algeria on August 10, 1979 between Mauritania and the POLISARIO Front, as well as the decision of

---

[386] *ORGA*: Resolutions 31/45 and 32/22 of the GA, approved December 1, 1976 and December 28, 1977 respectively.

[387] *ORGA*: A/33/364.

[388] *ORGA*: Resolutions 33/31 A and 33/31 B of the GA approved both December 13, 1978. As had happened before in the GA, both resolutions had very different results in their voting; Resolution 33/31 A was approved by 90 votes in favour (among which were Algeria and Spain), 10 votes against (among which were Morocco and Mauritania) and 39 abstentions. Resolution 33/31 B was approved by 66 votes in favour (Spain, Morocco and Mauritania), 30 votes against (Algeria among others) and 40 abstentions.

[389] *ORGA*: Resolution 34/37, approved November 21, 1979 by 85 votes in favour (among them Algeria and Mauritania, and by this supporting Mauritania the decolonization process of Western Sahara), 6 against (among them Morocco), 41 abstentions (among them Spain).

[390] *ORGA:* A/34/552, annex II, Decision AHG/Decl.114 (XVI).

Mauritania to withdraw its forces from Western Sahara[391]. However, the most notable part of this resolution was the affirmation of the legitimacy of the struggle being carried out by the POLISARIO Front, "the representative of the people of Western Sahara", whose participation is recommended in the search for solutions to the conflict. Finally, this important resolution

> "deeply deplores the aggravation of the situation resulting from the continued occupation of Western Sahara by Morocco and the extension of that occupation to the territory recently evacuated by Mauritania"[392].

Resolution 35/19, which continues the evolution that had begun the previous year, requests Morocco and the POLISARIO Front, "representative of the people of Western Sahara, to enter into direct negotiations with a view to arriving at a definitive settlement of the question of Western Sahara"[393]. This resolution will serve as a model for those that the General Assembly, almost routinely, would approve, all of which would have the common characteristic that they placed the UN at a second level as regards the OAU, which would be given the initiative in the decolonization process of the territory[394].

2.4. *Causes of nullity of the Madrid Agreements*

The first question to be highlighted is that, in accordance with what is set out in paragraph *a)* of Article 2 of the Vienna Convention on the Law of Treaties, regardless of its name ("Declaration of Principles") and, despite the fact that at

---

[391] The Mauritanian-Saharan agreement stated that: "the Islamic Republic of Mauritania declares solemnly that it does not and will not have any territorial claims or of any other type over Western Sahara; the Islamic Republic of Mauritania decides to definitely stand back in the unjust war of Western Sahara following the modalities adopted in agreement with the representation of the Saharan peoples, the POLISARIO Front; the POLISARIO Front declares solemnly that it has no territorial claim nor of other type towards Mauritania".

[392] ORGA: Resolution 34/37 de la AG, approved November 21, 1979.

[393] ORGA: Resolution 35/19, approved November 11, 1980.

[394] Resolutions 36/46, approved by the GA on November 24, 1981; 37/28, approved November 23, 1982; 38/40 approved December 7, 1983; 39/40, approved December 5, 1984; 40/50, approved December 2, 1985; 41/16, approved October 31, 1986; 42/78, approved December 4, 1987. It must be mentioned that from 1984 Spain changed its traditional abstention's attitude towards the conflict, voting from then on in favour of direct negotiations between Morocco and the POLISARIO Front. The reasons that took the Spanish Government to change of attitude, *cfr.* MARQUINA BARRIO, A., "El Tratado libio-marroquí, repercusiones e incidencia en la política exterior española", *Revista de Estudios Internacionales*, vol.6, n° 1 (1985): 125-136.

the request of the Spanish Government at the time the opposite was stated[395], this was a real international treaty, insofar as it was an "international agreement concluded between States in written form and governed by International law".

Once settled this question, it should be stressed that there is practical unanimity in the international doctrine when classifying the Madrid Agreements as null. Generally, it can be openly stated that the agreements are radically null because their purpose was to deprive a people of its right to self-determination. However, starting from this first consideration, we consider the basis of the arguments put forward by those who defend the validity of the agreements and the basis of the arguments of those who propose the nullity of these agreements.

Two main arguments have been put forward to justify the validity of the Madrid Agreements. It has been stated that the fact that in Resolution 3458 B (XXX) the General Assembly expressly referred to the agreements supposed the acceptance of its content by the General Assembly[396]. Nevertheless, as we have been able to see, the text of this resolution was the result of difficult negotiations which endeavoured to please both parties in the conflict which was, obviously, not possible. In our opinion, this resolution was a sad example of the weakness of the General Assembly and a regrettable concession to the expansionist pretensions of Morocco and Mauritania. Despite this, as Bedjaoui pointed out in 1977, for the then Algerian representative at the United Nations

---

[395] Carro maintained that Madrid Agreements do not have the same nature as an International Treaty. In his opinion it was a Declaration. The signature of the signed text says in an expressive way "Declaration of Principles" (CARRO MARTÍNEZ, A. (1976): 30). But this, from an International law point of view, and specifically, from the point of view of the Convention on the Law of Treaties of 1969, is undefendable.

[396] Fougerouse stated that, consequent to the approval of the GA resolution, with the support of the United Nation, the retrocession to Morocco of Río de Oro and Saguia El Hamra was irreversible. (FOUGEROUSE, M. (1987): 90). The Moroccan representation before the Third Commission pointed out on November 7, 1996, that, "by the Madrid Agreements, Spain had proceeded to the retrocession to Morocco of the Sahara", avoiding in this way, after more than twenty years, that among other things, the agreements of Madrid were tripartite (*ORGA*: AG/SHC/270).

Regarding what has been mentioned, Barbier had stated in 1978 that, even if it was regrettable and could be criticized, from a legal point of view it should be recognized that (the agreement of Madrid) had a real value (BARBIER, M., "Le Sahara Occidental et le Droit International", en *Sahara Occidental: un peuple et ses droits*. Colloque de Massy (1-2 avril 1978), Ed. l'Harmattan, Paris (1978): 99-101). Nevertheless, the author modified later this statements, pointing out that even if a resolution of the GA would have practically authorized it, it was completely contrary to International law regarding decolonization (BARBIER, M. (1982): 170).

this resolution "did not undermine in any way the right of the Western Saharan people to self-determination" as on three occasions it reaffirmed the "inalienable right of all the Saharan populations to self-determination"[397]. It is true that the drafting of this controversial resolution reminds us of some lines of the opinion of the Court since, as regards certain concessions to Morocco and Mauritania, it contains a blunt affirmation which is intended to save the decolonizing policy of the UN: the General Assembly tried to leave the right of the Western Saharan people to self-determination beyond doubt.

A second argument that was alleged in favour of the legal validity of the agreements is its registration in the Register of Treaties of the United Nations (Article 102 of the Charter)[398]. However, in accordance with what is established by the Regulations of the Register of Treaties, the fact that a treaty is registered at the General Secretariat of the UN neither prejudges nor confirms its validity[399], therefore, this argument must not be taken into consideration.

Having presented the main arguments affirming the validity of the Agreements, we now analyse those, which, in our opinion, justify their nullity. For this purpose, we will classify the arguments in the following three groups: nullity due the subjects intervening, due to their purpose, due to the content and due to the effects of the agreements.

---

[397] *ORGA*: A/C.4/32/SR.10, par. 106.

[398] The Declaration of Principles of Madrid was registered by Morocco in the United Nation Secretariat on December 9, 1975, and figures as incorporated to the document S/11880 (*ORSC*). It can also be consulted in the text *United Nations Treaty Series*, vol. 988, I, num. 14450.

[399] The registry procedure of treaties was regulated by a Regulation- Resolutions 97/1, December 14, 1946, 364 B-IV, December 1, 1949, and 482-V, December 12, 1950- that specifies expressly that the Secretary General has no legal capacity to assess whether or not the document which is submitted to the registry is a treaty, though he could consult with other Members any matter related to the registry (*cfr.* REMIRO BROTONS, A., *Derecho Internacional Público*, vol. II, *(Derecho de los Tratados)*, Tecnos, Madrid, 1987, p. 255). This author has underlined the relative value of the registry of treaties: registration and publication do not constitute conditions for the validity of treaties or essential acts for its constitution; so, it is doubtful that the Court has recourse to this disposition (article 102 of the Charter of UN) to ignore in the deciding process a valid, in force and pre-existing treaty (REMIRO BROTONS, *Ibid.*: 220 et seq.). The starting presumption is that, when transmitting to the Secretariat a certain text, "the Member of the United Nation that has done has considered that it constituted a treaty in compliance with the article 102 of the Charter" (GONZALEZ CAMPOS, J. D., SÁNCHEZ RODRÍGUEZ, L. I., ANDRÉS SAENZ DE SANTA MARIA, M. P. (2008): 216).

2.4.1. *The nullity of the agreements due to the subjects involved*

In general, it can be stated that none of the contracting States were competent to dispose of a territory and of a people alien to them since, through these agreements, the handover of the territory is undertaken by one "who is not legitimated to do so, to those who have no right to it"[400], together with the aggravating circumstance that this occurs outside the framework of the UN, or rather, counter to the decolonization policy established by the United Nations and in breach of International law. In this regard, it should be remembered that the *Waldheim Plan* was absolutely ignored and that the signing of the agreements led to the withdrawal of Spain and to the immediate occupation of the territory by two neighbouring powers, which is especially serious as these were precisely the powers that had made claims over the territory.

A) *The lack of legitimacy of Spain*

From a general perspective, it should be pointed out that, in accordance with what is established by General Assembly Resolution 2625 (XXV) of the General Assembly, as a Non-Self-Governing Territory, Western Sahara has a status "separate and distinct" from from the territory of the State administering[401]. Due to this, and as a first approximation to the question, it can be said that Spain was not legitimated to cede the territory as the administrator or the sovereign of a Non-Self-Governing Territory[402], which

---

[400] VILLAR, F. (1982): 346.

[401] In the same sense M. Bedjaoui intervention before the Fourth Commission, October 31, 1977 (*ORGA:* A/C.4/32/SR.10, par. 98).

[402] The same argumentation was defended by the President of the SADR, when, before the Fourth Commission, stated that "Spain used a disposal power for which it had no faculty (...) Spain trespassed severely its competence and its faculties of administering power (...) Spain is obviously non-competent to sign with third parties an agreement about the destiny of a territory that is unknown" (*ORGA:* A/C.4/31/SR.22, par. 12, of November 11, 1976). "Spain is still responsible, taking into account article 73 of the Charter (...)" (*ibid.*, par. 32). This approach is shared also by the Chief of States Assembly of the OAU, that already in 1979 (16th period of sessions, in Monrovia, Liberia, July 17 to 20) stated that "in the tripartite agreement between Spain, Morocco and Mauritania, only the territory administration was transferred on to Morocco and Mauritania, but not the sovereignty over it" -Decision AHG/DEC.114 (XVI)-. In the same sense, *cfr.* BARBIER, M. (1982): 170; LIPPERT, A., "The Western Sahara: an emerging State in Northwest Africa?", in *Hearing before the Subcommittees on International Organizations and on Africa of the Committee on International Relations House of Representatives*, October 12, 1977, U.S. Government printing Office, Washington (1977): 60.

CHAPTER V

was evident in the light of the context in which the study of the Western Saharan conflict was included within the framework of the UN from the time that Spain joined the UN, through Chapter XI of the Charter, that is to say, within the framework of the decolonization[403]. On this point, it should be remembered that even at the present time, the Fourth Commission continues to examine the Western Sahara question despite the repeated attempts of Morocco to prevent this[404].

It is clear that Spain was the administrator of the territory, and still is, as stated by the General Assembly,

---

Also, the argumentation used by Judge De Castro in his own opinion, as we have referred to above, when, unfortunately as a premonition, he pointed out that, even if Spain would have accepted Morocco's proposition to approach the matter before the Court via litigation, the possibility would not have been feasible, because "This skilful approach was in fact no more than a piece of camouflage. Even if Spain had accepted Morocco's proposal to bring before the Court by way of contentious proceedings the two questions raised in the letter of 23 September 1974, the case would not have been viable. Spain did not have at that time, and does not have today, capacity to be party to a dispute with Morocco, or with any other State, as to the present or past titles to sovereignty concerning a territory which has the status of a Non-Self-Governing Territory, and of which it is the administering Power. Spain does not have what is called in procedure a legitimation passive. Once it is established that the status of Western Sahara is that of a Non-Self-Governing Territory, Spain cannot recognize the right of another State to claim the territory, nor can it concede the existence of the titles of sovereignty of any State whatsoever, nor agree to arbitration over the sovereignty, nor make an agreement for partition of the territory, nor decide on its joint exploitation, nor attribute sovereignty over it to itself. Spain could not be party to a dispute involving the settlement, directly or indirectly, of any question concerning the sovereignty over the territory under its administration. Nor could the administering Power disregard the fact that it did not have the power to dispose of the right to self-determination of the Sahrawi, recognized by eight resolutions of the General Assembly by the parties which are interested or concerned, nor the power to disregard that right" (*Western Sahara, Advisory Opinion, I.C.J.*, Reports 1975, p. 145).

[403] In the same sense M. Bedjaoui set before the Fourth Commission (*ORGA*: A/C.4/32/SR.13, par. 21), and before also had Judge Gros and De Castro stated: "Spain cannot recognize the right of another State to claim the territory, nor can it concede the existence of the titles of sovereignty of any State whatsoever, nor agree to arbitration over the sovereignty, nor make an agreement for partition of the territory, nor decide on its joint exploitation, nor attribute sovereignty over it to itself" (*Western Sahara, Advisory Opinion, I.C.J., Reports 1975*, p. 145).

[404] Though documentation over the matter is logically very extensive, it would be as hard as useless to include a relation of all. As an example the intervention of Morocco before the Fourth Commission, September 30, 1977 when it claimed that the Commission dismiss the consideration of the Western Sahara question, "as this is a Moroccan territory" and also feared "that a debate on the question could affect the members of the Security Council" (*ORSC*: CPSD/127, section 5, September 30, 1997).

"in the absence of a decision by the Assembly itself, that a Non-Self-Governing Territory had attained a full mesure of self-government in terms of Chapter XI of the Charter, the interested administrating Power concerned should continue to transmit information under Article 73 *e* of the Charter with respect to that Territory"[405].

Thus, it is very significant that, despite the position taken up by the Spanish Government at the time when it "decided" to terminate its obligations concerning the territory[406], in the annual reports presented by the Secretary General to the General Assembly, Spain continues to appear as the administering Power of Western Sahara, although with a footnote to the document which records the declaration of February 26, 1976, by virtue of which Spain terminated its presence in the territory. Similarly, and up to the time of the referendum in East Timor, in August 1999, this territory appeared as a Non-Self-Governing Territory administered by Portugal, with a footnote to the document including the annual declaration of the Portuguese Government which stated the impossibility of providing the information referred to in section *e)* of Article 73 of the Charter, as it was *de facto* prevented from exercising its responsibilities in the territory. The Secretary General did

---

[405] *ORGA*: A/50/100, July 6, 1995, par. 88 and A/50/458, September 22, 1995, annex. In the same sense, *cfr.* NALDI, G.J., "The Statehood of the Saharan Arab Democratic Republic", *Indian Journal of International Law*, vol. 25 (1985): 480 et seq

[406] On September 27, 1976, Marcelino Oreja, the Spanish Minister for Foreign Affairs, stated before the GA that, "free from all responsibility inherited from History, we have forwarded this year to the Secretary General of the United Nations, for that last time, the information collected in article 73 of the Charter, as administering Power of the non-self-governing territories during the period that ended the 26 of February 1976".

Even if its consideration as a compulsory unilateral declaration would be a little unnatural, it should be reminded the public declarations of different Spanish representatives before organs of the United Nations and also before diplomatic means of correspondence, promising to carry out the referendum of self-determination in the territory. So, for example, De Piniés on December 1966, before the Fourth Commission, stated that "Spain has solemnly committed to follow the self-determination principle" (*ORGA*: A/C/SR.1660.), declarations that were repeated by Alba, that would take over De Piniés in the post for some time (*ORGA*: A/C.4/SR.2004), or Arias Salgado before the Security Council or the Secretary General of the United Nations. But apart from these declarations there is also the document that the Chief of State himself, F. Franco, sent in 1973 to the *Yemáa*, simultaneously sent to the Secretary General of the United Nations, in which, regarding the Statue of Autonomy mentioned above, asserted that "the Spanish State reiterated and guaranteed solemnly that Sahara population would determine freely their future" (the complete text of the letter can be consulted in CRIADO, R (1977): 298-300, and in CARRO MARTÍNEZ, A. (1976): 17, note num. 2).

not make any pronouncements regarding the core of the question in either of these cases, however, undoubtedly these were territories on which information had to be provided, and this had to be forwarded by the aadministering Powers that appeared in the document[407].

The fact that Spain withdrew from the territory leaving the way clear for the two neighbouring States to occupy it means that the agreements cannot be considered as "management agreements", which would come under the powers attributed by the United Nations to the administering Powers, and the only option is to consider these as agreements "on disposal and transfer"[408]. As stated by Bedjaoui, this is "an act of execution and not one of mere administration"[409]. In the Madrid Agreements the term "administration" of the territory is expressly mentioned while the term "sovereignty" is not mentioned. It is obvious that the Madrid Agreements did not entail the transfer of sovereignty of the territory, among other reasons because, as was pointed out above, Spain was only the administrator of the territory[410]. As regards this point, the *Joint Hispano-Algerian Communiqué* issued a few years later must be interpreted (May 1, 1979), in which Spain stated its position,

---

[407] *ORGA*: A/51/316, Annex.

[408] *ORGA*: A/32/303, Annex, Memorandum of POLISARIO Front, October 5, 1977.

[409] *ORGA*: A/C.4/32/SR.10, par. 99.

[410] Both for doctrine and for the politicians themselves that took part in the process, the references to a "sovereignty cession" are very strange. In this sense, *cfr.*, for example, RUPÉREZ, J., "La política exterior de la transición", *Cuenta y Razón*, n° 41, 12 (1988): 53. The policy followed by the different holders of the Spanish Ministry for Foreign Affairs that had arrived immediately after democracy (José María de Areilza and Marcelino Oreja) was to interpret in this same way the Spanish approach in the sense of not considering as concluded the decolonizing process until the peoples of the territory had exercised the right of self-determination (in this sense, *cfr.* MIGUEZ, A., "Le Sahara occidental et la politique maghrébine de l'Espagne", *Politique Etrangère*, n°. 2 (1978): 176 et seq.). In the complicated situation of the Spanish diplomacy in those moments, Areilza even asserted that "even if the Agreements of Madrid were technically bad, as all that is improvised, they will be respected" (AREILZA, J.M., *Diario de un ministro de la Monarquía*, Ed. Planeta, 1977, p. 167). Furthermore, when the P.S.O.E. reached the Government, Fernando Morán, then Minister for Foreign Affairs, maintained similar approaches than those of his predecessors in the seat (*Actividades, Textos y Documentos de la Política Exterior Española*, Ministry de Asuntos Exteriores, Madrid, 1983, p. 100).

As pointed out by González Campos, the withdrawal of Spain would have required a territory administration under the auspices of the United Nations, but never an arranged one between these two States (Morocco and Mauritania), and followed by the military occupation (GONZALEZ CAMPOS, J., "Los acuerdos nulos de Madrid", *El País*, September 18, 1977).

"that the fact that it had definitively ended its administration of the territory on February 26, 1976 could not entail a transfer of sovereignty as it was a Non-Self-Governing Territory, in the sense of Article 73 of the United Nations Charter".

This same interpretation was made by the *ad hoc* Committee of the OAU, that, on June 23, 1979, approved Resolution AHG.92 (XV), which stated that "the Madrid Agreement does not establish the transfer of the administration of the territory to Morocco and Mauritania and does not constitute a transfer of sovereignty".

Thus, the agreements were intended to establish equivalence between "decolonizing the territory of Western Sahara" and "terminating the responsibilities and powers which Spain has over the territory as the administering Power"[411]. Spain, as the administering Power, therefore, responsible before the International Community for the administration of the territory, permitted the establishment of a Moroccan and Mauritanian administration in the territory, which would conclude with an agreement between these two States[412]. Through this agreement, the international frontier between both States was established, partitioning the territory of Western Sahara, and thus breaching the obligations which corresponded to it as the administering Power: "the Western Saharan people were not the holders of an abstract right to self-determination; the people of Western Sahara had a material right stated in many acts of the organs of the United Nations (...)"[413].

Not only did Spain not cease to be responsible for the administration of the territory of Western Sahara (on occasions the Spanish Government itself has insinuated its possible responsibility in the inconclusive decolonization of the

---

[411] Likewise, *cfr.* ABELLÁN HONRUBIA, V., entrevista en la obra colectiva Cistero Bahima, J.M. y Freixes Sanjuan, M.T., *Sahara, una lección de la Historia*, Imprenta Altagraf, Barcelona (1987): 159; VILLAR, F. (1982): 346. Also, it should be reminded that the Spanish Government had pointed in October 1975 to the Visiting Mission that "its military forces were in the Territory solely for the purpose of maintaining security and protecting its borders. So long as tension existed on the Territory's frontiers, such protection was necessary. The Government would be prepared to withdraw these forces during a referendum, provided that they were replaced by United Nations forces and that the United Nations assumed responsibility for guaranteeing the security of the Territory" (*ORGA*: A/10023/Add.5, par. 275).

[412] Mauritanian-Moroccan agreement of April 14, 1976 (*United Nations Treaty Series*, vol. 1035, I, num. 15406).

[413] GONZALEZ CAMPOS, J.D., participation in Conference about the fourth anniversary of the Madrid Agreements, ASOCIACION DE AMIGOS DEL SAHARA, *Madrid, 14 de Noviembre de 1975: la traición*, Ed. Sedersa, Madrid (1980): 36-39.

CHAPTER V

territory[414], classifying the form in which the territory was abandoned as *"desaguisado"* ("disaster")[415], but it was also responsible for the damages suffered by the population from the signing of the agreements, responsibility which grew due to the fishing agreements between, at first Spain in its own name, and then, the European Union, and Morocco concerning the jurisdictional waters of Western Sahara, a question which we will analyse below.

Furthermore, section 1 of the Madrid Agreements evidently contradicts what is set out in Article 73 of the Charter in relation to Article 103 as "Spain could not freely dispose of the Sahara, not even transfer its administration to other countries, something which Article 73 of the Charter does not authorize in any case"[416]. In the best scenario, Spain should have ceded the provisional administration of the territory to that which had authorized its administration, the United Nations[417]. Thus, it is significant that Resolution 3458 A (XXX) ignores the agreements and refers to Spain as the administering Power, in clear contradiction with the content of Resolution 3458 B, where these agreements are referred. In addition, neither the General Assembly nor the Secretary General refer to Morocco or Mauritania as administering Powers of the territory, nor do they allude to the duty to facilitate information in accordance with what is established in Article 73 *e)* of the Charter as regards these States, which endorses the thesis that they are not considered to be the holders of any legal entitlement to the territory. Although there are some references in Spanish case law which affirm that Morocco and Mauritania "were going to succeed Spain both as regards the administration and the sovereignty of the territory"[418] in conformity with the International law in force, there can be no interpretation other than the one we defend.

---

[414] Appearance of the Secretary General of Foreign Policy, Francisco Villar before the Commission of Foreign Affairs of the Congress to answer to various questions raised by the Parliamentary Group IU-IC (*Actividades, textos y Documentos de la Política Exterior Española*, 1992, p. 851, and *B.O.C.G.* of June 25, 1992). Precisely the volume of this collection of the Ministry for Foreign Affairs of the year 1992 inaugurated an autonomous voice dedicated to Western Sahara, when until then any information referring to that territory appeared under the title "Morocco".

[415] *Cfr.* The appearance of the Minister for Foreign Affairs, Javier Solana, before Plenary Session of the Senate (*Actividades, textos y Documentos de la Política Exterior Española*, 1994, p. 415, y *B.O.C.G.* September 13, 1994).

[416] BARBIER, M. (1982): 170.

[417] GONZALEZ CAMPOS, J., "Los acuerdos nulos de Madrid", *El País*, September 18, 1977.

[418] Due to its literal content, we comment a surprising passage of the Sentence of December 28, 1980: "the Law of November 19, 1975 abolished specifically all former rules

Without prejudice to a question we will return to by analysing the illegality of the fishing agreements made between the EU and Morocco, it should be borne in mind that the report issued in 2002 by the Legal Advisory Service of the UN expressly stated the following,

> "The Madrid Agreement *did not transfer sovereignty over the Territory, nor did it confer upon any of signatories the status of an administering Power*, a status which Spain alone could not have unilaterally transferred. The transfer of administrative authority over the Territory to Morocco and Mauritania in 1975 did not affect the international status of Western Sahara as a Non-Self-Governing Territory (...). Following the withdrawal of Mauritania from the Territory in 1979, upon the conclusion of the Mauritano-Sahraoui agreement of 19 August 1979 (...), Morocco has administered the Territory of Western Sahara alone. *Morocco, however, is not listed as the administering Power of the Territory* in the United Nations list of Non-Self-Governing Territories (...)"[419].

B) The lack of legitimacy of Morocco and Mauritania

Both Morocco and Mauritania also lacked the legitimacy to conclude the agreements although obviously for reasons other than those of Spain. It should not be forgotten that, as clearly established in the Opinion of the ICJ, there were no ties of sovereignty between either of these States and Western Sahara at the time of the Spanish colonisation[420], and moreover, as stated above, even though there had been some type of tie in the past, these supposed ties could not have been an obstacle to the right of the Western Saharan people to self-determination in any way. On concluding the agreements, these States

---

pronounced by the Administration of Sahara, therefore it was clear that the Spanish Administration could not be made the only responsible of something that happened when sharing administration with other two powers, that would succeed them not only in the administration, but also in the sovereignty of the territory" (Sentence December 28, 1980, CONT.-ADM., Courtroom 3, *Aranzadi*, num. 4125).

[419] Report on the "the legality in the context of International law, including relevant resolutions of the Security Council and the General Assembly of the United Nations, and agreements concerning Western Sahara of actions allegedly taken by the Moroccan authorities consisting in the offering and signing of contracts with foreign companies for the exploration of mineral resources in Western Sahara" (*ORGA*: S/2002/161, February 12, 2002).

[420] *ORGA*: A/32/303, Annex, Memorandum POLISARIO Front, October 5, 1977.

breached the prohibition to hinder the exercise of the right to self-determination by peoples subjected to colonial domination, contained in Resolution 2625 (XXV)[421]. In addition, the change in the position of Morocco as regards the right of the population of Western Sahara to self-determination, admitted by this country until September 1974, is openly against the acts of this State, and places it in *estoppel* because the statements of the Moroccan authorities in this regard are both abundant and unequivocal[422].

2.4.2. The nullity of the agreements due to their purpose

The agreements are also null due to their purposes as they violate a *ius cogens* norm, the right of peoples to self-determination, and the obligation of the States to comply in good faith with the obligations established by the UN Charter.

Nevertheless, before addressing the analysis of the first two arguments, we believe that it is necessary to make, at least, a brief reference to a principle which has inspired the whole decolonization process, and which was totally ignored by the Madrid Agreements: the *uti possidetis iuris* principle. Although it is obvious that the reason for the nullity of the Madrid Agreements does not lie precisely in the breach of this principle, as it is not imperative law, its general character has been stressed by international case law on numerous occasions. Undoubtedly the share out of the territory carried out as a consequence of the Madrid Agreements clashes head on with the content of this principle, considered by the OAU from its constitution as one of the basic principles in

---

[421] Resolution 2625 (XXV) states that "Every State has the duty to refrain from any forcible action which deprives peoples referred to in the elaboration of the principle of equal rights and self-determination of their right to self-determination and freedom and independence".

[422] In this sense, *cfr.* TOMAS ORTIZ DE LA TORRE, J. (1975): 603. The same approach is maintained by Rigaux when analyzing the similarities between Western Sahara and East Timor. In the opinion of this author, Indonesia would have been in *estopp*el situation, regarding East Timor, as a consequence of the repeated statements of the Indonesian government representatives denying their interest and claims over the territory of East Timor (*cfr.* RIGAUX, F., "East Timor and Western Sahara: a comparative view", *International Law and the Question of East Timor*, Catholic Institute for International Relations & International Platform of Jurist for East Timor (1995): 172). These statements confirm the approach we defend in the sense that not only Spain, but also Morocco went against their own acts. Likewise, Mariño states that "Morocco and his King are internationally committed from a political and legal point of view in the sense to allow and cooperate in the celebration of the consultation. So that any delay or annulment or interruption that would be imputable to them would be considered a grave violation of their international duties" (MARIÑO MENÉNDEZ, F. M., "El Derecho Internacional..." (1991): 53).

this regard. It is significant that the states concerned or interested in the conflict refer to this principle on several occasions. Thus, the Mauritanian representatives referred to it in the course of the debates of the Fourth Commission, held a few days after the Madrid Agreements were concluded, in order to deny its applicability in the specific case of Western Sahara as it understood that this refers only to the "frontiers between States which had already achieved independence, and was not applicable to the 'reconstruction' of frontiers before independence was achieved"[423], an argument which was not a new one. Morocco had already made a similar interpretation of the principle when, without expressly mentioning it, it referred to the cases of Nigeria/Biafra and Congo/Katanga, concluding that if Biafra or Katanga had had the opportunity to pronounce on their independence, neither Nigeria nor the Congo would have the configuration they have at the present time[424]. However, this argument avoids a decisive component when establishing the applicability of the self-determination of peoples, closely linked to the *uti possidetis iuris* principle: in both cases the frontiers established in the colonial epoch served precisely to delimit the confines of both States when they achieved this condition, therefore the exercise of the right of the peoples of Biafra and Katanga to self-determination did not correspond to them, in the light of International law established by the United Nations, as they formed part of already constituted States. In this regard, the "territorial" concept of people used by International law based on the *uti possidetis iuris* principle cannot be ignored. As expected, the POLISARIO Front also referred to this principle, however, clearly counter to the States mentioned in order to affirm its necessary applicability to the Saharan conflict[425].

A) *The nullity of the agreements due to the breach of a norm of ius cogens*

The Madrid Agreements are null in application of Article 53 of the Vienna Convention on the Law of Treaties as "at the time it was made" the Treaty was

---

[423] The Mauritanian representation referred initially also to the self-determination principle to point out that legally it could not be alleged in a legitimate way to put in danger the territorial integrity of an independent State, reminding its support to measures taken by the GA regarding the cases of Goa, Gibraltar, Ifni, Hong Kong and Macao (*ORGA*: A/C.4/SR.2173).

[424] *ORGA*: A/10023/Add.5, Appendix II, par. 14.

[425] In this respect, *cfr*. Intervention of Mansour Salim before the Fourth Commission on November 11, 1976. *Cfr.* also HODGES, T. (1983): p. 320, n. 1.

Chapter V

"in opposition to an imperative norm of General International law", namely the right of self-determination of peoples[426].

Based on the consideration that, due to all the arguments put forward, the Madrid Agreements are null, it is not necessary to evaluate the possible consequences of the conclusion of the Peace Agreement reached in Algiers on August 10, 1979 by Mauritania and the POLISARIO Front and the subsequent recognition by Mauritania of the POLISARIO Front and the SADR[427], once these are analysed from the perspective of the possible termination of the Madrid Agreements[428], in conformity with what is

---

[426] This opinion is also shared by the representation of the POLISARIO Front (*ORGA*: A/32/303, Annex, Memorandum POLISARIO Front, de 5 de October de 1977). Also in this same sense, Mariño points out that the agreements "are nullity grounded in International law because it seems there was no other purpose and aim than to refrain, even if only 'provisionally', that the Saharan people exercised their right to self-determination and their independence. Western Sahara was and is, until the celebration of the referendum, formally a Non-Self-Governing Territory" (MARIÑO MENÉNDEZ, F. M., "El Derecho Internacional..." (1991): 49).

[427] Even if Mauritania had harshly attacked the recognition of SADR by Algeria, whom it considered its creator, and described the SADR as a "prefabricated" "artificial" republic and of being composed of "especially" by Mauritanians, as said, would end up by granting recognition on February 27, 1984 (*ORGA*: 31st period of sessions, 20th plenary session, October 6, 1976).

[428] Some authors think that the Algeria agreement would mean the withdraw of Mauritania from the Madrid Agreements. In this sense, *cfr.* BRIONES VIVES, F. (1994): 57; MARIÑO MENÉNDEZ, F.M., "El Derecho Internacional..." (1991): 49; of the same author, "El conflicto del Sahara Occidental desde una perspectiva histórica", in the collection *Procesos de cambio y retos pendientes: Este de Europa, China y Sahara Occidental*, Centro Pignatelli (ed.), Zaragoza (1991): 183; MARQUINA, A., ECHEVERRIA, C., "La politique de l´Espagne au Maghreb", *Monde Arabe: Maghreb-Machrek*, n° 137, Juil/Sept. (1992): 45.

Otherwise, among the various interventions in the Congress of Deputies of various parliamentary groups and representation of the Spanish Governments themselves related to the Saharan matter, some think that, *de facto*, the tripartite agreements were overcome. So, in August of 1983, Secretary of the State stated that "the Spanish Government thought that it is not necessary to denounce the Madrid Agreements of 1975. The Spanish Government considered that the historical evolution itself had leaded to overcome these Agreements, taking into account, especially, the Mauritanian Agreement with the POLISARIO Front of 1979 and the position of that party in the Declaration of Madrid, regarding Sahara; so that the denouncement would be a gratuitous act, that probably, would only lead the involved parties of the conflict to mistake. The position of the Spanish Government is to wait that the Sahara people exercise its right to self-determination and decided its political future, that should not be prejudged as a recognition of the SADR in these conditions would introduce elements of confusion" (*"Contestación formulada por el Gobierno en relación con la pregunta del Diputado López Raimundo, relativa a la política española hacia el Sahara"*, B.O.C.G., September 23, 1983, and *Actividades, textos y Documentos de la Política Exterior Española*, 1983, p. 482 et

established in Articles 54 et seq. of the Vienna Convention on the Law of Treaties as this agreement eloquently confirms that Mauritania admitted the nullity of the agreements.

B) *The nullity of the agreements as they breach the obligation of States to comply in good faith with the obligations established by the UN Charter*

Section 5 of the Madrid Agreements states that its content is "the best contribution to the maintenance of international peace and security", which is surprising in the light of its consequences. It is difficult to accept the grounds of the agreements as having the objective of peace since the war that began shortly after they were signed was foreseeable. In fact, the intention was to provide cover for an occupation that was flagrantly illegal, in breach of the good faith that must prevail in international relations.

---

seq.). In the same sense, Fernando Morán, Minister for Foreign Affairs, stated in 1983 that it was "unnecessary to denounce the agreements because they are not in force". The reason was that the essence of the Agreements of Madrid was the constitution of a tripartite administration. Otherwise, Spain did not participate in the Administration, that was not even set up, so these agreements were not in force and the admission or denouncement of these agreements were not put forward, nor as an urgent problem nor as a formal problem (*Actividades, Textos y Documentos de la Política Exterior Española*, Ministerio de Asuntos Exteriores, Madrid, 1983, p. 100).
The Spanish Communist Party signed a joint communiqué with the POLISARIO Front (September 5, 1977) in which both delegations considered urgent that the Spanish Government denounced the Madrid Agreements, that had no legal validity" (text in COLA ALBERICH, J. (1977): 9). This author refuses Spanish responsibility in its withdrawal from the territory and denies that Spain should again assume its responsibilities in Western Sahara, as this is a "closed matter". Though these are purely political approaches, that we obviously do not share, we describe below some of their unusual arguments: "Spanish people do not have to put in danger the lives of their sons —Spanish soldiers- to solve colonial disputes that do not either affect or interest them. Let "concerned parties" solve it! What would be the benefit for Spain denouncing the tripartite agreement? Not at all! It would only bring us a new enemy, the Moroccan-Mauritanian one. In Foreign Policy of States, interest is the essential rule to follow, and Spain is not interested reviving that question, that should be definitely cancelled" (*ibid.*, p. 52).
This question was also set out by the representation of the POLISARIO Front in their appearance as petitioners before the Fourth Commission, before the approval of Resolution 34/37 (*ORGA*: A/C.4/34/SR. 14 y 15). In the same session of the Fourth Commission, Morocco criticized the inclusion of the Sahara question in the Decolonization Commission agenda, understanding that "the territory had been decolonized for once and for all, in compliance with International law"(*ORGA*: A/C.4/34/SR. 23).

CHAPTER V

Furthermore, the agreements are incompatible with the decolonization policy followed by the United Nations from the very beginning of a process which would lead the great majority of the territories subjected to colonial domination to independence[429], a policy which precisely Morocco and Mauritania had benefited from. Moreover, this is not a "solution for the peaceful settlement of a dispute in accordance with the UN Charter ", as stated in section 4 of the agreements, but a negotiation concerning the sovereignty of people and their natural resources. The affirmation that the agreements reached are the fruit "of the negotiations proposed by the UN" (section 2) does not correspond with reality either as the Security Council addressed the breakdown of peace in the specific case of Western Sahara, but did not prejudge the decolonization process, which had been carried out by the General Assembly. This was precisely the intention of Morocco in its interventions before the Security Council[430]. Contrary to this attitude of Morocco, in no case did the Security Council intend to analyse the problem of the Sahara in the context of the decolonization process, but to attend to the situation of the territory before and after the invasion, evidence for which can be found in the position of the Spanish delegation before the Security Council when it separated the situational problem of the *Green March* from the core question, which lies within the competence of the General Assembly. Thus, to pretend that, when Resolution 380 (1975) of the Security Council urges the parties to cooperate fully with the Secretary General "without prejudice to any action which they might take under the terms of its Resolution 3292 (XXIX) of 13 December 1974 or any negotiations which the parties concerned or interested might undertake under Article 33 of the Charter", it is referring not to negotiations whose purpose might be to resolve the threat to peace as a consequence of the *Green March*, but to negotiations on the future of the territory, is an approach undoubtedly based on bad faith.

As pointed out by the Spanish representative before the Security Council, although it is obvious that all the Member States have the obligation to resolve their controversies peacefully, it is also obvious that the core question of decolonization remains beyond the capacity of the states to negotiate, as it is a

---

[429] In the same sense, *cfr. Avis sur le Sahara Occidental*, par. 41 in JOUVE, E. (1983): 62.

[430] *Cfr.* sessions 1849, 1850, 1852, 1853 y 1854 of the Security Council (*ORSC*); especially intervention of the Moroccan representation, Saloui (session 1854th, par. 28-60), to whom Arias Salgado replied in the following expressive terms: "to expect that in those moments we should debate the essential problem of the decolonization of Sahara without attending the fundamental question posed by the illegal seizing and occupation of the territory, seems a claim completely out of reality (...)" (par. 64).

competence that corresponds to the General Assembly[431]. Also significant is the position adopted by the Secretary General in his third report submitted to the Security Council in compliance with Resolution 379 (1975) when he points out in his conclusions that,

> "The Council will remember that it was convened (...) in order to study the tense situation in Western Sahara created by the 'Green March' (...). Algeria, one of the 'parties concerned and interested' formally stated that it considered the declaration 'null and with void' (...)" so, given that the aforementioned declaration "refers to the decolonization of Western Sahara, a subject which is currently before the General Assembly, it seems proper that the Assembly pronounce on the question".

2.4.3. *The nullity of the agreements due their content and effects*

One more argument that endorses the nullity of the Madrid Agreements consists in the violation of the essential component of self-determination: the consultation of the population. The agreements are intended to equate the "will of the *Yemáa*" to the "will of the Saharan people", which obviously does not correspond to reality. Undoubtedly this was the objective of the States which were signatories to the Agreements although the position of Spain was always an enigma, a consequence of the impossible balance it pretended to maintain between the pressure from Morocco and Mauritania, on the one hand, and that of the UN, on the other. In this regard, the Spanish representative before the Fourth Commission expressly stated that, although the Declaration of Principles "referred to the opinion of the population expressed through the *Yemáa*, this does not mean that other possibilities for the expression of the will of the population are excluded"[432], which is the same as saying that the consultation of the *Yemáa* "could be valid" as a way to know the will of the population, but other ways of consulting the population were not excluded. The drafting of the document whereby Spain notified the Secretary General of the decision to terminate its presence in the territory ("a valid expression of the opinion of the Western Saharan people") sowed other doubts rather than cleared up the existing ones[433]. However, this schizophrenic position of the Spanish representation ceased when Spain

---

[431] *ORSC*: S/PV.1854 (1854th session, par. 66).
[432] *ORGA*: A/C.4/SR.2177.
[433] *ORGA*: A/31/56, S/11997, and Supplement num. 23 (A/31/23/Rev.1), Vol. II, chap. XI, Annex I, par. 50.

expressly stated that "the meeting of the *Yemáa*, held on February 26, did not constitute the consultation of the population stipulated in the Madrid Agreements nor in the resolutions of the General Assembly"[434]. From then on, this declaration established the opinion of Spain in this regard.

The Secretary General, who was never in favour of the Madrid Agreements, expressly denied the legitimacy of the meeting of the *Yemáa* as representing the will of the Western Saharan people, and, due to this, he decided not to send his Special Representative to the meeting of the Western Saharan General Assembly, which he had been expressly invited to[435]. Although we have already analysed the main questions related to the *Yemáa*, it should not be forgotten that the *Yemáa* could hardly represent the will of the population of Western Sahara due to the way in which it was constituted, its composition, and its self-dissolution on November 8, 1975[436].

Professor Abellán put forward another argument against the validity of the agreements, regarding its effects: the implementation of the Madrid Agreements "has led to a situation involving the permanent violation of International law" as they gave rise to an annexation, first partially by Morocco, and then completely after the withdrawal of Mauritania from the Territory, given that Resolution 2625 (XXV) establishes that "no territorial

---

[434] The text can be consulted in DE PINIÉS, J., (1990): 218.

[435] To this respect, the Secretary General reminded in a press release, that, on the one hand Resolution 3458 A (XXX) required him to adopt the necessary measures to supervise the act of self-determination, which organization had been entrusted to Spain, and on the other hand, Resolution 3458 B (XXX) asked him to design a representation that would participate in the organization of a free consultation in order to carry out the exercise of self-determination. Nevertheless, in the invitations sent by Mauritania and Morocco he had not been asked to assist in the consultation or referendum, but to simply, sent an Observer that would take note of the decisions of the *Yemáa*. The Secretary General decided "even if he would have had the time" not to send a special representation, because "nor the Spanish Government, as administering Power, nor the temporary administration, of which Spain was part, have adopted necessary measures to guarantee the exercise of the right of self-determination of the peoples of Western Sahara" *(ORGA:* the Secretary General/SM/2306, February 26, 1976). On this particular, *cfr.* WEEXSTEEN, R., (1976): 262.

[436] *ORGA:* A/32/303, Annex, Memorandum POLISARIO Front, de 5 de October de 1977. On the contrary, Carro asserted that the colonial situation would continue until Saharan themselves decided freely their future through their vote, express through the *Yemáa*, as affirms the Madrid Agreement (CARRO MARTÍNEZ, A. (1976): 31).

In relation to the *Yemáa*, it must be reminded that the Moroccan Government tried to join them to ratify the integration of Western Sahara in Morocco "expressing freely the will of the Saharan people" and that this failure to legitimate the illegal annexation of the territory had its reply in the Declaration of El Guelta, in which the *Yemáa* decided to dissolve itself (text and documents *ORSC:* S/11902 y A/10481).

acquisition resulting from the threat or use of force shall be recognized as legal". It must also be taken into account that some resolutions of the General Assembly as well as official documents of other organs of the United Nations, such as the Human Rights Commission, referring to the situation of the territory expressly classify it as an occupation[437].

From the point of view of the effects of the Madrid Agreements, since we are dealing with a serious violation of an obligation of essential importance for safeguarding the right of peoples to self-determination, such as the maintenance or establishment of a situation involving colonial domination[438], we are faced with an authentic "international crime", or a "serious breach of an obligation araising un der a peremptory norm of general International law"[439], which therefore must have as its principal consequence the international responsibility of Morocco, Mauritania and Spain for the handover and subsequent occupation and division of the territory[440].

2.5. The Madrid Agreements and Spanish Law

Besides the declaration that we have analysed, the text of the Madrid Agreements also contained three annexes referring to economic questions. The first of these contained the minutes of the conversations held between the three signatory States; the second contained the minutes of the meetings held by Spain and Morocco; finally, the third referred to the meetings held by Spain and Mauritania. Although the text of the agreement was made public at a press conference in December 1975, it was never submitted to the Spanish

---

[437] In this sense, for example, Resolution 34/37, section 5, "deeply deplores the aggravation of the situation resulting from the continued occupation of Western Sahara by Morocco and the extension of the occupation to the territory recently evacuated by Mauritania" (ORGA). In the same sense, *cfr.* Resolution 34/37 (apart. 6), and 35/19 (Preamble, sections 3 and 9). There are also specific references to the occupation in resolutions adopted by the Commission On Human Right. For example, *cfr.* E/CN.4/L.1489, Resolution 12 (XXXVII), March 6, 1981 about "The right of peoples to self-determination and its application to peoples under colonial or alien domination or foreign occupation - Denial to the people of Western Sahara of its right to self-determination and other fundamental human rights, as a result of the occupation of its territory by Morocco" and "deplores the continuance of the occupation of Western Sahara by Morocco". In the same sense, *cfr.* the Resolution 4 (XXVI), February 15, 1980.

[438] As pointed by González Campos, the Madrid Agreements "sentenced the Saharan people to a new colonial domination" (GONZALEZ CAMPOS, J., "Los acuerdos nulos de Madrid", *El País*, September 18, 1977).

[439] Expression used by the Project of the ILC, approved in second reading in 2001.

[440] GONZALEZ CAMPOS, J., "Los acuerdos nulos de Madrid", *El País*, September 18, 1977; ABELLAN HONRUBIA, V. (1987): 161.

CHAPTER V

Parliament, which approved the Bill without knowing the full content of the agreements, and these were never published in the *Boletín Oficial del Estado* (*Official State Gazette*)[441].

The Law on the Decolonisation of Western Sahara, of November 19, 1975[442], which contained no reference to the Madrid Agreements of November 14, 1975[443] and the *Ordenanza* (Ordinance) of November 24[444] empowered the Spanish Government to execute these agreements when they came into force in Spanish legislation. They would come into force on the day the law was published in the *Boletín Oficial del Estado* (*Official State Gazette*), by virtue of section 6 of the Declaration of Principles, which authorised the Spanish Government "to acquire the commitments which are conditionally contained in this document (this refers to the Declaration)", which took place on November 20, 1977.

As highlighted by Remiro Brotons, the fact that these agreements, which were never officially published, entered into force on the same day as they were published in the *Boletín Oficial del Estado* had as its main consequence "to

---

[441] Diego Aguirre points out that the main reason of the non-publication of the agreements in the *Boletín Oficial del Estado/Official State Gazette* was the opposition of the then Government President, Arias Navarro (*cfr.* DIEGO AGUIRRE, J. R. (1988): 794).

[442] The Draft of Decolonization Law, published in the *Boletín de las Cortes Generales* on October 25, passed on November 10 to the Fundamental Law Commission, for its urgent procedures. Diego Aguirre states that one of the most discussed questions was the title of the Law: "decolonization or de provincialization"? (*cfr.* DIEGO AGUIRRE, J. R., "La verdad sobre la entrega del Sahara" (1991): 27). On November 18, the Project was presented to the Plenary Session of the Parliament, were it was finally approved. During the defence of the Project, Carro, in the name of the Government, surprisingly refused that it supposed legalizing tooth and nail concluded decisions or agreements" (VILLAR, F. (1982): 354), even if agreements had been signed four days before.

[443] The only article in the Law of Decolonization shortly pointed out that the Government was authorized to act and adopt the necessary measures to decolonize Sahara, guarding Spanish interests, and that the Government would inform the Parliament. On the controversy about the broad authorization of the Parliament to the Government to carry out the decolonization of the territory, *cfr.* REMIRO BROTONS, A. (1978): 90 et seq. As states this author, in a democratic system the question that should have been raised, with prosecuting attitude, was why instead of forcing the approval of the Law of Decolonization, hiding clearly relevant documentation and reports to form opinion, it was not decided the submission to the Cortes Generales of the negotiated Agreement. But Spain was not democratic at that moment, and from the perspective of the legal system in force, is forced to recognize that the broad terms of authorization given by the Law of Decolonization offered an excellent protection umbrella to the Agreements of Madrid (*ibid.*, p. 96).

[444] Ordenanza del Gobernador General del Sahara, November 24, 1975, on the collaboration of the Moroccan and Mauritanian representation in the administration of the territory (*Aranzadi*, num. 2531).

embargo all the information during the legislative procedure". In the opinion of this author, "practice encourages an interpretation in which the publication becomes a mere condition for a treaty to be opposed upon people", which would be the equivalent to affirming the full validity of the Madrid Agreements in Spanish Law. Despite this, obviously, this circumstance would not rectify its nullity in the international order[445].

It is surprising that even the *Tribunal Supremo* (Supreme Court) referred to the Madrid Agreements in one of its paragraphs of the Sentence of November 28, 1980 when, considering a claim for compensation for damage suffered due to a fire in a warehouse in El Aaiún, it pointed out that,

> "it has to be taken into account that, by virtue of the Madrid Agreements of November 14, 1975, the Administration of the territory of Western Sahara was shared by Spain, Morocco and Mauritania (...), therefore, it is evident that the Spanish Administration cannot be held solely responsible for something which happened when it shared the administration with another two powers, which were going to succeed it in the administration and in the sovereignty over the territory (...)"[446].

However, as is evident, this Sentence incurred in two crass errors: firstly, during the period of the three party administration, there was no de *facto* joint government as referred to in the agreements and which is mentioned by the Sentence[447]. Secondly, the sovereignty of the territory was never handed over, but the administration was ceded, the process of which was openly contrary to International law and to the UN Charter. Despite the hesitation of the successive democratic governments, the Spanish position regarding the status of the Territory was finally clearly established in January 2010, when, due to

---

[445] BROTONS, A., *"Derecho Internacional Público, (Vol.II)..."* (1987): 269.

[446] Sentence of the *Tribunal Supremo*, November 28, 1980 (*Aranzadi, Repertorio de Jurisprudencia*, núm. 4125).

[447] As states Diego Aguirre, Morocco displayed only a police and political work of attracting natives, especially the elder "notables", while Spain proceeded to give all that remained in the territory, and Mauritania was the blind witness, waiting to see what would come out from the distribution (DIEGO AGUIRRE, J. R. (1988): 804). It must be mentioned that Rodríguez de Viguri proposed to the Spanish Government, in the name of the Sahara Government, that the Spanish representation should remain until the moment of the consultation to the population (declaration of Rodríguez de Viguri, March 13, 1978 before the Foreign Affairs Commission. *Diario de Sesiones del Congreso*, num. 30, p. 8).

Otherwise, as we reminded before, the Sentence of of the *Tribunal Supremo* of December 28, 1980, maintained that the mentioned shared administration had really existed in the territory (*Aranzadi*, num. 4125).

the Hispano-Moroccan conflict provoked by the expulsion by Morocco of the Western Saharan activist Aminetu Haidar when she attempted to enter Western Saharan territory, The Secretary of Organization of the Spanish Socialist Party (P.S.O.E.), Leire Pajín, rejected the accusations of the opposition Partido Popular (P.P.), and bluntly stated that, "Spain does not recognize the sovereignty of Morocco over Western Sahara".

3. The Rabat Agreements of April 14, 1976

Subsequent to the implementation of the Madrid Agreements, Morocco and Mauritania concluded two agreements in Rabat (April 14, 1976), which regulated the situation of the territory under the occupation of both States. Thus, due to the first of these agreements, the territory was shared out between the two States so that the northern strip of territory came under Moroccan occupation, and the southern zone of the territory "corresponded" to Mauritania and the "state frontier" was established between both States[448]. The second agreement was intended to start up cooperation of an economic nature between the two States.

As was expected, and in coherence with its attitude to the agreements of November 1975, these agreements were immediately denounced by the Algerian Government, which considered them to be "null and void"[449] as they were contrary to the UN Charter and constituted a violation of what was established in the principal resolutions of the General Assembly concerning decolonization, mainly in resolutions 1514 (XV), 2625 (XXV), and 3314 (XXIX), regarding the Definition of Aggression, where aggression is characterised as the failure to comply with "the duty of all States to refrain

---

[448] "Convention concerning the State frontier line established between the Islamic Republic of Mauritania and the Kingdom of Morocco", that is the name of the agreement, pointed out that "the State frontier established between the Islamic Republic of Mauritania and the Kingdom of Morocco shall be defined by a straight line running from the point at which the Atlantic coastline intersects the 24th parallel North to the point of intersection of the 23rd parallel North and the 13th meridian West; the intersection of that straight line with the present frontier of the Islamic Republic of Mauritania constituting the south-eastern limit of the frontier of the Kingdom of Morocco. From the latter point the frontier shall follow the present frontier of the Islamic Republic of Mauritania northwards to a point represented by the co-ordinates824/500 and 959 as shown on the initialled map annexed to this Convention" (Article 1 of the Agreement, text that can be consulted in United *Nations Treaty Series*, vol. 1035, I, num. 15406; *Bulletin Officiel*, Royaume du Maroc, num. 3311 bis, 16 avril 1976, and also *Documents d'Actualité Internationale*, num. 21, 1976, p. 419).
[449] ORGA: A/31/92 and S/12079, May 19, 19776.

from all acts of armed force to deny peoples of their right to self-determination, freedom and independence".

In a first approach to the subject, it can be stated that the agreements on the partition of the territory are undoubtedly contrary to International law as they violate the right of the people of Western Sahara to self-determination, they violate the general policy of the UN on decolonization and they violate, *inter-alia*, the stipulations in Resolution 3458 B (XXX), which we have analysed above and which had had the favourable votes of Mauritania and Morocco.

If we concluded the nullity of the Madrid Agreements in the previous section, the reasons which led us to such a conclusion justify even more definitively the nullity of this agreement given that is does not even discuss the possible capacity of Spain to cede a Non-Self-Governing Territory but the physical share out of this territory between Morocco and Mauritania. In addition, once Mauritania signed the peace agreements with the POLISARIO Front, it is obvious that if the agreement had had any possibilities, from then on it ceased to have any. However, as pointed out by Carrillo, these agreements are even contrary to the Madrid Agreements[450], which stipulated a temporary administration of the territory under the charge of Morocco and Mauritania, but in no case its share out, and, even less, the establishment of new international frontiers. In short, and as graphically stated by Judge Elias,

> "This is a situation in which Third World States, pre-beneficiaries of Resolution 1514 (XV), which guarantees the self-determination of all peoples, become modern colonisers of less fortunate populations in their geographical areas"[451].

In compliance with what is established in Article 6 of the Mauritanian-Moroccan agreement ("from its entry into force, this convention will be registered with the Secretary General of the United Nations, in accordance with Article 102 of the UN Charter"), both States requested the registration of these agreements in the Register of Treaties of the United Nations, which presented the Secretary with the additional problem of deciding on his capacity to register an agreement which divides a Non-Self-Governing Territory, a question whose analysis, as we have pointed out above, in accordance with what is set out in the regulations governing the Procedure for the Registration of Treaties, does not correspond to him. Faced with this

---

[450] *Cfr.* CARRILLO SALCEDO, J.A., "La posición de España respecto de la cuestión del Sahara Occidental: de la Declaración de Principios de Madrid al Comunicado Conjunto hispano-argelino", *P.I.*, n° 163, mayo-junio (1979): 123.
[451] ELIAS, T.O., "The role of the ICJ in Africa", *African Journal of International and Comparative Law*, vol. 1, n° 1, Mar. (1989): 8.

difficult situation, the Secretary General finally decided to provide a questionable solution to the problem, and drafted a footnote to the registration proceedings in which reference is made to the special circumstances of this territory[452].

---

[452] *Cfr.* DE PINIÉS, J., *(1990)*: 224. The agreement was registered by Morocco and Mauritania on February 9, 1977, and entered into force on November 10, 1976 (*United Nations Treaty Series*, vol. 1035, num. 15406, p. 117 et seq.).

CHAPTER VI

THE PEACE PLAN (I). THE MISSION OF THE UNITED NATIONS FOR THE WESTERN SAHARA REFERENDUM (MINURSO)

1. The reactivation of the process

The activity of the Security Council concerning the Western Sahara question was interrupted in 1975[453] and reactivated on the occasion of the approval of Resolution 621 (1988)[454], which again took up the question of the referendum. This resolution took note of,

> "the agreement in principle given by the Kingdom of Morocco and the Popular Front for the Liberation of Saguia el-Hamra and Rio de Oro on 30 August 1988 to the joint proposals of the Secretary General and the current Chairman of the Organization of African Unity (...) with a view to the holding of a referendum for self-determination of the people of Western

---

[451] The activity of the SC in this period comes down to several of letters referred to the SC Chairman by Mauritanian, Algerian, Moroccan, Arab Libyan and French Jamahiriya relating incidents during the war. For example, ORSC: S/12360, S/12375, S/12430, S/12431, S/12442, etc., underlining as interesting the 2151st session of the SC, on June 20 of 1979, to which the POLISARIO Front where invited to intervene before the SC for the first time (ORSC: S/PV.2151), and the 2153rd, on June 22, 1979, in which the representation of the POLISARIO Front, Madjid ABDALLAH, made a memorable intervention (ORSC: S/PV.2153)-.

On the other hand, in this stage of the process, consecutive General Secretaries of the UN and the OAU were key factors. For a detailed description of the steps followed by both figures to succeeding in achievement of the "agreement in principle", *cfr.* Report of the SG of the UN of October 5, 2988, that describes period between November 1987 and September 1988 (*ORGA:* A/43/680). *Cfr.* also SOROETA LICERAS, J., "El plan de Paz del Sahara Occidental, ¿viaje a ninguna parte?", *Revista Electrónica de Estudios Internacionales*, n. 10 (2005): 1-33.

[454] Resolution 621 (1988) of September 20, approved unanimously during session (*ORSC*). Prior to the approval of UN Resolution the SG exposed to the members of the Council the main characteristics of the Settlement Plan (*ORSC:* S/PV.2826).

Sahara, organized and supervised by the UN in cooperation with the Organization of African Unity"[455].

Through this resolution the Security Council also authorized the Secretary General to appoint a Special Representative for Western Sahara, a figure who will play a decisive role in the development of the conflict, and asked him to submit a report "on the holding of a referendum on the self-determination of the people of Western Sahara", together with the resources required to ensure that it would be properly carried out as soon as possible.

Thus, thirteen years after the approval of its last resolution concerning the Western Sahara conflict, the Security Council again took up its study with renewed energy. However, despite this promising re-launching of the process within the Security Council, it would be precisely within its sphere of action where the difficulties to be addressed would be most evident. Although in a short period of time following this Resolution, the Security Council would adopt more resolutions on the question than it had during the whole conflict and and reached important achievements, such as the creation of the MINURSO and the establishment of criteria on which the referendum should be based[456], it was unable to take any measures which would in fact be effective to systematically implement the content of its own resolutions when faced with the obstacles which Morocco would place in the way of a referendum. Faced with these difficulties, the Security Council would restrict itself to approving the successive reports of the Secretary General, to point out again and again "its concern about the difficulties the process was going through", and "to request the maximum collaboration from both parties" in order to achieve a just solution, which must consist of the holding of a referendum on self-determination.

As regards the General Assembly, after stressing that the question of Western Sahara falls within the framework of the decolonization process and pointing out that the solution to this entails the implementation of Resolution AHG/Res.104 (XIX) of the OAU, Resolution 43/33 welcomes the

---

[455] It is clear that one of the main reasons of the Moroccan Government to initiate the peace process was the enormous economic cost that would imply to maintain the war. On this question, amongst others, *cfr.* DAMIS, J., "Morocco and the Western Sahara", *Current History*, 89 (546), Apr. (1990): 166 and seq. Also, the reasons of the change of attitude of the Moroccan Government are related to the uncertainty aroused on the future of the Algerian unconditional help to the POLISARIO Front, confronted to the changes in this country, as a consequence of the civil war started in 1991.

[456] As pointed by GROS, people submitted to a colonial or foreign domination cannot express freely its will in a referendum organized and controlled exclusively by a colonial of foreign power (GROS ESPIELL, H., (1979): par. 62).

aforementioned *Agreement in principle* of 30 August 1988 and the unanimous adoption of the Resolution 621 (1988) of the Security Council.

In this context of optimism[457], Resolution 44/88 highlights the fact that the General Assembly welcomes the Marrakesh Conversations, which finally took place directly between the King of Morocco and a high level delegation of the POLISARIO Front, and hopes that these meetings take place more often, as it is convinced that "direct dialogue between the two parties of the conflict would contribute to its positive conclusion" concerning the Western Sahara question[458].

The following resolutions of the Security Council would complete some of the most important aspects included in the Settlement Plan, mainly related to the creation of the MINURSO. Thus, Resolution 658 (1990)[459] first addressed a number of questions of substantial importance included in the 1988 Settlement Plan, such as the ceasefire, the presence of both Moroccan and Western Saharan military contingents in certain agreed areas, the release of prisoners and political detainees or the exchange of prisoners of war, and then established a timetable for the process, which would have to conclude with the holding of a referendum, approximating a duration of 24-26 weeks from the time that the creation of the MINURSO is approved by the Council. This

---

[457] In words of the SG of the UN, "proposals aimed at the restoration of peace in the region provide a framework for the conclusion of a cease-fire and the establishment of conditions necessary for the organization of a credible referendum that will make it possible for the people of Western Sahara to exercise its inalienable right to self determination without military or administrative constraints (...)" (*ORGA*: A/43/680, par. 13). European Community and the Assembly of Heads of States of Non-aligned Governments declared in favour of these proposals (respectively, *ORGA*: A/44/139 and *ORGA*: A/44/551 and S/20870).

[458] Resolution 44/88, approved by the GA on December 11, 1989. Resolution 45/21, of November 20, 1990, reproduces without any novelty some of the content of Resolution 44/88. According to Castel, even if the content of direct Saharan-Moroccan conversations, that took place mainly in Marrakech (city in which was created the Arab Maghreb Union in February of 1989), have not been revealed, the king would have proposed a federal statute for the territory. The proposal would have been refused by the Saharan representation (CASTEL, A., "La batalla politica I militar pel referendum", *L'Avenc*, n. 153 (1991): 43).

[459] Resolution 658 (1990) of June 27, 1990, approved unanimously at the 2929th session. This resolution approved the SG report, in accordance with Resolution 621 (1988), had been presented to the SC (*ORSC*: S/21360 and corr. 1), and presented also a petition to both parties of complete collaboration with the UN SG and the Chairman of the Assembly of Heads of State and Government of the OAU, clause that would become habitual in later resolutions.

possibility came about through Resolution 690 (1991)[460], which finally established, under the authority of the Security Council, "a United Nations Mission for a Referendum in Western Sahara" (MINURSO) and, at the same time, it proposed that the transitional period would come into force, "no later than sixteen weeks after the General Assembly approves the budget for the Mission".

Added to this was the start of the long and slow peace process, marked by the entry into force on September 6, 1991 of a ceasefire in the territory, recorded in Resolution 46/67 of the General Assembly[461].

Once these premises were established, everything seemed to indicate that the necessary conditions for the commencement of the Settlement Plan had already been tabled. However, despite the establishment of the MINURSO in the territory, questions related to the drawing up of the census, which, as we will see later, would become the real central issue of the referendum and would lead to the practical stoppage of the process.

2. Peacekeeping operations and the intervention of the UN in the electoral process

Having considered the reasons for the general atmosphere of optimism in the United Nations at the end of 1991 concerning the Western Sahara decolonization process, we now move on to the study of a key problem in this process: the establishment of the MINURSO. To do so, although we do not consider it necessary to analyse the multiple operations carried out by the

---

[460] Resolution 690 (1991) of April 29, 1991, approved unanimously April 29, 1991, at the 2984th session. Curiously, the Gulf conflict, provoked by the invasion of Kuwait by Iraq on August 2, 1990, drove indirectly the United Nations to intervene in the Western Sahara conflict (*cfr.* MADDY-WEITZMAN, B., "Conflict and conflict management in the Western Sahara: is the endgame near?", *Middle East Journal*, n° 45, Autumn (1991): 594-607 and ZOUBIR, Y., PAZZANITA, A.G., "The United Nations' failure in resolving the Western Sahara conflict", *Middle East Journal*, n° 49, Autumn (1995): 617). Also, this Resolution approved the report that the SG had presented to the SC, in accordance with Resolution 658 (1990) (*ORSC*: S/22464). This report described concrete features of the Settlement Plan object of the prior report (*ORSC*: S/21360), in particular, questions related to the financial and personnel needs of the MINURSO, concreting an estimation of the global cost.

[461] Resolution 46/67, approved by the GA on December 11, 1991, celebrates this event and underlines also the importance of the process of establishing the United Nations Mission for the Referendum in Western Sahara (MINURSO), approved by Resolution 690 (1991) of the SC. In the following period of sessions, Resolution 47/25, approved by the GA on November 25, 1992, will underline the need that both parties respect scrupulously the accorded ceasefire and that both parties cooperate with the SG in achievements of the Peace Plan process.

CHAPTER VI

United Nations since this would divert us from the true objective of this work, it does seem necessary, at least, to make a brief reference to some of the most important operations in order to better delimit the subject of our study, taking into account the possible parallelisms as regards the case in question so that we may analyse the operation started up in Western Sahara in the following section.

The operations carried out by the United Nations in the area called "strengthening of the efficacy of the principle for holding authentic, periodical elections" and in collective security have been of very different types. However, it should be said in advance that, although it may seem that these are clearly differentiated types of operations, the truth is, although not always, that the classification is often due to purely academic reasons. Thus, it is quite common to use indistinctly the terms which define each type of operation in many of the documents of the organs of the United Nations which deal with the question, which, of course, has not contributed to clarifying their content. In the specific case of the Western Sahara conflict it is common to include the MINURSO among both peace-keeping operations and those corresponding to electoral processes. Despite this, it must be admitted that, as we will see below, this operation has such special characteristics that the apparent confusion is perfectly explicable as both types of operations are complementary.

The question of the peacekeeping operations is so complex, and is currently subject to such intense debate that it would be very pretentious of us to attempt to sum up their most important aspects in a few lines. However, due to their relationship with the Western Sahara conflict, we consider it necessary, at least, to specify the following aspects of these operations:

- On the one hand, the main characteristics of each of the different and "multidimensional"[462] operations which the United Nations carries out or has carried out[463], and the main requirements which must be complied with in order to implement them;
- On the other hand, the specific characteristics of the operations in which the United Nations has intervened concerning electoral processes and the main characteristics for their implementation.

---

[462] *ORGA*: A/48/403 and ORSC: S/26450, par. 5.

[463] This classification does not pretend in any case, to be definitive, and has no other aim than to be able to set MINURSO in the frame of the United Nations in this field, and this being aware that even in the most important sectors of international doctrine considers useless to make such an effort as to classify peacekeeping operations, due to their diversity and speciality (in this sense, *cfr.* PICONE, P., "Il peace-keeping nel mondo attuale: tra militarizzazione e amministrazione fiduciaria", *Rivista di Diritto Internazionale*, 1 (1996): 31 and seq.).

2.1 Main characteristics of the operations carried out by the United Nations and the main requirements that must be complied with for their implementation

As pointed out by Sanchez Rodriguez, the end of the cold war was a key moment in the history of peacekeeping operations. Together with the "classical" type operations, characterized by their link to directly or indirectly inter-State conflicts, at this time a new type of operations of a multi-functional nature arose. These, which can be classified as second generation operations, must address new or insufficiently known challenges as a consequence, mainly, of two factors which have recently exploded with force onto contemporary international society: on the one hand, the proliferation of conflicts of an ethnic or religious nature and, on the other hand, the rise of a new type of inter-state armed conflict characterized by the disappearance and breakup of institutional structures and social organization. The difference between both generations of operations lies principally in going beyond the strictly military functions which characterized the first, so that other diverse and complex functions have been incorporated, involving a spectrum which is so wide that it ranges from control of internal public order and the re-establishment of administrative normality to the protection of fundamental rights and liberties and the guarantee of the implementation of humanitarian International law, with the organization and guarantee of a range of electoral processes somewhere in the middle[464].

Starting from these premises, the Secretary General of the UN made an attempt to typify the operations which the United Nations carries out or has carried out, arranging them in five groups, each under a name "which is becoming more and more familiar for the international community"[465]:

a) *Preventive diplomacy*, which has three main objectives: to prevent controversies from araising between the parties, to prevent existing

---

[464] *Ibid.*, p. 199.
[465] Terms used by the SG for each of the United Nation types of operations are result of a very slow evolution of the Organization in this field. It started with the creation in 1965 of the Special Committee on Peacekeeping Operations, through Resolution 2006 (XIX) of the GA. On the evolution of the different concepts and terms used by the UN throughout these three decades, the following resolutions are very significant: 2053 (XX), 2220 (XXI), 2308 (XXII), 2451 (XXIII), 2576 (XXIV), 2670 (XXV), 2835 (XXVI), 2965 (XXVII), 3091 (XXVIII), 3239 (XXIX), 3457 (XXX), 31/105, 32/106, 33/114, 34/53, 35/121, 36/37, 37/93, 38/81, 39/97, 40/163, 41/67, 42/161, 43/59 A and B, 44/49, 45/75, 46/48, 47/71 and 47/72.

disputes from escalating into conflicts, and to limit the spread of the latter when they occur.
b) *Peacemaking*, "diplomatic action to bring hostile parties to a negotiated agreement through such peaceful means as those foreseen under Chapter VI of the Charter". In order to implement these, it is not necessary to have the authorization of any organ of the UNO, unlike the actions explained below.
c) *Peace-keeping*, which has its legal basis in Chapter VII of the Charter, normally consists of a military and civil presence of the UN on the ground, with the consent of the parties, with the following objectives, which must be achieved excluding the possibility of the use of force: to implement or monitor the implementation of arrangements relating to control of conflicts (cease-fires, separation of forces, etc.), ans their resolution (partial or comprehensive settlements), and/or to protect the delivery of humanitarian relief. In this case it is obligatory to have the authorization of the General Assembly or of the Security Council in order to start up the operation.
d) *Peace-enforcement*. This involves the measures adopted under Chapter VII of the Charter, involving, logically, the use of armed force to maintain or restore international peace and security in situations where the Security Council has determined the existence of a threat to the peace, breach of the peace or act of aggression. For these types of operations the authorization of the Security Council is required.
e) *Peace-bilding*. This consists of identyfing and supporting measures and structures wich will solidify peace and build trust and interaction among former enemies, in order to avoid the relapse into conflict.
Subsequent reports of the Secretary General[466] classify the UN created instruments for the control and resolution of conflicts between and within States depending on the previous consent of the parties involved for their implementation. Thus, the Secretary General refers to those which require this consent, such as preventive diplomacy, peacemaking and peace-keeping, as opposed to those others which do not require consent due to their coercive

---

[466] Among others, *cfr. ORGA*: A/50/60 or *ORSC*: S/1995/1, of January 25, 1995, par. 23 et seq. In our opinion, this report of the SG is especially interesting for the bitterness with which it refers to the imposed limitations to its work by States, members of the of the Organization that, "collectively encourage the Secretary-General to play an active role in this field" and "individually they are often reluctant that he should do so when they are a party to the conflict" (*ibid.*, par. 28).

nature, such as sanctions and the peace-enforcement[467], and stresses the importance of maintaining well established limits to separate both types of actions since in cases such as those of Somalia or Bosnia-Herzegovina new mandates were superimposed onto the original ones, initially intended as peacekeeping function, and thus their content was distorted and they were destined to fail. We insist that, despite the fact that, on occasions, the distinction may seem to be unnecessary since these are interchangeable in appearance, as pointed out by the Secretary General himself, "To blur the distinction between the two can undermine the viability of the peacekeeping operation and endanger its personnel (...). In reality, nothing is more dangerous for a peacekeeping operation than to ask it to use force when its existing composition, armament, logistic support and deployment deny it the capacity to do so"[468].

Furthermore, the Security Council has pointed out the following factors as requirements for putting these into practice[469]:

- A clear political objective, with a precise mandate, and subject to periodical review;
- The consent of the government concerned and, when applicable, the consent of the parties concerned, "except in exceptional cases". Just as the Secretary General has pointed out on several occasions, the acquiescence in the action of the United Nations "is a *sine qua non*"[470];
- The support provided to a political process or the peaceful settlement of a controversy;
- Impartiality in the implementation of the decisions of the Security Council[471];

---

[467] Some authors understand that even in cases of imposition of peace, it is necessary that the Parties give their consent to the basic agreements, not being necessary the consent for the concrete measures to adopt for their applications. Among others, *cfr.* DIETHELM, R., *Die Schweiz und friedenserhaltende Operationen 1920-1995*, Berna, Viena, Stuttgart, Paul Haupt Verlag, 1997.

[468] ORGA: A/50/60, par. 35 and 35. The need that the peece-keeping and peace-enforcement should not be mixed in the mandate of the same United Nation operation has been stressed by several delegations before the Special Committee on Peacekeeping Operations (to that respect, *cfr. ORGA*: A/51/130, par. 8).

[469] ORSC: S/24111.

[470] ORGA: A/50/60, par. 28.

[471] This impartiality cannot be referred to the character of the United Nation intervention because, as pointed by Bertram, "the maintenance of peace is not a neutral act" (BERTRAM, E., "Reinventing governments: the promise and perils of United Nations peace building", *Journal of Conflict Resolution*, n. 39 (1995): 394).

- The disposition of the Security Council to adopt adequate measures against the parties that do not comply with its decisions;
- The right of the Security Council to authorize the use of all the resources necessary for the forces of the United Nations to comply with its mandate, as well as the immanent right of the forces of the United Nations to adopt the measures required for their legitimate defence.

2.2. *Specific characteristics of the operations in which the United Nations have intervened in electoral processes and the principal requirements for their implementation*

The interventions of the United Nations in electoral processes can be classified as follows[472]:

A) Operations involving the supervision of an electoral process

These operations reached their culmination in the decolonization process, therefore, its principle characteristic can be said to be the fact that they are carried out on territory which is not yet independent. Another highly relevant aspect is the need for the Special Representative of the Secretary General to certify and confirm the validity of certain fundamental aspects of the process. The complexity of the process requires a preparatory mission that visits the territory to verify compliance with the pre-requisites set out by the General Assembly. The United Nations must be in the territory, at least, four months in advance, and it is also necessary to have an agreement on the status of the mission to be concluded with the authorities of the territory.

As regards the mandate, although it will not always be the same as it may be modified depending on the territory in question, it will usually include the following factors: the impartiality of the electoral authorities; freedom of organization, movement, assembly and speech for the political parties; the presence of observers of the political parties throughout the process; equality as concerns the use of the State radio and television; the verification that the electoral census is taken properly; that the electoral authorities will be informed of the complaints, irregularities and interference notified or observed and, possibly, be requested to adopt the measures required to address these; observation of the electoral campaign, voting, counting, calculation and announcement of the results.

---

[472] ORGA: A/47/668/Add.1, of November 24, 1992.

As examples of these types of supervisory operations, we could bring to mind the decolonization processes of British Togo (1956), British Cameroon (1959), Ruanda-Urundi (1961), Western Samoa (1961), South Africa (1994) and Namibia (1989).

B) Operations for the verification of an electoral process

The main characteristic of these types of operations carried out by the United Nations consists of the fact that they are carried out in a sovereign State at the request of its Government; otherwise the verification operation would not be possible. Moreover, a national organ will be in charge of organizing and managing the electoral process with the role of the UN being one of the verification of the freedom and impartiality of fundamental aspects of this process.

As in the previous case, a preparatory mission is needed to visit the territory beforehand, and the United Nations must be present in the territory four months previously. Likewise, agreement is required on the status of the mission.

As regards the characteristics of the mandate, these are very similar to the mandates of the supervisory operations although, in this case, besides the factors pointed out, the key question of the operation lies in information. In fact, an extensive information network is essential as this will serve as a database for the reports, which must, periodically, be issued by the Mission on freedom and impartiality during the stages of the electoral process. After the voting, a final report must be issued about the execution of the election, the procedures used in the counting process and the final results of the election. Therefore, the mandate must clearly establish the information procedures to be used by the Mission.

As an example of these types of operations, besides some which were carried out in territories under trusteeship, mention must be made of Nicaragua and Haiti which, being the first States involved in this, had to address questions which had not arisen until then, just as Angola and Mozambique. In addition, as regards the form in which the mandates of the Missions were established, it is not possible to speak of a common model as the specific characteristics of each case determine the form of the mission.

C) Operations for monitoring an electoral process

The main objectives of these types of operations are the reports on the carrying out of the electoral process which must be issued by the United

Nations Resident Coordinator of the system in a country which requests international observers, and these reports will be sent exclusively to the Secretary General of the Organization. This is done when the United Nations is asked to participate in the process with an excessively brief period of notice, thus preventing adequate monitoring of all the process. Consequently, the mandate is also brief, and may be restricted to the Mission being present in the territory for a few days. Neither is it necessary to have an agreement on the status of the Mission. Operations with these characteristics were carried out in some territories that were under trusteeship, such as Papua-New Guinea (1972), Gilbert and Ellice Islands (1974), New Hebrides (1979) or the most recent case of the Palau Islands (1986, 1987 and 1990).

D) Technical assistance as regards electoral questions

As is obvious, this is the most common type of participation of the United Nations in electoral questions, and it normally forms part of the most important verification missions. The function of the operation takes in questions such as the contribution of technical analysis, advice, equipment, materials or training at Government institutions.

E) Organization and execution of an electoral process

This is the most ambitious operation within the area of the United Nations, as well as the most complex. This is the most pretentious operation as the United Nations takes on a task normally reserved for the authorities of the territory; it is the most complex because it includes such delicate questions as the establishment of a system of laws, procedures and administrative measures which enable free and impartial elections to be held, or the administration of the electoral process itself.

As is logical, considering its extreme complexity, a list of characteristics common to these types of processes cannot be made. Until now, there has been only one successful precedent: the case of Cambodia. But there is another example of subjection to an operation of this kind, also assigned to the UN, which constitutes the subject of this study. This is the case of Western Sahara, which, so far, represents the other side of the coin as regards this type of operation; as we shall see presently it is a reflection of the utter failure of the Organization.

As regards the *requisites common to all the types of operations* mentioned to be implemented, the following four should be mentioned[473]:
- The requests must primarily have a relationship with situations which have a "clear international dimension" and which are related to peacekeeping and international security;
- The operation must "geographically and chronologically" take in the totality of the electoral process, from the initial stages of the drawing up of the census until the elections themselves;
- There must be an express, specific request of the Government involved, as well as "wide public support and political support for the work of the United Nations";
- The competent organ of the United Nations must give its approval.

3. The Mission of the United Nations for the Referendum in Western Sahara (MINURSO)

The action of the United Nations in the peacekeeping operations has obtained very unequal success. Thus, compared with successes whose value, it must be remembered, is not exclusively attributable to the UN, such as the cases of Namibia (where the colonization and occupation of a territory for more than a century was ended), El Salvador (which saw the conclusion of a cruel war which lasted more than a decade), and Cambodia (which enjoyed the first free elections held in two decades of conflict), bloodier examples of operations during the decolonization process in East Timor (in which the resolution of the conflict was badly affected by the internal problems of Indonesia, while the United Nations was criticised for remaining more than discretely in the background) and Western Sahara show the extreme lack of organization in this field. Now that the decolonization process is nearly concluded, which is one of the principal and undoubted achievements of the United Nations throughout its existence, it seems that those territories which could not take advantage of the driving force of decolonization in the sixties are condemned to suffer the consequences of an Organization, ready for anything at that time but, in the 21st Century severely lacking keenness in this area and ceding to the interests not only of world powers, but regional powers too. To analyse the MINURSO case, we are going to follow the steps taken by successive Secretaries General of the UN, which, as can be seen easily, as well as playing a key role throughout the process, have a role in shaping in the activity of the Organisation.

---

[473] *Cfr. ORGA*: A/47/668, November 18, 1992, par. 53.

CHAPTER VI

3.1. The Pérez de Cuéllar phase: the Peace Plan

3.1.1. Resolution 621 (1988) of the Security Council: the Special Representative of the Secretary General

As was mentioned above, the first resolution of the Security Council from which it can be deduced that it was necessary to create a peacekeeping operation in Western Sahara coincides with the organ's return to the issue following the abandonment of its involvement in 1975. This was Resolution 621 (1988)[474], where, for the first time, the Council authorised the Secretary General to appoint a Special Representative for Western Sahara, a post that would be successively occupied by different persons, with varying degrees of success[475].

The Resolution was approved after the report of the Secretary General was heard by the Members of the Council. The report succinctly explained the agreement reached by both parties in the conflict on August 30, 1988 in Geneva, and requested the authorization of the Council to appoint a Special Representative for Western Sahara, who would be "the sole and exclusive authority, particularly with regard to all questions pertaining to the referendum, including the organization, monitoring and conduct of the referendum"[476]. The need to appoint a Special Representative of the Secretary General in Western Sahara had been stipulated in the "Settlement Proposals" of the agreement of August 30, 1988: the post had to be occupied by a person proposed by the Secretary General of the UN, in consultation with the Acting President of the OAU, and with the consent of the two parties in the conflict.

The mandate and the functions given to the Special Representative are very broad, although in the main are limited to the transitional period, which had to begin with the entry into force of the ceasefire and terminate with the

---

[474] ORGA: Resolution 621 (1988) of SC, approved unanimously on September 20, 1988.

[475] The charge would be occupied consecutively by H. GROS ESPIELL (October 19, 1988) and Johannes MANZ (January 19, 1990), named by PÉREZ DE CUÉLLAR; Sahabzada YAQUB-KHAN (March 23, 1992) named by BUTROS GALI; Charles F. DUNBAR (December 30, 1997-February 16, 1998), William EAGLETON (May 18, 1999), William L. SWING (December 1, 2001), Alvaro DE SOTO (August 7, 2003) and Francesco BASTAGLI (August 5, 2005-August 31, 2006), named by KOFI ANNAN; Julian HARSTON (February 5, 2007) and Hany ABDEL-AZIZ (November 5, 2009), named by BAN KI-MOON, and Wolfgang WEISBROD-WEBER, named also by BAN KI-MOON on June 15, 2012. On the action of GROS in his charge, that he would abandon to become the new Minister of Foreign Affairs of Uruguay, cfr. MADDY-WEITZMAN, B. (1991): 602 and seq.

[476] ORGA: S/PV.2826, September 20, 1988.

proclamation of the results of the referendum. During this period, he will have "sole and exclusive authority over all matters relating to the referendum, its organization and realisation"[477], and will be assisted by a "Support Group", composed of a civilian unit, a military unit and another security unit (civil police). With regard to the powers attributed to the Representative, he can adopt "all the measures considered necessary to guarantee the freedom of movement and the security of the population, as well as the impartiality of the referendum". He can also adopt "all the measures of an administrative and technical nature or security measures as he deems appropriate in the territory during the transitional period". Finally, he has the option to suspend all laws or measures, which, in his judgement, might be an obstacle to the referendum.

From a simple reading of the previous paragraph, it is clearly deduced that the functions attributed to the Special Representative of the Secretary General act as the corner stone of the peace plan. Thus, the success or failure of the operation depends to a great extent on the role played by him. However, the truth is that not being able to deploy all of his powers until the start of the transitional period, originally scheduled for 1992, so far his role has been limited. For this reason, the post has been gradually losing its relevance, in favour of that of the Personal Envoy to the Secretary General, occupied by those of the relevance of James Baker (1997-2004), Alvaro de Soto (2004-2005), Peter Van Walsum (2005-2008) and Christopher Ross (2009-present), which on occasions performs the functions of a mediator.

3.1.2. The report of June 18, 1990: the Peace Plan

The real starting point for the creation of the MINURSO is the report that the Secretary General submitted to the Security Council on June 18, 1990 as it constituted the basis of the Peace Plan. It has two parts: the first includes the "Proposals of the Secretary General of the UN and of the current President of the Assembly of Heads of State and Government of the OAU in order to achieve a settlement of the Western Sahara question accepted, in principle, by the parties on August 30, 1988", (hereinafter "The Settlement Plan") while the second refers to the "Implementation Plan proposed by the Secretary General in accordance with Resolution 621 (1988) of the Security Council".

---

[477] ORSC: S/21360, Section 8.

CHAPTER VI

A) *The Settlement Plan of August 30, 1988*

Without prejudice to the fact that some of the specific aspects of the Settlement Plan are dealt with below (mainly those referring to the census of the Western Saharan population, the Identification Commission, nature of the voting, etc.), the following questions regarding the Plan must be highlighted:
- The criteria are established in accordance with those whereby the ceasefire of September 6 was achieved. Besides specifying determined aspects concerning the form in which the ceasefire had to be carried out, and as a question to be stressed, it should be mentioned that there was a commitment acquired by the two parties concerning the situation of the troops "in order to be able to organize the referendum with no military pressure" as from the entry into force of the ceasefire. Thus, "Morocco undertakes to carry out an appropriate, substantial and gradual reduction of its troops in Western Sahara", while the POLISARIO Front undertakes to confine all its troops under the vigilance of the Group of Observers of the United Nations[478];
- Both parties undertake to accept and obey the result of the referendum;
- The options that the participants in the referendum must decide on are limited to two: independence or integration although the text of the question to be made on the ballot paper is not specified;
- The preconditions for holding the referendum are established, and must be verified by the Special Representative of the Secretary General. Thus,

---

[478] As established by paragraph 20 of the SG Report (S/21360), the Group of Observers of the United Nations will be named by the SG, and will "function in accordance with the general principles applicable to United Nations peace-keeping operations". Though the report does not specify the number of persons that will be member of the group; it points in a very general way that "the group will be large enough and its composition sufficiently broad for it to be able to perform the functions envisaged in the present proposals". Their principal functions are: supervision of the ceasefire, provision of supplies to the troops of the parties in the conflict and prisoner exchanges.
Regarding military organization, it is significant to underline the fact that, in accordance with the Houston agreements, Morocco would reduce its troops to a maximum of 65,000 in the territory, that will remain confined, but in the case of the POLISARIO Front the only troops that will remain confined will be those "who would not be eligible to vote would also be confined by that date, while all others would be regrouped with their immediate families and return to the Territory under the UNHCR repatriation programme" (*ORSC:* S/1997/882, par. 20). So it is obvious that the Moroccan soldiers are not Saharan, nor can they try to be included in the Referendum census, while the POLISARIO Front will practically be deactivated during the Referendum celebration, as most of its members will participate in it.

among the important functions of the Special Representative are those stated in Resolution 621 (1988), and the following[479]:
1) He will head and direct MINURSO, and these functions will be carried out by a Deputy Special representative when the special representative is absent from the territory;
2) He may, if he considers it necessary, suspend of any law or measure, which, in his view, might limit or prevent the achievement of this objective (the organization of a free and equitable referendum);
3) He will take steps to ensure that all Saharan political prisoners and detainees are released;
4) He will designate various entry points for the Saharan refugees who return to the territory to participate in the referendum;
5) With the assistance of the United Nations High Commissioner for Refugees, the Special representative will make sure that Saharans residing outside the Territory are able to choose freely and voluntarily whether or not to return to the Territory;
6) He will determine the starting date of the referendum campaign and will be the guarantor of freedom of speech, assembly, movement and press;
7) He will be responsible for maintaining law and order in Western Sahara during the transitional period and will also ensure that no one can resort to intimidation or interfere in the referendum process;
8) He will have authority over the Identification Commission, which must carry out its work during the transitional period.

B) The Implementation Plan proposed by the Secretary General

After being informed of the positions of Morocco and the POLISARIO Front regarding the timetable project which had been previously forwarded to both parties, the Secretary General drafted the present Implementation Plan, which repeats the main aspects of the Settlement Plan (functions of the Special Representative, Creation of the United Nations Support Group, ceasefire, etc.) and has an impact on new aspects of substantial importance, such as the new functions attributed to the United Nations in the process. Thus,
- "The United Nations (...) will issue rules and instructions which will provide the fundamental basis for the organization and conduct of the referendum (...)", which will prevail "over the laws or measures in force in the Territory, to the extent of any incompatibility"[480], and it will be the Secretary General

---

[479] *ORSC*: S/22464, par. 10.
[480] *ORSC*: S/21360, par. 58.

Chapter VI

who will be responsible for dictating the regulations, while the Special Representative will be responsible for the norms and instructions required for their implementation[481];

- "Will organize and conduct a referendum (...) in wich the people of Western Sahara will choose between independence or integration with Morocco", and
- "Will monitor (...) the maintenance of law and order, to ensure that the necessary conditions exist for the holding of a free and fair referendum (...)"[482].
- In addition, a provisional timetable was established, culminating in the holding of the referendum "24 weeks after the ceasefire comes into effect". Despite the establishment of this period of time, the Special Representative is granted the possibility to alter these time periods if "circumstances demand this".

In this report, the Secretary General proposed the creation of the MINURSO (*Mission of the United Nations for the Referendum in Western Sahara*), which would be composed of civilian, military and civil police personnel of the United Nations, under the command of the Special Representative and a Deputy Special Representative. It was also specified that "arrangements concerning the status of MINURSO and its personnel will be made with the parties and with neighbouring States involved in the implementation of the settlement proposals".

With regard to the transitional period, the Secretary General stated that, despite the fact that this would begin as from the entry into force of the ceasefire and would terminate at the time the results of the referendum were made official, "the United Nations would continue to have responsibilities for monitoring either the withdrawal of Moroccan troops or the demobilization of POLISARIO Front troops, depending on the outcome of the referendum". The initial forecast, which was quickly surpassed by the reality of the facts, was a maximum of 35 weeks with the MINURSO in the territory.

According to the calculations of the Secretary General, the withdrawal of the Moroccan troops should take place within a period of 12 weeks counting from the date on which the MINURSO personnel were definitively deployed in the territory, which had been calculated as approximately 14 weeks from the ceasefire. In any case, the forces which would remain in the territory during the campaign and the holding of the referendum should be composed exclusively of "the personnel deployed in static or defensive positions along the wall of

---

[481] ORSC: S/22464, par. 9.
[482] ORSC: S/21360, par. 47, f) and g).

sand[483] built by Morocco near the eastern and southern frontiers of the territory", with the sole exception of "certain logistical and support units required to back up the Moroccan troops deployed along the wall of sand (...), who will not carry weapons in the cities nor move about the cities in uniform". The Moroccan air force will continue to provide air traffic control services and radio communications, and the Moroccan navy will continue to provide functions, such as coastal patrols. All these activities must be closely watched by the MINURSO. As is logical, this vigilance extends to the personnel of the POLISARIO Front, who will be confined to places determined by the Special Representative.

On referring to the referendum campaign, and more specifically to the measures considered necessary to guarantee its free nature, among other things, the Secretary General pointed out that his Special Representative must "guarantee freedom of movement, the security of the population, freedom of speech, assembly and the press", and "allow the organization and holding of political meetings, assemblies, demonstrations and marches". Along these same lines, and within the Chapter entitled "other responsibilities of the Special Representative during the transitional period", the Secretary General again insisted on the fact that if the Special Representative had reached the conclusion that there are activities or measures which place the impartiality and free nature of the referendum at risk, "he will point this out to the authorities in order to achieve an amicable settlement" and, if the situation persists, this will oblige the Special Representative to inform the Secretary General "so that he might take the measures considered to be advisable".

In addition, he pointed out that the Special Representative would have "exclusive authority in all the premises of the United Nations related to the referendum and in their vicinity, such as the offices for registering the voters and the polling stations (...)".

With regard to the functions of the MINURSO, which would have its headquarters in El Aaiún, the Secretary General classified these into three groups, depending on the three units: civilian, security and military.

---

[483] Nowadays the consecutive walls constructed by Morocco in the Territory cover seven eights of it, with an approximate length of 2.500 kilometres. The construction of wall, II, III and the start of IV were possible thanks to the agreement between Libya and Morocco in Uxda and to the later decision of Libya (1983) of not provisioning weapons, and logistical and military material to the POLISARIO Front. This led to a diminished logistical and military capacity of the Front. *Cfr.* to that respect the intervention of de Fernando MORÁN before the Foreign Affair Commission of the Senate (*B.O.G.C.*, Senate, March 5, 1985, y *Actividades, Textos y Documentos de la Política Exterior Española*, Ministerio de Asuntos Exteriores, Madrid, 1985, pp. 325-326).

Chapter VI

- *The civilian unit*, composed mainly of civil servants of the United Nations, was in charge of questions such as the administration, political and legislative matters, those concerning refugees and political prisoners, information and public relations.
- *The security unit*, made up of members of the civil police, has the following tasks "to ensure tranquillity and maintain law and order in the vicinity of, and at, voter registration offices and polling stations, to ensure that no person is denied entry for the purposes of registration or voting (...), to monitor the activities of the existing police force so as to ensure that they are acting in strict accordance with the settlement proposals (...) and to prevent any possibility of intimidation or interference from any quarter". The report of the Secretary General did not define what the mandate of this unit consisted of, postponing its drafting to a later time, in order to define its supervision tasks and the procedures to be followed in the event of infringements to the Settlement Plan.
- *The military unit* will have the principal task of supervising the ceasefire, the reduction and confining of troops, and other questions related mainly to military work. The report pointed out that this unit would be under the authority of the Secretary General, who, in turn, would be under the authority of the Security Council.

As was expected, the report of the Secretary General was unanimously approved on June 27, 1990, by Resolution 658 (1990), which also requested the Secretary General to send the Security Council another report as soon as possible. This report would include, in particular, an estimate of the cost of the MINURSO, as a prior step to its creation[484].

---

[484] In accordance with the request of the SC, the SG delivered another report on April, 19, 1991 (*ORSC*: S/22464), that completed the content of the first, not only regarding the global cost estimation of the MINURDO -already evaluated in this report in approximately 200 million dollars- (*Ibid.*, par. 50), but also other many aspects, such as the concrete number of persons necessary to cover the different civil, military and security units (*Ibid.*, par. 39-50), the proposal of a calendar for the action plan (*Ibid.*, par. 51-53), concrete aspects relating the identification process and the announcement of the intention of preparing a conduct code to establish criteria regarding freedom of political campaign (*Ibid.*, par. 28).

On the other hand, the SG report pointed also the sending of a Technical Mission to the Territory and to the neighbouring countries to obtain information about the different positions of the States part of the conflict regarding the Settlement Plan. In this sense, he held conversations with the Moroccan king, with the Secretary General of the POLISARIO Front, and the Mauritanian and Algerian representatives, that contributed to delimit precisely the approximate cost of the operation. Also, the report consigned the first figures referring the number of Moroccan soldiers that should stay in the Territory during the process, that derived from the Moroccan commitment of reducing troops to "a level not

A) Resolution 690 (1991): the creation of the MINURSO

Finally, the Security Council decided to create the MINURSO through Resolution 690 (1991)[485], establishing that the transitional period had to begin within a period of, at least, 16 weeks from the approval of the proposal of the Mission by the General Assembly.

In accordance with the classification of the operations of the United Nations provided above and, in conformity with the mandate established by this resolution, the MINURSO would have to be included among peace-keeping operations since, in order to start it up, it was necessary to have the prior consent of both parties in the conflict. This previous agreement was the one concluded on August 30, 1988, which established the main characteristics of what would become the United Nations mandate:

- To control the ceasefire;
- To verify the reduction of Moroccan troops in the territory;
- To control the confining of the troops of Morocco and the POLISARIO Front in determined places;
- To ensure the freedom of all the political prisoners and detainees of Western Sahara;
- To supervise the exchange of prisoners of war;
- To make the repatriation programme effective;
- To identify and register the legitimate voters;
- To organize and ensure a free referendum and proclaim the results.

In the light of this data, it is evident that, at the time of its creation, the MINURSO constituted one of the most ambitious operations of the United Nations within the area of peace-keeping[486]. However, after a year, the MINURSO had only deployed ten per cent of its personnel, which was a measure of the true political will which supported it. As discussed below, the fact that the mandate does not include the possibility of the monitoring of respect for human rights in the territory by the Mission is a something which will become more relevant with time, especially from when, once the census has been drawn up for the referendum, Morocco withdraws from the peace process. Indeed, uprisings of the population of the territory and protests in favour of independence will only lead to intensification of repression by Morocco and various international organizations will ask the Security Council

---

exceeding 65,000 all ranks, within a period lf 11 weeks from the coming into effect of the cease-fire on D-day" (*Ibid.,* par. 14).

[485] *ORGA:* Resolution 690 (1991), approved unanimously by the SC on April 29, 1991.

[486] *Cfr.* DURCH, W.J., "Building on sand: UN peacekeeping in the Western Sahara", *International Security,* n° 17, Spring (1993): 151.

CHAPTER VI

to widen the mandate to protect the civilian population from the continuing excesses of the police and occupying army, an organ which benefits from unconditional French support.

B) *The Report of December 19, 1991: the stoppage of the identification process*

The Report of December 19, 1991, the last one made by Pérez de Cuellar as Secretary General, was also the most controversial one of his mandate. Besides the most controversial questions, related to the drafting of the census, and which we will refer to in the following Chapter, the Secretary General discusses the entry into force of the ceasefire in the territory as from September 6, 1991, as well as the establishment of the MINURSO in the capital of Western Sahara, El Aaiún, with three regional centres in the northern, central and southern sectors of the territory, and a linking office in Tinduf (Algeria). Furthermore, the Report stated that the deployment of the MINURSO in the territory "has contributed considerably to a calming of the situation"[487]. It also stresses the promulgation of the General Regulations that will govern the organization of the referendum and of the instructions concerning the responsibilities of the Identification Commission (these are analysed in detail in the following Chapter).

One of the most relevant aspects of the Report is the reference to what has been called "the Second Green March", as it stated that "a number of persons who claim to belong to Western Sahara have been moved into the Territory", and stressed the danger that actions such as this can put at risk the holding of the referendum. It also regrets the resignation of the Special Representative, Johannes Manz, who "is to assume his functions as his country's Permanent Observer to the United Nations, with effect from 1 January 1992"[488]. However, the resignation of J. Manz was not a casual event and, as is obvious, it was not exclusively a response to his concern about occupying the new post in the United Nations, but instead to his disagreement and distrust at the new direction which events seemed to be taking following the Report submitted by the Secretary General[489].

---

[487] *ORSC*: S/23299, par. 6.
[488] *ORSC*: S/23299, par. 11 and 12.
[489] Even after explanations of the SG regarding the resignation of Johannes Manz to his post of Special Representative, as pointed by Zoubir and Pazzanita, the causes of this resignation are directly related to the report of Pérez de Cuéllar to which we are referring. In a confidential letter, that Manz addressed to the SG when he resigned, that was published in *Le Monde Diplomatique* (November 1992, p. 13), he pointed as a cause of resignation the fact that after several of meetings with Moroccan officials, the SG had introduced changes in the

These bad omens were echoed in Resolution 725 (1991) of the Security Council[490], which stresses the serious concern within the Security Council due to the difficulties and delays in the implementation of the Settlement Plan, "approves the efforts of the Secretary General" and "welcomes the report of the Secretary General"[491]. This became the first time that the Security Council did not expressly approve the Report of the Secretary General, the final one drafted by Pérez de Cuellar as Secretary General which used a formula of diplomatic courtesy in order to highlight the difficulties to be addressed by the Security Council at the time of the approval of the resolution. The two main reasons for the disagreements among the members of the Security Council, both related to the question of the census, lay in the absence of an agreement between the parties, a premise which until then was inexcusable in the Peace Plan, and the absence of the approval of the OAU, which did not approve a Plan which could continue its course without the consent of one of the parties, the POLISARIO Front. As can be appreciated, these were strong reasons which motivated the reaction of some of the Security Council members who were radically opposed to the position of the Secretary General[492].

3.2. *The Butros Gali phase: towards the dismantling of the MINURSO*

Although the appointment of Butros Gali as Secretary General of the UN brought a breath of fresh air and gave rise to renewed hope that the process would emerge from its stagnation, in reality he did not bring substantial innovations to the policy of his predecessor: successive reports insisted on the significant difficulties in continuing the peace process in order to later propose a progressive reduction of the MINURSO operations.

Peace plan without any consultation. He also disagreed with the way United Nations controlled the Moroccan violations of the cease-fire (ZOUBIR, Y.H., PAZZANITA, A. G., (1995): 619).

[490] *ORGA*: Resolution 725 (1991), December 31, 1991, approved unanimously at 3025th session.

[491] *ORSC*: S/23330, December 19, 1991.

[492] While France, unconditional allied of Morocco during the whole conflict, approved this change of attitude of Pérez de Cuéllar, experienced, let us underline this, in the last days of his mandate, other members of the SC (especially USA, represented by Thomas Pickering, and several African States (like Zimbabwe) expressed openly their opposition to it and made pressure on France to withdraw its support to Pérez de Cuéllar and to give to the new SG a new chance to reconsider this attitude (*ORSC*: 3025th period of sessions).

CHAPTER VI

3.2.1. The 1992 reports: the progressive reduction of the MINURSO

In his first report to the Security Council[493], in which he stressed the impossibility of carrying out the referendum on the planned date (January 1992) due to the constant differences when interpreting the implementation of the Peace Plan, he proposed a maximum period of three months in order to achieve an agreement which would put an end to these differences and he recommended that the mandate of the military components of the MINURSO continue to be restricted to ensuring the ceasefire. He also underlined his efforts to limit the cost of the MINURSO; due to this, he decided to close the office of the Special Representative in New York, and redistributed the personnel of this office in their respective functions at the UN Headquarters. This shows the pessimism of the new Secretary General regarding the holding of the referendum.

In addition, the Secretary General informed the Security Council of his attempts to achieve the agreement of the parties for the appointment of the person who would occupy the post of the new Special Representative of the Secretary General, which would eventually go to the former Minister of Foreign Affairs of Pakistan, Sahabzada YAQUB-KHAN[494]. In his next report (May 29, 1992), he informed on this appointment and recommended another extension of three months for the MINURSO, whose role would continue to be limited to ensuring the ceasefire.

Once the premises for the beginning of another stage were set out in his third report[495] Butros Gali stressed the "principle of agreement" obtained from both parties by the recently appointed Special Representative, as regards the need to focus the conversations at the beginning, "on the formulation of safeguards to protect the political, economic, social and other rights and liberties of the losing side in the referendum, whatever the outcome", as this would serve to eliminate or mitigate at least the suspicion and distrust between both parties. The Report underlined the need to create a new climate that

---

[493] Report of SG of February 28, 1992 (*ORSC:* S/23662).

[494] The appointment of the new Special Representative of the SG, Yaqub-Khan, took place on March 23, 1992 without taking into account doubts put forward by the POLISARIO Front regarding his impartiality, because of the friendship relation between the new Special Representative and Hassan II. Also by the fact that he came from a State with a non-democratic regime (BUJARI, A., "The Western Sahara conflict", *Middle East International*, n° 422, april 3 (1992): 14). On this matter *cfr.* DAMIS, J., "The UN settlement plan for the Western Sahara: problems and prospects", *Middle East Policy*, 1, n. 2 (1992): 41 and seq. Also, ZOUBIR, Y.H., PAZZANITA, A.G. (1995): 620 and seq.

[495] *Report of the Secretary General of 20th August 1992* (ORSC: S/24464)

would permit a better understanding between the parties. In response to these approaches, the POLISARIO Front presented a document in which it defined two sets of safeguards: those which it would be prepared to respect in the event of a victory in the referendum, and those which it would want to be applied in the event that this was not the result of the referendum.

As regards the former, the POLISARIO Front undertook

"to govern on the basis of the principles of democratic freedoms, good-neighbourly relations, regional stability, non-interference in the internal affairs of other countries and even-handedness in relations with neighbouring countries, including Morocco", and was prepared "to establish the fullest possible economic cooperation with Morocco, both bilaterally and in the framework of the Arab Maghreb Union, and to study any proposal Morocco might wish to make for cooperation as long as it does not prejudice Western Sahara's sovereignty and territorial integrity".

With regard to the latter, in the event that the integration option triumphed, the POLISARIO Front requested the Government of Morocco "to guarantee freedom from any form of political persecution or discrimination and to allow free emigration ".

The Government of Morocco accepted the petitions of the POLISARIO Front in the case of integration, and undertook to decree an amnesty and a general pardon, and to honour all "national and international undertakings and to abstain from any action harmful to the dignity of others".

3.2.2. *The report of January 26, 1993: first suggestion of the dismantling of the MINURSO*

This report[496] constituted the change of direction in the policy of Butros Gali, tending to the dismantling of the MINURSO. After repeating the difficulties in the identification process, which on occasions seemed to him to be insurmountable, he pessimistically pointed out three possible options to resolve the conflict:
- The "continuation, and if possible, intensification of talks", but, in his opinion, "the chances for success under this option are very slim";
- The "immediate implementation of the Settlement Plan on the basis of the instructions for the review of applications for participation in the

---

[496] *ORSC:* S/25170.

referendum", which appear in the annex to the previous report drafted by the Secretary General in December 1991[497]. In the opinion of the new Secretary General, this possibility could mean the implementation of the Plan "without the cooperation of one of the parties";
- Finally, the third operation would entail a new approach to the resolution of the question, regardless of the Settlement Plan.

The report also described the military aspects of the MINURSO, and pointed out that its military mandate remained restricted, until the transitional period entered into force, to "monitoring and verifying the ceasefire in effect since 6 September 1991"[498], despite which, with regard to possible infringements of human rights in the territory during the holding of the referendum on the reform of the Moroccan Constitution and municipal elections held in Morocco and in the territory of Western Sahara, it affirmed that,

> "While MINURSO's current military mandate is strictly limited to the monitoring and verification of the ceasefire, MINURSO, as a United Nations mission, could not be a silent witness to conduct that might infringe the human rights of the civilian population. Hence, MINURSO patrols were alerted to possible unrest (...)"[499].

It is a shame that this affirmation has not been followed in subsequent years, during which the image of MINURSO has severely deteriorated in the eyes of the Sahrawi people, because hiding behind the content of the mandate, the UN looked the other way following human rights violations (some of which occurred in the gates of the MINURSO Headquarters in El Aaiún).

Though Resolution 809 (1993), the Security Council[500] "welcomes" the report of the Secretary General of January 26, 1993, it does not provide a clear response to the orientation that the Secretary General requested as regards how to follow the process. Thus, although it insists on pointing out the concern of the Council as regards the difficulties and delays encountered as regards the Settlement Plan and, in particular, "the persistent divergences between the two parties on the interpretation and application of the criteria for voter eligibility set out by the Secretary General in his report of 19 December 1991", it does not expressly refer to any of the options proposed by the

---

[497] ORSC: S/23299.
[498] ORSC: S/25170, par. 6. This same point of view is followed by the SG in his reports, for example, that of March 10, 1994 (ORSC: S/1994/283) and November 5, 1994 (S/1994/1257).
[499] Ibid., par. 25.
[500] ORSC: Resolution 809 (1993), approved by the SC, March 2, 1993.

Secretary General. What seems to be evident is that it rejects the possibility of abandoning the route opened up by the Settlement Plan as it invites the Secretary General implement the Plan which must conclude with the holding of the referendum, by making the preparations required for its organization and maintaining consultations with the parties for the purpose of "commencing voter registration on a prompt basis starting with the updated lists of the 1974 census", signalling the deadline for the holding of the referendum as the end of 1993. Furthermore, it requests the Secretary General to include in the report which he must submit to the Security Council in May 1993 the latest "proposals for the necessary adjustments to the present role and strength of the United Nations Mission for the referendum in Western Sahara (MINURSO)"[501].

In June 1993 the POLISARIO Front changed its attitude, as regards the report of Pérez de Cuéllar: the Western Saharan national liberation movement decided to accept the criteria for the registration of voters established by the former Secretary General of the UN[502], which will facilitate the meeting between representatives of the POLISARIO Front and of the Government of Morocco, held in El Aaiún between July 17 and 19. This meeting was not very fruitful as regards results but it was the starting point for the intensification of direct meetings between the representatives of both parties, which little by little, was becoming more common. In this new context, the report of the Secretary General of May 21 that same year[503], points out the coincidence in the positions of both parties when stating the need that the referendum be carried out as soon as possible. The report announces the creation of the Identification Commission, "which is due to establish itself in the Territory, together with ancillary staff, in the first half of June", and which will begin to register voters in El Aaiún and Tinduf, and stipulates the need to increase the budget planned in principle for the MINURSO.

The decision of the POLISARIO Front to accept the identification criteria which had established unilaterally by Pérez de Cuéllar constitutes the first in a long line of concessions made by the Sahrawi movement, throughout the process coming to accept, one after another, conditions established by Morocco, often sponsored by the Secretary General, while this State refuses to move an inch as regards its approaches.

---

[501] *ORSC:* S/25170, 26 January, 1993
[502] *ORGA:* A/AC.109/1163, 8, July, 1993, p. 11.
[503] *ORSC:* S/25818,

3.2.3. *The "Commitment Proposal" of the Secretary General (of June 1, 1993). The stoppage of the identification process*

On June 1, 1993, Butros Gali sent both parties the "Commitment Proposal of the Secretary General"[504], which basically included the Moroccan approaches as regards the interpretation of the criteria for the inclusion of voters in the census, a question which, as we stated above, we will analyse in the following section.

Obviously, Morocco accepted the proposal while the POLISARIO Front sent its confirmation of the flexibility of its stance to the Secretary General (11 of August) as it was prepared to admit the five criteria for the registration of voters, but with two conditions:

- Only the oral testimony of the *Sheikhs* mentioned on previous occasions by the Special Representative of the Secretary General, who had been elected in 1973, would be accepted, and
- The fact that a person was included in the 1974 census did not necessarily entail that the whole tribal sub-fraction was Saharan. For this to occur, it would be necessary that the majority of its members were included in the 1974 census[505].

At first sight, although it is not easy to evaluate its importance, it is clearly not an insignificant question since, as we will see below, it will constitute the main obstacle to be addressed by the process[506] as the failure to apply the conditions put forward by the POLISARIO Front would mean that the census would be increased by approximately 60,000 people, belonging to families of Moroccan citizens who were in the territory at the time the census was drawn up but, obviously, they were not Western Saharans. The acceptance of the conditions put forward by the POLISARIO Front would be the principal aim of the Houston Agreements (1997), which would make it possible to unblock the process, which had come to a stop since the POLISARIO Front proposed the conditions and Morocco refused to accept any modification to the identification criteria in this regard.

---

[504] The text of the Proposal figures as Annex I to the Report of SG, *ORSC*: S/26185, July 28, 1993.
[505] *Cfr. ORGA*: S/1994/283, Annex II.
[506] The SG himself did foresee the paralyze of the process if this question should not be resolved, as in fact, unfortunately happened (*cfr. ORGA*: S/26797, November 24, 1993, par. 28).

3.2.4. The report of 10 March 1994: specific proposals for dismantling the MINURSO

The report of 10 March 1994 of the Secretary General proposes three different options to the Security Council on how to complete the decolonisation process in Western Sahara. After taking stock of the situation in the territory, with specific reference to the electoral census[507], he presents the three options:

- Option A: that the Security Council would decide that the United Nations should proceed "to hold the referendum *regardless of the cooperation of either party*", and this will be held between 7 and 15 of December 1994, beginning on this date and continuing until 31 of December that same year, together with the withdrawal of the personnel of the MINURSO from the Territory[508].
- Option B: the Security Council would decide that the Identification Commission *should continue* its work during a prescribed period, while the United Nations would continue its efforts to obtain the cooperation of both the parties.
- Option C: that the Security Council would conclude that reaching an agreement between the two parties would be impossible would decide either that *the whole MINURSO operation should be phased out* within a given time frame or that the registration and identification process should be suspended. A reduced United Nations military presence should be retained in either case to encourage respect for the ceasefire[509].

Based on purely economic reasons, the Secretary General seemed to want to sew discouragement in the Security Council as regards the first two options since, as regards *Option A* he stated that the maintenance of the MINURSO in these conditions would entail the need for "very considerable additional

---

[507] To that respect, the SG stressed that the census lists of the population of 1974 and the supplement listing of names of additional persons expected to reach 18 years of age by 31 December 1993 (being these lists accessible in El Aaiún and in the camps of Tinduf) were ready at the end of November 1993. In the opinion of the SG, the identification process "appears to be proceeding smoothly", though "the completion of the identification and final registration of all eligible voters remains uncertain in the absence of agreement by the Frente POLISARIO to the compromise as a whole" (*ORSC*: S/1994/283, par. 16 y 19).

[508] *ORSC*: S/1994/283, par. 24.

[509] *Cfr. ibid.*, par. 26. As points Durch, the acceptance of the Referendum by Morocco was not an open compromise in favour of the right of self-determination of the Saharan people, but, counting that time was on their side, the Moroccan government supposed that the members of the United Nations would not agree to finance forever the operation. *Cfr.* DURCH, W.J. (1993): 151-171.

resources " (the gross cost would amount to approximately 8.7 million dollars per month for a period of nine months, as compared to 617,000 dollars monthly which Option C would suppose, for an indeterminate period of time), he also pointed out that both Option A and Option B would require "Member States to be willing to provide the military personnel needed" and, moreover, "maintenance of MINURSO at its present strength would require urgent action to obtain replacements for the contingents whose withdrawal has already been announced by their Governments". It was surprising that, as opposed to the logical duty of the Secretary General to propose the need to provide the MINURSO with more financing in this "critical stage in the efforts that the United Nations has made to implement the Settlement Plan", he understood the problem in pecuniary terms: obviously it would be much more economic for the UN to withdraw the MINURSO from the territory.

It is evident that Option A at the time was considered to be almost impossible as the Peace Plan involved questions such as the cantonment of troops and a code of conduct, which were impracticable without the cooperation of the parties. For the first time, the Secretary General openly put forward his proposals, and intended to discourage the Security Council as regards the maintenance of the MINURSO as he pointed out that Option A involved the highest cost of the three options, as opposed to the most economic which was Option C[510]. Fortunately, the Security Council decided against this approach and, through Resolution 907 (1994), of 29 March 1994, it went ahead with negotiations between the parties, continued the identification process, tending thus towards Option B, in the hope that the referendum might be held at the end of 1994, a decision which Spain was not alien to as a member of the Council[511].

---

[510] "Option A" would suppose 8.700.000 American dollars gross per month during a period of 9 months going from April 1, 1994, to December 31, 1994, while "option C" would mean a reduction to 617 American dollars gross per month during a non determined period.

[511] The role played by Spain in the period in which it belonged to the SC undoubtedly had effects on the development of the process, especially at critical moments in which the SG, Butros Gali, presented the three different proposals to the conflict when, according to the events that were occurring at that moment in the world -Bosnia, Rwanda-, the support to "Option C" seemed to grow within the members of the Council for economical and political reasons. This option proposed by the SG was withdrawn from the beginning of deliberations within the SC, which meant an implicit undermining of the authority of the SG, decision with no precedents in the conflict, for which the specific position of Spain in the Council was determinant. To that respect, *cfr.* the appearance of the Minister of Commission for Foreign Affairs of the Chamber to inform on the evolution of the Western Sahara situation in *Actividades, textos y Documentos de la Política Exterior Española*, 1994, p. 340., and *B.O.C.G.* June 1, 1994. Spain was member of the SC during the period between

In his next report (12 July 1994)[512], the Secretary General proposed for the first time a date (1 of October 1994) for the commencement of the transitional period, postponed indefinitely since the date it should have been started (6 of September 1991), and another for holding the referendum (14 of February 1995). In accordance with these dates, the Secretary General proposed the reduction of the presence of Moroccan troops in the territory to the minimum accepted by this State (65,000 soldiers) before 31 of December 1994, and the MINURSO would be in charge of supervising the cantonment of the troops.

These factors were again analysed by the Secretary General in his report of 5 of November 1994[513], which again stressed the question of the functions of the civil police, which are, basically, the following:

> "a) To ensure tranquillity and maintain law and order in the vicinity of, and at, voter registration offices and polling stations, to ensure that no person is denied entry for the purposes of registration or voting and, when specifically so ordered, to maintain order at other locations where activities in connection with the referendum, under MINURSO auspices or authority, are taking place;
>
> b) To monitor the activities of the existing police forces so as to ensure that they are acting in strict accordance with the Settlement Plan and the current Implementation Plan, which is intended to secure the organization of a free and fair referendum without military or administrative constraints and to prevent any possibility of intimidation or interference from any quarter".

The Secretary General pointed out that, since, in compliance with the stipulations of Resolution 907 (1994) of the Security Council, the work of the Identification Commission began previous to the commencement of the transitional period (the operation for the identification and registration of potential voters began on 28 of August 1994), although the fact that the transitional period had not yet begun, from that time, the MINURSO assumed the functions stated in paragraph a). This is practically the first real step of the MINURSO carrying out more important functions than the simple

---

January 1, 1993 and December 31, 1994, period in which Morocco was also a non-permanent member of the Council. *Cfr.* also *Actividades, textos y Documentos de la Política Exterior Española*, 1994, p. 412, and *B.O.C.G.* September 13, 1994.
[512] *Cfr. ORSC:* S/1994/819.
[513] *ORSC:* S/1994/1257, November 5, 1994.

Chapter VI

verification of the ceasefire. At that time, the impression was that the Peace Plan was finally being put into action, given that until then the intervention of the MINURSO had been very limited. As we shall see below, although the deployment of the MINURSO was not nor has been really efficient, at this time there were renewed expectations regarding the process. The Secretary General announced the impossibility to conclude the process on the dates arranged in his previous report, postponing the arrangement of new dates for time when the process is more advanced, which led to the Security Council stating that "it was concerned about the slow speed of the identification process", and encouraged the parties to collaborate with the MINURSO in order to avoid further unjustified delays[514].

As was mentioned, the identification process finally started on August 28[515], but it was soon evident that it was impossible to respect the proposed dates. In addition, the Secretary General insisted on his intention, already announced in a previous report, to present the parties with a code of conduct.

The suspension of the identification process, provoked by the floods that had occurred in Tinduf, was taken advantage of by Morocco in order to carry out an operation aimed at igniting the process. The Secretary General referred to this when he pointed out that "in the second half of October, there was a flood of completed application forms"[516], which officially amounted to 232,000. Of these, 180,000 were sent by the Government of Morocco, 150,000 of which dated from the day of the "last minute flood of applications", referred to in the report. This would kill the identification process due to the evident difficulties involved in examining 180,000 new applicants and the attitude adopted by the Secretary General, who radically changed his opinion in less than four months, passing from establishing the date of the referendum for 14 of February 1995 to considering that "many months will be required to make sufficient progress in the identification process to be close to determining a date for the referendum". In order to speed up the process, the number of identification centres was increased and, logically, so too were the costs associated with the MINURSO, a consideration recorded in the report of the Secretary General of 14 of December 1994[517], in which the Secretary General also referred to his visit to the territory with his new Special Representative for Western Sahara, Erik Jensen[518]. Finally, he proposed a

---

[514] ORSC: S/PRST/1994/67, November 15, 1994.
[515] Report of SG November 5, 1994. ORSC: S/1994/1257, par. 9.
[516] *Ibid.*, par. 15.
[517] *Cfr.* ORSC: S/1994/1420.
[518] Erik Jensen had been head of the Identification Commission until the moment of his appointment as new Special Representative of the SG (June de 1995).

further extension of the mandate of the MINURSO, and another date for holding the referendum, which would take place in October 1995[519].

Resolution 973 (1995) of the Security Council[520], after reiterating that the main objective of the UN was the holding "without further delay" of a "free, regular and impartial" referendum on self-determination in the territory, in accordance with the Peace Plan approved by the two parties, and "welcoming" the commencement of the process for the identification of electors, it decided to extend the mandate of the MINURSO until May 31, "on the basis of a further report from the Secretary General and in the light of progress achieved towards the holding of the referendum and the implementation of the Settlement Plan", an extension which would come about through Resolutions 995 (1995)[521], 1002 (1995), 1033 (1995) and 1042 (1996). This last Resolution extended the mandate of the MINURSO in order to continue with the efforts involved in the preparation of the referendum, although it requested of the Secretary General that in the event that there is no significant progress in the voter identification process he proposes a slow withdrawal of

---

[519] *Cfr. ORSC*: S/1994/1420, par. 22.

[520] Resolution 973 (1995) was approved by the SC January 13, 1995.

[521] Resolution 995 (1995) of the SC extended the mandate of the MINURSO to June 30, 1995 and decided to send a SC Mission to the Territory. The results of this mission are described in the Report of the Mission Visit of the SC, of June 21, 1995 (*ORSC*: S/1995/498, and SC/6062 -Press Release Security Council-, June 30, 1995), though due to the fact that the questions analysed are related to the census, its analyse corresponds to the next chapter of this work. The mentioned Resolution was approved by the SC on May 26, 1995, in a tense situation, because on May 11, 1995, during a small demonstration in favour of the independence of Sahara that took place in El Aaiún, eight Saharan were arrested, and later convicted by a Military Court (Judgment June 21) to sentences of up to 20 years of prison for "attack to foreign security of the State" (*El País*, July 10, 1995). Nevertheless, because of the international press pressure, Hassan II reduced the sentence to a year. This reduction was later a grace petition from the families of the arrested, that had to declare publicly that they had been "victims of propaganda cheatings" (CESSOU, S., PRAZ, H. (1995). The decision of King Hassan II was not considered enough by the European Parliament, which in a Resolution, approved on July 14, asked for the immediate liberation of the eight Saharans. The European Parliament had already pronounced itself on other occasions against arbitrary arrests in occupied territories by Morocco (*cfr*. Resolution December 17, 1987, *OJEU*, num. C 13/102, January 18, 1988, p. 102; Resolution February 15, 1990, *OJEU*, num. C/68/143-144, March 19, 1990, Resolution October 11, 1990, *OJEU*, num. 284/132, November 12, 1990; Resolution B3-1443, 1452 and 1476/92, October 29, 1992, *OJEU* num. C 305/153, November 23, 1992; and Resolution B3-0699, 0711 and 0746/93, May 27, 1993, *OJEU*, num. C 176/158, June 28, 1993). This last resolution states that Morocco has "made disappear" during the last fifteen years (1978-1993) more than a thousand Saharan, and keeping another five hundred arrested secretly (sections C y D).

the MINURSO, in accordance with the proposal made by the Secretary General to the Security Council in his report of 19 of January 1996[522].

As was pointed out above, since the report of Butros Gali of 10 of March 1994, there was a feeling of pessimism about the resolution of the conflict, and attention was drawn to the dangerous statement, which until then was unknown in the policies of the UN, that a resolution to the conflict could be achieved without the approval of the two parties. However, the subsequent report of the Secretary General of 19 of May 1995 on the Settlement Plan did not mention this possibility. It was surprising that the Secretary General changed his position in this report, and with an optimism which was apparently groundless, considering the slow pace of the identification process[523] and the fact that the question of the interpretation of the identification criteria were still pending agreement, he concluded that, despite this, the process would continue, and the referendum would be possible if both parties collaborated, at the beginning of 1996.

In his report of 8 of September 1995[524], the Secretary General pointed out that he sent the parties the *Code of Conduct*, and that both disagreed with its content[525]. As concerns the civil unit, the Secretary General referred to the functions attributed to it for the transitory period and the need for its presence in order to ensure the freedom of the persons who present themselves at the identification centre in order to "ensure that no one can resort to intimidation or interfere in the referendum process". Finally, the Secretary General requested another extension of the mandate of the MINURSO, until 31 of January 1996, although, on this occasion, he pointed out that, in the event that the conditions required for the commencement of the transitory period were

---

[522] *ORSC*: S/1996/43. The following reports of the SG (March 30, 1995, *ORSC*: S/1995/240 and May 19, 1995, *ORSC*: S/1995/404) bring no novelty to the MINURSO and its functions. Only to the fields of costs of the operation (the calculation of the extra cost of the operation figure in the document *ORSC*: S/1995/240/Add.1), insisting the second that the military mandate of the MINURSO is limited to verification of the cease-fire, maintaining the relative to the civil police in the terms of prior reports, delaying once again the date of the referendum to January 1996 (*Ibid.*, par. 39).

[523] On May 15, 1995 the identification of 44,4% (12.819 from a total of 28.831) of the persons that have to be identified in the camps next to Tinduf, and of 28,1% (23.032 from a total of 81.855) of the population centres of the Territory. *ORGA*: Report of SG, S/1995/404, May 19, 1995, that confirms, practically in all its extent, on March 30 of the same year.

[524] *Cfr. ORSC*: S/1995/779

[525] Though the Code of Conduct of the SG was never published, Zoubir and Pazzanita state that it contained an implicit recognition of the Moroccan authority over the Territory. *Cfr.* ZOUBIR, Y. H., PAZZANITA, A. G. (1995): 628.

not met, he would present for the consideration of the Security Council "different options, including the possibility of the withdrawal of the MINURSO".

Resolution 1017 (1995) of the Security Council[526] continued the general trend established by the previous resolutions, and extended the mandate of the MINURSO again (until 31 of January 1996), although it expressly included the possibility stipulated by the Secretary General for a withdrawal of the MINURSO from the territory, in the light of the slowness of the identification process. The Secretary General was also asked to reduce the cost of functioning of the MINURSO[527].

Among the little progress made in the process at the end of the mandate of Butros Gali was the liberation of 186 Moroccan prisoners of war by the POLISARIO Front[528] and another failed attempt to reach an agreement on the Code of Conduct which, as was mentioned above had been proposed by the Secretary General and rejected by both parties, was revised and sent to them again.

3.2.5. *The report of May 8, 1996: the dismantling of the MINURSO*

The process received another hard blow with the report of the Secretary General of 8 of May 1996[529], in which the Secretary General highlights the fact that, despite having identified 60,000 people and more than 77,000 have been convened, 156,924 applicants remain to be identified. Taking into account the frustrated attempts to overcome the problems involved in the identification process being carried out by the Special Representative, the Secretary General himself, the Special Mission of the Security Council, the Special Envoy and the independent jurist, Emmanuel Roucounas, and since, in his opinion, "the required willingness does not exist to give MINURSO the cooperation needed for it to resume and complete the identification process

---

[526] *ORSC:* Resolution 1017 (1995) of SC approved September 22, 1995.

[527] The Report of SG of November 24, 1995 (*ORSC:* S/1995/986, November 24, 1995), reiterates the approach of the prior report regarding the possibility that the MINURSO should leave the Territory, and explains questions relating the problems during the identification process, so Resolution 1033 (1995), December 19 1995, that reports nothing new on the process, reiterates the possibility that MINURSO should withdraw from the territory.

[528] Report of SG, January 19, 1996 (*ORSC:* S/1996/43), in which the visit of a Mission, headed by the Vice Secretary General of the Organization and the Special Representative of the SG for Western Sahara, is described. After the visit, on November 19, 1995, some of these prisoners were liberated.

[529] *ORSC:* S/1996/343.

within a reasonable period of time", he felt obliged "to recommend that the identification process be suspended until such time as both parties provide convincing evidence that they are committed to resuming and completing it without further obstacles".

As a consequence of these, the Secretary General proposed the withdrawal of most of the personnel of the identification centres "with the exception of a few who will be required to ensure the orderly closure of the remaining centres and the storage of the identification data as is appropriate". He also proposed the withdrawal of the civil police "except for a small number of officers to maintain contacts with the authorities on both sides and to plan for eventual resumption of the identification process", thus reducing the personnel of the military component of the MINURSO by 20%.

In the opinion of the Secretary General, this did not entail the end of the Peace Plan as "the United Nations cannot abandon its responsibilities", so he proposed to maintain "a political office, headed by my Acting Special Representative and staffed by a small number of political officers", which would be located in El Aaiún, with a liaison office in Tinduf. The Secretary General thus proposed to the Security Council that the mandate of the MINURSO be extended for a period of six months.

Resolution 1056 (1996) of the Security Council[530] followed the recommendations of the Secretary General to the letter and decided to suspend the identification process "until such time as both parties provide convincing evidence that they are committed to resuming and completing it without further obstacles", to reduce the components of the military unit by 20%, to maintain a political office, in the terms referred to in the proposal of the Secretary General, and to extend the mandate of the MINURSO until 30 of November 1996.

On 20 of August 1996 the Secretary General submitted another report to the Security Council[531] in which he explained the permanent efforts of his Special Representative, in command of the political office referred to in Resolution 1056 (1996) of the Security Council, to make progress with the negotiations in order to get the process moving. Moreover, he informed of the closure of the offices in Bojador, Dahla, Smara, El Aaiún and Nouadhibou, and the transfer of records to the offices of the UN in Geneva. He also insisted that the task of the MINURSO be limited to the verification of the ceasefire. The conclusion of the report was pessimistic as regards the possibility of renewing the identification process in the short term, which would not change

---

[530] *ORSC:* Resolution 1056 of the SC was approved unanimously May 29, 1996.
[531] *ORSC:* S/1996/674.

substantially in the following report, in which he informed on the liberation of 66 prisoners of war of the POLISARIO Front on 31 of October 1996[532]. Despite this, he considered that it was necessary to maintain the MINURSO and he proposed the extension of its mandate until 31 of May 1997, which would be approved by Resolution 1084 (1996) of the Security Council[533].

3.3 The Kofi Annan Phase: the conclusion of the process of identification and the abandonment of the Peace Plan

3.3.1. The Report of 27 of February 1997: the unblocking of the process

Faced with the stagnation of the process after the withdrawal of a large number of personnel of the MINURSO, the appointment of Kofi Annan as the new Secretary General of the United Nations, after a bitter struggle carried out by the United States against the renewal of Butros Gali to the post, the latter accused by the United States of causing many of the problems of the UN, including those of Western Sahara[534], led to progress being made in the process. In his report of 27 of February 1997[535] and using an approach that was much more optimistic than his predecessor, the Secretary General proposed three grand areas concerning the feasibility of the conclusion of the Western Sahara conflict:

"a) Can the Settlement Plan be implemented in its present form?

---

[532] Report of SG of November 5, 1996. *ORSC:* S/1996/913.

[533] *ORSC:* Resolution 1084 (1996) of the SC approved November 27,1996.

[534] Mistrust of representation of the POLISARIO Front are similar to that of USA, and was confirmed when after the take over of the mandate in the General Secretary, Butros Gali was named General Secretary of French speaking countries, during the seventh Conference of French speaking countries, that took place in Hanoi, in November 1997. During this Conference the President of Congo, Laurent Kabila, decided to abandon the Summit, considering that "French speaking extended neo-colonialism". This is precisely the main reason of the American interest of his dismissal and the worry of the POLISARIO Front for his near approach to French thesis (*cfr. El País,* November 17, 1997). In this sense, *cfr.* the statement of Jarat Chopra against Butros Gali becoming General Secretary of the United Nations, and the questioning of whether consecutive interpretations of the SG in matters relating census criteria are or are not among the competences of the SG (*cfr.* CHOPRA, J., *An Agenda for Western Sahara,* Intervention before the *International Association of Lawyers for Western Sahara,* Barcelona, November de 1996. *Internet: http://www.arso.org//Chopra2-96.htm*).

[535] *ORSC:* S/1997/166.

b) If not, are there adjustments to the Settlement Plan, acceptable to both parties, which would make it implementable?

c) If not, are there other ways by which the international community could help the parties resolve their conflict?"

Although the approach is more feasible than its predecessor, the reference to "other means" of resolving the conflict is worrying as they would be parallel to the legal route already taken. This thus refers to the political route, which would be shortly launched by James Baker. The report of the Secretary General, as expected, was met without difficulty with the approval of the Security Council[536].

3.3.2. James Baker, Special Envoy of the Secretary General

In his following report[537], the Secretary General made it known how he was going to modify the policy of the United Nations in this question. The new Secretary General created a new post, which, together with the Special Representative, would have specific weight in the process. This was the Special Envoy of the Secretary General for Western Sahara, an appointment which, not by chance, was given to the former Secretary of State of the United States, James Baker, the man who would negotiate the end of the Cold War, organize the coalition against Iraq after the invasion of Kuwait, and would sit Palestinians and Israelis at the negotiation table, and he was asked "to assess the implementability of the plan, to examine ways of improving the chances of resuming its implementation in the near future and, if there were none, to advise me on other possible ways of moving the peace process forward". In addition, and in order to provide margin for manoeuvre for the new post, the Secretary General proposed an extension of the MINURSO, in the minimum conditions referred to in previous reports, until 30 of September 1997. Resolutions 1108 (1997), of 22 of May, and 1131 (1997), of 29 of September 1997, of the Security Council would confirm the petitions of the Secretary General.

During his work, James Baker commenced a number of visits to the countries considered to be "involved and interested", which resulted in direct conversations held by the parties in Lisbon, London and Houston, which would manage to unblock the identification process. The Special Envoy called

---

[536] *ORSC*: S/PRST/1997/16, of March 19, 1997.
[537] Report to SC May 5, 1997 (*ORSC*: S/1997/358).

the parties to London, where he met each one separately, and, after concluding that there was a need for the following round of conversations to be held directly between the parties, the bases for the future negotiations were established. As a starting point, he clarified that the conversations would be of a private nature, and would not constitute an international conference, that Mauritania and Algeria would be informed of this, "as observers", but that they would intervene in the negotiations "as regards the questions which directly affect them" and that, in the course of the negotiations, he would act as mediator, making specific proposals to solve the differences which might arise, although he would not have the capacity to impose solutions nor to veto any agreements[538].

3.3. The Agreements of London, Lisbon and Houston

In accordance with these premises, the first direct meetings were held in Lisbon (23 June), where the main question concerning the drawing up of the census was addressed. Faced with the differences between the positions of both parties, Baker made a specific proposal in order to make progress in the negotiations and, as the representatives of the parties expressed that they needed to consult their respective Governments, the first round of negotiations was suspended, and the parties undertook to respond within a period of forty-eight hours. The result of this response was another convening of conversations to take place in London.

In London, an agreement was reached on questions related with identification, which will be analysed in the following Chapter, and the preparations for the return of the refugees, as well as the commitment of the parties to accept the provisions of the Settlement Plan as concerns the reduction and the confining of Moroccan forces during the transitional period.

During the third round of negotiations held again in Lisbon, questions related to the confining of troops was addressed[539], together with the releasing of prisoners of war and Western Saharan political prisoners, reaching agreement on the questions. Moreover, the Special Envoy proposed that the

---

[538] Report of SG of September 24, 1997 (*ORSC*: S/1997/742, par. 5 and 6).

[539] The agreement arranged that Moroccan troops would be confined in the same terms as established in the Settlement plan and that the forces of the POLISARIO Front would do the same in locations and in the number determined by the Representative of the SG (according to the Settlement Plan) under the condition that, not more than 2,000 should be confined in the territory East of the sand wall of the Western Sahara (so to say, "in the occupied areas"), and more than 300 persons in Mauritanian territory. The rest of the POLISARIO Front forces should be confined in Algerian territory (*ORSC*: S/1997/742, Annex II, I, par. 2).

negotiations would include a code of conduct project for the referendum campaign, but given that this was not included in the agenda and as Morocco stated that it did not have the experts required to address this question, the negotiations were postponed until September in Houston.

Finally, in Houston an agreement was reached on the agreement on the code of conduct that would govern the referendum campaign, another on the role that the United Nations must play in the transitional period, and finally a number of practical measures were agreed to in order to renew the identification process. As regards the code of conduct, "drafted and dictated by the Special Representative of the Secretary General after holding consultations with the two parties", the most important aspects are the following:

- "Sole and exclusive authority over all matters relating to the referendum, including its organization and conduct, shall be vested in the United Nations", and the Special Representative must exercise this power. Again we must draw attention to the practically all embracing power of the Special Representative[540], who will also establish the date of commencement of the referendum campaign, "at such time as he is satisfied that all conditions are met for a free and fair campaign".
- As well as prohibiting, as is logical, any type of intimidation and coercion, the agreement includes what, in another process, could be considered to be an "unusual precaution", and points out that,

> "It is understood that, apart from those returning under the auspices of UNCHR in accordance with the Settlement Plan, no party shall encourage, support or facilitate the transfer or movement of people in substantial number into the Territory without the express authority of the Special Representative".

It is significant that "it is understood" must be expressly mentioned in the text of the agreement. Obviously this refers implicitly to the "Second Green March" organized by Morocco during the peace process and, in our opinion, it constitutes an unfortunately late problem, which must be stopped by the United Nations at the time they occur in order to prevent any aggravation.

In addition, the agreements refer to the flags that may fly in the Territory during the campaign. The text states that in the activities related to the referendum, and in the places where these are held, "No national colours or flags, other than the UN flag, shall be displayed in any campaign activities or locations. Nor shall any national colours or flags be displayed except those that

---

[540] *ORSC*: S/1997/742, Annex II, II, par. 1.

were on government buildings as at 14 September 1997". In the course of the negotiations, the POLISARIO Front was obliged to cede in this question since the only flag that should be flown in the territory was the flag of the United Nations. It is plain to see that the official buildings flying the flag of Morocco could continue to do so, and this might condition the opinion of many of the inhabitants who would consider that the option put forward in the referendum was not real. Obviously, this was not the best way to demonstrate the impartiality of the referendum and could give the impression that the impartiality of the United Nations was in doubt.

Furthermore, as it had been agreed in the first conversations that none of the partial agreements which might be adopted in the course of the negotiations would come into force until a definitive agreement had been reached regarding all the issues pending, on the conclusion of the negotiations in Houston, the previous agreements of Lisbon and London would come into force.

In his report of 24 of September 1997, the Secretary General stated that following his consideration of the three issues in his first report, the parties had clearly chosen the Settlement Plan, so he was obliged to request the reactivation of the MINURSO in the territory, when only a few months had elapsed from the commencement of its dismantling. Thus, he had to ask the Security Council that the identification registers which had been forwarded to the United Nations Office in Geneva in 1996 be transferred to the MINURSO centres in El Aaiún and Tinduf, and that the mandate of the MINURSO be extended until 20 of April of 1998 in order to be able to address the identification tasks[541]. He also had to request the supply of the corresponding budget in order to be able "to have the identification centres restored"[542]. At that time in the conflict, it was evident that the appointment of Annan as the Secretary General had had the effect of unblocking the identification process, although alongside these lights were gradually appearing new shadows.

As discussed below, and although Kofi Annan had managed to unblock the identification process, he was then already aware that Morocco would end up abandoning the Peace Plan, so that in parallel with the resumption of the peace process, James Baker would be charged with finding a political solution to the conflict or in other words, with leaving the referendum in search of a solution outside of International law. Although, as we shall see in the following pages, the intervention of the Secretary General lead to the creation of a census for the referendum, the withdrawal of the Peace Plan and the fact that it was to

---

[541] *Cfr.* ORSC: S/1997/742, par. 30 and 31.
[542] Report of SG of November 13, 1997 (ORSC: S/1997/882, par. 5).

continue to develop within the framework of Chapter VI of the Charter meant that the peace process was at a dead end, which is where today we find the MINURSO. Ban Ki-Moon, the Secretary General of the UN since 1 January 2007 has barely managed to revive the process, meaning that the activity of the MINURSO has become a relic of the past.

3.4. Lights and shadows of the MINURSO

In a very brief summary, one can say that the most significant achievement of the MINURSO has been, after a very long process in which it was necessary to overcome obstacles which at times appeared insurmountable, the drawing-up of a census for a referendum, the principal mission for which it was created. To analyse this question, we are going to dedicate the final chapter of this work, in which it will be possible to see how, despite significant limits in its mandate, the MINURSO managed to get that far.

Its greatest failure was as consequence of the limitations to its mandate, established by the Security Council, and its incapacity to, in line with Chapter VII of the Charter, impose on the parties the holding of a referendum of self-determination. But it has also been a consequence of the not fair intervention of the Secretary General and the limitations that the MINURSO has placed on itself.

The role played by those who have occupied the post of Secretary General throughout the peace process has been as relevant as it has been negative, in that the peace process has suffered from successive stoppages and revivals, depending on the person holding the post. So, if in some moments everything appeared to suggest that the process was on track (1988, 1991), within months the outlook would radically change and when the process appeared to be at a dead end (1993, 1997) it arose from its own ashes. The successive Secretaries General have significantly shaped the development of the conflict, at times verging on crossing the line of what is permitted by the UN Charter.

It is true that MINURSO has been limited by the content of its mandate, but it also always interpreted too restrictively the powers that it had been conferred, renouncing some of the functions which, by virtue of its very raison d'être, correspond to it. It practically limited itself to the simple verification of the cease-fire and the finding of sporadic and minor violations of some aspects of the agreement (such as movements of troops, live ammunition practice etc.), openly favouring the Moroccan pretensions to the extent that, on too many occasions, the occupying State has been seen by it as more of an ally than an impartial observer. Since the launch of the process, both the Secretary General and, although with notable exceptions, his successive Special Representatives, have shamelessly positioned themselves on the Moroccan side. For example, we recall the passivity of the MINURSO and the Security Council itself during the development of, as referred to by the Secretary General himself, the "Second Green March", which saw the massive transfer of Moroccan settlers into the territory. Although this was publically acknowledged and justified by Morocco, although it constitutes a violation not only of the Settlement Plan but also of the IV Geneva Convention and although it provoked the resignation of the Special Representative of the Secretary General, Johannes Manz[543], it did not have any major consequences and the Secretary General did no more than "point out the dangers involved in such action", as if the movement of thousands of people from the occupying State to the occupied territory was a minor issue.

The limitations imposed on the functions of the Organization by the will of permanent members of the Security Council, which, as highlighted by the Secretary General himself[544], are more obvious as regards its peace-keeping operations than other ambits of its activity, should not serve to exempt the Organization from responsibility in the Sahrawi conflict given that the Secretary General could compensate for some of these short comings with his considerable powers. The MINURSO mandate provided for the entry into force of the transitional period from the moment that the cease-fire was put into practice. This cease fire was implemented on 6 September 1991, but the start of the transitional period, during which the operational capacity of MINURSO is much larger and it is even competent to derogate from Moroccan laws which, according to the Special Representative of the Secretary General, prevent the holding of a referendum in free conditions, has been repeatedly postponed at the request of the Secretary General. The facts show that when the Secretary General has decided to take a step towards the implementation of specific questions contained in the Peace Plan which have been held up by Moroccan obstructionist action, progress has been made in the process. Thus, for example, using one of his powers, the Secretary General

---

[543] In this sense, Johannes Manz lamented the movement of approximately 40,000 people into the Territory, "despite the fact that he had made very clear recommendations (to King Hassan II) on this matter". The Special Representative of the Secretary General stated: "the movement of non-identified people within the Territory, in the so called 'Second Green March' constitutes, in my view, a violation of the spirit, if not the exact words of the Peace Plan" (cfr. HUMAN RIGHTS WATCH, "Western Sahara", *Human Rights Watch Middle East*, vol 7, no 7, October 1995, p43)

[544] Report of the Secretary General entitled "Supplement to 'a Peace Programme': a document on the position of the Secretary General on the occasion of the fiftieth anniversary of the UN" (ORGA: A/50/60 and ORSC: S/1995/1, of 25, January, 1995)

decided that, given that for the satisfaction of Resolution 907 (1994) of the Security Council the work of the Identification Commission would begin before the transitional period and *despite the fact that this transitional period had not begun, the MINURSO would assume* from that moment some of the functions of the civil police unit, specifically those functions related to the obligation

> "To ensure that the peace and law and order is maintained in voter inscription offices, in voting centres and in their vicinity to guarantee that there is no obstruction to any person who wants to vote or register, and, when so ordered, to maintain order in those places where activities related with the referendum under the auspices or authority of the MINURSO are taking place"[545]

As mentioned above, amongst the functions of the Special Representative can be found the power to adopt necessary measures to ensure that potential voters have free access to identification centres. This and other functions, the most basic in order to make a census, were postponed until the commencement of the transitional period[546] …which never occurred. Thus, until the conclusion of the identification process, the functions of the MINURSO police were linked to those of the Identification Commission, maintaining their presence twenty-four hours a day in the identification centres but acting strictly within the buildings where they were located, which facilitated the Moroccan police in restricting access to potential voters since the police could freely control and intimidate candidates to be included in the

---

[545] *ORSC:* S/1994/1257, of 5, November, 1994

[546] The MINURSO chose to get involved in the identification process as little as possible, abandoning part of its control over the process by deciding that it should be the parties themselves who should be charged with the distribution and collection of applications from candidates to be registered on the census, admitting an exceptional case of those applicants residing in Mauritania (*cfr.* HUMAN RIGHTS WATCH, "Western Sahara", Middle East, vol. 7, no. 7, October 1995, p24), a decision which deserved the labelling of "very foolish" given to it by the then Vice-president of the MINURSO Identification Commission, Frank Ruddy (*Review of United Nations Operations and Peacekeeping*, 25, January, 1995, *op. cit.*). As Ruddy also lamented, in Moroccan occupied territories "only those people who have been accredited by Moroccan authorities may enter MINURSO Identification Centres or UN Offices"; although those who were excluded from the process for this reason still had the possibility of going to any of the MINURSO offices in the Territory, this was highly unlikely if you consider the presence of the Moroccan military who could have prevented their access, as the Under-Secretary General for Internal Security Services (*ORGA:* A/49/884, para. 12)

census[547]. Moreover, despite the cease-fire, the freedom of expression and assembly, guaranteed by, *inter alia*, Articles 19 and 22 of the International Covenant on Social and Political Rights of 1966, still did not exist in the territories occupied by Morocco[548]. The indefinite postponement of the commencement of the transitional period has prevented the UN from exercising all of the powers attributed to it in the Settlement Plan, in the sense that from the start of the identification process on 28 August, 1994, the MINURSO became "an instrument of Moroccan domination of the identification process", leaving the freedom of movement of the members of the territory restricted and monitored[549].

The Implementation Plan provided that during the referendum the Special Representative should "guarantee the freedom of movement, the security of the population, the freedom of expression, assembly and press" and "allow the organization and holding of political meetings, assemblies, rallies and marches" and should have "exclusive authority in all UN premises in relation with the referendum and in its surrounding area, such as in the voter registration offices and polling stations (…)". However, given that the transitional period has not been implemented, all of these eventualities have been ignored. As reported by Ruddy, the Moroccan Government "always denied the MINURSO permission to buy space in Moroccan newspapers or on the radio to advise people about registering to vote and participating in the

---

[547] *Cfr.* HUMAN RIGHTS WATCH, *"Western Sahara"*, op. cit., p35. Ruddy signalled, in front of the US Congress, that Moroccan "journalists" photographed all the Sahrawis appeared to apply for inscription in the electoral census, pressuring in this way not only those who appeared, but also those who subsequently passed through the Identification Centres. Those people who appeared before the Commission were required to hand in a register receipt to be redeemed for a credential to vote. In this situation, many people were forced to give these receipts to the Moroccan police leaving the possibility open for a person other than the registered voter to obtain a credential to vote (*Cfr.* RUDDY, F, *Review of United Nations Operations and Peacekeeping*, Statement before the Subcommittee on the Departments of Commerce, Justice and State, The Judiciary and Related Agencies, 25, January, 1995)

[548] There are numerous reports to this regard by *Amnesty International*, for example *cfr.* AMNESTY INTERNATIONAL, *Continuing Arrests, "disappearances" and Restrictions on Freedom of Movement, Expression and Movement in Western Sahara*, London, A.I. Index MDE 29/03/93, February 1993, p.2; also from the same organization *Breaking the Wall of Silence: The Disappearance in Morocco*, London, A.I. Index MDE 29/01/93, April, 1993.

[549] Ruddy signals that Moroccan police control over the MINURSO even involved phone tapping, the interception of mail and even the searching of personal rooms (RUDDY, F, *Review of the United Nations Operations and Peacekeeping*, statement before the Subcommittee on the Departments of Commerce, Justice and State, the Judiciary and Related Agencies, 25 January 1995).

CHAPTER VI

identification process (...), controlled access to voter identification centres" and also ordered the withdrawal of the UN flag from the Identification Centre in El Aaiún the evening before the commencement of the identification process. Morocco had insisted throughout the negotiations for the Code of Conduct that neither the Sahrawi flag nor any distinctive symbol of Sahrawi national identity could be flown during the transitional period, so as not to give the electorate the impression that the status of the land is immovable.

Despite the severe shortcomings in the MINURSO operation and despite the existing difficulties one must highlight and celebrate its impeccable work in the preparation of the census, which has revealed at least two things: the first is the manipulation of the Plan by Morocco, which used the process not as an end to get to the referendum, but instead a means of avoiding it, and secondly when the Security Council has allowed it to work, attributing it real functions, and in spite of pressures of all kinds to which it has been subjected, it was able to perform with absolute rigor. As discussed below, and despite the allegations by Morocco of technical difficulties which will frustrate the holding of the referendum, the fact is that if the Security Council decided to implement it, the exercise of the Sahrawi people of their right to self-determination would be made. Unfortunately since the completion of the preparations of the census, in light of Morocco's withdrawal from the peace process, the functions of the MINURSO have declined so far as to becoming a purely token presence in the territory; the MINURSO has the dubious record of being the only peacekeeping operation in effect not to have competences relating to the protection of human rights.

Finally, regarding the position of MINURSO in relation to this last issue, the human rights violations in the territory, one must criticise the attitude of MINURSO's responsible parties, who by using as an excuse the limits of the mandate approved by the Security Council, whereby the French veto prevents any extension of its functions, pretend to ignore that, for the mere reason of being a peace-keeping operation, the monitoring of respect for human rights is one of its functions[550]. In this regard, and to conclude this Chapter VI, we must

---

[550] "International human rights law is an integral part of the normative framework for United Nations peacekeeping operations. The Universal Declaration of Human Rights, which sets the cornerstone of international human rights standards, emphasizes that human rights and fundamental freedoms are universal and guaranteed to everybody. United Nations peacekeeping operations should be conducted in full respect of human rights and should seek to advance human rights through the implementation of their mandates (...) They must be able to recognize human rights violations or abuse, and be prepared to respond appropriately within the limits of their mandate and their competence"

remember what the Secretary General stated years before (1993): "While MINURSO's current military mandate is strictly limited to the monitoring and verification of the ceasefire, *MINURSO, as a United Nations mission, could not be a silent witness to conduct that might infringe the human rights of the civilian population*"[551].

(*Peacekeeping Best Practices Section. Division of Policy, Evaluation and Training. Department of Peacekeeping Operations.* United Nations Secretariat, 2010, pages 14-15)

[551] ORSC: S/25170, par. 25 (stressed characters by author).

CHAPTER VII

THE PEACE PLAN (II). THE PROBLEM OF CONSULTING THE POPULATION

1. **The Waldheim phase. The Report of the Visiting Mission of October 10, 1975**

The first text of reference when examining the Peace Plan must be the *Report of the Visiting Mission* of the United Nations, which, in compliance with Resolution 3292 (XXIX), travelled throughout the territory in 1975. At the time, this document correctly forecast the most important difficulties involved in the organization of the when it stated that,

> "It is evident from the above that, if the Territory were to become independent, the criteria for determining nationality would be very important. Likewise, problems would arise in determining eligibility to participate in a referendum".

In this regard, it pointed out that, in the opinion of the administering Power and of the population of the territory, those who belonged to a family group in the territory and whose identification would not be excessively complicated should have the right to participate in a referendum since,

> "All the members of such groups are known to each other and that the authenticity of a claim to belong to a family group can be verified by the sheiks and notables of that group in consultation with their members"[552].

The report[553] also pointed out that, as a previous question to any approach to consulting the population, that,

> "If it is to be truly an expression of the opinion of the majority, any consultation of any nature whatsoever organized in the territory must be based on the *participation of all the Western Saharans indigenous to the Territory*. Therefore, it is important to

---

[552] *ORGA*: A/10023/Add.5, par. 157 and 158.
[553] *ORGA*: A/10023/Rev. 1, Volume III, Chapter XIII, annex

determine those who are and those who are not indigenous to the Territory".

In addition, it stated that, if the solution to the conflict were to be lasting and permit peace in the region, any settlement of the situation "must carried out with the agreement and the participation of all the parties involved and concerned". To this end, the decolonization "must take into account the wishes and aspirations of all the Western Saharan population in the territory, including those who now live abroad as political exiles or refugees". Despite the fact that the participation of the parties involved and concerned as regards achieving the agreement was considered to be necessary, as pointed out by the Cuban representative of the Visiting Mission, Marta Jiménez Martínez "the exercise of this right cannot be limited, much less subordinated to the interests of other nations".

In order to achieve these objectives, the so-called "Parties involved and interested" gave a number of *previous conditions* for the referendum so that it might be carried out in a climate of freedom:
- The withdrawal of the armed forces and the Spanish administration;
- The return of the political exiles and the refugees, and
- A Transitional Period, during which the United Nations would be present and would assume responsibility for the administration and the maintenance of peace and order in the territory.

As regards the *modalities of the referendum*, the report we refer to is not very clear as it only pointed out that these,

> "Should be drafted by a new Visiting Mission designated by the Secretary General of the United Nations in close cooperation with the administering Power and the other parties involved and concerned ".

The positions of the parties involved in the conflict were as follows:
- Spain was in favour of carrying out a referendum in the terms of Resolution 1541 (XV): independence, association or integration, although the General Assembly should decide the text of the question;
- Morocco defended a "procedure for the transfer of administration" as was the case for the enclave of Ifni and, although it opposed the holding of a referendum, in the event that one were to be held, it would accept only one question, "Do you want to remain under the authority of Spain or to re-join Morocco?";
- The POLISARIO Front proposed to ask the voters, "Whether they wished to be free or to remain under Spanish rule".

- Algeria explained to the Mission that, regardless of the question which would finally be asked in a referendum, the main question consisted of verifying whether the population wanted to be freed from the yoke of colonization and that, on a second occasion, once the territory had free political institutions, the question of association or integration in another State could be asked.
- Finally, although Mauritania opposed the holding of a referendum on self-determination, since, the "situation had been tailored by the Spanish authorities so that a referendum could have only one result, that sought by the administering Power", so it proposed that, if there was a referendum, this would be based on universal adult suffrage or, "as in the case of West Irian, on the vote of their representatives". The question put to the population would have to be proposed by the organ in charge of making the census, "taking into account the objective facts of the situation and the need to respect the national unity and territorial integrity of States".

In the light of these positions, it was not difficult to deduce where the problems would arise in a theoretical referendum: Morocco would refuse to accept the possibility of asking the Western Saharan electorate about the "third option", namely, the independence of the territory, and Mauritania proposed the method used in Western Irian as an example for the resolution of the conflict, and, as we pointed out above, this constituted the conflict in which the impartiality of the United Nations was most called into question throughout the whole decolonization process.

2. The Pérez de Cuéllar phase

2.1. The Settlement Plan

Once the Visiting Mission had carried out its task in the territory, a long period of hopelessness began and the questions related to the census passed into the background, as the war prevented any debate on this question. It was not until November 1987 that a period of peace began in the territory and the question was again taken up seriously. At this time, a mission composed of representatives of the UN and of the OAU[554] visited the territory in order to

---

[554] Paragraph 6 of Resolution 42/78 of the GA, approved on December 4, 1987, takes note of the joint decision of the current Chairman of the Assembly of Heads of State and Government of the Organization of African Unity and the Secretary-General of the United Nations to send a technical mission to Western Sahara in order to collect the relevant technical information to assist them in discharging the mandate entrusted to them under General Assembly resolutions 40/50 and 41/16 and by the present resolution; Also, in the

carry out a technical evaluation of the conditions for holding the referendum. After holding successive meetings with King Hassan II[555] and with the representatives of the POLISARIO Front, the Secretary General of the UN, who was also visiting the territory, in his report of October 5, 1988[556] welcomed the fact that, on August 30, 1988, both parties to the conflict had agreed to the "*proposals for a peaceful settlement*" presented by the President of the OAU and the Secretary General of the UN. In the opinion of the Secretary General, these proposals, aimed at restoring peace in the region "provide a framework for the conclusion of a ceasefire and the establishment of conditions necessary for the organization of a credible referendum that will make it possible for the people of Western Sahara to exercise its inalienable right to self-determination without military or administrative constraints". As stated in the previous Chapter, the proposals established that their application be directed by a Special Representative of the Secretary General, assisted by civil, military and security units in order to comply with his organization and control functions, whose appointment was authorized by Resolution 621 (1988) of the Security Council.

On June 30, 1989, the Secretary General constituted the *Technical Commission*, whose main mission would be to specify, together with the parties, the conditions and the resources that would make it possible to implement the peace proposals agreed to on 30 August the previous year[557].

---

advisory opinion of the ICJ of October 16, 1975, it was referred to in a general way, noting that the decolonization process in Western Sahara envisaged by the General Assembly will respect the right of the population of Western Sahara to determine their future political status by their own freely expressed will, not mentioning any possible option (independence, association, integration in another State, or any other) between which the population should be able to choose (*CIJ, Recueil* 1975, p. 36, par. 70).

[555] King Hassan II, as noticed before, had already accepted the following commitment "the Secretary General has been assured of Morocco's full cooperation and support in his efforts. And has indicated that his country was fully prepared to see the United Nations entrusted with the responsibility for the organization and conduct of a referendum in the Territory through which the inhabitants could express their right to self-determination" (*RGA:* A/42/601, par. 26, October 1, 1987).

[556] *Cfr. ORGA:* A/43/680, October 5, 1988 (Annual report of the SG on the application of the implementation of the declaration of the granting of independence to colonial countries and peoples).

[557] This Commission is integrated by the SG himself, that will assume the function of President, the Special Representative, Gros Espiell, the Personal Representative of the current Chairman of OAU, the Under-Secretary-General for Special Political Questions, Regional Co-operation, Decolonization and Trusteeship, the Under-Secretary-General for Special Political Affairs, the Legal Counsel and the Military Adviser to the Secretary-General (*ORGA:* A/44/634, par. 11).

Chapter VII

As was stated above, the report submitted to the Security Council by the Secretary General on June 18, 1990[558] includes the proposals for a peaceful settlement accepted by both parties in the conflict, and would provide the bases for holding the referendum, which had to be, "organized and supervised by the United Nations, in cooperation with the OAU, will be carried out during a Transitional Period", with the following characteristics[559]:
- 18 is the minimum age established for the right to vote of "all the Western Saharans who are registered in the census of 1974 made by the Spanish authorities", while the Special Representative of the Secretary General

---

[558] *ORSC:* S/21360.

[559] While the Saharan question was submitted to study by the OAU, a series of Decisions of the Organisation established certain criteria regarding how to carry out the self-determination referendum. Though, due to existing tensions at the time between the Parties in conflict, these criteria were not in fact implemented. They are nevertheless of undoubted importance, for having concreted, even at a very early stage, the criteria that would later on form the Settlement Plan. So, already in 1981, some criteria had been accepted by "all parties of the conflict". In the first ordinary period of the Implementation Committee for Western Sahara of the OAU (Nairobi, 24-26 August, 1981), and in application of the AHG/Res.103 (XVIII), the aforementioned Committee decided to "organize and conduct a general and free referendum in the Western Sahara, establish and maintain the cease-fire (...) in the territory in which the main features would be: 1) All Saharans listed in the census conducted in 1974 by the Spanish authorities who have attained the age of 18 or above, shall be eligible to vote; 2) In determining the Saharan refugee population in the neighbouring countries, reference should be made by the records of the UNHCR; 3) In establishing the population of the Western Sahara, account shall be taken of the internationally recognized rate of population growth"; 4) The people of the Western Sahara shall be given the following choice: independence or Integration with Morocco (AHG/IMP.C/WS/DEC.1 (I), that figures as annex to document of the UNO, *ORGA:* S/14692, or also *ORESC:* E/CN.4/1982/14, p. 13, and E/CN.4/1982/17, Annex 1).

The criteria established by the Decision of this Implementation Committee of the OAU where also complemented, if not "retouched", during the second ordinary period of sessions of the mentioned Committee ((Nairobi, 8-9 February 1982), in which it was pointed that the requirements to have the right to vote would be established during the basic agreement and would conclude in an Order that would be promulgated by the Commission, who would be in charge during the referendum of a register of eligible voters. Also, it establishes as the first requirement of the celebration of the referendum a "register of the eligible voters, for which must be taken into account the figures of the census of 1974". Furthermore, it insisted on the fact that the options for the referendum would be two: independence or integration to Morocco (AHG/IMP.C/WS/DEC.2 (II), Rev.2, that figures as annex to document of the UNO, *ORGA:* A/37/570/Rev.1 and E/CN.4/1982/17, Annex 2).

As it can be appreciated the development of the project is still at early stage of what will become the Settlement Plan, being especially important the participation of the United Nations in its making from the very start. To this respect, *cfr. ORGA:* A/37/570/Rev.1, Report of the SG to the UNO

assisted by the High Commissioner of the United Nations for Refugees (UNHCR) is responsible for the Western Saharan refugees outside the territory. As was later pointed out by the representative of the POLISARIO Front before the Fourth Commission[560], respect for these criteria as a basis for determining the updating of the census should entail a maximum increase of 3-6% of the electorate registered in the 1974 census. However, this first criterion would later be "reinterpreted", in such a way that this percentage was only symbolic;

- An *Identification Commission* was created with the principal function of examining and *updating the 1974 census*, which involved calculating the real growth of the Western Saharan population in the period between the aforementioned census and the date of organization of the referendum (taking into account the births and deaths and the displacements of the Western Saharan population), a function which had to be finalized prior to the commencement of the referendum campaign.

In order to resolve the questions more strictly related to the characteristics of the population, this Identification Commission would be made up of "an expert in demography, familiarised with the problems and the structure of Western Saharan society, assisted by a group of three to five specialists in the demographic study of countries where nomads predominate". In order to achieve an improved guarantee of success in the work of the Identification Commission, the participation of the *chiefs and tribal leaders* in the territory was guaranteed, as these "can make comments and provide their contribution", considered by the Secretary General as "essential for the peaceful and swift resolution of the question", as well as the participation of the *representatives of the two parties* in the conflict and those of the OAU at the meetings of the Commission with the tribal leaders, as observers;

- There were only two *options* included in the referendum on self-determination for the accredited Western Saharan: *independence or integration* with Morocco. The limitation of the possibilities included in Resolution 1541 (XV)[561] and 2625 (XXV)[562] of the General Assembly to

---

[560] October 7, 1996.

[561] "A Non-Self-Governing Territory can be said to have reached a full measure of self-government by: a) Emergence as a sovereign independent State; b) Free association with an independent State; or c) Integration with an independent State" -Principle VI Resolution 1541 (XV)-.

[562] "The establishment of a sovereign and independent State, the free association or integration with an independent State of the emergence into any other political status freely determined by a people constitute modes of implementing the right of self-determination of that people" (-Principle of equal rights and self-determination of peoples. Resolution

these two options clearly shows the difficulties encountered by the representatives of the two parties involved in the conflict when attempting to reach a base agreement to enable the process of self-determination in the territory[563];
- The *ballot* will be *secret*, and special arrangements will be made for people who cannot read or write;
- Although the absence of references to the withdrawal of the Moroccan Administration during the referendum is particularly notable[564], the following factors are established as *previous conditions*:
  a) before the commencement of the electoral campaign, the Special Representative can request the suspension of any law or measure which might be a risk to a free and fair referendum;
  b) all the *political prisoners* must be released so that they can participate in the referendum;
  c) once they have been included in the census, Western Saharan *refugees* can return to the territory freely and participate in the referendum;
  d) the Western Saharans who are *resident outside the territory* can freely decide whether they wish to return or not and will be assisted by the Special Representative of the Secretary General and by the UNHCR;

(XXV)-.
[563] In 1973, when the Spanish Government was studying different possibilities regarding the future of the territory, Fernández de la Mora proposed to grant it with the statute of a Free State associated to Spain, by which the consultation to the people would be made under the auspices of the UNO (*vid.* FERNÁNDEZ DE LA MORA, G., *Río Arriba. Memorias*, ed. Planeta, Barcelona (1995): 164).
[564] In respect to this, answering the questions of the SG, the Moroccan government had pointed already in May 1986 that not only Moroccan Administration would not leave the territory, but also if it were to take place, it would be materially impossible to carry out the referendum. So the Moroccan administration "to whom electoral consultation is no novelty", offers all its cooperation and goodwill to accept any suggestions with the aim of "adapting certain rules in force to the particular demands of the referendum". The text of the Moroccan answer can be consulted in GRIMAUD, N. (1988): 99 and s.
This approach was openly in contrast with the SADR claims. The Information minister had pointed a month before (April 11, 1986) the necessary conditions for the celebration of the referendum: 1) complete withdrawal of Moroccan; 2) complete withdrawal of Moroccan Administration and presence in any form, including the colony population; 3) return of all Saharan refugees; 4) liberation of all Saharan prisoners and detainees; 5) peace-keeping force of the UNO and the OAU in the territory; and 6) set up of an internal international administration, constituted by the OAU and UNO to administer the territory during the transitional period to prepare, organize and lead the celebration of the referendum (Text in *Sahara Libre*, num. 285, April 1986).

THE PEACE PLAN (II) – THE PROBLEM OF CONSULTING THE POPULATION

e) *absolute freedom of speech, assembly, movement and press* will be established;
- Once it is verified that all these prerequisites have been complied with, the Special Representative will establish the date of commencement of the *referendum campaign*, and will be responsible for the maintenance of law and order in the territory during the Transitional Period;
- As regards the *holding of the referendum* itself, the representatives of the two parties in the conflict, as well as those of the OAU, will be invited to observe how it is carried out, and may submit any possible complaints for the consideration of the Special Representative, whose decision cannot be appealed against. In addition, the parties are committed to cooperate fully with the Special Representative, as well as to accept and obey the result of the referendum.

In January 1989[565] technical conversations began at the United Nations Headquarters as regards preparations for updating the census that had been made by the Spanish authorities in the territory in 1974, which should serve "as agreed by the two parties, to draw up of a voters' list for the proposed referendum". This previous agreement of the parties constituted the starting point of the search for agreements intended to achieve the holding of the referendum in the territory. However, an event of special importance was to take place in the context of these pre-agreements, strengthening even more the progress of the negotiations: in February 1989, in Marrakech, direct contact between the two parties in conflict was established for the first time, between King Hassan II and a high level delegation of the POLISARIO Front.

In May 1990 the preparations to establish the Identification Commission stipulated in the Agreement Proposals were being finalized so that the identification process could be carried out in conditions of security. Since it was going to be necessary for the heads and tribal leaders to meet, a month later the Secretary General gathered thirty-eight tribal leaders and elders of the territory and explained the mandate and the methods of work of the Identification Commission to them. Thus, they had the opportunity to formulate the suggestions they considered to be advisable for the Commission both in relation to the best way to identify the persons with a right to vote in the referendum and the possible methods so that the leaders and elders could help the Commission to carry out its task[566].

---

[565] *ORGA:* A/44/634, October 12, 1989 (Report of the SG).
[566] *Cfr. ORGA:* A/45/644, p. 5, par. 13.

2.2. The Implementation Plan

Furthermore, the Secretary General proposed an *Implementation Plan for the referendum on Self-Determination*[567]. On July 12, 1989, the Technical Commission, constituted on June 30, 1989 in order to carry out a study of the resources required to implement the settlement proposals we have just analysed, delivered this study to the two parties, together with a timetable plan for its implementation. This Plan, which includes the content of the agreement of August 30, 1988, had the following most innovative aspects:

a) For the first time a *period* for holding the referendum was established: which would be "24 weeks after the ceasefire came into force", and its results "must be publicly announced within a period of 72 hours", although the possibility to alter these periods was left to the Special Representative, depending on the circumstances;

b) The need for the creation of "an integrated group of United nations civilian, military and civil police personnel which he will head and direct" was established, and this would receive the name *Misión de las Naciones Unidas para el Referéndum del Sahara Occidental (MINURSO)[United Nations Mission for the Western Sahara Referendum]*. Its presence in the territory would last, with the proviso mentioned in the previous paragraph, "for up to 35 weeks from the coming into effect of the ceasefire". The main function of the MINURSO[568] would consist of resolving all the questions concerning the referendum, its organization and execution, and it could take the measures needed to guarantee freedom of movement and the security of the population, as well as the impartiality of the referendum;

c) A *Transitional Period* was also established and this would begin with the ceasefire and would terminate when the results of the referendum were publicly announced;

d) Finally, the Secretary General pointed out the impossibility of calculating the *cost which the MINURSO* might entail for the UN, therefore, he decided to send a technical mission to the territory and to the neighbouring countries in order to make an in-depth study of the administrative aspects of the Plan which would make it possible to make an approximate evaluation of this cost (as we have seen above, the creation of the MINURSO was decided by Resolution 690 (1991) of the Security Council of April 29).

---

[567] *Cfr. ORSC:* S/21360.
[568] *Cfr.* in this respect the work of ORTEGA TEROL, J.M., "Una operación de mantenimiento de la paz: la MINURSO", *A.D.I.*, XI (1995): 243-259, especially , pp. 249 et seq.

The content of some of the aspects of the Implementation Plan was subsequently extended through the *report that the Secretary General submitted to the Security Council on April 19, 1991*, in compliance with Resolution 658 (1990)[569], which also developed other aspects already stipulated in the report. This specified the estimation of the global cost of the MINURSO (approximately 200 million dollars), developed some questions related to the referendum census and modified other aspects, stressing the following points:

a) Some of the functions to be implemented by the Identification Commission had to be carried out "outside and inside the Territory before the ceasefire comes into effect " thus contradicting the previous report, which limited these to the Transitional Period;

b) As regards the updating of the 1974 census, *the functions to be carried out by the Commission were extended*, when it pointed out that this must "a) remove from the lists the names of persons who have since died and b) consider applications from persons who claim the right to participate in the referendum on the grounds that they are Western Saharans and were omitted from the 1974 census", and the tribal leaders of Western Sahara would be asked to contribute to this work;

c) Moreover, *two stages in the process that would lead to the drafting of the definitive census of voters* were established:

- In the first phase the 1974 census list would be updated. In order to achieve this, the Secretary General previously sent both parties a copy of the census list drawn up by Spain, accompanied by a request for information on the location of persons who were in or outside the territory at the time the census was made, and had not been included in it. Once the corrections are made to the list, it must be published in the territory and "in places outside where numbers of Western Saharans are known to be living", and at the same time instructions had to be published before a determined date concerning the submittal of applications in writing by "those Western Saharans wanting to be included in the list who were omitted from the 1974 census". As a culmination to this first phase, the Commission had to meet in New York or Geneva together with the tribal leaders in the presence of observers from the OAU and from the parties in order to examine the applications under the supervision of the Special Representative. The resulting lists of this phase of the process had to be published in the territory and in the places referred to above on a determined date, when the Commission had to be "installed in the mission zone".

---

[569] *ORSC*: S/22464, April 29, 1991.

- In the second phase, which was planned to last for a maximum of eleven weeks, the Commission had to address two tasks: identify the persons on the lists, hand over their registration cards and establish the procedure for appeals against the decisions taken by the Commission concerning the drafting of these lists. In this second phase, the Commission also had to take the measures required to identify and register "at the designated locations, all Frente POLISARIO troops who are eligible to vote", as well as "any Western Saharans who are similarly eligible and may be serving in the Moroccan forces". Once this second phase finalized, the Special Representative had to submit the lists drafted to the Secretary General to be examined in consultation with the Acting President of the OAU, then, the definitive list of voters would be published. The process, including the carrying out of the referendum, was planned to last for 36 weeks starting from the date on which the establishment of the MINURSO was approved.

The report reaffirmed that the options the voter could choose from amounted to two: integration with Morocco or independence, and that the ballot would be secret and carried out "only in the Territory". Moreover, it was established that the result of the referendum would be determined by a simple majority of the votes validly cast. As regards the question of the refugees, the Office of the United Nations High Commission for Refugees was assigned to implement the repatriation programme[570]. Finally, as was stated above, through Resolution 690 (1991), the establishment of the MINURSO was approved.

2.3. *The Report of December 19, 1991[571]. The modification of the identification criteria and the types of evidence admissible*

As recorded in what would be the last report of Pérez de Cuéllar as Secretary General of the UNO, as a previous question to the implementation of the Settlement Plan of the Secretary General, on September 6, 1991 the *ceasefire* proposed in the Plan and expressly agreed to by Morocco and the POLISARIO Front came into force[572]. From that same date, the headquarters of the MINURSO was established in the capital, El Aaiún, with three regional

---

[570] The main functions of UNHCR are: 1) to ascertain and record the repatriation wishes of each Western Saharan as he or she is registered as a voter by the Identification Commission. 2) to issue the necessary documentation to the members of his or her immediate family and 3) to establish and manage, in cooperation with MINURSO which will provide security, the reception centres that will be established in the Territory for the returning of Western Saharans" (*ORSC*: S/22464, par. 35).

[571] *Cfr. ORGA*: S/23299.

[572] *Cfr. ORSC*: S/22779.

centres in the northern central and southern sectors of the territory, together with a "liaison office" in Tinduf, assisted by the Government of Algeria. Although it was sporadically breached by both parties, the establishment of the ceasefire made it possible to start up the parts of the Plan regarding the identification of voters.

Furthermore, the report of the Secretary General stressed the failure to comply with the periods established in the Settlement Plan, but despite this he considered that progress had been made in the process since, although an agreement on its publication had not been reached, at least the first of the phases planned in the previous report for the updating of the census had been completed, and there was a revised list of the 1974 census[573].

In an annex to his report[574], the Secretary General took time to analyse the principal *difficulties involved in the identification process*, and highlighted the following:

- The first is in relation to the peculiarities of the Western Saharan population, insofar as it is a *nomadic society and tribal structure*. The difficulties deriving from these characteristics of the population had already been underlined by the Visiting Mission to Western Sahara, when it mentioned that,

    "Because of their nomadic way of life, the peoples of the Territory move easily across the borders to the neighbouring countries, where they are received by members of their tribes or even of their families. This ebb and flow of people across the borders of the Territory makes it difficult to take a complete census of the inhabitants of Spanish Sahara and also poses the complex problem of the identification of the Saharans of the Territory and makes it even more difficult to take a satisfactory census of refugees"[575];

- The second is related to a question that the Visiting Mission had also pointed out. This was the added difficulty when determining who is and who is not an inhabitant of the territory deriving from the *affinity*, "between the Saharans of the Territory and those in neighbouring countries, and their nomadic tradition";

---

[573] *Cfr. ORSC:* S/23299 (Report from SG, December 19, 1991), par. 9.

[574] "Instructions relating to the tasks of the identification Commission", written in accordance with article 3 of General Ruling of the organization of the referendum (November 8, 1991), and figures as annex to document *ORGA:* S/23299.

[575] *ORGA: 30th period of sessions, supplement num.* 23: A/10023/Rev.1, par. 11.

- A third question concerned the *conflicts occurring previously* in the territory, which gave rise to a large number of Western Saharans seeking refuge in neighbouring countries on several occasions, and the *emigration due to natural reasons* (drought, the search for employment, etc.)[576];
- Finally the problem deriving from the *Green March* must not be forgotten since, when it ended, part of the participants settled in the territory and became new settlers[577]. The Secretary General may have alluded to this question in his report, and such a neutral approach points to a shift in his outlook, aligning himself to the Moroccan position. The brief report states that "a number of persons who claim to belong to Western Sahara have been moved into the Territory". The use of the impersonal grammatical structure to refer to a situation which constitutes a violation not only of the content of the Settlement Plan but also of the obligations of Morocco as the occupying Power in the territory in conformity with the IV Geneva Convention, is more than a mere slip by Pérez de Cuéllar, and is the first step taken by a Secretary General to align himself with approaches of the occupying Power.

Despite this, the Secretary General states that "only those persons who have been duly identified by the UN will eventually be eligible to vote in the referendum", an assessment which, although obvious, is surprising coming from the person who holds the ultimate representation of the UN, and he casts doubt on his conviction that the conflict will be resolved, especially when he later points out that,

> "it is clear that only members of tribes whose connection with the Territory within the limits of recognized international

---

[576] *Cfr. ORSC:* S/23299, par. 10.

[577] Segura stated that approximately 50,000 Moroccans constituted the social base for the new occupation (*vid.* SEGURA PALOMARES, J., *El Sahara, razón de una sinrazón*, Ed. Acerbo, Madrid (1976): 194). Also, the third report that the SG presented to the SC in accordance to Resolution 379 (1975), in which he referred to the Madrid Agreements, pointed that "After the withdrawal of the participants in the 'Green March' from the Territory of Western Sahara, Spain resumed negotiations with Morocco and Mauritania and on 14 November the three parties agreed upon a 'declaration of principles' relating to the future of the Western Sahara" (*ORSC:* S/11880, par. 7), setting in this way that the totality of the participants left the territory already for November 19, 1975. Nevertheless, declarations of the Moroccan representative before the GA, M. Laraki, seem to confirm the contrary, as he states "Sahara lives in a peaceful atmosphere *and of great activity of reconstruction and organization*" (*ORGA:* 31st period of sessions of GA, 21st session, October 7, 1976, highlighted by author), which seems difficult to understand after the withdrawal of the territory of great part of the Saharan population, if it is not done by Moroccan colonists.

borders is clearly established should participate in the referendum".

The main problem of drafting the census derives precisely from the lack of respect to this last sentence. As we will see later, the pretensions of Morocco to include in the census members of tribes presumably linked with the territory but who reside outside "the limits of its recognised international borders" would take the process to the verge of collapse.

As a basis for a possible solution to the first two questions, the report of the Secretary General again referred to the Visiting Mission, to the effect that the census of the referendum should be based on the demonstrated composition of the social and family groups (fractions and sub-fractions of tribes) within the territory[578]. In relation to these last two points, another question practically stopped the identification process, or rather almost killed it off. This was the intention of the Alawite monarch to include 170,000 new voters in the census, "Western Saharans" who had fled from the territory in 1958 as a consequence of the war and subsequent military operations[579]; this was in open contradiction with the data used by the organs of the United Nations and expressly mentioned by the Moroccan representatives before these organs, and with the data provided by the POLISARIO Front and by Algeria[580] as well as contrary to the report of the Secretary General which excluded from the census tribe members who do not live within the limits of the internationally recognised borders. In addition, the Western Saharan representation before the Committee of Twenty-Four appeared on October 15, 1990 before this Committee and stated that together with a military contingent of more than

---

[578] *Cfr. ORGA: 30th Period of sessions, supplement num. 23*: A/10023/Rev.1, par. 125.

[579] The claim came from the Moroccan King by a letter sent on September 15, 1991 to the SG of the UNO. From the beginning of the seventies, when Morocco accepted for the first time that the solution to the conflict should be a self-determination referendum (where only two options would be eligible: remain under the Spanish *status quo* or integrate to Morocco), the government of this country mentioned the possibility that nearly 150,000 "Saharan refugees in Morocco under the Spanish repression" would be able to participate in the referendum. *Cfr.* DESSENS, P. (1976): 33.

[580] Morocco had stated to the Visiting Mission of the UNO that they had an *official calculation* of Saharan refugees in the southern part of Morocco of between 30,000 and 35,000 (*ORGA*: Supplement num. 23 (A/10023/Rev.1), Report of the Visiting Mission, par. 124). Furthermore, the Decolonization Committee had collected similar statements from the Moroccan government that situated the number of Saharan refugees between 30,000 and 40,000 (Decision November 7, 1975, apart. 9). The POLISARIO Front stated to the Visiting Mission that the number of political refugees and exiled persons was of 50,000, while Algeria calculated that the Saharan refugees in its territory was over 7,000 (*ORGA*: Supplement num. 23 (A/10023/Rev.1), Report of the Visiting Mission, par. 156, note *ff*).

CHAPTER VII

100,000 soldiers, there were 50,000 civil servants in Western Sahara, and "a Moroccan civil colony whose number exceeds 150,000"[581].

Furthermore, besides this serious situation, there was what has been called *"the Second Green March"*, which consisted of the movement of a large contingent of Moroccan citizens to the territory, and the Moroccan Government intended to include these in the census of the referendum[582]. Although this was the most important colonization of the territory as regards numbers, before this occurred, Morocco had already carried out an intense colonization policy in the territory[583].

With regard to another factor, in a section called *"Instructions for the examination of the applications to participate in the referendum"*[584], the Secretary General specified the *profile of the inhabitants with a right to vote in the referendum*, based on "recognized sources such as custom, international

---

[581] ORGA: A/AC.109/PV.1376.

[582] As stressed by Remiro Brotons, the systematic inflow of immigration leads the colonised territory to a situation where free election is infringed by colonists, even if the new population does not figure in the census of the referendum (*vid.* REMIRO BROTONS, *"Derecho Internacional"* (1997): 119).

[583] In this way, for example, the growth of the population of El Aaiún had been important. From 30,000 inhabitants in 1975, to 90,000 in 1984 (Centre d'Etudes et de Recherches Démographiques, Situation démographique régionale au Maroc: Analyses comparatives, Ministère du Plan. Rabat, 1988, pp. 248-257), and to 130,000 in 1992 (BERRADA GOUZI, N., GODEAU, R., "Laayoun, plus fort que le désert", in the collective work "Que font les Marocains au Sahara?", *Jeune Afrique*, num. 34, supplement num. 1722, January (1994): 73). As Kroner says, the spectacular increase of inhabitants of occupied territories of Western Sahara can only be explained by the massive inflow of Moroccan settlers (*cfr.* KRONER, D.H., "The maroccanization of the Western Sahara", *Swiss Review of World Affairs*, 34 (9), Decembre (1984): 10). Likewise, Seddon numbers in 38,000 the Moroccans moved to the territory during the "Second Green March" (*cfr.* SEDDON, D., "Briefing: Western Sahara Tog-of-War", *Review of African Political Economy*, n° 52 (1991): 110-113). On this same matter, *cfr.* JOFFE, G. (1995): 111. Also, the moving population from Morocco, moved by military transport to Western Sahara territory has been repeatedly denounced before the United Nations. Among these, *cfr.* CHOPRA, J., "Statement regarding the issue of the Western Sahara before the Fourth Committee of the United Nations General Assembly, October 19 1992", *Internet:* http://heiwww.unige.ch/arso/Chopra-92.htm;

Otherwise, in the case that the POLISARIO Front should win the referendum, there is no doubt of the problem that the new State would have to face: approximately a hundred thousand Moroccans could claim their staying in the Territory. As underlines Bookmiller, the Saharan thesis victory at the referendum would be the beginning and not the end of a long political process (*cfr.* BOOKMILLER, R.J., "The Western Sahara: future prospects", *American-Arab affairs*, n.37, Summer (1991): 75 and s.).

[584] ORSC: S/23299.

practice, generally recognized norms as well as laws in force in the region". After clarifying that "the determining factor is the membership of a family group (sub-fraction of a tribe) existing within the territory which can be attested to by the sheiks and notables of the family group", the Western Saharans in the following circumstances could be registered in the census:
1) The persons whose names are on the original 1974 Spanish census list, as well as on the revised list[585].
2) The persons who lived in the territory as members of a Western Saharan tribe when the census was made in 1974 and who could not be registered by virtue of individualised applications which had to be studied by the Identification Commission, which must apply criteria of justice and fairness. The applications of these persons must be accompanied by testimonies or documents that provide the grounds for their request.
3) The members of the immediate family (father, mother and children) of these first two groups, on account of kinship. In both cases, the relationship will be established in response to individual applications, that is to say, it will be necessary for each one of the persons concerned to make an individual claim to have his right recognized.
4) The children of Western Saharan parents born in the territory and were not there at the time of the census made by the Spanish authorities. Although these persons are not denied their *a priori* right to participate in the self-determination referendum, they are required to demonstrate strong ties with the territory. Moreover, in order to ensure that, the scope of this possibility was not excessively wide and was limited to the possibility of a single generation.
5) Finally, and generically, the Report points out that, when these guidelines of the United Nations were established, the interest of the parties and the customs of Western Saharan society were taken into consideration. Thus, generically, it was established that, "it is considered that a member of a Saharan tribe belonging to the Territory is eligible to participate in the referendum if he or she has resided in the Territory for a period of six consecutive years before 1 December 1974", although a twelve year period of intermittent residence previous to this date was established in order not to harm the Western Saharans who had to enter and leave the territory frequently due to their circumstances. The establishment of these periods was not arbitrary as six consecutive years was the average period of

---

[585] *Cfr. ORSC:* S/23299, par. 23. On questions related to the making of the census by Spanish authorities both in the Western Sahara case, as in other Spanish administered territories in Africa, *cfr.* GOZALVEZ PEREZ, V., "Descolonización y migraciones desde el África española (1956-1975)", *Investigaciones geográficas*, n. 12 (1994): 45-84.

residence required by law in the countries in the region in order to acquire nationality.

Thus, the Secretary General extended the possibilities of acquiring the condition of voter in the referendum, without the approval of one of the parties, and openly contradicted the agreements stipulated in the Peace Plan. According to the report, there were five groups of persons with the right to participate in the referendum, while in the Settlement Plan, accepted by both parties, only the first group mentioned was referred to in the following terms, "eligibility to vote will depend either on the presence of a person's name in the 1974 census list, or on a person's ability to convince the Identification Commission that he or she is a Western Saharan who was omitted from the 1974 census"[586]. Even considering some of the criteria concerning the family ties as correct, and which had been admitted by the norms of the *Yemáa* Commission analysed above[587], this extension seems to be excessive, especially, if the statement in the Settlement Plan is taken into account a this refers to Western Saharan society as, "a society that is nomadic and to a large extent illiterate and where such criteria as place of birth or residence are of limited relevance"[588]. The attitude of the Secretary General which modified the criteria which would give the right to participate in the referendum was denounced by the POLISARIO Front and, in the end, this would become the main reason for stopping the process, which was only unblocked after Kofi Annan[589] became the UN Secretary General. Morocco considered these criteria to be correct as they were clearly advantageous considering its intentions, which were, if possible, even more ambitious[590].

The conclusions of the Report of the Secretary General also contained a component that was of decisive importance for drafting the lists, which, considering its significance, would constitute one of the main obstacles to the process, and would contribute to accentuating the differences between the parties. This involved the *evidence* admissible by the Identification Commission

---

[586] *ORSC*: S/22464, par. 62, a).

[587] *Cfr. ORSC*: S/10023/Rev.1, annex, par. 160.

[588] *ORGA*: S/22464, par. 62, a).

[589] In these conditions, the Saharan representative denied even to receive Marrack Goulding, Under-Secretary General of the UNO, that in 1992 travelled to Western Sahara in a good offices mission (*vid.* DAMIS, J. (1992): 39).

[590] Damis states that Morocco wanted to extend these criteria to two generations back in time that would lead us to approximately to the year 1900. Also, the application of this new criterion would enable to participate in the referendum between 25,000 and 35,000 Saharans that had abandoned the territory during the last years of the fifties. And the new criteria would extend in 7,000 approximately the possible voters in favour of the POLISARIO Front (*Ibidem*).

while carrying out its work. According to the report of the Secretary General, these could be of two types: written documents -"the official documents, well known by the Western Saharans and used by them"-, and oral testimony - "given the fact that in Western Saharan society (...) this is an important component of all social activity".

As regards the *written evidence*, the report stated that all types of official documents would be accepted, and this was openly rejected by the POLISARIO Front as, in its opinion, only written documents issued by the colonial Power should be admitted, never those issued by Morocco. Morocco doubted the impartiality of the Spanish authorities and considered that those issued by its Administration should also be admitted.

Neither was an agreement reached on the admissibility of *oral testimony*. Thus, while Morocco defended its admissibility in all cases, the POLISARIO Front established the following limitations:

- The oral evidence for registering applicants for the census through the 5th criteria will not be admitted;
- The oral evidence will be purely complementary to the written evidence, therefore, this alone will not be considered to be sufficient evidence;
- This will only be taken into account in order to prove that an applicant belongs to a tribe, or to physically identify a person;
- Only the *Sheikhs* will be able to testify that they were included in the list drawn up by Spain.

Since belonging to a family group is a key component when including an applicant in the census, another controversial question, present throughout all the report, consisted in determining when it should be understood that this family group or sub-fraction of a tribe *is settled in the territory*. The differences between the Western Saharan and the Moroccan approaches to this point are evident since, as opposed to the broader interpretation of Morocco, according to which the fact that a single representative of a tribe was recorded in the 1974 Spanish census would give the totality of the members of this tribe to participate in the referendum, the representation of the POLISARIO Front maintained that only the family group whose majority of members were registered in the 1974 could be accepted as settled.

Despite the difficulties mentioned above (the nomadic nature of society, affinity, etc.), in 1974 the Spanish authorities had managed to achieve a census of the population, according to which the total number of Western Saharans who lived in the territory amounted to 73,497. The Visiting mission had been informed that "all the members of such groups are known to each other and that the authenticity of a claim to belong to a family group can be verified by the sheiks and notables of that group in consultation with their members".

CHAPTER VII

Therefore, between 1970 and 1976, the Spanish authorities had issued 32,516 identity cards, which served as a basis for the census, issued due to the norms established by a Permanent Commission of Tribal Leaders (a Commission of the *Yemáa*) which used the criteria of belonging to a family group (*ahel*) in the territory[591].

Moreover, at the final communiqué of the meeting of the tribal leaders organized by the United Nations in June 1990, referred to above, "the flaws and imprecision" of the 1974 census were stressed, as numerous Western Saharans had not been interviewed, and these had been included in the census of the territory, but were out of the territory when the 1974 census was carried out, and, if this had been taken into account, it would logically have increased the number of persons in the census. However, when mention was made of the imprecision of the 1974 census, this also involved an express reference to the refugees outside the territory who were not included in the census due to their situation. The Report of the Secretary General stated that the Identification Commission had to appeal, particularly, to the Western Saharan notables and tribal leaders faced with the rectification of the defects affecting the 1974 census which, as we pointed out above, would have to be the basis of the new

---

[591] According to the approved rules by the *Yemáa* on November 1974 governing the issue of identity documents to Saharans, which were promulgated by the Governor-General on 18 December 1974 and could eventually form the basis for such law (*ORGA*: Supplement num. 23 (A/10023/Rev.1), Report of Visiting Mission, par. 160-163), "the following persons *shall be deemed* Saharans: 1) All persons born of Saharan fathers; 2) Persons born of Saharan mothers and fathers of foreign nationality, provided that the laws of the country of the father's nationality do not require that the children have the same nationality as the father; 3) Persons born in the Territory of parents of foreign nationality provided that the latter were also born in the Territory and were resident there at the time of birth; 4) Persons born in the Territory of unknown parentage, except that, should the latters' nationality become know, the foregoing provisions should apply".

Also, the rule provides that persons may opt for Saharan nationality if they were born in the Territory or born outside the Territory of Saharan parentage. Where marriage is involved, the wife of a Saharan automatically acquires the nationality of her husband; the converse also applies, the children automatically having the nationality of the father. So, it *was possible to choose the Saharan*. Finally, these rules provide that a non-Saharan may be granted Saharan nationality, on the recommendation of the appropriate commission of the *Yemáa*, provided the applicant has resided in the Territory for not less than five consecutive years immediately prior to the application, or exceptionally, for three years if the applicant has made significant contribution to the Territory for example, by virtue of having introduced an important industry or by being the director of a major agricultural, industrial or trading enterprise. This last possibility aroused criticism by the POLISARIO Front before the Visiting Mission, as it could be used to grant Saharan nationality to non-local persons that occupied at that moment important posts in Spanish Administration.

census[592], thus, attributing an important role to the collaboration of the Western Saharans in the process for the identification of voters.

With regard to the *identification procedure*, until the present time, this was carried out in twelve identification units, distributed as follows: four in the territories occupied by Morocco (El Aaiún, Villa Cisneros, Smara and Bojador), four in the Western Saharan "provinces" in the refugee camps located in Algerian territory (El Aaiún, Villa Cisneros, Smara and Auserd[593]), two in Mauritania (Nuabidú and Zuerat) and another two mobile units. As regards their composition, there was a civil servant of the UN, two *Sheikhs* appointed by the parties (Morocco and the POLISARIO Front), two observers appointed by Morocco and the POLISARIO Front, and a third designated by the OAU.

The procedure is as follows: the possible voters, distributed geographically among the identification units, had to appear before their corresponding units. In the event that there was an agreement between the two *Sheikhs* regarding the Western Saharan identity of the applicant, he would be registered in the census and would be given a census card, which would enable him to participate in the referendum. In the event that there was no agreement, it would be necessary to resort to written evidence if there is any. If there were no agreement as regards this evidence, the UN civil servant would decide. The provisional lists of those registered may be appealed against, and these appeals will be resolved by an international jurist.

This final report of Pérez de Cuéllar was undoubtedly a setback for the process as it modified the criteria and the evidence agreed to from the beginning as regards the drafting of the census and these criteria had always been defended by the Secretary General but he had decided to abandon them on leaving his post. The POLISARIO Front flatly opposed this change of criteria decided by the Secretary General, "since it viewed the 1974 census as a key provision of the Settlement Plan, to which the two parties had agreed and which could not be changed without their consent"[594].

One sign of the conflict concerning the content was the unusual controversy in the Security Council; through its Resolution 725 (1991),

---

[592] The importance of the cooperation and assistance of tribal chiefs and other notables of the Territory refers to the following aspects: 1) to assist the Commission in refining its operational procedures; 2) to assist in the review of the written applications from people who were not counted during the 1974 census; and 3) to assist in identifying and registering voters, and in connection with the process of appeals (*cfr. ORSC*: S/23299, par. 16-18).

[593] The Saharans organized the refugee camps of Tinduf in several geographical organisations, which they named after the main locations of Western Sahara.

[594] *ORSC*: S/25170, par. 16.

approved by unanimity, the Security Council approved "the efforts of the Secretary General", but not the report that it merely "welcomed". Approving the report of the Secretary General is quite different from "welcoming" it; the latter expression only entailing diplomatic courtesy[595]. In addition, the impartiality of the Secretary General was called into question when, after this resolution was approved, some of the media published news referring to his participation in an important Moroccan company linked to Hassan II[596].

3. The Butros Gali phase

The first report drafted by Butros Gali as Secretary General of the United Nations[597] highlighted the deep discrepancies between the Moroccan and the Western Saharan representatives as regards the census. The POLISARIO Front insisted that in the Settlement Plan the two parties in the conflict had agreed that the 1974 census would be the exclusive basis for the determination of the right to participate in the referendum, meaning therefore that the persons registered in this census should constitute the majority of the persons with the right to participate in the referendum, and those born in Western Sahara and omitted from the 1974 census would be the exception to the rule. The POLISARIO Front also insisted on the criteria already explained to the Secretary General[598] concerning the conditions of admissibility of oral evidence. However, Morocco considered that the 1974 census was only a reference to be taken into account.

---

[595] BRIONES VIVES, F. (1994): 92. Likewise, *cfr*. DAMIS, J. (1992): 39.

[596] There are several press releases that refer to this question. In this regard, for example, *cfr*. the following: "Pérez de Cuéllar signs up for the main Moroccan holding" (*El País*, February 1, 1993, p. 14); "Pérez de Cuéllar affirms having rejected the post of head of a firm as it was going to be bought by a Moroccan group" (*El País*, February 4, 1993); The SG pointed that "it is true they made an offer, but I asked for time to think... They considered my lack of answer as an acceptance of the post, and made it public" (*Abc*, February 7, 1993); "Pérez de Cuéllar has been appointed Vice-president of a subsidiary company of the Moroccan Consortium ONA, related to Hassan II" (*El Mundo*, February 2, 1993).

[597] *Cfr*. *ORSC*: S/24464, August 20, 1992. The prior reports of the new SG (*ORGA*: S/23662, of February 28, 1992, and S/24040, of May 29, of the same year) give faith of the same aspects that are related in this one, with the exception that for the first time the SG attributes in part the delay in the celebration of the referendum to "the fact that the United Nations has never before organized a referendum of this kind", wich "explains in large measure the delay that has occurred" (S/23662, par. 32).

[598] These criteria were collected by the SG in his Report of December 19, 1991 (*ORSC*: S/23299).

THE PEACE PLAN (II) – THE PROBLEM OF CONSULTING THE POPULATION

The report of the Secretary General of January 26, 1993 clearly indicated the intention of the new Secretary General to put an end to the peace process. He untruthfully insisted on stating that the reports of his predecessor[599] "are based on proposals to which the parties had freely agreed in August 1988"[600], given that, as mentioned above, Pérez de Cuéllar had included identification criteria which was not planned in these proposals, and he attributed the failure of the negotiations to the lack of willingness of the parties. In this situation, the Secretary General put forward three options regarding the future of the process, mentioned above: to continue with the negotiations, to apply the Plan even without the collaboration of the parties, or to propose a new way to resolve the conflict apart from the Plan.

3.1. The "agreement on the interpretation which must be given to criteria 4 and 5" (January 26, 1993)

The report of the Secretary General informed the Security Council of the scant progress in the process and notified it that, as a result of the negotiations between its Special Representative and the parties on the interpretation of the *"Instructions for the examination of the applications for participation in the referendum"*[601], an agreement had been reached on the interpretation which must be given to criteria 4 and 5 of these "Instructions"[602], as these were the criteria "which present the POLISARIO Front with the greatest problems in terms of applicability, compatibility and legality with regard to the relevant provisions of the Settlement Plan". Once it was established that discussing the interpretation of these criteria did not entail their acceptance, the representatives of the POLISARIO Front were prepared to accept these criteria with a single non negotiable condition: the exclusive use as evidence of authentic documents issued by the Spanish Administration. Morocco rejected a reopening of the debate on this question.

As was expected, the extent of the agreements reached in these circumstances was rather mediocre. In our opinion, they did not even reach

---

[599] *Cfr.* ORSC: S/21360, June 18, 1990, and S/22464 and corr.1, April 19, 1991.
[600] ORSC: S/25170, par. 28.
[601] ORSC: S/23299, annex. Negotiations took place in the headquarters of the United Nations between the 25th of August and the 25th of September of 1992, and later the SG communicated its content to the President of the SC (Letter of October 2, 1992, ORSC: S/24644).
[602] The agreements figure as Annex to the document ORSC: S/25170, under the title "an interpretation by the parties of the criteria for eligibility to vote and other instructions relating to the tasks of the Identification Commission".

this level. This is shown by the significant drafting of the agreements. In the case of *"Criteria 4"*, the two parties agreed that "if this is applied", the evidence that the father was born in the territory would be a *sine qua non* condition for the person to have the right to vote. Moreover, this is the only agreement reached regarding this criterion as the POLISARIO Front considered that this was unacceptable as it reduced the stipulations in the Settlement Plan[603], but despite this, it was prepared to examine "any compromise proposals on this issue"[604].

With regard to *"Criteria 5"*, the POLISARIO Front held that, in accordance with this criteria, if a person had been abroad at the time of the 1974 census, he would have to prove that he had been resident in the territory for six consecutive years or twelve non-consecutive years between 1958 and 1974 (if he was in Morocco), between 1960 and 1974 (if he was in Mauritania), and between 1962 and 1974 (if he was in Algeria) in order to be registered in the census. As is logical, these dates are not arbitrary, but correspond to the dates when these three neighbouring States became independent. Morocco referred to the nomadic nature of Western Saharan society and to the movements of the population due to the colonization as it considered that the period to be taken into account should begin in 1884, the year in which Spain entered the territory. It is clear that there was no agreement on the question, and the Secretary General simply restricted himself to collecting the contradictory positions of both parties, so it is not appropriate to speak of an agreement.

As regards the *evidence,* the report of the Secretary General repeated the differences between the parties, with no more comments. Finally, on the question of *belonging to a tribe*, the parties did agree that belonging to a tribe did not, in itself, grant the right to participate in the referendum, meaning that "the individual must in all cases meet one of the criteria for eligibility in order to vote in the referendum". However, despite this, the positions of the parties remained immovable as regards when a sub-fraction should be considered "to be established in the Territory".

After successive failed attempts to close the gap between the parties, and as consequence of the efforts of the Special Representative of the Secretary General, the parties held direct conversations in El Aaiún (17-19 of July 1993), in which agreements were reached on a new revised timetable and on a new form for registration with two versions, one in Arabic and French and the other in Arabic and Spanish[605]. As a result of these agreements, on November

---

[603] Par. 24 and 61 of document *ORSC:* S/21360.
[604] *ORSC:* S/25170, par. 6.
[605] *Cfr.* Report of SG November 24, 1993, (*ORGA:* S/26797, par. 19).

3, 1993, the commencement of the identification and registration process was officially announced. However, the re-launch of the process was only apparent. Although the POLISARIO Front modified its position as regards the type of evidence admissible, and accepted oral testimony in support of individual applications to participate in the referendum, it requested the inclusion of amendments to the transaction proposal of the Secretary General, which were immediately rejected by Morocco.

3.2. *"The Compromise put forward to the two parties by the Secretary General" (July 28, 1993)*[606]

The most controversial question continued to be the determination of what should be understood by "settled sub-fraction of the territory"; so the SG presented the Parties a concrete compromise on the matter. The proposal of the SG could not be accepted by the POLISARIO Front and neither by Morocco due to reasons that will be analysed later on. The most important aspects of the proposal are that it:
- Reaffirms the previous five criteria of the SG Report;
- Establishes that a sub-fraction belonging to the territory is a sub-fraction included in 1974 census;
- Regarding supporting evidence it affirms that:

    "Exceptionally, where an applicant does not possess the above documents or has incomplete or inadequate documents, the Identification Commission may determine eligibility to vote taking into account testimony by tribal chiefs (Sheikhs)

- Regarding chiefs (Sheikhs) it points that

    "Only sheikhs of the Saharan subfractions included in the 1974 census will be eligible to testify before the identification Commission in support of individual applications to participate in the referendum"

This proposal could not be accepted by the POLISARIO Front, because the fact that if a single person belonging to a tribe, including those not settled in the territory, should figure in the census of 1974 it would give the right to participate in a referendum to all the members of that tribe, which, obviously, would distort the census, and therefore the Peace Plan. In their opinion, the

---

[606] Report of SG, June 28, 1993 (*ORSC*: S/26185).

formula proposed by the SG lacked of any kind of basis: neither historical nor related to the 1974 census.

Morocco was also dubious with the proposal, with the surprising argumentation that the decision to consider as settled in the territory "all Saharan subfractions whose members had been included in the census of 1974"[607] could arbitrarily exclude subfractions of which no member was present in the Territory during the 1974 census, but which were none the less an integral part of a Saharan Tribe of the Territory. To accept this position would throw be to directly discard the Settlement Plan, since the Spanish census would become the base criteria for create a further identification criteria.

Given this situation, the SG considered that neither of the conflicting interpretations of the two parties would be easily applicable, "the first being too imprecise and too broad and the second being mathematically impossible to formulate accurately", especially considering that "the notion of 'people of Western Sahara' cannot be defined clearly and precisely". Regarding the *Sheikhs* who could participate in the identification of the members of the different sub-fractions, the SG underlined "that two lists of *Sheikhs* are in existence: one from 1973, the other of those who at the time of realization of the census claimed to have this status, meaning that it was very difficult to reach an agreement on this question".

Even if the SG was aware that "the identification process and registration of potential voters cannot proceed beyond a certain point unless the particular problem of linkage with the Territory is settled", in his report of July 12, 1994[608] he reported to the SC the situation of the work of the Identification Commission and underlined that the Identification Commission focused its efforts on achieving the agreement and cooperation of both parties in order to proceed with the identification of potential voters. The agreement refers to the two Saharan tribal subfractions with which the operation should start, the pertinent *Sheikhs* who would help the Commission to identify the applicants and the Parties representatives in charge of the observation of the process. In virtue of this process, the SG recommended that the Transition Period should start on October 1, 1994, and that the referendum should take place on February 14, 1994.

---

[607] Report of SG of March 10, 1994, (*ORSC*: S/1994/283, Annex I, par. 5 a 17).
[608] *Cfr. ORSC*: S/1994/819.

3.3. Stalling of the process after "the flood of application forms at the last moment" (October 15, 1994). Decisions of the Secretary General (November 24, 1995) and his later disavowal by the Security Council -Resolution 1033 (1995)-

Although on August 28 1994 the identification and registration operation was finally launched[609] in El Aaiún and in the Tinduf camps (precisely in the "Wilaya" in "El Aaiún") and even after the initial understandable optimism at the start, the process had to be suspended for a few days. This was at the request of the POLISARIO Front, when the political and procedural difficulties inherent in the process were joined by those of nature, which seemed to ally itself with the misfortune Sahrawi people, punishing them with unprecedented heavy rainfall and consequent flash flooding in the Tinduf area, which caused widespread damage and disruption. The suspension for a few days of the process would not merit mention here if this unfortunate circumstance had not been used by Morocco to set up an operation that would ruin the whole process. The SG refers to it with a certain "surprise" pointing that "in the second half of October, there was a flood of completed application forms" but this mere "surprise" cannot cover the situation, given the significant extent of the violation of the Peace Plan. This is especially so if it is taken into account that, if the heavy rainfalls had not occurred, this "avalanche" of application forms would have arrived after the deadline, set in a letter to the parties from the Deputy Special Representative to set 15 October 1994 as the deadline for the receipt of the applications.

In a letter addressed to the President of the Security Council by the POLISARIO Front on November 10, 1994, the Saharan representatives fiercely criticized the Moroccan manoeuvre but also the Secretary General's attitude towards it, since faced with the flood of applications, the SG only pointed that "this inevitably means further lengthy delays in the identification process"[610]. 180,000 from the 232,000 demands received by the Identification Commission (data officiated by the MINURSO) were sent by the Moroccan government, of which 150,000 were sent on the day of the "last minute avalanche of applications" referred to in the report[611]. Including the new applications in the voter's census would mean, compared to the 1974 census, an increase of 296%, when the initial previsions were of an approximate increase of 3-6%. Furthermore, the great majority of the new applications

---

[609] Report of SG, November 5, 1994 (ORSC: S/1994/1257, par. 9 and 12).
[610] Report of SG of November 5, 1994 (ORSC: S/1994/1257).
[611] Par. 1 of letter of November 10, 1994.

CHAPTER VII

belonged to tribal sub-fractions that only represented 14% of the 1974 census (approximately 10,000 persons)[612]. The POLISARIO Front expressed their surprise and indignation to what they considered a "grave omission", as the SG's report referred neither to the mentioned data, nor to the origin of the mentioned "flooding of applications"[613]. This event without doubt marks the turning point of the identification process and another step in the drift of the attitude of the Secretary General towards Moroccan interests, since less than four months later he changed the course of the process, from setting the date for the referendum (February 14, 1995) to later considering that "it is clear that it will take many months to make sufficient progress in the identification process to be able to determine a date for the referendum"[614].

---

[612] Data from the newspaper *El País*, May 11, 1996.
[613] In a memorandum of the POLISARIO Front, of June of 1995 (unpublished), the Saharan representation presents concrete data on the identification process expressing their doubts on the credibility of the process and, deducing in practice the impossibility of the commencement of the "transitional period", that should take place after the final preparation of the voter list. In this way, it is stated that among the common features of the members of the big contingent of applicants of residence in the South of Morocco and in the occupied territories that claim to be included in the referendum census, the lack of identity documents is outstanding: documents issued by Spanish authorities or by Moroccan ones. But the memorandum draws attention about a paradigmatic case, the "most flagrant and symbolic" that took place in the Centre of Identification of the occupied location of Smara, where more than 3,000 applicants claimed in their inscriptions the following data: that they were born near Smara and that, following the drought, emigrated to Morocco in 1971, lived in Marrakech and returned to Sahara in 1991; that they were orphans of mother and father, and had no brothers or sisters; that they knew the designated *Sheikh* by Morocco; that they had no Spanish or Moroccan documentation. The POLISARIO Front considers that the following data are inconceivable among the Saharan population, and that it is also "too systematic to be accidental". The memorandum also states that the *Sheikh* appointed by the POLISARIO Front checked the falseness of the data after a few questions. But the most worrying issue is related to the future of the identification process: "how will the Commission resolve in the case of thousands and thousands of persons that a) do not figure in the 1974 census, b) do not present any kind of document to prove their own identity or allegations, c) about whom both Sheikhs do not agree?". The POLISARIO Front draws attention also on the problems that the post-referendum phase would cause and in the case it should be favourable to independence, how the United Nations should guarantee the mechanisms of peaceful transfer of the Territory Administration to the POLISARIO Front.
[614] ORSC: S/1994/1257, par. 20. The POLISARIO Front continues to insist on this approach. In this sense, for example, *cfr.* intervention of his representative before the Fourth Commission, October 7, 1996. In public statements of the President of the SADR, the POLISARIO Front outlined its intention to return to arms in the case the Peace plan should fail (*cfr. El País*, June 10, 1995).

Once Butros Gali accepted this situation, in his next reports[615] he would comment on the progress of the identification process, underlining exclusively the circumstance that the Government of Spain decided to forward to the Special Representative the Sharia Civil Register for Western Sahara my Deputy Special representative. We do not understand the reason for which this material should not have been forwarded at the beginning of the process, but now nearly twenty years after the Spanish withdrawal from the Territory.[616].

The two main questions of the identification process during this phase are related to the *designation of the Sheikhs for both parties and the identification of the tribes proposed by Morocco*. Butros Gali took decisions concerning both matters. Regarding the first, and since on numerous occasions the POLISARIO Front could not present a *sheikh* to identify these groups when dealing with tribes which, in its opinion, are not Western Saharans, the Secretary General decided that the procedure should be followed regardless of the cooperation of the parties. Firstly, both parties will be invited to present a *sheikh*, or deputy from the sub-fraction concerned who would act as representatives during the identification process. The OAU is also invited to name an observer. In these circumstances, as well as in the situation where one of the parties does not name a *sheikh* or deputy, "identification will take place on the basis of appropriate documentation, with the assistance of one of the *sheikhs* present" and anticipating that "in the situation where neither party wants to or is able to present a *sheikh* or deputy, identification will be based solely on documentary evidence"[617].

This proposal once again violated the spirit of the Peace Plan, which always took the agreement of both Parties as the starting point during the whole identification process. This question could have been overcome, maybe, during the Transitional Period, in which the power of the Special Representative would have allowed a decision to be made without taking into account the opinions of the parties, but during the identification phase this is not possible, not even if the SG proposed so, as time would show. According to the decision of the SG, the identification of 85 of the 88 resident subfractions of the territory and camps of Tinduf posed no problem regarding the designation of *sheikhs* and alternates and was carried out in the same conditions as before, with one exception: in the case of there being was no representative for one of

---

[615] Reports of the SG of March 30, 1995 (*ORSC*: S/1995/240); of May 19 of 1995 (*ORSC*: S/1995/404); of May 21, 1995 (*ORSC*: S/1995/498); of September 8, 1995 (*ORSC*: S/1995/779); of November 24, 1995 (*ORSC*: S/1995/986).
[616] Report of SG of 30 March, 1995 (*ORSC*: S/1995/240, par. 7).
[617] Report of SG of 24 November 1995 (*ORSC*: S/1995/986).

CHAPTER VII

the Parties, one of the *sheikhs* and/or the observer from the OUA would continue the identification process as long as the established formal procedures were followed (communication to the Parties of the date of identification and publication of the lists). In the case of the rest of the three tribal groups (H41, H61 y J51/52)[618], and in the case of all identification which took place outside the Territory and in the camps of Tinduf, the SG decided to continue the process even in the absence of a representative of the Parties, one of the *sheikhs* and/or an OAU observer, but in this case "although the *sheikh* who is present will be able to assist in identifying the applicant, the latter's claim for inclusion in the electoral roll, under any of the five criteria, will be evaluated on the basis of documentary evidence"[619]. For this purpose two documents will be required: first, a birth certificate issued by the competent authorities in the country of the applicant's birth to substantiate that he or she is the child of a father born in the Territory; secondly, a document issued by the competent authorities within the internationally recognized frontiers of the Territory before 1974 to substantiate the father's birth in the Territory.

As it was expected, both Parties rejected the proposal, though each one for different reasons. Since it had already refused that the only valid documents

---

[618] The POLISARIO Front refused to include in the census applicants that belongs to groups of tribes H41, H61 and J51/52, belonging to the "Tribes of the North", "Chorfa" and "Costeras and del Sur", respectively, because, in its opinion, they were groups of tribes and are not formed by subfractions in the strict sense of the Spanish census of 1974. In this census tribes were classified in alphabetic order (A, B, C, D, E, F, G, H, I, J), subdividing the seven first letters (A to G) in subfractions (A11 to A62; B11 to B81; C11 to C35; D11 to D22; E11 to E21; F11 to F51; G11 to G61). But, the most controversial aspect is the one related to tribes H, I and J, because these are not classified in subfractions, being groups of tribes: H41 is composed of a non determined number of tribes, H61 by more than 17 tribes and J51/52 by nearly 62. The most complicated question is related precisely to determine the subfractions and the *Sheikhs* of these groups, being in the majority persons that, according to Morocco, had been expelled by Spanish authorities during the colonization of the then Spanish Sahara. Among 242,000 applications to be identified, 181,000 were by Morocco and 61,000 by the Frente POLISARIO, and among those presented by Morocco approximately 110,000 belong to these three tribal groups. According to the census made by Spain, 7,908 of the persons in the census belonged to these three groups, which means 14% of the census. The Moroccan proposal of increasing the solicitors to 110,000 would increase the participation of these groups from the 14% mentioned to 45%, which logically, was rejected by the POLISARIO Front. In this sense, for example, regarding group H61, in the census of 1974 there were a total of 536 persons and Morocco has presented for their identification 56,000, from which 46,000 continue to live in Morocco (*ORSC*: S/1996/366, p. 10). This is precisely the key-point of the census, so consecutive interruptions of the process, until its reactivation by Kofi Annan, will be related nearly always to this question.
[619] Report of SG of November 6, 1995 (*ORSC*: S/1995/924).

should be the ones issued by the Spanish authorities, Morocco considered the reference to appropriate documentation as too vague and therefore liable to a restrictive interpretation. It further found unacceptable the proposal that identification could take place without the participation of any *sheikh* since this would exclude the oral testimony that this State believed should take priority over documentary proof. The POLISARIO Front would not subscribe the proposal but rejected it from a very different approach. In its opinion, the implementation of the new proposal would again give Morocco the opportunity to introduce, by means of a *sheikh* of its choice and its own documents, 13,000 applicants who had no ties with Western Sahara, which would be tantamount to holding a referendum for a people "other than those from Western Saharan", and according to M. Abdelaziz, it would prompt the POLISARIO Front to draw "appropriate" conclusions as to its involvement with regard to the Settlement Plan[620]. Resolution 1033 (1995) of the SC confirmed the need that in order to make progress in the identification process, both Parties should cooperate, though it asked the SG that in the case that no significant progress should be made he should inform the Council about the possible options, including the option of a progressive withdrawal of the MINURSO[621]. In this way, the Council came to reflect the feeling of both Parties (the decision of the Secretary General was unviable with the collaboration of the Parties) and set an important precedent which fatally wounded the political future of Butros Gali as Secretary General of the UNO by rejecting the draft of the resolution that endorsed the proposals of the SG[622].

As a way of unblocking the process, deadlocked since the POLISARIO Front's decision of not taking part in the identification of the applicants belonging to groups H41, H61 and J51/52 (with the exception of those part of groups included in 1974 census), and the corresponding denial of Morocco to continue the identification of other tribal groups in identification centres of Tinduf and as an attempt to regain credibility following the disavowal by the Security Council, the SG proposed to enter into direct talks between the Parties, and even proposed, for the first time, the possibility of creating a

---

[620] Report of SG of November 24, 1995 (*ORSC*: S/1995/986, par. 11).
[621] *ORSC*: Resolution 1033 (1995) of the SC, approved December 19, 1995.
[622] In opinion of Morocco this regretful precedent, by which "nothing can be done without the agreement of both parties, even though the settlement plan does not demand their cooperation" gives advantage to the "obstinate refusers", the POLISARIO Front, unique guilty of the paralysis of the process. Letter of May 10, 1996 addressed to the SG by the permanent representative of Morocco before the United Nations (*ORSC*: S/1996/345, Annex, p. 3).

"contact group" which could consist of regional and non-regional States"[623]. Nevertheless, after recommendation of the Secretary General in May of 1996, the Security Council decided to suspend the identification process until "such time as both parties provide concrete and convincing evidence that they are committed to resuming and completing it without further obstacles, in accordance with the Settlement Plan"[624].

In these circumstances the Security Council was not able to retract from the inertia that the SG had given to the process and set out a gradual dismantling of the MINURSO[625], approving a 20% reduction of the military component, although he decided to maintain an "Acting Special Representative" in charge of pursuing the dialogue between the Parties. The dismantling of the MINURSO followed the path traced by Butros Gali, closing the identification centres of the Territory (centres of Bojador, Dajla, Smara and El Aaiún) and those of the camps of Tinduf (Auserd, El Aaiún, Smara and Dajla), and then moving the identification registrations to the Offices of the United Nations in Geneva (16-23 July 1996).

Against this attitude of the Security Council, the USA launched into action its overwhelming diplomatic machinery, in view to obtaining two clear objectives: on the one hand, to avoid the reappointment of Butros Gali as the Secretary General of the UN, and on the other, to start up direct contact between the Parties "to explore direct dialogue between them that enables the situation to come out of the impasse" which the process was in[626]. As expected, this effort was successful.

4.   The Kofi Annan phase

4.1.   *The Houston Agreements. The unblocking of the identification process*

The appointment of Kofi Annan as Secretary General of the UN[627] was very well received by the representatives of the POLISARIO Front, given that they

---

[623] Report of SG, January 19, 1996 (*ORSC*: S/1996/43, par. 11).

[624] *ORSC:* Resolution 1056 (1996), approved by SC May 29, 1996.

[625] In words of the SG himself, "It is for this purpose that I have proposed and carried out, with the consent of the Security Council, considerable reductions in the size and functions of MINURSO in the past few months" (*ORSC:* S/1996/913, par. 25).

[626] *El País*, September 11, 1996. Apparently, these activities were communicated by the USA Embassy in Madrid to the Spanish Minister for Foreign Affairs before his visit to Algeria in those days.

[627] The renewal proposition of Butros Gali as SG, for a second mandate, between 1st of January 1997 and the 31st of December, 2001, proposed through a resolution draft

were now to deal with an individual with significant experience in decolonization processes and one who was a national in a State (Ghana) which recognised the SADR. His first steps in the process seemed correct to those who considered that he was the correct person to unblock the identification process and find an appropriate way to bring the Settlement Plan to fruition. However, this optimism only lasted a few months, time which showed that if it seemed that the unblocking of the process would allow the advancement towards the holding of a referendum, in reality the Secretary General had assumed that once the census was drafted, Morocco would retire from the peace process and had entrusted James Baker with the task of finding a solution outside of the Peace Plan. But let's break it down.

Kofi Annan's interest in reactivating the MINURSO was not coincidental, given that since March 1996 he occupied the position of Under-Secretary-General for Peace-keeping operations, after having assumed, during the transitional period which followed the signing of the Dayton Agreements, the functions of Special Representative of the Secretary General for the former Yugoslavia and Special Envoy before NATO. Regarding the census, negotiations carried out by the Personal Envoy of the SG, James Baker, initiated on April 22 and concluded with the signing of the Agreements of Lisbon, London and Houston on September 16, 1997, achieved a concrete agreement on the controversy referring tribal groups H41, H61 and J51/52, in the following terms:

> "1. The parties agree that they will not *directly or indirectly sponsor* or present for identification anyone from tribal groupings H41, H61 and J51/52 other than persons included in the Spanish census of 1974 and their immediate family members, but the parties shall not be obligated to actively prevent individuals from such tribal groupings from presenting themselves. The parties agree that identification of any such individuals who may present themselves shall proceed as soon as possible.

---

presented by Germany, Botswana, Chile, China, Egypt, France, Guinea-Bissau, Indonesia and the Russian Federation, was rejected by 14 votes in favour and one against, that of USA, that in exercise of its right of veto right did not allow such renewal (*ORSC: CS/749*, November 19, 1996). The 13th of December 1996, the SC approved unanimously the appointment of Kofi Annan as the new SG of the UNO, for the period for which the second mandate had been to Butros Gali (*ORSC: CS/760*).

2. The parties agree that persons from all other tribal groups from census categories H, I and J may come forward to be identified.

3. *The parties agree that the Special Representative of the Secretary - General shall notify the parties of the results by number, but not name, of the identification process to date.*

4. *The parties acknowledge that, from the time of the original Settlement Plan, they have understood that* credible oral testimony to the Identification Commission would be required, *and the parties agree that the Identification Commission shall receive and consider oral testimonies, as provided for in the Settlement Plan"*[628].

It is not difficult to appreciate the subtlety of the reached agreement. So, on the one hand, the first paragraph corresponds, though not categorically given the farfetched formula used, with the POLISARIO Front approach that limits the danger that, being presented by Morocco, the applicants of these controversial groups should reach excessive figures. On the other hand, the third (the second paragraph is not really an agreement, as it had already been set out during the process up until this time) corresponds partially to an express demand of the POLISARIO Front demanding that the result of the identification process should be notified to the Parties (number and also name of identified person). But, the fourth paragraph is closer to the Moroccan intentions to give more weight to the oral testimony. The truth is that even as a result of the first paragraph's confusing drafting, as expected, the process would again find the same obstacle, but at least it reactivated the process at a moment when, once again, it was doomed to failure.

These agreements led to the gradual reactivating of the MINURSO. The first and most significant step was that identification files stored in the United Nations Office in Geneva were returned to El Aaiún and Tinduf and the initial reopening of four identification centres with the intention of reaching a total of twelve, nine of which should function concurrently[629]. Finally, the identification process resumed on December 3[630], during the course of which the problems related to the identification of applicants belonging to the three

---

[628] *ORSC*: S/1997/742, annex I (underlined by the author).
[629] These movements were made between October 23 and November 6, 1997 (Report of SG to the SC on November 13, 1997, *ORSC*: S/1997/882, par. 5 and 6).
[630] Letter of the SG to the President of the SC on, December 12 of 1997 (*ORSC*: S/1997/974).

controversial tribal groups again came up[631]. But, after the long succession of reports and resolutions, stoppages and reactivations of the process, all seemed to point that this time problems were going to be overcome. In effect, the process was reactivated after the appointment of the new Special Representative of the Secretary General, the American Charles F. Dunbar[632].

Despite the continuing problems faced by the identification process, the Houston agreements had an important virtuality: though the identification of the "contested" tribal groups by the POLISARIO Front were the main obstacle of the process (the number of persons of these the tribes included in the 1974 census was of 603, while Morocco increased this number to 65,000 persons to identify)[633], the agreements lead, in the first stage, to the conclusion of the identification process of all of the rest of the eighty five groups[634] and in the second stage and with a surprising rapidity[635], to the identification of the controversial three tribal groups.

During the months that followed the Houston agreements, the identification process continued to proceed with success. So, even if it had been the most controversial issue during the peace process, as it could alter substantially the referendum census, the POLISARIO Front finally felt forced to accept that the Commissions were to proceed to identify the applicants belonging to tribal groups H41, H61 and J51/52. The reasons of such concession, another but not the last, were that they were backed up by the reference data of the number of applicants that completed the provisional list of voters, corresponding to the eighty five non contested groups, which, in opinion of the Saharan movement, allowed them to trust the seriousness with which the UN had acted during the long identification process, and that the Organization would maintain during the identification of the aforementioned groups. As the only way out of the deadlocked process, the POLISARIO Front felt forced to take the risk that the census should be extended by including the

---

[631] The fact that in a few days, 8.613 people, without being invited and most of whom belonged to the H61 group, presented themselves at El Aaiún led to the protests of the POLISARIO Front, which believed that Morocco had failed to comply with the Houston Agreements (Report of the SG, January 15, 1998, ORSC: S/1998/35)

[632] February 9, 1998 (cfr. ORGA: S/1998/316, April 13, 1998).

[633] Cfr. ORGA: S/1998/634, par. 5.

[634] The consecutive reports of the SG announced clearly the more than probable deactivation of the identification process once concluded the one regarding the "non contested" tribal groups (cfr. ORGA: S/1998/534, June 18, 1998; S/1998/634, July 10, 1998; S/1998/775, August 18, 1998; S/1998/849, September 11, 1998).

[635] Even if the groups were the most disputed ones, its identification took place from the 15th of June to the 30th of December 1999 (ORGA: S/2000/131, Report of SG of February 17, 2000).

mentioned tribal groups, trusting that, acknowledging previous data, the increase of the census would not be too big. As a counterpart of this concession was the fact that it was the concession of the weak party, and implies the acceptance of the main obstacle put in place by Morocco in the Peace Plan since its commencement: Morocco did not give way in its restrictions to the normal functioning of the MINURSO (for example, as some which have caused most problems to it, the one can mention the limitations on the use of MINURSO aircraft, which are "not in accordance of peacekeeping practices and could bring negative consequences to the process (…)"[636], the obstacles to UNHCR in their "preparatory work for the repatriation of Saharan refugees eligible to vote and their inmediate families"[637], or those related to the operational capacity of the technical support unit of the MINURSO[638]). As a result, it is clear that the concessions made by the Parties to allow the process to succeed were not of the same weight.

The faith of the POLISARIO Front was fruitful, as the United Nations continued the identification process with the rigor with which it had been carried out in precedent stages. So, on January 17, 2000 the SG published the results of the first part of the identification process and according to it, from the 198,469 applicants interviewed since the identification process began in 1994, the total number of persons included in the census was 86,386. Out of 147,249 from Saharan tribes other than the three controversial groups, 84,251 were eligible applicants and from the 51,220 corresponding to the three other groups (tribal groups H41, H61 and J51/52), 2,135 were accepted. These data, together with the rapidity with which the identification was carried out during the last months, reflect eloquently the "soundness" of the proof presented by the applicants. By that stage of the process, these data show at least two of the key issues of the process: on the one hand, the bad faith of Morocco in its demand that 65,000 persons should be considered residents of Western Sahara, and, on the other hand, the rigor of the United Nations in the identification of applicants. If the first issue was well known, the second was a good and encouraging news.

As expected, after publishing these data, Morocco resorted to the "penultimate" argument that was left to reject the right to self-determination of the peoples of the territory: the presentation of an appeal regarding practically all the applicants that the different Identification Commissions had rejected.

---

[636] *ORGA*: S/1998/634, July 10, 1998.
[637] *ORGA*: S/1998/849, September 11, 1998, par. 22.
[638] *ORSC*: Resolution 1204 (1998) of SC, approved October 30, 1998.

We say "penultimate" argument because only one was left: once this second stage of appeal was concluded, the Moroccan Government would reject the census drafted by the MINURSO on the grounds that the Organisation had acted with bias. Thus, the report of the Secretary General of 17 February, 2000 called to the Security Council's attention the reaction of the Moroccan Government on discovering the results: "the Moroccan officials questioned again the impartiality and objectivity of Identification Commission members, and warned that the referendum would not be held if any person originating from the Sahara were denied the right to participate"[639].

Nevertheless, the certainty of this attitude will come after the last obstacle put by Morocco in the Peace Plan, consisting of provoking a "duplication" in the identification process, by appealing the majority of rejected applicants rejected by the MINURSO. The Secretary General himself pointed out in his report of October 28, 1999 that the overwhelming majority of the 79,000 appeals received by the Identification Centres in the last two weeks before the deadline for their presentation "correspond very closely to the number of persons omitted from the first part of the provisional list of potential voters issued on 15 July 1999", so predictably "we might be confronted with a lengthy appeals process, involving almost all applicants rejected in the first instance, as well as a large number of applicants whose inclusion in the provisional voter list has been challenged"[640]. The doubts on whether these 79,000 could be increased with another 60,000, belonging to the applications rejected belong to persons from the controverted three tribal groups, were unfortunately confirmed when published, showing that they were increased in the "second identification process" to nearly 140,000 applicants[641]. Once these data were published, which in reality constituted an open secret, the SG, surprisingly, affirmed in his report of 6 December 1999 that "the problem posed by the current number of appeals and the opposing positions taken by the parties on the issue of admissibility seem to allow little possibility of holding the referendum before 2002 or even beyond"[642].

---

[639] *ORGA:* S/2000/131, par. 5.

[640] *ORSC:* S/1999/1098, October 28, 1999, par. 26.

[641] The fact that among the presented appeals only a few hundred correspond to the Saharan part is eloquent. The Moroccan party interprets the high number of appeals as a sign of dissatisfaction of applicants due to the MINURSO attitude. In this respect, and regarding the eighty five tribal groups whose "Saharan" nature is no doubt for neither Party, the number of appeals presented by the Moroccan side is of approximately 68,000, for not including certain persons in the voting lists, and 10,000 for including certain persons that the appealing part consider as non Saharan. On the Saharan part, the numbers are of 840 and 2,000 respectively.

[642] *ORSC:* S/1999/1219, December 6, 1999, par. 28.

CHAPTER VII

Given the circumstances, the President of the SADR, M. Abdelaziz stated before the SG of the UN what was only obvious: if the dispositions referring to admissibility of appeals were to be applied with rigor[643], the majority of the appeals presented should not be admitted. To this effect, it must not be forgotten that the applicants excluded from the census in the first phase have the right to appeal such decision, but only if the basis of the appeal is the testimony of witnesses that may give additional information to support their inclusion. Furthermore, in the second phase, only persons who have been previously included in the electoral census can testify as a witness. If the person wishing to testify had been excluded in the first phase of the MINURSO or was not an applicant to be included in the census, obviously, the witness cannot be considered as Saharan; given the tribal structure of the society, non-Saharans could hardly be expected to testify that the applicants are Saharan.

Once again we encounter a Moroccan move to delay the celebration of the referendum, just as the main obstacle of the process had been overcome and it at last seemed that it should have a smooth ending. Nevertheless, in his report of February 17, 2000 Kofi Annan noted the effects of the Moroccan move, making a particularly concerning statement, given who it was coming from: "even assuming that a referendum were held pursuant to the settlement plan and agreements of the parties, *if the result were not to be recognized and accepted by one party, it is worth noting that no enforcement mechanism is envisioned by the settlement plan,* nor is one likely to be proposed, calling for the use of military means to effect enforcement"[644]. That after nearly ten years of the Peace Plan the Secretary General calls attention to this issue, instead of requesting that the Security Council adopts the necessary measures to ensure that both Parties abide by the outcome of the referendum, resorting if necessary to Chapter VII of the Charter, was not reassuring.

As expected, at first the POLISARIO Front refused to accept that this huge quantity of applicants would go through the Identification Centres, since this would practically entail the re-commencement of a process which had already taken over five years, especially considering that about 95% of them could not provide new evidence which could justify the appeal in accordance with the criteria established in the Settlement Plan and subsequent adjustments[645]. However, the Sahrawi national liberation movement would eventually accept this latest affront to the Plan by the Moroccan Government, allowing even the possibility that the MINURSO would carry out the identification of the

---

[643] *ORSC*: S/1999/483/Add.1, p. 13 et 14.
[644] *ORSC*: S/2000/131, February 17, 2000, par. 36.
[645] *ORSC*: S/1996/343.

appeals without the approval of the *sheikhs* or tribal chiefs proposed by the POLISARIO Front and Morocco[646].

But by this time, Morocco had already decided to definitively abandon the possibility of holding the referendum for self-determination in the territory at any point; although the Moroccan position was clear from the time of Pérez de Cuéllar[647], it was at this time that it openly expressed its total opposition to any type of referendum.

4.2. Reasons for the abandonment of the Settlement Plan. The "slips" of the Secretary General

Although Kofi Annan expressly welcomed the POLISARIO Front's conciliatory attitude and its confidence in the UN in proposing that the final decision about the inclusion or not in the census of the appellants be left to the MINURSO, accepting even the absence of Sahrawi tribal chiefs in the process of identification, the Secretary General finally decided to propose to the Security Council the abandonment of the route agreed on by the Parties in 1988 (the Settlement Plan) and the commencement of a search for a political solution to the conflict. The arguments that underpin this proposal cannot be more disappointing. We will consider the most important[648].

Firstly, the reason for the inability to advance in the peace process could be found in the "fundamental differences between the parties *over its interpretation*" because of the "*ill-defined* nature of tribal affiliation with the Territory"[649]. Inasmuch as the positions of the parties over the different aspects of the Settlement Plan that make reference to the issue of the census and its criteria have already been analysed, this issue requires no further commentary. The fact that Morocco uses this argument is unacceptable although understandable; however, that the Secretary General does it is neither acceptable nor understandable.

---

[646] ORSC: "Official proposals submitted by the POLISARIO Front to overcome the obstacles to the implementation of the Settlement Plan", S/2001/613, Annex IV, appendix, para. 1

[647] Among the many examples that could be mentioned, in 1996, during a time of stoppage of the Plan Morocco explained to Butros Gali that meetings with the representatives of the POLISARIO Front "would not take place until such a time as when Morocco's sovereignty was accepted as a prerequisite [sic] for the consideration of any proposal" (Report of the SG June 20, 2001, S/2001/613, para. 32). Given this Moroccan approach, the SG often "reiterated the promise of the POLISARIO Front to respect the outcome of the referendum".

[648] ORSC: Report of the SG, June 20 2001, S/2001/613.

[649] *Ibid.*, par. 21.

Secondly, even in the situation that the MINURSO finally proceeded with the examination of the pending appeals and called a census in conformity with the criteria accepted by the parties, it lacks "an enforcement mechanism for the results of the referendum"[650]. The very likely veto from France in the Security Council would have prevented recourse in the situation to Chapter VII of the Charter and more worryingly, the Security General tiptoed around the mechanisms provided in Chapter VII for such situations and avoided recommending their application. It must also be remembered that we are dealing here not only with an obligation on a State to comply with general International law, obligatory on all States, such as that of self-determination for all peoples but also an agreement (the Settlement Plan) entered into freely and voluntarily by it. It is inadmissible that an obligation voluntarily entered into by a State can be breached with absolute impunity and pretends that International law offers no mechanisms to enforce it.

Thirdly, the Secretary General argues that to move the process forward would require the agreement of Morocco, and that any alterations to the Settlement Plan would be unless since at the end with would still be *"a winner and a loser"*. He reiterates this idea by stating that "it is perhaps understandable that this full cooperation is difficult to achieve given the '*winner-take-all*' nature of the referendum called for under the settlement plan"[651]. This perverse expression is a constant in the reports of the Secretary General and deserves severe criticism since it seeks to put on the same plane the State who is illegally occupying a Non-Self-Governing Territory, and the people, its legitimate owners, who suffer from this illegal occupation. Can we really say that in the decolonization process one sees the sharing of territory, resources or rights between the colonizer and colonized? Must it be considered a "loser" the State, which, after years of violating International law, meets, or is bound to meet, its international obligations?

However, the most serious "mistake" of the Secretary General is the repeated affirmation that Morocco is acting "as the administering power". Given that this is total legal nonsense and that its use by the person who holds the ultimate representation of the United Nations is not innocent, since even though this claim was disqualified by the Legal Department of the Organization it continues to figure in his reports, we will return to this issue later to analyse it further.

---

[650] *Ibid.*, par. 29.
[651] *Ibidem.*

This report of the Secretary General opened the doors to "plan Bs", "fourth routes" or political solutions to the conflict, outside of the Settlement Plan. James Baker had already been working on them since he took office[652].

4.3. *"The Framework Agreement on the Status of Western Sahara" (Baker Plan I)*

In June 2001, Kofi Annan presented to the Security Council the draft "Framework Agreement"[653] which, if agreed to by the parties, would not entail the definitive abandonment of the peace process but it would be "suspended", a term difficult to understand in reality.

4.3.1. *The powers of the "Sahrawi" organs in the Territory*

The Framework Agreement shares the competencies and powers in the Territory between "the population of Western Sahara" on one hand and Morocco on the other. In respect of the former, this theoretical "Sahrawi Government" would consist of an executive, a legislature and a judiciary and would have exclusive competence in respect of local government administration, territorial budget and taxation, law enforcement, internal security, social welfare, culture, education, trade, transport, agriculture, mining, fisheries and industry, environmental policy, housing and urban development, water and electricity, roads and other basic infrastructure.

An Assembly with a life of four years would exercise legislative power, and its members would be elected by those people who have lived continuously, without interruption, in the territory since 31st October, 1998 and those who were included in the repatriation list of 31st October, 2000.

Executive power would be elected for four years by those people included in the census made by the MINURSO, published on 30th December, 1999. However, after this first mandate of four years, the new executive would not be voted for using this electoral census but instead by the Assembly. Thus, the

---

[652] Given this snub by Morocco of the Settlement Plan, one should not be surprised by the POLISARIO Front's response, in which it highlighted that if the process continued to suffer severe delays there would be no point in the MINURSO remaining in the Territory and that it may even act to resume the hostilities. As M. Abdelaziz claimed "if the UN does not intend to move the process forward, it is best to call it a day, proclaiming the mission a failure and leaving the Territory. The Sahrawi people would assume its responsibilities. It is not our preferred option, but it is the only one we are left with in the face of such delays and Moroccan stalling tactics" (*El País*, 19 February 2000)

[653] *ORSC*: S/2001/613, June 20, 2001.

first executive would be chosen by those who, according to the United Nations itself, are Sahrawi, while the Assembly would also be chosen by those who have resided in the Territory since October 1990.

Finally, judicial authority would be exercised by courts composed of judges originating from the Territory but selected by a Moroccan body, such as the National Institute of Legal Studies. These courts would have competencies as regards territorial law.

Further, both the laws passed by the Assembly and the decisions of the courts would have to respect the Moroccan Constitution, especially as regards the protection of civil liberties.

A) *The powers of Morocco in the Territory*

The Framework Agreement gives Morocco exclusive competencies as regards foreign relations (including international treaties), national security and external defence (including the determination of maritime, air and land borders, and their protection by "all appropriate means"), all matters related to the production, sale, ownership and use of arms and explosives and the preservation of territorial integrity "against secessionist attempts" (*sic*), whether they come from within or outside the territory. Further, the flag, currency, customs and postal and telecommunications systems of the Kingdom shall be the same for Western Sahara.

B) *The referendum on the final status of the Territory*

The status of Western Sahara would finally be submitted to a referendum that should be held at a date agreed on by the parties no later than five years after the initial actions of application of the agreement. The census would be comprised of those persons who have resided continuously in the Territory during the year prior to its celebration.

C) *The virtuality of Baker Plan I*

In view of these data, it does not escape the mind of anyone that we are here dealing with a project that ignores the decolonization doctrine and practice of the United Nations, especially as regards the critical moment of the consultation of the population, since it will involve Sahrawi's…and Moroccan residents. Obviously, as is only logical, there is no precedent in this regard. Moreover, specific aspects of the powers conferred to Morocco, especially the applicability of its Constitution in the Territory, are totally and openly in contradiction to the content of Resolution 2625 (XXV), which establishes a separate and distinct legal status of the Non-Self-Governing Territory from the metropolis. The same can be said about the attribution of exclusive competence to Morocco as regards foreign affairs.

Moreover, the attribution of exclusive competence to Morocco as regards the preservation of territorial integrity "against secessionist attempts", related to the idea that part of the territory of this State intends to separate from the rest, which is to admit the Moroccan pretensions of Western Sahara forming part of its territory, which is unacceptable. As noted by the Algerian representative "this project ratifies the illegal occupation of the territory of Western Sahara and it is a report of a planned integration, in violation of International law"[654].

For its part, in response to this report, the POLISARIO Front reiterated that the only way to resolve the conflict was through the agreement of both parties to the Settlement Plan, reaffirmed its strong commitment to accept the result of the referendum and recalled the responsibility of the United Nations and the Security Council itself when it comes to enforcing the results. Needless to say that Morocco expressly accepted the Framework Agreement.

4.4. *"The Peace Plan for the self-determination of the people of Western Sahara" (Baker Plan II)*

A) *The powers of the "Sahrawi" organs in the Territory*

The second Baker Plan[655] modified some of the aspects of the Framework Agreement, although it maintained a very similar structure to its predecessor. Thus, it maintains the share of competences between "the population of Western Sahara" and Morocco, but with some alterations. The future "Sahrawi Government" would have the same composition as that proposed by the Framework Agreement (to be made up of executive, legislative and judicial powers), and it would have exclusive competences in relation to local government administration, territorial budget and taxation, law enforcement, internal security, social welfare, culture, education, trade, transport, agriculture, mining, fisheries and industry, environmental policy, housing and urban development, water and electricity, roads and other basic infrastructure.

---

[654] Memorandum of Algeria to the proposed Framework Agreement (ORSC: S/2001/613, Annex II)
[655] ORSC: S/2003/565, Anex II.

An Assembly, that would have practically the same competences as in the prior project, would exercise the legislative power, but, differently, it would be elected by a census that would not include residents. This same census would elect the executive power, which would be exercised by a *Chief Executive* which would have similar powers to those proposed in the first Baker Plan. Elections would take place a year after the entry into force of the Plan, and would be for a term of four years or "until the governmental authority of Western Sahara is modified in conformity with the referendum on its final status". Finally, the judicial power would be exercised by the Supreme Court of Western Sahara, which, together with the inferior courts, could form the Western Saharan Authority. Its members would be named by the Chief Executive, with the prior consent of the legislative Assembly. The Supreme Court would have competence to determine the compatibility of any Western Saharan law with the Plan with the exception on those relating to competencies reserved to Morocco, in which case the Supreme Court of this State would be competent. Moreover, the Supreme Court of Western Sahara would be the court of last instance as regards the interpretation of the law in the Territory.

B) *The powers of Morocco in the Territory*

The competences attributed to Morocco are very similar to those in the Framework Agreement. The only ones that change are firstly those related to the production, sale, ownership and use of arms and explosives, in the case of "of weapons by the law enforcement authorities of the Western Sahara Authority" and secondly, although again it makes an unfortunate reference to the "preservation of territorial integrity against secessionist attempts", it states that "the right to preserve territorial integrity shall not authorize any action whatsoever that would prevent, suppress, or stifle peaceful public debate, discourse or campaign activity, particularly during any election or referendum period". Finally, it is noted that the authority of Morocco as regards the foreign affairs of the Territory shall be exercised in consultation with the Western Saharan Authority in the case of questions that directly affect the interests of the Territory. In this sense, it points out that "Morocco may authorize representatives of the Authority to serve as members of the Kingdom's diplomatic delegations in international meetings concerned with economic issues and other issues of direct interest to Western Sahara".

THE PEACE PLAN (II) – THE PROBLEM OF CONSULTING THE POPULATION

C) *The referendum*

a) *The right to self-determination of "bona fide residents"*

The Plan provides for a transitional period during which there will be a sharing of responsibilities between the parties before the celebration of the referendum on self-determination, which, in the words of the Secretary General himself "would provide the bona fide residents of Western Sahara with an opportunity to decide their future". The reference to "the Sahrawi people" or "the people of Western Sahara" is abandoned as the true recipient of self-determination in favour of the *"bona fide residents"*. We find ourselves before an innovation in International Law in which, surprisingly, new subjects are discovered: from now on, together with those people subject to colonial, foreign and racist domination and insurgent movements, we will see the inclusion of "residents in good faith". For reasons discussed later, despite the obvious affront to International Law posed by this idea, the POLISARIO Front will eventually accept this so called "Peace Plan for the self-determination of the people of Western Sahara", which would be rejected by Morocco.

Under the Plan, those individuals over 18 years of age may participate in the referendum if:
- They figure in the provisional list of voters of 30th December, 1999 made by the Identification Commission of the MINURSO (without the possibility of appeal or objection), or if
- They are included in the repatriation list drawn up by UNHCR on October 31st, 2001, or if
- They have lived continuously in the Territory since 30th December 1999.

The United Nations will determine which individuals have the right to vote and its decision shall be final and appeal shall not be possible. New voters may only be included in the event that their permanent residence in the Territory since 30th December 1999 can be "supported by testimony from at least three credible persons and/or credible documentary evidence" which will be analysed by the UN which will take the decision which will be final and without appel.

b) *The third option of the referendum: autonomy*

The Secretary General noted in his report that the main objection of Morocco to the Plan is the inclusion of the option of independence among the possibilities in the referendum and he mentions two reasons why Morocco should accept it, reasons that perplex even the most expert analyst. Firstly, for the "the stated commitment of Morocco to the settlement plan" (should this not in fact be used as an argument to enforce the implementation of the entire Settlement Plan?) and secondly for the inclusion in the electorate for the referendum of "all of those who have resided continuously in Western Sahara since 30 December 1999, as opposed to only those who would be included in the voter list, wich was created on the basis of the work of the Identification Commission"[656]. In other words, Morocco should accept the option of independence because in recognizing the right to participate in the referendum not only to Sahrawis but also to Moroccan settlers it means that the chances of victory for the independence option would be practicly non-existent. But Morocco, which saw it as completely logical that residents would participate in the referendum (it considered it literally "just, equitable and in accordance with democratic practices"), asked why the mentioned date, 30th December 1999, should be the limit for residence in the Territory.

To overcome the problem posed by the refusal of Morocco to accept this option, the Secretary General suggested a third option along with those agreed by the parties (integration and independence): autonomy. In case none of the three options won a majority of votes, the option that receives the fewest votes would be eliminated and a second round of voting would take place to allow the voters to choose between the two remaining options. Should the third option prevail, that of self-government or autonomy, the electorate for future elections for the executive and legislative authority of the Territory would be made up of the aforementioned "bona fide residents of Western Sahara" who are over 18 years old.

c) Other issues

The Baker Plan II tries to concretize more questions related to its implementation, including:
- It ensures the commitment of the parties "not to hinder the ability of persons to campaign peacefully for or against any person standing for election or any option or ballot question offered to the voters in the referendum on final status".
- It guarantees the respect of the Statute of the Territory by noting that neither Morocco nor the Western Saharan Authority can unilaterally "change or abolish the status of Western Sahara, except for the adoption of

---

[656] *ORSC*: Report of the Secretary General, 23 May 2003, S/2003/565, par. 52.

such laws as may be necessary to conform to the results of the referendum on final status".
- It also ensures the release of all political prisoners and prisoners of war.
- Finally, the Plan advances the surprising prevision of the Security Council to modify the name and mandate of the MINURSO "to enable it to assist in the implementation of this plan, in particular during the period between the plan's entry into force and the holding of the election for the Chief Executive and the Legislative Assembly of the Western Sahara Authority". This attempt to change the name of the MINURSO is not innocent since it would suppose an attempt to abandon its real raison d'être: the organization of the referendum for self-determination.

4.5. Farewell to the Baker Plan: Morocco is left on its own

The Security Council, through Resolution 1495 (2003) of 24th July, "acting under Chapter VI of the Charter", decided to support Baker Plan II, "as an optimum political solution based on agreement between the parties". For his part, the Secretary General urged Morocco "to seize the opportunity and to participate positively in the plan by accepting and implementing the Plan"[657]. Despite this, Morocco representatives noted to the Secretary General that "over the years, the proposed referendum has always been inapplicable in the way it has been planned and it has lost its raison d'être", since with a referendum, "after all, there would be a winner and a loser"[658]. As shown, Morocco did not have time to dig deeper into the on-going slips of the Secretary General.

Among other arguments for refusing to accept the Peace Plan, Morocco claims that it is in clear contradiction with its Constitution[659]. If this argument had any truths, many of the decolonization processes could not have come about, since in the majority of, if not in all, Constitutions of colonial powers the colonial territories are considered as an integrated part of their territory. For the same reason, Morocco considered incompatible its domestic laws with the judicial decentralization envisaged by the Plan. It even came to criticize the fact that the Secretary General should reserve to himself the power to interpret the Plan and that his decision should be binding and without appeal in order to

---

[657] ORSC: Report of the Secretary General 16 October 2003, S/2003/1016, para. 27.

[658] "Observations of Morocco to the new proposal of James Baker entitled 'Peace Plan for the Self-Determination of the people of Western Sahara'" (ORSC: S/2003/565, Annex III).

[659] On the incompatibility of the Baker proposal with the Moroccan Constitution, cfr. RUIZ MIGUEL, C., "La tercera vía ante el Derecho constitucional marroquí: una autonomía imposible" (http://sahara_opinions.site.voila.fr).

CHAPTER VII

accuse him expressly of trying to place in an "untenable position of being both judge and party"[660]. Judge, yes, but party? As we have examined so far, the Sahrawi's have more reasons to question the impartiality of the Secretary General.

As a result of the intransigence of Morocco, on 11th June 2004, the Secretary General announced the resignation of James Baker, who left the post of Personal Envoy having done "everything in his power" to find a solution to the conflict. He was replaced in office by Peter van Walsum, who as we shall see later, was as a fleeting as a disastrous step in the conflict[661].

The POLISARIO Front noted in a comprehensive report[662] many of the reasons for its refusal to accept the Peace Plan, despite the fact that eventually it ended up agreeing to it. As a starting point, it lamented that the new plan would entail the abandonment of the Settlement Plan, the only one agreed to voluntarily by both parties, to substitute it for another which left unresolved many issues of significant importance, including the cantonment of military contingents, the time and guarantees of the return of Sahrawi refugees, the release of prisoners of war[663], the need to prevent future "Green Marches", as well as the fact that the Plan did not guarantee respect for the result of the referendum.

It also reiterated the main mistake contained in the Plan: Morocco is not the administering Power but instead the occupying Power of the Territory, so it cannot be the representative of the Sahrawi people in foreign affairs nor can it conclude agreements relating to the exploitation of Sahrawi natural resources, nor can it determine the international borders of the Territory. For this same reason, the symbols of Moroccan sovereignty over the Territory (flags, currency) are also not acceptable. In this sense, it recalled that reference in the

---

[660] *ORSC*: S/2003/565, Observations of the Kingdom of Morocco on the new proposal of James Baker entitled "peace plan for self-determination of the people of Western Sahara", par. 22.

[661] Report of the SG 11 June 2004 (*ORSC*: S/2004/492). In later declarations, Baker expressly blamed Morocco for the failure of the peace process and did not hesitate to refer to the possible return to armed struggle by the POLISARIO Front against the Moroccan intransigence as "logical" (text from an interview of 19 August 2004 at http://arso.org.site.voila.fr/BakerPBSes.htm).

[662] Letter of 8 March 2003 to the SG from the Secretary General of the POLISARIO Front (*ORSC*: S/2003/565, Annex III).

[663] At the height of repression in the occupied Sahrawi territories, the POLISARIO Front decided unilaterally to release those Moroccan prisoners of war who remained in their power, while Morocco does not even recognise this status of prisoner of war and has not disclosed the whereabouts of more than 500 Sahrawi soldiers who are desappeared since the time of the war.

Plan to possible "secessionist interference" was another unforgivable *lapsus linguae* given that it is based on the idea that Western Sahara forms part of the territorial integrity of Morocco, which is openly contrary to the doctrine of the UN itself.

The report of the POLISARIO Front also details some of the times when the peace process has been halted as a result of obstructions by Morocco, to highlight that after each of these the Sahrawi movement backed down or compromised, as well as the United Nations, while Morocco maintained absolute intransigence.

Finally, the POLISARIO Front considered the census for the referendum proposed by the Plan unacceptable, since in it would participate 86,425 Sahrawis and a far higher number of Moroccan settlers, without any guarantees that the results of the referendum would be respected in the situation that the independence option won.

Although, as we have seen, specific aspects of the Baker Plan II clearly contradict the provisions of the Settlement Plan and it aligns itself to the pretensions of Morocco, in June 2003, the POLISARIO Front decided to accept it, "to show their sincere commitment to peace and cooperation with the work done by Mr Baker and the Secretary General"[664], probably convinced that Morocco will never give its approval to the Plan, once again using its spot on diplomatic intuition to show the true intentions of the occupying State.

The stagnation of the peace process led different representatives of the POLISARIO Front to note the possibility of re-employing weapons in the event that the deadlock was indefinite, about which Kofi Annan expressed concern, urging the parties to "refrain from inflammatory statements or taking any action, including legal, political or military, which would have the effect of further complicating the search for a solution or cause unnecessary friction"[665]. Although it is conceivable that what the Secretary General asked of the parties is prudence, the request to the party who for more than three decades has been on the receiving end of violations of International law to avoid taking any *legal* action is simply grotesque. Indeed if any aspect of the approach of the POLISARIO Front can be criticized, it is not the lack of prudence or patience, but instead the lack of legal initiatives involving not only Morocco but also those States and international organizations (including the

---

[664] Memorandum on the question of Western Sahara directed to Member States of the UN by the POLISARIO Front (*ORGA*: A/59/314 and S/2004/704, 1 September 2004).

[665] Report of the Secretary General 19 April 2005 (*ORSC*: S/2005/254).

EU) which negotiate with the occupying State over the exploitation of natural resources in the Territory or which make significant investments in it.

5. The Ban Ki-moon phase: The Mansahett round of talks, negotiations without a future

On 1st January 2007 Korean Ban Ki-moon became the eighth Secretary General of the United Nations. In the last half of his term, it is certain that his involvement in the Western Sahara has been more discreet. His first steps were accompanied by the so-called "Moroccan initiative for negotiating a statute of autonomy for Western Sahara" presented on 11th April, 2007, a proposal for resolving the conflict through the establishment of autonomy in the Territory, which would be approved through a referendum, incorrectly referred to as one of "self-determination" since it excludes the option of independence[666]. It did not get any further since it was in effect a proposal to integrate the Territory into Morocco.

The negotiations driven by the new Secretary General, which took place in Manhasset (New York) over four rounds[667], were of limited scope, since in the erroneous words of the Personal Envoys to the Secretary General, Van Walsum and Christopher Ross, the differences between the parties as to the way in which self-determination should be exercised in the Territory are insurmountable. And they are wrong, because given that Morocco will never accept independence as an option, one cannot speak of "differences as to the way in which self-determination should be realized"; one must instead speak of the differences as to the acceptance or not of self-determination as a way to end the conflict.

Reports from the Secretary General would not deserve even a mention if they were not aimed almost exclusively at issues relating to respect for human rights. Indeed, while highlighting that both parties criticize the other for violations of human rights in the occupied territory and the refugee camps (the Secretary General treats with the same value those criticisms made by "different NGO's", including none other than *Amnesty International* and

---

[666] On this initiative, *cfr.* RUIZ MIGUEL, C., "La propuesta marroquí de autonomía para el Sahara occidental de 2007: una antigua propuesta sin credibilidad", *Revista d'Estudis Autonòmics i Federals*, num. 7, Octubre (2008): 268-291; and ABDELHAMID EL OUALI, *Towards territorial autonomy as a right to democratic self-determination*, Stacey International, London, 2008, which supports the Moroccan arguments.

[667] 18 and 19 June 2007 (*ORSC*: S/2007/385), 10 and 11 August 2007 (*ORSC*: S/2008/45), 8 and 9 January 2008 (*ORSC*: S/2008/45) and 16 and 18 March 2008 (S/2008/251)

Human Rights Watch, as those made by the "Moroccan media"), the reports resemble more of a request to the Security Council and less of a lamentation that:

> "The MINURSO has no specific mandate to defend human rights, has no staff to observe the situation of human rights in the Territory and the refugee camps near Tinduf (...) and the Office of the High Commissioner of Human Rights is not integrated into the operations of the Mission".

Indeed, one of the main criticisms of the functioning of the MINURSO is that after 20 years in the Territory, it does not have the competence to denounce human rights violations occurring in the occupied territories under its helpless gaze: not only can it not intervene, it cannot even report a violation. It is true that the reason for this bizarre limitation lies in its mandate from the Security Council, but it is also the case that the MINURSO itself has taken an unduly restrictive view of its competencies, since, as the Secretary General has noted,

> "The United Nations recognizes its duty to uphold human rights standards in all of its operations, including the Western Sahara, where the two conflicting parties often accuse each other of violating human rights in the media and in communications with the UN".

Attempts to expressly expand the powers of the MINURSO into the ambit of human rights have always proved unsuccessful given the persistent and shameful veto exercised by France, who does not shudder at denying a UN Mission the ability to ensure the respect of human rights[668]. But the most unfortunate of all of this is that in these circumstances the MINURSO does not itself act exclusively in line with human rights; some of its own members have committed exploitation and sexual abuse, and this has been reported in numerous reports of the Secretary General. As if that weren't enough, the Secretary General himself acknowledged that in 2008 members of MINURSO committed acts of vandalism on sites of archaeological and cultural importance in the areas of Tifariti and Agwanit (Western Saharan

---

[668] In debates prior to the adoption of Resolution 1871 (2009), approved by the Security Council on 30 April 2009, and in the face of the proposal of extension of the mandate in field of the human rights championed by Costa Rica, Uganda, Mexico and Austria, France was the only State to reject it, which had been met by silence from the other permanent members of the Security Council. Moreover, although the Spanish Government in 2005 supported the possibility of extending the MINURSO's mandate, the EU's lack of influence is very clear, at least on this issue.

territories under control of the Saharawis) and that he had to require the Organization to fund the restoration work[669], a sad image of a Mission that during the process of identification of voters had managed to gain the trust of the weakest party.

The truth is that until the time of writing the position of the Secretary General in relation to the conflict leaves a lot to be desired. It is true that, under pressure from the POLISARIO Front, he was forced to dismiss[670] the Special Envoy who had replaced Baker, Peter van Walsum, after the latter stated that despite International law being openly sided towards the Sahrawi's, given that the Security Council was not going to use the powers conferred to it by Chapter VII of the Charter to enforce its respect by Morocco, the option of independence "was not realistic". Sahrawi hopes now lie in the new Special Envoy[671], Christopher Ross, former US Ambassador to Algeria, but as yet his actions have not borne fruit.

Giving him the benefit of the doubt, it is still surprising that the highest representative for the United Nations has come to strongly argue that the role of the UN in Western Sahara is limited to "facilitating negotiations", reducing it to merely offering its good offices and forgetting, evidently, that there exists a Peace Plan which has been voluntarily negotiated and agreed upon by the parties. Also, it is not encouraging at all that, on the occasion of the celebration in 2010 of the 50th anniversary of the International Declaration of Independence to Colonial Countries and Peoples- Resolution 1514 (XV)- and, in order to complete this historic task, to ask the international community for "creative solutions for the remaining territories without self-government", as if one was dealing with a vulgar competition of ideas; solutions which should be adopted should be "pragmatic and realistic, taking into account the specific circumstances of each case".

---

[669] ORSC: S/2009/200, 13 April 2009.

[670] The formula of dismissal used was the non-renewal of his mandate, although in reality this was a full dismissal because it is a mandate that, barring resignation, automatically renews itself.

[671] Relating to the Special Envoy, cfr. SOROETA LICERAS, J., "Las Naciones Unidas, entre la *realpolitik* y el Derecho. Algunas reflexiones en torno al papel del Enviado Especial en los conflictos de Kosovo y del Sahara Occidental, in *El Derecho Internacional en el Mundo Multipolar del Siglo XXI. Obra Homenaje al Profesor Luis Ignacio Sánchez Rodríguez*, ed. Iprolex, Madrid (2013): 585-595.

CHAPTER VIII

CONSEQUENCES OF THE FAILURE OF THE DECOLONIZATION PROCESS: THE ILLEGAL EXPLOITATION OF NATURAL RESOURCES IN WESTERN SAHARA

Given the inherent inferiority of the status of territories subject to colonial domination, the United Nations have since the nineteen fifties stated that States and international organizations shall "strictly and conscientiously respect the sovereignty of peoples and nations over their natural wealth and resources in accordance with the Charter". This concern is reflected in many General Assembly resolutions, which during the first thirty years came to establish a complete system of protection, even if their efficacy has been limited in the Territory with which we deal.

Among the first achievements of the General Assembly in this area is the creation of the *Commission on Permanent Sovereignty over Natural Resources*[672], an organ wich, in theory, was called to play a significant role in the decolonization process, but in reality was merely a first step that achieved few results. Greater success was seen following subsequent resolutions, based on the consideration that "natural resources in developing countries are one of the bases of their development"[673], which argued strongly that "the violation of sovereign rights of peoples and nations of their wealth and natural resources is contrary to the spirit and to the principles of the UN Charter and it hinders the development of international cooperation and the preservation of peace"[674], and in which they "resolutely support the efforts of the developing countries and of the peoples of territories under colonial and racial domination and foreign occupation in their struggle to regain effective control over their

---

[672] *ORGA*: Resolution 1314 (XIII) of the AG, approved on 12 December 1958
[673] *ORGA*: Resolution 2158 (XXI) of the AG, approved on 25 November 1966
[674] *ORGA:* Resolution 1803 (XVII), of the AG, approved on 14 December 1962. The concern of the United Nations for the permanent sovereignty of peoples over their natural resources goes back to the nineteen fifties, when the most important resolutions on the matter were approved. (*cfr.* Resolutions 523 (VI), 12 January 1951 and 626 (VII), 21 December 1952).

natural resources"[675]. Thus, from a general point of view, one cannot doubt the success of the UN in their fight to defend effectively natural resources in dependent territories, resources whose exploitation in many cases was the main reason for the original respective colonisations.

In the case of Western Sahara, from the moment at which the decolonization process was launched, the UN has been conscious of the economic interests of Spain as well as those States with claims on the Territory and of the need to protect the resources from indiscriminate exploitation. Nevertheless, and although the proclamations against the exploitation of these resources were already common in the general context of decolonization, one would have to wait until 1970 for the General Assembly to explicitly call for the necessity to safeguard the natural resources in the Territory. Resolution 2711 (XXV) invited Spain to comply with the resolutions of the General Assembly on the activities of foreign economic, financial and other interests operating in colonial countries and territories and to refrain from any action likely to delay the process od decolonization of the territory" [676]. As mentioned above, it was the first time that the General Assembly pronounced on the defence of natural resources in the Sahrawi territory, contrary to the traditionally passive attitude of the Organization as regards this question, an attitude which unfortunately would return following the division of the Territory between Morocco and Mauritania.

In this same line of action, and as a last reference to the Assembly General resolutions in question, Resolution 3292 (XXIX) reiterated the invitation to all States "to observe the resolutions of the General Assembly regarding the activities of foreign economic and financial interests in the Territory" and "to abstain from contributing by their investments or immigration policy to the maintenance of a colonial situation in the Territory.

The wording of the resolutions makes it clear that the General Assembly included among the activities which involve or promote the illegal exploitation of natural resources in the Territory not just strictly exploitative activities (phosphate mining, fishing etc.) but also all of those which drive it including investments, which at the time were mainly of Spanish capital, as well as the establishment of settlers themselves in the Territory. The fact that after the military occupation the General Assembly avoided any reference to these two issues shows that there are two different standards for measuring colonizing policy: a "hard" standard against the historical colonial Power, Spain, which

---

[675] ORGA: Resolution 3171 (XXVIII), of the AG, approved 25 November 1966.

[676] ORGA: Resolution 2711 (XXV) of the AG, approved 14 December 1970, by 103 votes in favour, 0 against and 11 abstentions.

was openly pressed during its last years in the Territory, and a "soft" approach to the State which militarily occupied the Territory, Morocco, practicing an undisguised policy of the establishment of settlers, which left the country with nothing to envy as regards the previous practices of the former colonial power. But let's first consider what the principal natural resources of Western Sahara actually are.

Although there are those who considered that the resources of the Territory were not the primary reason for Morocco's annexation claims, which they claim have more strategic-political objectives[677], it is clear that these resources have attracted and continue to attract interest amongst States in the region. We are now going to analyse the principal natural resources in the Territory, focusing especially on phosphates, fisheries and the possible existence of hydrocarbons, without forgetting the increasing exportation of sand and the growing tourism sector which, although until the ceasefire of 1991 saw practically no activity, has since then enjoyed significant development and is destined to occupy a privileged position in the future economy of the Territory[678].

As a starting point, it should be stated that the exploitation of natural resources in the Territory without the consent of the only legitimate representative of the Sahrawi people, the POLISARIO Front, whether carried out by companies or States constitutes a violation of International law. It suffices to recall the attitude of the UN Council for Namibia, an organ created by the UN with the aim of protecting the population of Namibia and its natural resources from the voracity of the racist South African regime, in response to the illegal agreements made between the South African authorities and different foreign companies in order to exploit natural resources in Namibia, some of which came to be demanded by this organ before the domestic courts of the respective States[679]; this is unprecedented but in reality of limited scope

---

[677] In this sense, *cfr.* VILLAR, F. (1982): 23; ASSIDON, E., "Inventaire et exploitation des richesses économiques", en la obra colectiva *Sahara Occidental, un peuple et ses droits,* Ligue Française pour les droits et la libération des peuples. Colloque de Massy (1 et 2 avril 1978), ed. L'Harmattan, Paris, (1978): 33-67; BARBIER, M., "Essai d'interprétation du conflit saharien", in *Enjeux Sahariens* (Table ronde du CRESM, nov. 1981), Ed. Centre National de la Recherche Scientifique, Paris (1984): 212-229.

[678] The peculiarity of the sector lies in the exploitation agreements between Morocco and foreign companies, some of which have been carrying out their activity in the sector for decades, among which one can point out the French company *Club Méditerranée*. In this respect, *cfr.* JOFFE, G. (1995): 126; GRIMAUD, N. (1988): 102.

[679] *ORGA:* A/40/24, 4 December 1985, ("*Report of the United Nations Council for Namibia*"), pp. 11 and 513. The first lawsuit of the Council in the respect was presented before Dutch

given that three years after the start of these actions Namibia gained independence. It is also worth noting here the study by the European Parliament on the possibility of compensating the Government of Namibia for the harm caused by the exploitation of the fishery resources[680]. Therefore, it must be remembered that not only the States, but also the companies which negotiate with Morocco about the exploitation of natural resources in the Territory are violating International law, and that the future Sahrawi State could demand international responsibility for these violations.

Phosphates

The first resources to whet the appetite of Spain were phosphates. Paradoxically, despite the fact that their existence in the Territory was discovered in 1943[681], their real exploitation only began ten years before Spain's withdrawal, when the Bu-Craa deposits were discovered in 1963. Their exploitation by Spain was therefore very brief[682]. During this period, Spain launched the conveyor belt that took material extracted at Bu-Craa one hundred kilometres to the beach at El Aaiún, from which it was exported. The belt became one of the first military objectives of the POLISARIO Front, which during the first few years of the war managed to stop its production until the construction by Morocco of walls dividing the Territory into two prevented the Sahrawi military actions from reaching it. From then on, the extraction of phosphates has become a lucrative business for the Moroccan Treasury, or rather for the Alawite monarchy, which, thanks to this, has been scandalously increasing its personal fortune in recent years[683].

---

courts on 14 July 1987, against a uranium enrichment plant (*Urenco Nederland V.O.F.*) and against the company that managed it (*Ultracentrifuge Nederland N.V.*), controlled by the State.

[680] This study was conducted at the request of the Commission for Development and Cooperation, March 1989 (Series A, Doc. A2-402/88). *Cfr.* In this respect PIGRAU I SOLE, A., "Culminación del Plan de Naciones Unidas para la independencia de Namibia", *R.E.D.I.*, vol. XLII, 1 (1990): 321.

[681] Actually, this is the date on which the discoverer of the deposits, Manuel Alia Medina, informed the Spanish Government of the importance of such a discovery (*cfr.* HODGES, T., *Historical Dictionary of Western Sahara* (1982): 34).

[682] However, one must not forget that the Madrid Agreements provided for the sale to the Moroccan public company "Office Chérifien des phosphates" *of* 65% of the share capital of FOSBUCRAA, with the remaining 35% staying with the Spanish INI (National Institute of Industry).

[683] US magazine *Forbes* placed the fortune of the King of Morocco in seventh position amongst the that of all world Monarchs and it attributed this unstoppable growth to the considerable increase in the market Price of phosphates, of which Morocco is the leading

CHAPTER VIII

Hydrocarbons

The possibility that beneath the Western Saharan soil could exist oil deposits has attracted oil companies from all over the world to the Territory since the nineteen forties but despite having some influence in the nineteen seventies[684], the real importance of the resource came recently, in the early twenty-first century, when two important companies -one from the United States (*Kerr-McGee du Maroc Ltd.*) and the other French (*Total Final Elf E&P Maroc*)- each concluded with the Moroccan authorities contracts to allow for the exploration and the assessment of petrol off the coast of the Sahrawi territory.

But the issue came into the international spotlight when, at the request of the President of the Security Council, the Under-Secretary-General for Legal Affairs, Hans Corell, on 12th February, 2002 issued an opinion on "the legality, in the context of International law, including the relevant resolutions of the Security Council and the General Assembly of the UN and the agreements relating to Western Sahara, of the actions allegedly taken by the Moroccan

---

exporter and third largest producer behind China and the United States (*Forbes*, 27 December 2007). On the real extent of the exploitation of phosphates in Western Sahara, see the website of *Western Sahara Resource Watch*, an active NGO which details the exploitation operations of Sahrawi phosphates (http://www.wsrw.org/index.php?cat=110&art=1114). Despite this intense exploitation to which the phosphate deposits of Western Sahara have been subjected, the joint supply of Morocco and Western Sahara represent today more tan 60% of the global reserves.

[684] Since Morocco controlled the Sahrawi coast (after the constructions of the walls) many different companies have concluded illegal agreements for the investigation and extraction of oil resources or for the installation of port facilities in the Territory. For example, *inter alia*, Morocco concluded agreements *British Petroleum* and *Philips Petroleum* to carry out oil searches in the maritime areas of El Aaiún (8 September 1978); with the Dutch group *Royal Kalis Westmister* for the construction of a port at El Aaiún (29 February 1980); with the Australian company *Proken Hill Dropietarry Ltd. (Bhp)* for oil searches in the Dahla region (22 July 1985).

The POLISARIO Front since then has denounced fishery infrastructure works undertaken by Morocco on the Sahrawi coast to facilitate and improve the exploitation of resources in the Territory. For example, it claimed before the Committee of Twenty Four (6 June 1997) that the Moroccan Government were carrying out an important project of reform of the ports of Western Sahara, including the most important, Dahla, as well as others such as El Aaiún, which would cost up to 130 million dollars, and it called for the Committee to encourage States to avoid participating directly or indirectly in the exploitation of Sahrawi wealth (text in *Sahara Información*, August 1977, p. 3 onwards). On the works carried out by Morocco on the Western Saharan coast throughout the period of occupation, under the plan of "development of the Sahrawi provinces", *cfr.* FOUGEROUSE, M. (1987): 425 onwards.; "Que font les Marocains au Sahara?", *Jeune Afrique*, n° 34, supplement n° 1722, January (1994): 352-353.

authorities, namely the offering and signing of contracts with foreign companies for the exploration of mineral resources in Western Sahara". The question forced the Office of Legal Affairs to pronounce on the legal status of the Territory, and in consequence on the status of Morocco as well, which it did in the most orthodox way, affirming that the Madrid Agreements "did not transfer sovereignty over the Territory nor did it confer to any of the signatories the status of administering Power, since Spain, on its own, could not have transferred it unilaterally" so that the transfer of the administrative authority over the Territory to Morocco and Mauritania in 1975 "did not affect the international status of Western Sahara as a Non-Self-Governing Territory".

The report examines the right of peoples under colonial rule to permanent sovereignty over their natural resources, and aware that there is no other option than to affirm the illegality of their exploitation, he clarified this statement by recalling the developments in the area following the passing of Resolution 50/33 of the General Assembly of the UN[685], which established a key distinction between economic activities which harmed the peoples of these territories and those activities undertaken to benefit them. This resolution affirmed "the value of foreign economic investment undertaken in collaboration with the peoples of Non-Self-Governing Territories and according to their wishes in order to contribute validly to the socio-economic development of the territories[686]". In the opinion of Corell, recent State practice is illustrative of an *opinion iuris* of administering Powers as well as third States, under which activities of resource exploitation benefit the peoples of Non-Self-Governing Territories, carried out in its name or in consultation with its representatives, are considered compatible with the obligations imposed on administering Powers under the Charter, as well as in conformity with the resolutions of the General Assembly and the established principle of "permanent sovereignty over natural resources". In reality this affirmation was nothing new, but as we will see presently, it was invoked by the EU to defend, although with little success, the legality of fishing agreements.

The report concludes that the aforementioned contracts are not illegal in themselves, but the implementation of exploration and exploitation activities without regard to the interests and wishes of the people of Western Sahara is a violation of the international legal principles applicable to activities related to mineral resources in Non-Self-Governing Territories. Given that both the

---

[685] *ORGA:* Resolution 50/33, approved on 6 December 1995.
[686] This position was reaffirmed in many later resolutions (*ORGA:* 52/72, 10 December 1997, 53/61, 3 December 1998, 54/84, 6 December de 1999, 55/138, 8 December 2000, y 56/66, 10 December 2001).

SADR and the POLISARIO Front publically denounced these agreements there are no doubts regarding the illegality of these contracts.

Although in too many occasions the inefficacy of this type of non-binding international reports and opinions is the rule, in this case one can take some positive consequences. On the one hand, as a consequence of the complaints of the SADR and the pressure from certain NGO's, in June 2005 the Norwegian Government Pensions Fund (*The Petroleum Fund*) decided for ethical motives (the illegality of the exploration and exploitation of the natural resources of a Non-Self-Governing Territory) to sell all shares which it had in one of the companies which had negotiated with Morocco, the American multinational *Kerr-McGee*[687]. On the other hand, and in order to oppose Moroccan policy in this area, the SADR decided at the end of 2005 to offer to the international market a series of licences for the exploration of oil and gas in various parts of Western Sahara, and despite present circumstances meaning that it is impossible to put it into practice, it is encouraging that in the expectation of one day becoming a fully independent State it was able to attract various oil companies, with which in 2006 it concluded agreements for the development of these activities[688].

Fishing

Spanish activity in the Territory has been historically linked to fishing activity, mainly through the Canarian fleet. And this is not in vain, since the waters off the coast of the Territory are home to one of the richest fishing grounds in the world[689]. The idea to establish a base for fishing operations in the country came during the middle of last century. Thus, it is possible to say that fishing is the primary reason from Spain's decision to embark on its colonization of the Sahrawi lands, and it also formed a starting point to the Hispano-Moroccan

---

[687] This decision resulted in the disinvestment of 337 million Norwegian Krone (NOK). The text of the report of the *Government Petroleum Fund's Council of Ethics* (integrated organ of the Norwegian Finance Ministry) of 12 April 2005 can be found at: http://www.vest-sahara.no/files/pdf/kmg_analysis_norway_2005.pdf.

[688] The companies awarded these licences were: *Ophir Energy Company Ltd., Europa Oil & Gas plc., Maghreb Exploration Limited, Osceola Hydrocarbon Limited, Nighthawk Energy Limited,* y *Encore Oil Plc.*

[689] ASSIDON, E. (1978): 35. On this issue, *cfr.* BRAVO DE LAGUNA CABRERA, J., "La pesca en el banco sahariano", Instituto Español de Oceanografía, *El Campo*, n° 99 (1985): 69 (although this is not a legal study, it is very interesting because it provides data about the general characteristics of the Saharan Bank and its reserves); GAUDIO, A. (1978): 336-342; GOFFINET, T., "Development and fisheries management: the case of Northwest Africa", *Ocean and Coastal Management*, vol. 17, 2 (1992): 105-136 (especially, pp. 121-125).

Treaty of Tetuan (1860) which, in Article 8, attributes to Spain a territory on the Atlantic coast of the Moroccan Empire next to the ancient site of Santa Cruz de Mar Pequeña, for the establishment of a fishery[690]. Years later the ICJ would make it clear that this was an area which never came under the control of the Moroccan Sultan. However, the creation of the first fishery establishments in the Territory was not the product of actions of the Government, immersed at the time in the ups and downs of the country's internal politics, but instead was driven principally by private Spanish companies. In these circumstances, in March 1881, the Sociedad de Pesquerías Canario-africanas (the Canarian-African Fishing Companies) concluded an agreement with Sahwari notables from the Dahla region, under which the Spanish were permitted to install a fishery in this coastal area, which over time would take the form of territorial cession and would signify the colonial occupation of Rio de Oro.

Despite this, the Spanish-Moroccan fishing disputes have a more recent origin given that, since the independence of Morocco, it claimed the handover of three territories of "Spanish Sahara" (Ifni, Ceuta and Melilla) which it considered part of its territory[691]. The only one of these territories which is

---

[690] *Cfr.* GARCIA FIGUERAS, T., *"La Acción Africana de España en torno al 98 (1860-1912)"*, Madrid, CSIC, vol. II (1966): 19-28; MARTÍNEZ MILLAN, J.M., "Las pesquerías canario-africanas en el engranaje del africanismo español (1860-1910), *A.W.R.A.Q.*, n.11 (1990): 97-122; MORALES LEZCANO, V., "El africanismo español (1860-1975)", *España y el Norte de Africa: El Protectorado en Marruecos (1912-1956)*, Madrid, UNED, 1986, 2th ed. Art. 8 of the Tetuán Treaty signals the following: "His Majesty the King of Morocco undertakes to grant in perpetuity to His Majesty the King of Spain in the oceanic coast next to Santa Cruz la Pequeña, the sufficient territory for the formation of a fisheries establishment, like that which Spain once had there. To implement what is agreed upon in this Article, prior agreement will be made between the Governments of Spain and Morocco, which must appoint commissioners for each side to mark the limits of the said establishment" (text in PORTILLO PASQUAL DEL RIQUELME, J. (1991): 305.

[691] The first significant conflict between Morocco and Spain dates back to the early years of the existence of the Maghreb State with the passing of numerous internal norms. Thus, by a Dahir of 30 June 1962 and a later Decree of 21 June 1975, the Moroccan Government decided to extend its territorial waters from 6 to 12 miles, determining the cut of points of bays on the Moroccan coast and placing within Moroccan territorial waters the waters of Ceuta and Melilla. This measure would be in contradiction with Article 4 of the Geneva Convention on the Law of the Sea of 1958, which stated that "over territorial sea and the contiguous zone, the system of straight baselines may not be applied by a State in such manner as to cut off from the high seas the territorial seas of another State".

Meanwhile, the Spanish Government had already regulated the waters of the territory, via an Order of 23 May 1967, by which the law of 8 April 1967 on the extension of jurisdictional waters to twelve miles for fishing purposes was applied in Sahara (*Official Bulletin of Sahara*,

today under Moroccan sovereignty is Ifni, which under the Treaty of Fez (1969) was ceded by Spain. Annexed to this Treaty was a fisheries agreement, which granted certain privileges to Spain as compensation for the handover. However, as we have already had the occasion to mention, although Article 7 affirms that "any extension of the territorial water of one of the Parties made in the future in accordance with International law will not affect the regime established by this Convention, unless otherwise agreed by the Parties" this was denounced by Morocco on 2nd March 1973, the date on which, via a *Dahir* (decree), it approved the extension of its Exclusive Economic Zone to 70 nautical miles (this measure was the Moroccan reaction to the application made by the *Yemáa* to the Franco Government for a progressive institutionalization of Sahrawi society, in order to prepare itself for its future self-government).

In the ten years that followed the publication of the aforementioned Dahir (1973-1983), despite the conclusion of a series of transitional agreements of short duration and limited scope, there were many serious incidents in the waters of the Territory. After a turbulent two year period (1973-1975), the Madrid Agreements of 1975 came to substantially change the situation since, as we have already mentioned, the Fishing Protocols are annexed to the agreements; the most important aspects being the following[692]: Morocco gives Spain the right to fish "a maximum of 600 boats and for a period of 15 years" in "its territorial waters of the Atlantic coast" and a maximum of 200 boats in the "Moroccan waters of the Mediterranean coast"; Morocco and Mauritania recognise together the right to fish 800 Spanish boats for a maximum of 20 years in the Sahrawi waters.

As can be seen, at this time Morocco made a clear distinction between its territorial waters on the Atlantic coast and the Mediterranean and the "waters

---

n° 134) (text in *Legislación de Sahara. Años 1965-1973*, Dirección General de Promoción de Sahara e Instituto de Estudios Africanos (C.S.I.C.), Madrid, 1974, p. 170.

[692] The texts, which are listed under the names "Acta de las conversaciones mantenidas entre Marruecos y España relativas a aspectos económicos derivados de su cooperación mutua", and "Acta de las conversaciones mantenidas, de una parte, entre las delegaciones del Reino de Marruecos y de la República Islámica de Mauritania, y de otra, de España, a propósito de los aspectos económicos derivados de la transferencia de la Administración del Sahara", can be found in GONZALEZ CAMPOS, J., *El Sahara, un problema pendiente*, Instituto de Estudios Políticos para América Latina y Africa (IEPALA), Madrid, October (1978): 67-69, and *Posible*, n° 142, 29-5 September-October 1977.

The Spanish Minister for Foreign Affairs, M. Oreja, down-played the importance of the content of these protocols, which he said were "simply proceedings, which were not internationally listed as protocols, which reflect conversations which had been had" (*cfr.* DEL PINO, D., "España y el Sahara", *Leviatán*, n° 21 (1985): 50).

of Sahara". This distinction was to be maintained with different nuances in various fishery agreements, both between Spain and Morocco, and Morocco and the European Community and will be a standard reference in the statements of the Spanish authorities when addressing the issue of Western Sahara. In this sense, the Spanish Minister for Foreign Affairs at the time, Marcelino Oreja, said repeatedly that while the people of Western Sahara do not properly exercise their right to self-determination, Spain will consider that the decolonization of the Non-Self-Governing Territory of Western Sahara has not been completed[693] and that Spain recognised "the jurisdiction, but not the sovereignty" of Morocco over Sahrawi waters[694], expressions which clearly show the "judicial schizophrenia" which dominates many questions related to decolonization, when one tries to save the image of legality before the international community while at the same time it is involved in its most serious violations.

These contradictions would become more evident still on the ratification by the Spanish Congress (15th February 1978), despite the rejection by P.S.O.E., at the time the main opposition party, of the first Spanish-Moroccan fisheries Treaty. The conclusion of this Treaty was considered at the time by some authors as an implicit recognition of the annexation of the Territory by Morocco[695], but since it was never actually ratified by the Moroccan Parliament it didn't ever come into force. Following the entry into force of a temporary agreement (30th June 1979), whose content was rejected by the Canarian fleet, causing a considerable outbreak of conflict between the Moroccan patrol boats and the Canarian ships, the POLISARIO Front decided to implement a new strategy involving the seizure of Spanish fishing vessels for violating the sovereignty of the Sahrawi people over their fishing resources and the retention of their crews to allow for later bilateral negotiations with Spain over their release. In this way, the Sahrawi national liberation movement demanded both its international subjectivity and its right to control the exploitation of its national resources in the Territory. The incidents involving the Spanish vessels "Saa" (April 1977) and "Las Palomas"

---

[693] For example, before the Commission for Foreign Affairs of Congress, on 16 December 1977 and 11 January 1978; 15 February 1978 before the full chamber of Congress and 23 February before the Senate, on the occasion of the ratification of the fishing agreement with Morocco; 8 March 1978, before Congress, during a motion raised on the subject of Western Sahara; 9 March and 4 April 1978, before the Senate during its debates on foreign policy; 26 September 1977 and 2 October 1978 before the AG of the UN

[694] MERCER, J. (1979): 15.

[695] MIGUEZ, A. (1978): 180. The socialist and communist amendments were rejected by 142 in favour to 174 against and 8 abstentions.

Chapter VIII

(April 1978) and the many later conflicts occurring between 1978 and 1980, originated in this policy[696], which was modified significantly when P.S.O.E. came to power (28th October 1982), who until then had been a strong advocate of the rights of the Sahrawi people, from then on took at 180 degree turn, closing the POLISARIO Front office in Spain[697]. The POLISARIO Front's hopes that the fishing agreements with Morocco would be reconsidered by the new Spanish Government quickly vanished[698].

The agreement of 19th August 1983[699], the first agreement with Morocco as regards fisheries for the socialist Government, reduced the Spanish fishing capacity by 40% and raised the fees to be paid by Spain to Morocco by 70%[700]. Shortly after its approval, for "security reasons" Morocco decided to restrict certain zones in which traditionally the Spanish had been fishing, which would lead to a protest note from the Spanish Government[701]. It was precisely the coast next to Sahara and the Province of Tarfaya. Eventually, following pressure from the Government of the Autonomous Community of the Canary Islands, most affected by the agreement, the area of Tarfaya was excluded from the agreement. The part of the agreement referring to "sea fishing in waters under Moroccan jurisdiction" made a distinction between

---

[696] On April 20, 1978 the POLISARIO Front capture eight members of the crew of the Spanish ship "Las Palomas", which operated in the waters of Western Sahara. After long negotiations they were finally released on 14 October of the same year. During the period of captivity of the Spanish fishermen, Javier Ruperez, the then Secretary for Foreign Affairs for UCD, the party in power at the time, attended the IV Congress of the POLISARIO Front. By the end of this Congress, a joint UCD-POLISARIO Front statement was made which affirmed that the POLISARIO Front is the "only legitimate representative of the Sahrawi people in their struggle". On this question, *cfr.* DESSENS, A. (1979): 73-86.

[697] On this question *cfr.* MARQUINA BARRIO, A., "El conflicto del Sáhara y la cooperación global del Gobierno español con Argelia y Marruecos", *Revista de Estudios Internacionales*, vol. 4, n. 4 (1983): 755-773. Moreover, shortly after its arrival into the Government, the content of the agreement between PSOE and the POLISARIO Front was published in the press, an agreement in which the socialist party denounced the Madrid Agreements and regarded them as null (*cfr. El País*, 16 March 1983).

[698] On the change of the approach of the PSOE before and after its arrival into the Spanish Government, *cfr.* the detailed work of BERRAMDANE, A., *Le Sahara Occidental: enjeu maghrèbin*, Paris (1987): 217-231.

[699] The text of the Spanish-Moroccan fishing agreement was published in the *B.O.E. (Official State Bulletin)* on 11 October 1983.

[700] On the content of this agreement *cfr.* the reply of the Government to Deputy G. Kirkpatrick's question on the difficulties surrounding the signing of the fishing agreement with Morocco (*B.O.C.G.*, 28 October 1983 and *Actividades, Textos y Documentos de la Política Exterior Española*, Ministerio de Asuntos Exteriores, Madrid, 1983, p. 543).

[701] *Actividades, Textos y Documentos de la Política Exterior Española*, Ministerio de Asuntos Exteriores, Madrid, 1983, Crónica, 4 Feburary 1983.

two different areas of fishing: north of the Cape Noun and the Mediterranean and South of the Cape Noun, with the latter area corresponding directly to the waters of Western Sahara. One the other hand, the agreement made express reference to the future Spanish-Moroccan negotiations to take place once Spain had acceded to the EEC, which would involve a review and any modifications. It is very significant that the Secretary of State at the time pointed out, just three days after the conclusion of the agreements with Morocco, that "it must be made very clear that in the Fisheries Agreement with Morocco Spain has been very careful not to recognise the sovereignty of this country over Western Sahara. In these agreements, deliberately nuanced expressions have been used to distinguish Moroccan territorial water and the Sahrawi fishing bank[702]". Subsequently, the entry of Spain into the EEC would enable Morocco, under Article 16 of Chapter VI, to apply for fresh negotiations to revise the existing agreement between Spain and this State.

Despite the fact that in 1985 there occurred some serious incidents on the Sahrawi coast, among which the most serious was that involving the shipping vessel "Junquito", coming as a consequence of the Spanish Government's decision to close the POLISARIO Front office in Madrid[703], and that these

---

[702] "Contestación formulada por el Gobierno en relación con la pregunta del Diputado López Raimundo, relativa a la política española hacia el Sahara", B.O.C.G., 23 September 1983, or Actividades, textos y Documentos de la Política Exterior Española, 1983, p. 482 etc.

[703] Under the Madrid Agreements, and more specifically the secrete clauses, 1200 Spanish ships were authorized to fish in the Sahrawi coasts, for which Spain had to pay approximately 500 million dollars a year to the Moroccan Government. Despite this clear violation of the sovereignty of the Sahrawi people over their natural resources, the POLISARIO Front negotiated with the then President of the Government, A. Suarez, over the presence of Spanish trawlers, allowing them to fish as long as they carried the Spanish flag or were without flag. Morocco had imposed the condition that Spanish boats had to carry the Moroccan flag to be allowed to fish, causing the incident involving the Spanish trawler "El Junquito", which was shot down by forces of the POLISARIO Front (20 September 1985) when it fished in Sahrawi waters under the Moroccan flag. As a result, one of the crew was killed and six were taken prisoner by the POLISARIO Front. The situation endured longer when the Spanish patrol boat "Tagomago" went to the scene and was also the object of attack, in which a Spanish oficial was killed and two others were injured. Although the six crew members were returned to the Spanish authorities eight days later, on 30 September of this year the Spanish Government decided to close the POLISARIO Front Offices in Spain and to expel its representatives within 72 hours. To the question posed by the Deputy E. Tarragona in relation to the flag under which the trawler "Junquito" sailed, the Government representative said that, even though it did not fish under the Moroccan flag, it displayed it as a courtesy flag. However, the response acknowledged that the custom of the Spanish fleet to display the flag out of courtesy in Moroccan controlled waters "could be somewhat encouraged by Morocco which acts in conformity with International law in requesting that in its territorial waters its flag is shown out of courtesy" (Actividades, textos y

incidents continued until 1987[704], when Morocco took control of the whole Sahrawi coast having built walls IV and V in the occupied territories, the United Nations did not reflect these events, avoiding taking a decision on the matter. Without doubt, it would have been an excellent opportunity to reclaim the rights of the Sahrawi people over their natural resources that the General Assembly had set in motion two decades before.

The cooperation agreement concluded between Morocco and the EEC in 1988 definitively surpassed the bilateral framework in which up until then negotiations had unfolded[705]. In this way, the Spanish-Moroccan cooperation agreement of 1976 was replaced and adapted to the EEC through a trade protocol and another financial protocol, which logically included negotiations on fisheries[706]. Despite this seemingly new framework in which the negotiations took place, provisions relating to fisheries, concluded between Morocco and the EEC on 25th May 1988, retained the same formula which had figured in the previous agreements, avoiding any express references to the Sahrawi situation but with an ambiguous mention of "the waters under Moroccan jurisdiction"[707].

Documentos de la Política Exterior Española, 1985, p. 532, ó B.O.C.G., de 23 December 1985), which is false since the incident did not occur on Moroccan territorial waters. For an analysis of this and other incidents on the Sahrawi coast involving the POLISARIO Front, *cfr.* Cistero Bahima, J.M.and Freixes Sanjuan, M.T., *op. cit.*, pp. 66 et. seq. and 184 et. seq.; DIEGO AGUIRRE, J.R., *Guerra en el Sahara*, Madrid, ed. Istmo, D.L. (1991): 292-294; GONZÁLEZ, L.M., "La expulsión del Frente POLISARIO", *Gaceta Sindical*, n° 38 (1985): 44-45.

[704] These incidents, of which there were many in 1985, involved the Moroccan Navy and totalled 85 in the year. Of these, just three were freed without penalty, affecting a total of about 400 crew members. (*cfr. Actividades, textos y Documentos de la Política Exterior Española*, 1986, p. 252, and *B.O.C.G.* 30 May 1986).

[705] The agreement of August 1983 followed an interim agreement which was valid until 31 December of that year, in order to give the EEC time to negotiate the definitive one, given that, since the incorporation of Spain into the EEC, renegotiation has been within the competence of the Commission (Article 167 of the Act of Accession). However, should an agreement not have been made by this date, Community fishing would have had to stop in the fisheries of the Sahrawi coast between 1st January and 1st March 1998.

[706] On the general framework of this agreement, *cfr.* MARQUINA, A., ECHEVERRIA, C. (1992): 48 et. seq

[707] Article 1 of the agreement states that the agreement regulates "the modalities of cooperation (…) in the waters under the sovereignty or jurisdiction of Morocco, hereinafter referred to as Morocco's fishing zone". This avoids complication reference to sovereignty over waters corresponding to the Territory of Western Sahara, which correspond to the waters "under the jurisdiction" and not those "under the sovereignty" of Morocco. However, the text of the agreement cannot avoid references which are clearly although not to such an extent- contrary to the international order, such as "Moroccan port facilities" (Art 3), which

Subsequent agreements signed by Morocco with the EC in 1992[708], 1995 and 2005[709] maintained references to the two different fishing areas: "waters under the sovereignty" and "jurisdictional waters of Morocco", which are

---

include those of the Sahrawi Territory or its ambit of application (Art 13) which includes the territories of the EEC and "the Kingdom of Morocco".

Moreover, the question posed by the Deputy I. Callejo regarding of the attitude that the Government should take in respect of the opinion of the European People's Court, in which it affirmed that the EEC couldn't conclude agreements regarding fishing in waters that correspond to the sovereignty of the SADR, was to no avail. After highlighting that neither Spain nor any other member State of the EEC had recognised it, the response of the Government was to affirm that Spain considers that the Western Sahara case is one of unfinished decolonization "which will only be completed when the Sahrawi people can fully express themselves of their future in a referendum of self-determination with international due process", and that the fishing agreement with Morocco "does not prejudge the sovereignty or jurisdiction of Morocco over waters to which it do not belong" (*Actividades, textos y Documentos de la Política Exterior Española*, 1987, p. 364, and *B.O.C.G.* 3 October 1987). Moreover, on 15 May 1990 the Government of Morocco told to the EEC of the prohibition of fishing in certain areas of the coast of Western Sahara, which was "justified" by the Spanish Minister of Foreign Affairs, Fernandez Ordonez, because it is "a place where a conflict has taken many human lives" and it is a temporary measure which even affects Morocco's own fleet (*Actividades, textos y Documentos de la Política Exterior Española*, 1990, p. 494 et. seq., and *B.O.C.G.* 30 May 1990).

[708] The texts of the treaties concluded by the EC with Morocco until 1992 can be found in the *OJCE*, L232, of 19 August 1987, pp. 18 et. seq. (Decision 87/442, of 13 August 1987), L 99, of 16 April 1988, pp. 45 et. seq. (Decision 88/219, of 29 February 1988), L 181, of 12 July 1988, pp. 1 et. seq. (Decision of 23 June 1988), L 208, of 7 August 1990, pp. 39 et. seq. (Decision 90/408, of 27 July 1990), L 78, of 26 June 1991, pp. 10 et. seq. (Regulation 721/91 of 21 March 1991), L 195, of 18 September 1991 (Decision 91/360, of 8 July 1991), L 21, of 30 January 1992 (Regulation 188/92 of 27 January 1992), L 91 of 7 April 1992, pp. 27 et. seq. (Decision 92/211, of 30 March 1992), L 218, of 1 August 1992, pp. 135 et. seq. (Decision 92/395, of 20 June 1992 and L 407, of 31 December 1992, pp. 1 et. seq. (Regulation 3954/92, of 19 December 1992).

[709] This is the agreement on sea fishing relations between the EEC and the Kingdom of Morocco of 21 December 1992 (OD L 407, of 31.12.1992, pp. 3-14), which maintains references to the two distinct zones of fishing, but using more technical expression than the usual reference to the Cape Noun: area of the North Atlantic and Mediterranean, and the south zone, with the division between the two falling 28° 44' N (the duration of this agreement was reduced to three years, meaning that it terminated on 30 April 1995; *cfr.* in this respect the Resolution of the European Parliament of 29 April 1995; the Agreement of cooperation over sea fishing between the EC and the Kingdom of Morocco of 13 November 1995 (OD L 306, of 19.12.1995, pp. 7-43), which entered into effect on 1 January 1996 for a duration of four years, which returned to the rhetorical mention of "waters under the sovereignty or jurisdiction of Morocco" and the "Moroccan fishing zone"; and finally the Agreement of collaboration in the fishing sector between the European Community and the Kingdom of Morocco of 29 May 2006 (OD L 141, of 29.5.2006, pp. 4-37).

broadly referred to as "the fishing area of Morocco" and which are given the same treatment when it comes to their exploitation[710]. The Head of the negotiating delegation of the European Commission in this mencioned agreement justified the inclusion of the waters of Western Sahara in it stating that this is "not because the Commission considers that it is dealing with Moroccan waters" but because the waters "are under Moroccan administration", which can be derived from the Madrid Agreements. In his opinion, "the Sahrawi people also benefits from the economic income and job creation from this agreement"; the Commission "wants to avoid that a fisheries agreement, which is an act of economic cooperation, could be handled and affected by the political context". Almost thirty years on from the signing of these agreements, that the European Commission based this on the legality of the fishing agreement, adding that it benefits the people of Western Sahara, saves us any comment[711].

Although there is no doubt that the fishing agreements between EU and Morocco violate the right to self-determination of the Sahrawi people[712], it

---

[710] Article 2 of the Agreement of 2006 signals that the term "Moroccan fishing zone" must be understood to mean, "waters under the sovereignty or jurisdiction of the Kingdom of Morocco".

[711] Interview with César Debén (*El País*, 8 August 2005).

[712] On this question *cfr.* SOROETA LICERAS, J., "La posición de la Unión Europea en el conflicto del Sahara Occidental, una muestra palpable (más) de la primacía de sus intereses económicos y políticos sobre la promoción de la democracia y de los derechos humanos", *Revista de Derecho Comunitario Europeo*, núm. 34, Madrid, September/December (2009), pp. 1-42; BADÍA MARTÍ, A. M., "La cuestión del Sahara Occidental y la explotación de sus recursos naturales", in *El Derecho Internacional y Comunitario ante los retos de nuestro tiempo: Homenaje a la profesora Victoria Abellán Honrubia*, Vol. 1, (ed. Badia Martí, Antoni Pigrau i Solé, and Andreu Olesti Rayo), Madrid, Marcial Pons (2009): 29-53; CORELL, H., "The Legality of Exploring and Exploiting Natural Resources in Western Sahara", in *Conference on Multilateralism and International Law with Western Sahara as a Case Study: Pretoria, South Africa, 4 and 5 December 2008, ed.* by Neville Botha, Michèle Olivier, and Delarey van Tonder, Pretoria: VerLoren van Themaat Centre, University of South Africa (2010): 231-247; DAVANTURE, S., "Les limites de l'application du droit sur les ressources naturelles: Le cas des territoires palestiniens et du Sahara Occidental", PhD diss., Université du Québec à Montréal, 2006; HAUGEN, H. M., "The Right to Self-Determination and Natural Resources: The Case of Western Sahara", *Law, Environment and Development Journal*, 3 (2007): 70–81; OLSSON, C., ed. *The Western Sahara Conflict: The Role of Natural Resources in Decolonization*, Current African Issues 33. Uppsala, Sweden: Nordic Africa Institute, 2006; RIQUELME CORTADO, R., "La soberanía permanente del pueblo saharaui sobre sus recursos naturales", *Cursos de Derecho Internacional y Relaciones Internacionales de Vitoria-Gasteiz*, 31 (2011): 387–451 and RIQUELME CORTADO, R., "Derechos humanos y recursos naturales a la sombra de la berma", in *Estudios de Derecho Internacional y Derecho Europeo en homenaje al profesor Manuel Pérez González*. 2 vols. Edited by Jorge Cardona,

would be unfair not to recognise the willing, although inefficient, role played by the European Parliament where it specifically requested that the 2005 fisheries agreement be in the best interests of the Sahrawi population in the Territory. Its opinion on the legality of the matter[713], not binding, was rejected by the Commission, but it does contain important references to some of the issues pointed out by the Corell report which are worth highlighting. The amendments it demanded, amongst other things, requested that the EC's financial contribution should be used "for the development of the coastal population living on fishings in Morocco and Western Sahara and the creation of small and medium-sized local firms in the fishering sector"; it proposed the approval of the partnership agreement in the fishing sector "subject to its implementation in accordance with International law", since "The right to self-determination, including the right of permanent sovereignty over natural wealth and resources, is a norm of International law from which no derogation is permitted. Neither the Regulation nor the Agreement as they stand provide any safeguards for the Community (or the Member States) in the event of contraventions"; and it also proposed that "if there is evidence that the implementation of the Agreement is in contravention of international obligations, the Commission shall take measures to suspend the Agreement, following the procedure contained in Article 15 of the same". These amendments and the rest of the European Parliament's proposals were rejected by the European Commission, because, in its opinion, "the agreement is fully consistent with International law". In the opinion of the Commission:

> "The text of the agreement (...) neither defines nor prejudges the legal status of the waters concerned (....) the United Nations legal adviser gives a clear answer. Although the United Nations has never recognised Morocco as an administrative power in accordance with Article 73 of the Charter of the United Nations, and Morocco is not listed as an administering power of the territory in the United Nations' list of non-self-governing

---

Jorge Antonio Pueyo, José Luis Rodríguez-Villasante and José Manuel Sobrino, Valencia, Tirant lo Blanch (2012): 1167–1194.

[713] *Report on the proposed Regulation of the Council in relation to the celebration of the Agreement of association in the fisheries sector between the EC and the Kingdom of Morocco* (PE369.842, of 4.05.2006). This report, which was mandatory but not binding, was ignored by the Council, which would finally adopt on 22 May 2006 Regulation n° 764/2006 *on the conclusion of the fisheries partnership agreement between the EC and the Kingdom of Morocco* (OD C 297E de 7.12.2006, pp. 119-122), by which it approved the aforementioned agreement

territories (…), *agreements can be concluded with the Kingdom of Morocco concerning the exploitation of natural resources of Western Sahara.* The interpretation of the legal advisor to the UN recognises the competence of Morocco to sign such agreements, which implies that Morocco is a de facto administering Power of the Territory (…) In the framework of these agreements, International law seeks to assure the right of peoples and nations to use and dispose of the natural resources in their territories. In that respect, the agreements are considered compatible with the Charter obligation of the administering power and in conformity with the General Assembly resolution and the principle of permanent sovereignty of natural resources enshrined therein, *if the exploitation of the resources in non-self-governing territories is considered for the benefit of the peoples of those territories, on their behalf or in consultation with their representatives.* In that respect, Morocco is under an obligation to take all appropriate measures to ensure the full application of the EC-Morocco Fisheries Partnership Agreement in accordance with the obligations of International law. (…) The interpretation given by the UN legal adviser recognises the competence of Morocco to conclude these types of agreements and in this way implies that Morocco is a *de facto administrative power* of the territory of Western Sahara"[714].

As shown, the Commission took note of the paragraph of the legal advisor's opinion in which he affirmed the legality of the exploitation of natural resources in Non-Self-Governing Territories when this is in the benefit of the population, but it interpreted it as it pleased, since the fisheries agreement would not benefit the population nor did it have the permission of the only legitimate representative, the POLISARIO Front. It is important to note that Morocco is not the administering Power: neither *de facto* nor *de iure*.

The incorrect interpretation of his 2002 report by the European Commission led Hans Corell in 2008 to say that this criterion, mentioned in his report relating to oil resources, is logically applicable to fisheries agreements between Morocco and third States or International Organizations, and he denounced the Commission's interpretation as follows:

---

[714] Intervention of J. Borg, on behalf of the Commission (debate of 15 May 2006). Stressed characters by author.

"I find it incomprehensible that the Commission could find such support in legal opinion, unless, of course, it could show that it had consulted the people of Western Sahara, who would have accepted the Agreement and the way in which they would be benefitted from the income brought in from the activity. However, a review of the Agreement leads to a very different conclusion (…) In not one of the pages in this Agreement is reference made to the fact that this Moroccan "jurisdiction" is in fact limited by International norms of self-determination. As a European, I am ashamed (…) In any event, it should be obvious that an agreement of this type, which makes no distinction between the waters off Western Sahara and the territorial waters of Morocco, violates International law"[715].

Thus, through the conclusion of the fisheries agreements between Morocco and the EU, in which the occupying Power assumes title over "the waters of Western Sahara" and implicitly the EU recognises Moroccan sovereignty over the Territory, both parties are violating the right of the Sahrawi people to the permanent sovereignty over their natural resources. The EU is negotiating with Morocco in the absence of a valid interlocutor: it is practicing *realpolitik*, but at the same it is violating International law[716].

---

[715] CORELL, H. (2010): 2432 et seq.

[716] In effect, the Fisheries Commissioner, Emma Bonino, justified in 1995 the agreements with which occupied ilegally the Territory stating that "another valid interlocutor does not exist (…) I have to deal with what there is. If later this changes, I will negotiate with others (…) I cannot say that I am not going to negotiate with someone who is not recognised, nor can I leave the issue until things are clarified. That would be worse" (*El Mundo*, 10 December 1995). Curiously, the same argument was made before the ICJ by Australia to negotiate with Indonesia over natural resources in East Timor (*Case of East Timor (Portugal v. Australia)*, Decision of 30 June 1995, *CIJ Recueil 1995*).

CONCLUSIONS

The Western Saharan conflict constitutes one of the most glaring exceptions to the otherwise successful completion of the decolonization process, as four decades after the United Nations had almost totally completed the greatest success in its history -the decolonization of half of the world- the Sahrawi people have still not been able to exercise their right to self-determination, recognised and proclaimed time after time by the principal organs of the United Nations.

The work of the United Nations in the African decolonization context (1955-1975) led Western Sahara so close to self-determination. Its actions in the defence of the rights of the population of the Territory, which had a strong and promising start, have though, from start to finish, been uneven and sometimes puzzling. From the moment that it first joined the UN, Spain was instantly pressured to recognise the status of its African dependencies as *Non-Self-Governing Territory*, and once this was achieved, to organise a referendum for self-determination in the Territory. However, just as this pressure was about to pay off and one was about to see the achievement of the UN's objectives with Spain preparing to organize the referendum in which, as the UN Mission which visited the territory in 1975 pointed out, everything seemed to point towards a victory for the independence option, Moroccan actions managed to blur the clarity of the ideas which until then had characterised the work of the Organization. It managed to get the General Assembly to make a request for an opinion before the ICJ in a Resolution which annexed a request that while the issue is being considered by the Court, Spain should stop the preparations for the referendum; this was to derail the progress so painstakingly made up until that moment.

In 1975, the coincidence of three circumstances brought the Territory into a dark tunnel from which it has not been able to escape. The request for the opinion to the ICJ, with the parallel request to Spain that it stopped the referendum, the lack of a strong UN response to the *Green March* and finally the conclusion of the Madrid Agreements plunged the Territory into its darkest days. Although voices were raised in doubt at the necessity of the advisory opinion at a time when the process was so close to completion and, although the intention of King Hassan II to conduct a march on the Territory had become, by various means, the chronicle to an announced occupation, the General Assembly committed one of the most severe errors that it ever has during the decolonization processes in giving the ICJ a primary role in pronouncing on an issue which, regardless of other considerations, was not purely judicial, and in also supposedly favouring (innocently?) an invasion into the Territory. This error was endorsed by the Security Council, which saw how Morocco had invaded a Non-Self-Governing Territory without deciding to take action in the matter.

The advisory opinion of the ICJ made it clear that, at the time of colonization of the Territory at the end of the XIX Century, it was neither terra nullius nor did there exist any links of sovereignty over the population in respect of Morocco or the Mauritanian Entity. The Court also stated that the links that in its opinion did exist -ties of allegiance- could in no case affect the right to self-determination of the Sahrawi people. While it is clear that these affirmations put pay to Morocco's hegemonic pretensions over the Territory, however they do not make it clear how, the Court having concluded the existence of ties of sovereignty, these could have affected the right to self-determination. Since it is a right whose crystallization did not come until the beginning of the nineteen seventies, not in existence at the historical moment upon which the Court's investigations cantered, it is difficult to understand the usefulness of the opinion. Today it is undisputed that the essential element of the right to self-determination of peoples is the will of the population. If this is mostly in favour of independence, it is difficult to imagine how historical ties of allegiance -a concept which was alien even to Arab law at the time- and even those of sovereignty, could overlap the right of self-determination.

The occurrence of the so-called Green March, which culminated with the occupation of the Territory, constituted a violation of Article 2 of the UN Charter. Despite the condemnation of the Security Council, and their express request to Morocco that it immediately retires all of its participants, those who eventually had to leave the Territory where in fact the Sahrawi's, who saw that while the vast majority of those territories subjected to foreign colonization enjoyed independence, in their Territory the clock was put back to the darkest days of colonialism. The occupation by Morocco of the Territory abandoned by Mauritania after the signing of the Peace Treaty with the POLISARIO Front (1979), in the exercise of a presumed and surprising "right of first refusal" was another example of such a violation.

The signing of the Madrid Agreements, under which Spain tried to pass on their responsibilities and duties over the Territory to a temporary bipartite Moroccan-Mauritanian administration, undermined the Secretary General's efforts to continue with the decolonization process for Western Sahara, specified in the *Waldheim Plan*. There are many motives that confirm the nullity of the agreements, accepted almost unanimously by the most highly qualified publicists. On one hand, this comes from the lack of legitimacy of the *subjects* that participated in its conclusion. In the case of Morocco and Mauritania, the

Opinion of the ICJ left no room for doubt in this respect; in the case of Spain, and despite his unilateral decision to "terminate its presence in the Territory", considering "itself henceforth exempt from any from any responsibility of an international nature in connection with the administration of the Territory", continued to be the administering Power of the Territory since, as the General Assembly has stated on many occasions, a State does not lose its status as administering Power nor can it liberate itself from the obligations it derives from this status simply by saying so. On the other hand, the agreements are null because of their *purpose* (the violation of a *ius cogens* norm -that of self-determination- whose application to the Sahrawi people had been recognised on innumerable occasions by different principal organs of the UN), as well as for their *content* (it impeded consultation of the population which is an essential element in the right to self-determination of peoples, trying to replace its will with that of the *Yemáa* which had dissolved following the Green March), and for its *effects* (constant violation of International law, military occupation of a Non-Self-Governing Territory and violation of the sovereignty of the Sahrawi people over their natural resources which is provided in the annexes of these Madrid Agreements).

The Madrid Agreements deserved a lukewarm response from the General Assembly, which in an impossible equitable exercise opted to give them some virtuality, requesting of the non-existent "interim administration" that it takes the measures necessary "to ensure that all of the original Sahrawi populations can exercise fully and freely, under the supervision of the United Nations, their inalienable right to self-determination", which was, in the graphic expression of Thomas Frank "like inviting a cat to consult the canaries", while it also requested the same attitude of Spain, as the administering Power of the Territory. Thus, if the intervention of the United Nations in the conflict during Spain's first twenty years as part of the Organization (1955-1975) had been instrumental in putting the country on the verge of self-determination, the years which followed the Green March showed its inability to bring a successful outcome to this conflict, which remains the exception to the great decolonization work. The fruits of twenty years of sleepless nights defending the right to self-determination of the Sahrawi people were reduced to flames in just a few months.

The proclamation of the Sahrawi Arab Democratic Republic (SADR) and its recognition by more than eighty States is a decisive step towards the definitive establishment of an independent State in the Territory. As is well known, the constitutive elements of a State are a territory, a population and an organised Government, capable of effectively exercising power over the first two. The first question did not pose many problems in relation to the Sahrawi State, in that in application of the principle of *uti possidetis iuris*, the limits of a territory were drawn in the colonial era, and this has not been an object of contention for the parties. As regards the existence and delimitation of the human basis of the State, the realization of the census for the referendum has been the Gordian knot in the peace process. However, discussions have centred primarily on three of the eighty-eight tribal groups that make up the census, meaning that, regardless of an exact number, the Sahrawi population is also a defined element. Moreover, there also already exists a census which was drawn up by the MINURSO, which the Security Council could use to carry out the referendum if it one day decides to make recourse to Chapter VII of the Charter. The most delicate question lies in the third of the requirements since, even if the Government is perfectly organised with a structure comparable to that of a Government of any other State, the fact is that the power it is exercising over a territory is non-exclusive and is only over part of an area, the majority of which is under Moroccan military occupation. This means that the SADR's pretensions of Statehood may not be totally appropriate from a strictly legal standpoint, but reality shows that as well as being a full member of the African Union, almost half of the international community believe that it is a State. Even after forty years the annexation of the occupied territories has still not been recognized by any State, which is in a sense an express recognition that Morocco does not hold sovereignty over them, with sovereignty corresponding exclusively to the SADR. But it does also control part of the Territory, over which it exercises effective control of its administration. The fact is that this Territory is not in a state of legal limbo; instead it is part of the Sahrawi State, which will possess full international subjectivity on the day that it regains control over the rest of its territory. It is only a question of time.

The legal status of Western Sahara in the United Nations is that of a Non-Self-Governing Territory awaiting decolonization, in the process of the consolidation of the SADR. Despite intense opposition from the powerful Moroccan lobby, the situation in the Territory continues to be analysed annually by the Decolonization Commission. Amongst others, this the reason for which, after over three decades of occupation, no State, not even its most unconditional ally, France, has recognised annexation of Western Sahara by Morocco. The decolonisation of the territory will not be completed while the Sahrawi people have still not exercised their right to self-determination.

The legal status of Morocco in Western Sahara is not that of administering Power, but instead that of occupying Power in the Territory, similar to that of Israel in the occupied Palestinian territories. The *opinion of the ICJ on the legality of the construction by Israel of the wall in the occupied Palestinian territories* is applicable *mutatis mutandis* to the Sahrawi case. The Spanish withdrawal would have required the delivery of its administration to the only legitimate representative of the Sahrawi people, the POLISARIO Front, or failing that the United Nations, but never the agreement with Morocco and Mauritania and the military occupation by these States which followed. The implementation of the Madrid Agreements of 1975 led to a situation of constant violation of International law, because it led to an occupation, firstly partly by Morocco and then completely by the same following the withdrawal of Mauritania from the Territory, since Resolution 2625 (XXV) states that no territorial acquisition arising from the threat or use of force will be recognised as legal. The Madrid Agreements did not entail a transfer of sovereignty over the Territory, among other reasons because Spain merely administered it. The report of 29th January 2002 by the Legal Office of the United Nations confirmed this with clarity.

The agreements concluded by Morocco over the exploitation of natural resources in Western Sahara violate International Law. Consequently, States, international organisations and companies that negotiate with Morocco over the exploitation of natural resources in the Territory also violate International Law. Firstly Spain, and the European Community as well from the date that Spain joined in 1986, are internationally responsible for the exploitation of the natural resources of the Sahrawi people. The EU consciously violates International Law. The reports of the European Parliament relating to the legality of the fisheries agreements (May 2006 and January 2011) leave no room for doubt as to this. Despite this, both the Commission and the Council, allegedly involved in expanding across the world democracy and respect for human rights, prefer to look the other way when their economic interests are at stake.

The pending decolonization in the Western Saharan Territory also became a question of the nationality of its inhabitants, and until these exercise their right to self-determination it will continue to directly affect the Spanish legal system. Spanish law on the Territory passed through three different phases. In the first (1884-1958), the distinction between the colonial and metropolitan areas and the question of the inhabitants were never in doubt. In the second phase (1958-1968) the legislator tried to assimilate the Territory and its inhabitants under the status of "Overseas Provinces", rejecting therefore their colonial status. Finally, the third phase, which began in 1968, culminated in the Spanish withdrawal from the Sahrawi Territory, the publication of the Decolonization of Sahara law and the affirmation that it had never formed part of Spain's national territory. Two judgements also shed light on this question. On one hand, the Spanish Supreme Court (28th October 1998), with a very questionable legal technique, tried to settle the Spanish debt with the Sahrawi people, opening the door to people who they once recognised as Spanish citizens allowing individuals, if they wanted to, to claim nationality. On the other hand, the Supreme Court (20th November 2007) came to recognise the stateless status of the Sahrawi people. So, regardless of the rights which they can claim in Spanish law if they can show that they satisfy particular requirements, and more importantly if they want to, Sahrawi's are not and do not try to be Spanish or Algerian or, even less, Moroccan. The logical fact of many of them intending to have documentation which, like that of Spain, allows them to enjoy the rights enjoyed by EU citizens does not mean that they want to renounce their nationality, their Sahrawi nationality. With the exception of those who, for whatever reason, have acquired Spanish nationality, the Sahrawi's are nationals of the SADR in those States which recognise it, and stateless in the rest.

After fifteen years of war, the new international context which emerged following the end of the Cold War brought a newly relaxed atmosphere to the region, favouring the conclusion of a first agreement between the representatives of Morocco and the POLISARIO Front (30th August 1988), driven jointly by the UN and the OAU, which was the starting point of the Peace Process. Within this framework, the ceasefire came into effect (6th September 1991) and the Security Council decided to establish a peacekeeping operation (the MINURSO) that was charged with the task of implementing a process that should hopefully end with the celebration of a referendum for self-determination. Although at that moment there was heated debate within the POLISARIO Front between those who defended the continuance of the armed struggle, arguing that if Morocco had come to accept sitting down at the negotiating table it was because of both military and economic exhaustion caused by the war, and those who had faith in the UN's actions to finally decolonize the Territory, it was this latter peaceful option which was followed. After almost two decades of the UN's Peace Plan, the UN itself has been bent on showing that this was a wrong decision…

Although there are some who maintain that the main cause of the successive stoppages of the identification process lies in the narrow scope of the mandate given to the MINURSO, the design of the Peace Plan does give this operation the necessary instruments to allow for the carrying out of the referendum with every guarantee of success. Nor is it true that technical problems related to the census prevented the carrying out of the referendum. There is already a census that has been drafted by the UN with all guarantees of impartiality, and a plan perfectly designed and negotiated by the Parties; the only reason for not implementing them is the French veto to a Security Council resolution that would impose the plan and guarantee the celebration of the referendum. Despite this, one can also criticise the fact that the MINURSO's mandate was not changed at any point during its long existence, keeping the functions already provided in the Settlement Plan; given the circumstances, the introduction of some specific modifications could have helped to break the deadlock from which at numerous moments the process suffered.

The systematic obstruction of the Peace Plan by Morocco has enjoyed the complicity of successive Secretary Generals of the UN. Although it would be unfair to place the fault of the failure and the desperate prolongation of the conflict exclusively on the UN's shoulders, something that is all too common and easy, one can hardly ignore the decisive impact on the process of the attitude adopted by successive Secretary Generals. *Pérez de Cuéllar* unilaterally modified the criteria which gave the right to be included in the census and increased the terms of the agreement related to admissible evidence for identification, openly contradicting the content of the Peace Plan to benefit the approaches of Morocco, and he looked the other way when the *second Green March* occurred (this entailed the establishment in the Territory, in an organised manner, of a new avalanche of thousands of Moroccan settlers), which constitutes another violation of the obligations on occupying Powers contained in the Geneva Conventions. The arrival of *Butros Gali* to the Secretariat led to another step backwards since, as well as allowing the violation of the Peace Plan in matters relating to the identification of applicants, he promoted the progressive reduction of the MINURSO right up to its decommissioning, an objective that at one point was even overrule by the Security Council but he still managed to achieve, even if it did almost cost him his job. The appointment of *Kofi Annan* gave a new impetus to the identification process, although by then the new Secretary General was already aware that once the census had been drawn up, Morocco would withdraw from the process. This was eventually the case, and Annan charged James Baker, former US Secretary of State, to find a route alternative to the Peace Plan, or in fact alternative to International law. Annan managed to unblock the identification process and reactivate the MINURSO, but opened the dangerous route of finding a "political route which is acceptable for both parties", putting the party who violates International law and that which suffers the consequences on the same level. Finally, *Ban Ki-moon* until now has not shown any signs of life, limiting himself to asking Member States for imaginative solutions to resolve the conflict.

The unconditional support of France to the Moroccan occupation does not only impede the resolution of the conflict under the framework of Chapter VII of the Charter, but is also gives cover and impunity to the serious human rights violations carried out by Morocco in the Territory. In another example of its contempt for the respect of human rights in the occupied territories, even acting alone against the other fourteen members of the Security Council, in 2010 France expressly vetoed the possibility to extend the functions of the MINURSO in the human rights ambit to allow, at least, the body to be able to denounce severe violations which occur at the doors of its own headquarters in the Sahrawi capital of El Aaiún. The violent dismantling by Morocco of the Gdeim Izik camp, not far from the Sahrawi capital (8th November 2010), the intensification of the repression of the Sahrawi population in all occupied territories and the use of Moroccan settlers to carry out acts of vandalism against the people of the Territory has brought Sahrawi-Moroccan relations to a point of no return.

The Moroccan rejection of the Baker Plan II, a plan that openly favoured the annexation claims of the party that illegally occupied the Territory, clearly shows that for Morocco the Peace Plan was no more than an instrument to indefinitely postpone the celebration of the referendum. The forecast in this plan that within five years a referendum would have to be carried out, one in which all Sahrawis included in the census drawn up by the MINURSO and "the *bona fide* residents until December 1999" would take part, inaugurated a new institution of... International law? It substituted the right to self-determination of the peoples for the right to self-determination of the *bona fide* residents! The POLISARIO Front, which has ceded time and time again to the many obstacles put in place by Morocco throughout the whole Peace Plan, already approaching the limit of what it can accept, gave its approval to the Baker Plan II, showing that it knew perfectly its enemy, given that it knew that Morocco would never accept a self-determination referendum because, as Peter Van Waldsum would later accept in front of the French Parliament, the Moroccan Government does not trust the way in which its citizens would vote.

The United Nations has been acting in the conflict since the adoption of the first Security Council resolution in 1975 within the framework of Chapter VI of the Charter, and not since Morocco rejected the Baker Plan has there been any significant progress made. On the contrary, Mohammed VI has made it clear on numerous occasions that his Government will never *allow* the celebration of a referendum on self-determination. The situation of the Sahrawi people has worsened significantly in recent years. In the occupied territories, repression, denounced by prestigious organizations such as *Amnesty International* or *Human Rights Watch*, is the rule, and the peaceful uprising of the Sahrawi resistance against the occupier continues to make ground. The POLISARIO Front faces more problems in the Tinduf refugee camps to house the young generation, fed up of waiting and having never seen a world beyond these camps. Under these circumstances, only a change in the French attitude within the Security Council, something today which is highly unlikely, will allow an end to be put to the conflict, because acting within the framework of Chapter VII of the Charter, the Security Council could -and should- impose a situation: that of the pact freely agreed by the Parties in 1988. Hopefully we will not have to wait for this, like in the case of East Timor where it took another genocide of the population for the United Nations to intervene with the strong hand of International law.

In December 1991, the General Assembly declared the decade from 1991-2001 the *International Decade for the Elimination of Colonialism* (Resolution 46/181); ten years later the General Assembly declared the period from 2001-2010 the Second International Decade for the Elimination of Colonialism (Resolution 55/146). In 2004 the Assembly urged Member States to collaborate with the UN to make the world one free of colonialism in the Second International Decade and urged them to continue to fully support the Special Committee on Decolonization in its efforts to achieve this objective (Resolution 59/134). It is about time that the UN shows that these Declarations are more than just a mere manifestation of intentions empty of content. After fifteen years of war for national liberation, whose legitimacy is guaranteed by International law, in 1991 the POLISARIO Front decided to substitute weapons for polls, in the confidence that the UN would be able to bring fruition to a Peace Plan that had been negotiated freely by the Parties. Despite the Moroccan boycott of the work of the MINURSO, there already exists a census for the referendum, which was drawn up by the UN, but the French veto prevents the UN from acting within the framework of Chapter VII of the Charter to impose a solution. Meanwhile, in occupied Western Sahara there are serious human rights violations and the EU is illegally exploiting its natural resources. In this situation, if the Sahrawi people are eventually prevented from freely deciding their future via a referendum on self-determination, in the terms established by UN resolutions, no-one can accuse it of not having explored every peaceful means possible to put an end to their suffering.

BIBLIOGRAPHY

A) GENERAL WORKS AND WORKS ON INTERNATIONAL PRACTICE

ABELLAN HONRUBIA, V, *Prácticas de Derecho Internacional Público*, Ed. Jose María Bosch, 3th ed. Barcelona, 2005.

AKEHURST, M., *A Modern Introduction to International Law*, 4th ed., George Allen and Unwin, Londres, 1982.

ANDRÉS SAÉNZ DE SANTA MARÍA, P.: *Sistema de Derecho Internacional Público*, 2ª ed., Civitas, Madrid, 2012.

BEDJAOUI, M., (ed.) *Droit international. Bilan et perspectives*, 1991.

BROWNLIE, I., *Principles of Public International Law*, 4th ed., Clarendon Press, Oxford, 1990.

CARRILLO SALCEDO, J.A., *Soberanía del Estado y Derecho Internacional*, Tecnos, Madrid, 1969 (2th ed., 1976).

CARRILLO SALCEDO, J.A., *El Derecho Internacional en un mundo en cambio*, Madrid, Tecnos, 1984.

CARRILLO SALCEDO, J.A., *El Derecho Internacional en perspectiva histórica*, Tecnos, Madrid, 1991.

CARRILLO SALCEDO, J.A., *Curso de Derecho Internacional Público*, Tecnos, Madrid, 1992.

CARRILLO SALCEDO, J.A., *Soberanía de los Estados y Derechos Humanos en Derecho Internacional Contemporáneo*, Tecnos, Madrid, 1995.

CARRILLO SALCEDO, J.A., "Droit international et souveraineté des États", Cours général de Droit internacional public, *Recueil des Cours*, t. 257 (1996): 35-222.

CASSESE, A., *Il Diritto internazionale nel mondo contemporaneo*, Bologna, 1984 (English trasl., Oxford, 1990).

CHAUMONT, Ch., *L'Organisation des Nations Unies*, 14th ed., Ed. Puf, Paris, 1994.

DE VISSHER, Ch., *Teorías y realidades en Derecho Internacional Público*, Ed. Bosch, Barcelona, 1962.

DELBEZ, L, *Les principes généraux du Droit International Public*, 3th, ed., L.G.D.J., Paris, 1964.

DIEZ DE VELASCO, M.: *Instituciones de Derecho Internacional Público*, 18.ª ed., Tecnos, Madrid, 2013.

DIEZ DE VELASCO, M.: *Las Organizaciones Internacionales*, 16.ª ed., Tecnos, Madrid, 2010.

DUPUY, P. M., *Droit International Public*, Dallos, Paris, 2002.

GONÇALVES PEREIRA, A., DE QUADROS, F., *Manual de Direito Internacional Público*, Livraria Almedina, 3th ed., Coimbra, 1995.

GONZÁLEZ CAMPOS, J. D., SÁNCHEZ RODRÍGUEZ, L. I., ANDRÉS SAENZ DE SANTA MARIA, M. P., *Curso de Derecho Internacional Público*, 4th ed., Thompson-Civitas, Madrid, 2008.

GONZÁLEZ CAMPOS, J. D., SANCHEZ RODRIGUEZ, L. I., y ANDRES SAENZ DE SANTA MARIA, M. P., *Materiales de prácticas de Derecho Internacional Público*, Madrid, 1987.

GUTIERREZ ESPADA, C., *Apuntes sobre las Funciones del Derecho Internacional Contemporáneo*, Promociones y Publicaciones Universitarias, Murcia, 1995.

GUTIÉRREZ ESPADA, C., *Derecho Internacional Público*, 3ª ed. Trotta, Madrid, 1995.

GUTIÉRREZ ESPADA, C., CERVELL HORTAL, M- J., *El Derecho Internacional en la encrucijada*, Ed. Trotta, 2012.

HERRERO RUBIO, A., *Historia del Derecho de Gentes*, 3th ed., Valladolid, 1967 (10th ed. 1994).

JIMENEZ DE ARECHAGA, E., *El Derecho Internacional Contemporáneo*, Tecnos, Madrid, 1980.

JUSTE RUIZ, J.; CASTILLO DAUDÍ, M., y BOU FRANCH, V., *Lecciones de Derecho Internacional Público*, 2.ª ed., Tirant Lo Blanch, Valencia, 2011.

KELSEN, H., *La paz por medio del Derecho*, ed. Losada, Buenos Aires, 1946.

MARIÑO MENÉNDEZ, F., *Derecho Internacional Público (Parte General)*, 4.ª ed., Trotta, Madrid, 2005.

MAYER, P., *Droit international Privé*, Ed. Montchrestien, Paris, 1977.

MIAJA DE LA MUELA, A., *Introducción al Derecho internacional Público*, 7th ed., Madrid, 1979.

MIAJA DE LA MUELA, A., *Derecho Internacional Privado*, II, Parte Especial, Madrid, 10th ed. 1987.

NGUYEN QUOC, D., DAILLIER P. et PELLET, A., *Droit International Public*, 3th ed., Paris, 1987.

PASTOR RIDRUEJO, J. A., *Curso de Derecho Internacional Público y organizaciones internacionales*, Tecnos, 16ª ed., Madrid, 2012.

REMIRO BROTONS, A., *Derecho Internacional Público (Vol. I: Principios fundamentales)*, Madrid, 1983.

REMIRO BROTONS, A., *Derecho Internacional Público (Vol. II: Derecho de los Tratados)*, Tecnos, Madrid, 1987.

REMIRO BROTONS, A., *Derecho Internacional*, McGraw-Hill, Madrid, 1997.

REMIRO BROTÓNS, A., RIQUELME CORTADO, R., ORIHUELA CALATAYUD, E., DÍEZ HOCHLEITNER, J., y PÉREZ-PRAT DURBÁN, L.: *Derecho Internacional (curso general)*, Tirant Lo Blanch, Valencia, 2011.

REUTER, P., *Derecho Internacional Público*, Trasl Spanish. PUENTE EGIDO, Bosch, Barcelona, 1978.

ROUSSEAU, Ch., *Derecho Internacional Público*, 3th ed. Spanish, Ed. Ariel, Barcelona, 1966.

ROUSSEAU, Ch., *Droit International Public*, Paris, 1971-1983.

SANCHEZ RODRIGUEZ, L.I., *Derecho Internacional Público: Problemas actuales*, Eurolex, Madrid, 1993.

SEARA VAZQUEZ, M., *Derecho Internacional Público*, México, 1991.

SEPULVEDA, C., *Derecho Internacional*, México, 1991.

SHAW, M. N., *International Law*, 3th ed., Cambridge, 1991.

SORENSEN, M., (Ed.), *Manual de Derecho Internacional Público*, México, 1973.

STARKE, J.G., *Introduction to International Law*, 10th ed., Londres, 1989.

THIERRY, H., "Cours Général de Droit International Public", *Recueil des Cours*, 1990, III, t. 222.

TOUSCOZ, J., *Droit International*, Paris, 1993.

VERZIJL, J.H.W., *International Law in historical perspective. Part V: Nationality and other matters relating to individuals*, A.W.Sijthoff, Leiden, 1972.

B) INTERNATIONAL LAW ENCYCLOPEDIAS

MARAUHN, T.,"Sahara" In *The Max Planck Encyclopedia of Public International Law*. Vol. 8. Edited by Rüdiger Wolfrum, 1095–1106. Oxford: Oxford University Press, 2012.

RIQUELME CORTADO, R., and SOROETA LICERAS, J., "Western Sahara", Oxford Bibliographies, 2013, http://www.oxfordbibliographies.com

C) MONOGRAPHIC WORKS

ABI-SAAB, G., "Wars of National Liberation in the Geneva Conventions and Protocols", *Recueil des Cours*, IV, (1979): 366-436.

AGO, R., *Annuaire de la Commission du Droit International*, 1971, vol. II, 1th part.

ALI YARA, O., *La question sahraouie et la mutation strategique du Maghreb*, Tesis Doctoral Thesis, April 1991, Université Paris X-Nanterre, Paris, 1997.

AMEYAR, H., *Sahara Occidental: Que veut l'ONU?*. Algiers, Algeria: Casbah Editions, 2000.

AREILZA, J.M., *Diario de un ministro de la Monarquía*, Ed. Planeta, 1977.

BALAGUER, S., WIRTH, R., *Frente Polisario: La última guerrilla*, Barcelona, 1976.

BALTA, P., *Le Gran Maghreb, des indépendances à l'an 2000*, Ed. La Découverte, Paris, 1990.

BARBERIS, J.A., *Los sujetos del derecho internacional actual*, Tecnos, Madrid, 1984.

BARBIER, M., *Le conflit du Sahara occidental*, L'Harmattan, Paris, 1982.

BARDINI, R., *El Frente POLISARIO y la lucha del pueblo saharaui*, Cuadernos de la CIPAAL, Tegucigalpa, 1979.

BARDONET, VIRALLY, *Le nouveau droit de la mer*, Paris, 1983.

BEDJAOUI, M., *Nouvel ordre mondial et contrôle de la légalité des actes du Conseil de Sécurité*, Bruselas, 1994, trasl. Spanish by FERNANDEZ DE CASADEVANTE ROMANI, C. and QUEL LOPEZ, J., IVAP, Bilbao, 1995.

BEIGBEDER, Y., *Le controle international des élections*, Bruylant-Bruxelles, L.G.D.J., Paris, 1994.

BERISTÁIN, C.M., and GONZÁLEZ HIDALGO, E. eds., *El oasis de la memoria: Memoria histórica y violaciones de los derechos humanos en el Sahara Occidental*, ed. Hegoa, Bilbao, 2012.

BERRAMDANE, A., *Le Sahara Occidental: enjeu maghrèbin*, Paris, 1987.

BERRAMDANE, A., *Le Maroc et l'Occident (1800-1974)*, Ed. Karthala, Paris, 1987.

BONTEMS, C., *La guerre du Sahara Occidental*, Paris, 1984.

BRIONES, F., *Sahara: Cien años sin libertad*. Asociación de Amistad con el Pueblo Saharaui de Alicante, Librería Compás. Alicante, 1994.

BROWNLIE, I., *Basic Documents on African affairs*, The Clarendon Press Oxford, 1971.

BROWNLIE, I., *African Boundaries. A Legal and Diplomatic Encyclopaedia*, London, 1979.

BUSTOS GISBERT, R., *Relaciones Internacionales y Comunidades Autónomas*, C.E.C., Madrid, 1996.

CALOGEROPOULOS-STRATIS, S., *Le droit des peuples à disposer d'eux-mêmes*, Etablissements Emile Bruylant, Bruselas, 1973.

CARO BAROJA, J., *Estudios Saharianos*, CSIC, Madrid, 1955.

CARRERA HERNÁNDEZ, F.J., *Política Pesquera y Responsabilidad Internacional de la Comunidad Europea*, ed. Universidad de Salamanca, Salamanca, 1995.

CASSESE, A., *La guerre di liberazione nazionale e il Diritto internazionale*, Pisa, 1974.

CASSESE, A., *Self-Determination of Peoples. A legal Reappraisal*, Cambdridge University Press, Cambridge, 1996.

CHAUMONT, Ch. (Homage), *Le droit des peuples à disposer d'eux-mêmes, Méthodes d'analyse du Droit International*, Paris, ed. Pedone, 1984.

CHOMSKY, N., *Autodeterminación y Nuevo Orden. Los casos de Timor y Palestina*, ed. Txalaparta, Tafalla, 1998.

CISTERÓ BAHIMA, J.M. y FREIXES SANJUAN, M.T., *Sahara, una lección de la Historia*, Imprenta Altagraf, Barcelona, 1987.

COBBAN, A., *National Self-Determination*, London/New York/Toronto, 1945.

CORDERO TORRES, J.M., *Textos Básicos de Africa*, Parte General y Parte Especial, Madrid, 1962.

COT, J. (dir.), "Operations des Nations Unies. Leçons de terrain: Cambodge, Somalie, Rwanda, ex-Yougoslavie", Collection Perspectives Stratégiques, Fondation pour les Études de Défense, Paris, 1995.

COT, J. P. et PELLET, A. (dirs.), *La Charte des Nations Unies. Commentaire article par article*, 2th ed., Paris/Bruxelles, 1987.

CRAWFORD, J., *The creation of States in International Law*, Oxford, 1979.

CRAWFORD, J., *The rights of peoples*, Ed. J. Crawford, Clarendon Peperbacks, Oxford, 1992.

CRAWFORD, J., (ed), *Brownlie's Principles of Public International Law*, 8th ed., Oxford, 2012.

CRIADO, R., *Sahara: Pasión y muerte de un sueño colonial.* Ruedo Ibérico, Paris, 1977.

CRISTESCU, A., *El Derecho a la Libre Determinación. Desarrollo histórico y actual sobre la base de los instrumentos de las Naciones Unidas*, Naciones Unidas, ORGA:. E/CN.4/Sub.2/404/Rev.1, Nueva York, 1981.

DANIEL, D.C.F., HAYES, B.C., *Beyond traditional peacekeeping*, 1995.

DE BURLET, J., *Nationalité des personnes physiques et décolonisation. Essai de contribution à la théorie de la succession d'Etats*, Ed. Bruylant, Bruxelles, 1975.

DE CASTRO, F., "La nationalité, la double nationalité et la supra-nationalité", *Recueil des Cours*, I, 102 (1961): 521-632.

DE CHASSEY, F., *L'etrier, la houe et le Livre. "Sociétés traditionnelles" au Sahara et au Sahel occidental*, Ed. Anthropos, Paris, 1977.

DE LUPIS, I.D., *International Law and the Independent State*, 2th ed., Hants, 1987.

DE PINIÉS, J., *La descolonización del Sahara Occidental: Un tema sin concluir*, Madrid, 1990.

DE YTURRIAGA BARBERAN, J.A., *Participación de la Organización de las Naciones Unidas en el proceso de descolonización*, Madrid, 1967.

DIEGO AGUIRRE, J.R., *Historia del Sahara español*, Madrid, ed. Kaydeda, D.L. 1988.

DIEGO AGUIRRE, J.R., *Guerra en el Sahara*, Madrid, ed. Istmo, D.L. 1991.

DIEHL, P. F., *International peacekeeping*, 1993.

DÍEZ DE VELASCO, M., *Hacia un nuevo orden internacional y Europeo* (Libro homenaje), Tecnos, Madrid, 1993.

DIETHELM, R., *Die Schweiz und friedenserhaltende Operationen 1920-1995.* Berna, Viena, Stuttgart, Paul Haupt Verlag, 1997.

DIRECCIÓN GENERAL DE PROMOCIÓN DE SAHARA, *Legislación de Sahara. Años 1965-1973*, Instituto de Estudios Africanos (C.S.I.C.), Madrid, 1974.

DURCH, W.J. (ed.), *The evolution of UN Peacekeeping, Case Studies and Comparative Analysis*, New York, St. Martin's Press, 1993.

EL OUALI, A., *Saharan Conflict: Towards Territorial Autonomy as a Right to Democratic Self-Determination*, Stacey International, London, 2008.

EL-SAID, M.F., *The United Nations and Namibia: implications for institutional development of the Organization and the creation of norms of international behavior*, Nueva York, 1986.

EPSTEIN, P., "Behind Closed Doors: 'Autonomous Colonization' in Post United Nations Era: The Case for Western Sahara", *Annual Survey of International and Comparative Law* 15 (2009): 107–143.

ERICH, R., "La naissance et reconnaissance des Etats", *Recueil des Cours*, The Hage, III, t. 13, (1926): 427-507.

FALK, R.A., "The new States and international law order", *Recueil des Cours*, t. 118 (1966-II): 1-102.

FERNANDEZ DE CASADEVANTE ROMANI, C., *La interpretación de las normas internacionales*, ed. Aranzadi, San Sebastián, 1996.

FERNANDEZ DE LA MORA, G., *Río Arriba. Memorias*, ed. Planeta, Barcelona, 1995

FERNANDEZ ROZAS, J.C., *Derecho español de la nacionalidad*, Tecnos, Madrid, 1987.

FERNÁNDEZ SÁNCHEZ, P.A., *Operaciones de las Naciones Unidas para el Mantenimiento de la Paz. La presencia de la ONU en los conflictos internacionales e internacionalizados*, Servicio de Publicaciones de la Universidad de Huelva, Huelva, 1998.

FERRER LLORET, J., *La aplicación del principio de autodeterminación de los pueblos: Sahara Occidental y Timor Oriental*. San Vicente del Raspeig, Servicio de Publicaciones de la Universidad de Alicante, 2002.

FOUGEROUSE, M., *Le Maroc: vocations et realites,* Fondation Singer-Polignac, Paris, 1987.

GAUDIO, A., *Le dossier du Sahara Occidental,* Nouvelles Éditions Latines, Paris, 1978.

GIL RODRÍGUEZ, J., *La nacionalidad española y los cambios legislativos,* ed. Colex, Madrid, 1993.

GONZÁLEZ VEGA, J.A., *Conflictos territoriales y uso de la fuerza (un estudio de la práctica internacional a la luz del conflicto Irán-Irak),* ed. Beramar, Madrid, 1994.

GOYTISOLO, J. *El problema del Sahara,* ed. Anagrama, Barcelona, 1979.

GROS ESPIELL, H., *El Derecho a la Libre Determinación. Aplicación de las Resoluciones de las Naciones Unidas,* Naciones Unidas, Nueva York, 1979, ORGA: E/CN.4/Sub.2/405/Rev.1.

GUILHAUDIS, J. F., *Le droit des peuples à disposer d'eux-mêmes,* Presses Universitaires de Grenoble, 1976.

GUTIERREZ ESPADA, C., *El estado de necesidad y el uso de la fuerza en derecho internacional,* Tecnos, Madrid, 1987.

GUTIERREZ ESPADA, C., *El uso de la fuerza y el Derecho internacional después de la descolonización,* Cuadernos de la Cátedra S. J. Brown, Universidad de Valladolid, 1988.

HANNIKAIEN, L., *Peremptory norms (ius cogens) in International Law. Historical Development, Criteria, Present Status,* Lakimiesliiton Kustannusk, Hensilki, 1988.

HANNUN, H., *Autonomy, Sovereignity and conflicting rights (Procedural aspects of International Law),* University of Pennsylvania. Pr. Philadelphia, 1990.

HANNUN, H., (ed.), *Documents on Autonomy and Minority Rights,* Martinus Nijhoff Publishers, Dordrecht, Boston, London, 1993.

HIGGINS, R., *Problems & Process. International Law and how the use it,* Clarendon Press, Oxford, 1994.

HINOJO ROJAS, M., *A propósito de la jurisdicción consultiva de la Corte Internacional de Justicia,* Cuadernos de Derecho Internacional, n° 8, Servicio de Publicaciones de la Universidad de Córdoba, Córdoba, 1997.

HINZ, M.O., *Le Droit a l'autodetermination du Sahara occidental; le chemin difficile du peuple sahraoui,* ed. Progress Dritte Welt Verlag, Bonn, 1978.

HODGES, T., *Historical Dictionary of Western Sahara,* London, 1982.

HODGES, T., *The roots of a desert war*, Westport, Connecticut, 1983.

JAMES, A., *Peacekeeping in International Politics*, Studies in International Security, Londres, 1990.

JENSEN, E., *Western Sahara: Anatomy of a Stalemate?* 2d ed. Boulder, CO: Lynne Rienner, 2012.

JOUVE, E., (Dir.) *Un Tribunal pour les Peuples*, Serie Points Chauds, Paris, 1983.

LAROSCH, J., *Caught in the Middle: UN Involvement in the Western Sahara Conflict*. Clingendael Diplomacy Papers 11, Netherlands Institute of International Relations "Clingendael", The Hague, 2007.

LAURENT, E., *Hassan II. La memoria de un Rey*, Ed. B, Grupo ZETA, Barcelona, 1994.

LÁZARO MIGUEL, H., *Legislación de Sahara. Años 1965-1973.* Madrid, CSIC, 1974.

LÓPEZ MARTIN, A.G., *El ejercicio continuo y pacífico de funciones de Estado como modo de adquisición del título territorial en la jurisprudencia internacional: el problema de su prueba*, Universidad Complutense de Madrid, Servicio de Publicaciones Madrid, 2009.

LOZANO SERRALTA, M., *La nacionalidad en los territorios dependientes (apuntes sobre la nacionalidad en Derecho Colonial)*, Madrid, 1955.

MARIÑO MENÉNDEZ. M. y FUENTE COBO, I., *El Conflicto del Sahara Occidental*, conflictos Intrenacionales Contemporáneos, n. 4. Ministerio de Defensa, 2005.

MÁRQUEZ CARRASCO, M.C., *Problemas actuales sobre la prohibición del recurso a la fuerza en Derecho Internacional*, Tecnos, Madrid, 1998.

MERCER, J., *Spanish Sahara*, George Allen & Unwin Ltd. (ed.), London, 1976.

MIAJA DE LA MUELA, A., *La emancipación de los pueblos coloniales y el Derecho Internacional*, 2th ed., Tecnos, Madrid, 1968.

MIAJA DE LA MUELA, A., (Homenaje) *Estudios de Derecho Internacional. Homenaje al profesor MIAJA DE LA MUELA*, Madrid, 1979.

MISKÉ, A.B., *Front Polisario: l´âme d´un peuple*, Rupture, Paris, 1978.

MORAND, J., "Autodétermination en Irian occidental et à Bahrein", *A.F.D.I.* (1971): 513-540.

MORILLAS, J., *Sahara Occidental: desarrollo y subdesarrollo*, Madrid, Prensa y Ediciones Iberoamericanas, 1988.

MUSGRAVE, T.D., *Self-Determination and National Minorities*, Clarendon Press, Oxford, 1997.

NALDI, G. J., *The Organization of African Unity: an analysis of its* role, Ed. Mansell, London/New York, 1989.

NEVILLE, B., OLIVIER, M., and VAN TONDER, E., eds., *Conference on Multilateralism and International Law with Western Sahara as a Case Study: Pretoria, South Africa, 4 and 5 December 2008*, VerLoren van Themaat Centre, University of South Africa, Pretoria, 2010.

O'CONNELL, D.P., *The Law of State Succession*, Cambridge University Press, 1956.

OFUATEY-KODJOE W., *The principle of Self-Determination in International Law*, Nellen Publishing Company, Inc., New York, 1977.

OLIVER LOPEZ-GUARCH, P., *Sahara, drama de una descolonización (1960-1987)*, ed. Miguel Font, Palma de Mallorca, 1988.

PALACIOS ROMEO, F. (coord.) *El derecho a la libre determinación del pueblo del Sahara Occidental. Del ius cogens al ius abutendi*, Thompson Reuters Aranzadi, Pamplona, 2013.

PEASLEE, I., *Constitutions of Nations*, 1970.

PEYRÓ LLOPIS, A., Le Sahara occidental face à la compétence universelle en Espagne", *Revue Belge de Droit International* 43 (2010): 61–74.

PEREZ VERA, E., *Naciones Unidas y los principios de la coexistencia pacífica*, Tecnos, Madrid, 1973.

PLAYFAIR, E. (ed.), *International Law and the administration of occuped territoires*, Clarendon Press Oxford, Oxford, 1992.

POMERANCE, M., *Self-Determination in Law and Practice. The New doctrine in the United Nations*, Martinus Nijhoff Publishers, The Hage/Boston/London, 1982.

PORTILLO PASQUAL DEL RIQUELME, J., *Historia de los saharauis y crónica de la agresión colonial en el Sahara Occidental*, Doctoral Thesis not published, Madrid, 1991.

REMIRO BROTONS, A., *Civilizados, bárbaros y salvajes en el nuevo orden internacional*, McGraw-Hill, Madrid, 1996. Also in *Cursos de Derecho Internacional de Vitoria-Gasteiz*, Tecnos, Vitoria-Gasteiz (1994): 17-84.

REMIRO BROTONS, A., *Las Cortes y la Política Exterior Española (1942-1976)*, Valladolid, 1976.

REMIRO BROTONS, A., *Territorio y Constitución de 1978*, Madrid.

RÉZETTE, R., *Le Sahara Occidental et les frontières* marrocaines, Nouvelles Editions Latines, Paris, 1975.

RIGO SUREDA, A., *The evolution of the right of Self-Determination. A study of United Nations Practice,* A.W. Sijthoff, Leiden, 1973.

ROLDAN BARBERO, J., *Democracia y Derecho Internacional*, Civitas, Madrid, 1994.

RONZITTI, N., *La guerre di liberazione nazionale e il Diritto internazionale*, Pisa, 1974.

ROSENNE, S., *The Law and Practice of the International Court*, 2th ed., Martinus Nijhoff Publishers, Dordrecht/Boston/Lancaster, 1985.

RUIPEREZ, J., *Constitución y autodeterminación*, Tecnos, Madrid, 1995.

RUIZ COLOME, M.A., *Guerras civiles y guerras coloniales. El problema de la responsabilidad internacional*, ed. Eurolex, Madrid, 1996.

RUIZ MIGUEL, C., *El Sahara Occidental y España: Historia, Política y Derecho. Análisis crítico de la política exterior española*, Dykinson, 1995.

SAGAY, I., *The legal aspects of the namibian dispute*, University of Ife Press, Ile Ife, Nigeria, 1973.

SALMON J., *La reconnaissance d'Etat. Quatre cas: Mandchoukouo, Katanga, Biafra, Rhodésie du Sud*, Paris, 1971.

SÁNCHEZ RODRÍGUEZ, L.I., "L'*uti possidetis* et les effectivités dans le contentieux territoriaux et frontaliers", *Recueil des Cours*, vol. 263, (1997): 151-373.

SEGURA PALOMARES, J., *El Sahara, razón de una sinrazón*, Ed. Acerbo, Madrid, 1976.

SEVILLANO CASTILLO, R., *Los orígenes de la descolonización africana a través de la prensa española (1956-1962)"*, Madrid, Secretaría de Estado para la Cooperación Internacional y para Iberoamérica, Ministerio de Asuntos Exteriores, 1986.

SMITH, A.D., *Nationalism in the Twentieth Century*, Martin Robertson, Oxford, 1979.

SMITH, J., "From the Desert to the Sea: The Maritime Jurisdiction of Independent Western Sahara", MA diss., Tufts University, 2010.

SOLÀ-MARTÍN, A., *The United Nations Mission for the Referendum in Western Sahara*, Lewiston, Edwin Mellen, New York, 2007.

SOROETA LICERAS, J., *El conflicto del Sahara Occidental, reflejo de las contradicciones y carencias del Derecho internacional*, Servicio de Publicaciones de la UPV/EHU, Bilbao, 2001.

THORNBERRY, P., *International Law and the rights of minorities*, Clarendon Press, Oxford, 1991.

TIEDREBEOGO, P.R., *Le Droit des peuples à l'autodetermination et son aplication au Sahara Occidental*, Institut Universitaire de Hautes Etudes Internationales, Genève, 1988.

TOMUSCHAT, C., (ed.), *Modern Law of Self-Determination*, Martinus Nijhoff Publishers, Dordrecht/Boston/London, 1993.

TOUSSAINT, Ch.E., *The Trusteeship System of the United Nations*, Londres, 1956.

UMOZURIKE O.U., *Self-Determination in International Law*, Harden: Archon Books, London, 1972.

URRUTIA, L., *Sahara, diez años de guerra*, ed. Trazo, Zaragoza, 1983.

VAQUER I FANÉS, J., "The European Union and the Western Sahara Conflict: Managing the Colonial Heritage", in *European Foreign Policy in an Evolving International System: The Road towards Convergence*, edited by Nicola Casarini and Costanza Musu, Palgrave Macmillan, Basingstoke (2007): 144–162.

VEICOPOULOS, N., *Traité des Territoires Dépendants. Tome I: Le système de Tutelle d'après la Charte de San Francisco,* Athens, 1960.

VEICOPOULOS, N., *Traité des Territoires Dépendants. Tome II: L'oeuvre fonctionnelle des Nations Unies relative au régime de Tutelle.* Athens, 1971.

VEICOPOULOS, N., *Traité des Territoires Dépendants. Tome III: Les Territoires non autonomes.* Athens, 1985.

VILLAR, F., *El proceso de autodeterminación del Sáhara Occidental*, Fernando Torres, Valencia, 1982.

VIRALLY, M., (Homage) *Le Droit International au service de la Paix, la Justice et du Développement*, ed. Pédone, Paris, 1990.

WILSON, H.A., *International Law and the Use of Force by National Liberation Mouvements*, Oxford, 1990.

ZOUBIR, Y.H., "Stalemate in Western Sahara: Ending International Legality", *Middle East Policy* 14 (2007): 158-177.

ZUNES, S. and MUNDY, J., *Western Sahara: War, Nationalism, and Conflict Irresolution*, Syracuse University Press, Syracuse, NY, 2010.

Orígenes y Evolución del Problema Palestino (1918-1988), preparado por el Comité para el Ejercicio de los Derechos Inalienables del Pueblo Palestino, y con la orientación de este Comité. Naciones Unidas, New York, 1990.

D) JOURNAL ARTICLES AND WORKS IN COLLECTIVE WORKS

ABELLÁN HONRUBIA, V., "La ampliación del concepto de mantenimiento de la paz y seguridad internacional por el Consejo de Seguridad de las Naciones Unidas: Fundamento jurídico y discrecionalidad política", in *Hacia un nuevo orden internacional y Europeo* (Libro homenaje al profesor M. DÍEZ DE VELASCO), Tecnos, Madrid (1993): 3-18.

ABELLÁN HONRUBIA, V., entrevista en la obra colectiva Cistero Bahima, J.M. y Freixes Sanjuan, M.T., *Sahara, una lección de la Historia*, Imprenta Altagraf, Barcelona (1987): 159-162.

ABI-SAAB, G., "Les guerres de liberation nationale et la Conference diplomatique sur le droit humanitaire", *Annuaire d'Etudes Internationales*, t.8, (1977): 63-78.

AGENZIA GIORNALISTICA OLTREMARE, "La Spagna e il Sahara", *Quaderni di Documentazione*, Roma, vol. X, n° 20, 1 de diciembre de 1971.

AGO, R., "Les Avis consultatifs 'obligatoires' de la Cour Internationale de Justice: problemes d'hier et d'aujourd'hui", in *Mélanges Michel Virally, Le Droit International au service de la Paix, la Justice et du Développement*, ed. Pédone, Paris (1990): 9-24.

AHMED, M.M., "Le programme du Front Polisario" in *Ligue française pour les droits et la libération des peuples. Colloque de Massy* (1-2 avril 1978), Paris (1978): 158-190.

AMANKWAH, H.A. "Self-determination in the Spanish Sahara: a credibility gap in the UN practice and procedure in the decolonisation process", *The Comparative and International Law Journal of Southern Africa*, 14 (1981): 34-55.

ANDRES SAENZ DE SANTA MARIA, M.P., "Problemas actuales de la sucesión de Estados", *Cursos de Derecho Internacional de Vitoria-Gasteiz,* Tecnos, (1993): 157-213.

ANDRÉS SÁENZ DE SANTA MARÍA, M.P., "La libre determinación de los pueblos en la nueva sociedad internacional", *Cursos Euromediterráneos,* Bancaja de Derecho Internacional, ed. Aranzadi, vol. I (1997): 113-203.

ANDREYEV, K., "Western Sahara: difficult search for settlement", *New Times (Moscow),* n. 34 August (1979): 14-15.

ANDREYEV, K., "Western Sahara: the referendum issue", *New Times (Moscow),* n° 50 Dic. (1981): 12-13.

ANNACKER, C., "The Legal Régime of *Erga Omnes* Obligations in International Law", *Austrian Journal of Public and International Law,* 1994, vol. 46, pp. 131-159.

ARKELL, T., "International Involvement in the Western Sahara Conflict", *Rivista di Studi Politici Internazionali,* Anno LVII, n. 2 Aprile-Giugno (1990): 427-432.

ARTS, K. and PINTO LEITE, P. eds. *International Law and the Question of Western Sahara,* Leiden, ed. The Netherlands: International Platform of Jurists for East Timor, 2007.

ASSIDON, E., "Inventaire et exploitation des richesses économiques", en la obra colectiva *Sahara Occidental, un peuple et ses droits,* Ligue Française pour les droits et la libération des peuples. Colloque de Massy (1 et 2 avril 1978), ed. L'Harmattan, Paris, (1978): 33-67.

BACOT, G., "Réflexions sur les clauses qui rendent obligatoires les avis consultatifs de la C.P.J.I. et de la C.I.J.", *R.G.D.I.P.* (1980): 1027-1067.

BADÍA MARTÍ, A., "La participación de las Naciones Unidas en los procesos electorales: la Misión de Observación de las Naciones Unidas en Sudáfrica", *Cursos de Derecho Internacional de Vitoria-Gasteiz,* Tecnos (1994): 195-252.

BADÍA MARTÍ, A. y SAURA ESTAPÀ, J., *Informe sobre las elecciones palestinas de 20 de enero de 1996 y selección de textos sobre el proceso de paz,* ed. Asociación para las Naciones Unidas en España, Barcelona, 1996.

BADÍA MARTÍ, A. M., "La cuestión del Sahara Occidental y la explotación de sus recursos naturales", in *El Derecho Internacional y Comunitario ante los retos de nuestro tiempo: Homenaje a la profesora Victoria Abellán Honrubia,* Vol. 1, (ed. Badia Martí, Antoni Pigrau i Solé, and Andreu Olesti Rayo), Madrid, Marcial Pons (2009): 29-53.

BADÍA MARTÍ, A. M., "La cuestión del Sahara Occidental a la luz de la dimensión económica del principio de Autodeterminación de los pueblos colonials", in PALACIOS ROMEO, F. (coord.) *El derecho a la libre determinación del pueblo del Sahara Occidental. Del ius cogens al ius abutendi*, Thompson Reuters Aranzadi, Pamplona (2013): 51-78.

BARBIER, M., "L´avis consultatif de la Cour de la Haye sur le Sahara Occidental", *Revue Juridique et Politique Independence et Cooperation*, 30 (1976): 67-103.

BARBIER, M., "Le Sahara Occidental et le Droit International", en *Sahara Occidental: un peuple et ses droits*. Colloque de Massy (1-2 avril 1978), Ed. l'Harmattan, Paris (1978): 68-123.

BARBIER, M., "Le problème du Sahara Occidental et la crise de l´OUA", *Mois en Afrique*, 18, n° 207/208, (1983): 31-51.

BARBIER, M., "Essai d'interpretation du conflit saharien", in *Enjeux Sahariens* (Table ronde du CRESM, nov. 1981), Ed. Centre National de la Recherche Scientifique, Paris (1984): 212-229.

BARBIER, M., "La formation de la RASD", *Actes du colloque International de juristes tenu à l'Assemblée Nationale. Paris, le 20 et 21 octobre 1984*, Paris, 1984.

BARBIER, M., "Les pays d´Afrique noire et le problème du Sahara Occidental", *Afrique Contemporaine*, 24, 135 (1985): 10-37.

BARCIA TRELLES, C., "Polémica sobre el colonialismo", en *P.I.*, Centro de Estudios Constitucionales, núm. 50-51, julio-agosto/setiembre-octubre (1960): 47-60.

BARCIA TRELLES, C., "La O.N.U., la descolonización y el neocolonialismo", *R.P.I.*, 136 (1974): 17-37.

BARSOTTI, R. "Il tema di amministrazione diretta dei territori non autonomi da parte dell´ONU: il caso della Namibia", *Comunicazione e Studii* (1980): 53-135.

BEDJAOUI, M., "Commentaire à l'article 73", in *La Charte des Nations Unies*, (Dir. COT, J-P. et PELLET, A.), Ed. Economica / Bruylant, Paris / Bruxelles (1985): 1061-1076.

BEDJAOUI, M., "L´admission d´un nouveau membre à l´Organisation de l´Unité Africaine", in *Le Droit des peuples à disposer d´eux-mêmes.Mèthodes d´analyse du Droit International (Mélanges offerts à Charles Chaumont)*, Paris (1984): 35-58.

BEDJAOUI, M., "*Terra nullius, 'droits' historiques et autodétermination*", Exposés oraux prononcés devant la C.I.J. en l´affaire du Sahara Occidental, le 14 mai et les 14,15,16 et 29 juillet 1975. La Haye, 1975.

BELKHERROUBI, "Essai sur une théorie juridique des mouvements de libération nationale, *Revue Egyptienne de Droit International* (1972): 20 et seq.

BENCHIKH, M., "La décolonisation du Sahara occidental à travers les résolutions des Organisations internationales", in *Enjeux Sahariens* (Table ronde du CRESM, nov. 1981), Ed. Centre National de la Recherche Scientifique, Paris (1984): 149-159.

BENNET, T.W., "A Linguistic Perspective of the Definition of Aggression", *G.Y.B.I.L.* (1988): 48-69.

BENNOUNA, M., *Hearing before the Subcommittees on International Organizations and on Africa of the Committee on international elations House of Representatives*, 12 de octubre de 1977, U.S. Government printing Office, Washington (1977).

BENNOUNA, M., "L´admission d´un nouveau membre à l¨Organisation de l´Unité Africaine", *A.F.D.I. l*, (1980): 193-198.

BERNADAS, J.M., "Lels beidani: el Sahara occidental abans del Frente Polisario", *L'Avenc*, n° 153 (1991): 22-27.

BERAT, L., "The evolution of self-determination in International Law: South Africa, Namibia, and the case of Walvis Bay", *E.I.L.R.*, vol. 4, núm. 2 (1990): 251-290.

BERRADA GOUZI, N., GODEAU, R., ZNIBER K., in "Que font les Marocains au Sahara?", *Jeune Afrique*, n° 34, supplément n° 1722 (1994): 38-81.

BERRADA GOUZI, N., GODEAU R., "Laayoun, plus fort que le désert", in "Que font les Marocains au Sahara?", *Jeune Afrique*, n° 34, supplément° 1722 (1994): 72-73.

BERTRAM, E., "Reinventing governments: the promise and perils of United Nations peace building", *Journal of Conflict Resolution*, n. 39 (1995): 387-418.

BING, A., "Sahrawi Republic: ten years of desert war; last month the people of Western Sahara celebrated the tenth anniversary of their proclamation of the Sahrawi Arab Democratic Republic", *Africa*, n° 176, abril (1986): 38-40.

BLAY, K.N., "Changing African perspectives on the right of self-determination in the wake on the Banjul Charter on Human and People's rights", *Journal of African Law*, n. 29 (1985): 147-159.

BLAY, K.N., "Self-Determination versus territorial integrity in Decolonization revisited", *Indian Journal of International Law*, vol. 25, n. 3-4 (1985): 386-410.

BLAYDES, L.E. Jr., "International Law. International Court of Justice does not find ´legal ties´ of such a nature to affect self-determination in the decolonization process of Western Sahara. Advisory opinion on Western Sahara, (1975) I.C.J., *T.I.L.J.*, 11, (1976): 354-368.

BLUMANN, C., "Establissement et rupture des relations diplomatiques", in *Aspects récents du droit des relations diplomatiques*, Pedone, Paris, 1989.

BOLLECKER, B., "L'Avis du 21 juin 1971 dans l'affaire de la Namibie (Sud-Ouest Africain)", *A.F.D.I.*, vol. XVII (1971): 281-333.

BONNEFOUS, M., *Le Maghreb: repères et rappels*, Centre de Hautes Études sur l'Afrique et l'Asie Modernes, Paris (1990): 115-112.

BONTEMS, C., "The government of the Saharawi Arab Democratic Republic", *Third World Quarterly*, Vol. 9, n° 1, January (1987): 168-186.

BOOKMILLER, R.J., "The Western Sahara: future prospects", *American-Arab affairs*, n.37, Summer (1991): 64-76.

BOSCH, A., "La Katanga del Magrib o el proces de descolonitzacio del Sahara espanyol", *L'Avenc*, n° 153 (1991): 32-37

BRAVO DE LAGUNA CABRERA, J., "La pesca en el banco sahariano", Instituto Español de Oceanografía, *El Campo*, n° 99 (1985): 69-74.

BRILMAYER, L., "Secession and Self-Determination: A Territorial Interpretation, *Yale Journal of International Law*, vol. 16, 1 (1991): 177-202.

BUCHANAN, A., "Self-Determination and the Right to Secede", *Journal of International Affaires*, vol. 45, (1992): 347-365.

BUJARI, A., "El conflicto del Sahara Occidental desde la perspectiva saharaui", in *Procesos de cambio y retos pendientes: Este de Europa, China y Sahara Occidental*, Centro Pignatelli (ed.), Zaragoza (1991): 189-195.

BUJARI, A., "The Western Sahara conflict", *Middle East International*, n° 422, april 3 (1992): 14 et seq.

BUJARI, A., "Baker y el Sahara Occidental. Una nueva dinámica", *El País*, 26 setiembre 1997.

BUKARAMBE, B., "Nigeria and the Western Sahara conflict", *Nigerian Forum*, 2 (1982): 771-779.

BYMAN, A., "The march on the Spanish Sahara: A test of International Law", *Denver Journal of International Law and Policy*, 6 (1976): 95-121.

CALLIES DE SALIES, B., "La peur des urnes au Sahara Occidental", *Defense Nationale*, Avril (1992): 8-16.

CALOGEROPOULOS-STRATIS, S., "Le droit des peuples à disposer d'eux-mêmes. Théorie et Pratique", *Hellenic Review of International Relations*, vol. 2, n. II (1981-1982): 461-484.

CANO HERNANDEZ, G., MARRERO URBIN, D., "Aproximación a una evolución de la lucha anticolonial en el Sahara Occidental (1955-1989)", *Revista de Geografía Canaria*, vol. 3 (1988/1990): 9-23.

CAPOTORTI, F., "Cours Général de Droit International Public", *Recueil des Cours*, IV, t. 248 (1994): 9-344.

CARDONA LLORENS, J., "La responsabilidad internacional por violación grave de obligaciones esenciales para la salvaguarda de intereses fundamentales de la Comunidad Internacional (el 'crimen internacional')", *A.D.I.*, vol. VIII (1985): 265-336.

CARDONA LLORENS, J., "Nuevo Orden Mundial y Mantenimiento de la Paz y Seguridades Internacionales", *Cursos de Derecho Internacional de Vitoria-Gasteiz*, Tecnos, (1993): 215-264.

CARRILLO SALCEDO, J. A., "Libre determinación de los pueblos e integridad territorial de los Estados en el dictamen del T.I.J. sobre el Sáhara Occidental", *R.E.D.I.*, vol.XXIX, n°1 (1976): 33-49.

CARRILLO SALCEDO, J.A., "La cuestión de Namibia ante el Tribunal Internacional de Justicia", en *Homenaje a F. DE CASTRO*, vol. I, Madrid (1976): 368-396.

CARRILLO SALCEDO, J.A., "La posición de España respecto de la cuestión del Sahara Occidental: de la Declaración de Principios de Madrid al Comunicado Conjunto hispano-argelino", *P.I.*, n° 163, mayo-junio (1979): 117-126.

CARRILLO SALCEDO, J.A., prólogo a la obra de HINOJO ROJAS, M., *A propósito de la jurisdicción consultiva de la Corte Internacional de Justicia*, Cuadernos de Derecho Internacional, n° 8, Córdoba, 1997.

CARRO MARTÍNEZ, A., "La descolonización del Sáhara", *R.P.I.*, 144, Marzo-Abril (1976): 11-38.

CASLA, K., GARAY, J., VILCHES, M., BERISTAIN, C.M., SOROETA, J, and ANDA, J.M., *La situación de los derechos humanos en los territorios del Sahara Occidental*, Servicio Central de Publicaciones del Gobierno Vasco, Vitoria-Gasteiz 2008.

CENTRE D'ÉTUDES INTERNATIONALS, *Le différend saharien devant l'Organisation des Nations Unies*. Hommes et Sociétés Series. Paris: Karthala, 2011.

CHAPAUX, V., ed. *Western Sahara: Which Legal Remedies for Peoples under Foreign Domination?*, Bruylant, Brussels, 2010.

CASSESE, A., "La Carta dell'Organizzazione dell'Unità Africana", *Rivista* (1964): 430-441.

CASSESE, A., "*Commentaire à l'article 1.2*", in *La Charte des Nations Unies*, (Dir. by COT, J-P. et PELLET, A., Ed. Economica/Bruylant, Paris/Bruxelles (1985): 39-54.

CASSESE, A., "Le Droit international et la question de l'assistance aux mouvements de libération nationale", *R.B.D.I.*, vol. XIX, 2 (1986): 308-326.

CASSESE, A., "Powers and Duties of an occupant in relation to land and natural ressources", in *International Law and the administration of occuped territoires*, PLAYFAIR, E. (ed.), Clarendon Press Oxford, Oxford (1992): 419-442.

CASTEL, A., "La batalla politica I militar pel referendum", *L'Avenc*, n. 153 (1991): 42-44.

CESSOU, S., PRAZ, H., "Sahara occidental: l'interminable conflit", *Jeune Afrique Economique,* n° 206, 6 noviembre (1995): 106-111.

CHAABANE, S., "Réflexion sur la Charte Africaine des droits de l´homme et des peuples", *Etudes Internationales* (Tunisia), n. 40 (1991): 97-98.

CHAPPEZ, J., "L´avis consultatif de la C.I.J. du 16/10/1975 dans l´affaire du Sahara Occidental", *R.G.D.I.P.*, n. 4 (1976): 1132-1187.

CHARPENTIER, J., "*Commentaire à l'article 2.3*", in *La Charte des Nations Unies*, (Dir. COT, J-P. et PELLET, A.), Ed. Economica / Bruylant, Paris / Bruxelles (1985): 103-112.

CHARPENTIER, J., "Autodétermination et décolonisation", in *Mélanges Ch. CHAUMONT*, Paris, Pedone (1984): 117-134.

CHARPENTIER, J., "Le droit des peuples à disposer d'eux-mêmes et le droit international positif", *Révue Québécoise de Droit International* (1985): 196-213.

CHATTON, P.F., "La Namibie: un exercice practique de décolonisation pour l'ONU", *Trimestre du Monde*, núm. 7 (1989): 47-62.

CHINKIN, C., "Laws of Occupation", in *Conference on Multilateralism and International Law with Western Sahara as a Case Study: Pretoria, South Africa, 4 and 5 December 2008*. Edited by Neville Botha, Michèle Olivier, and Delarey van Tonder, Pretoria (2010): 196–221.

CHOPRA, J., Testimony before the Committee on Foreign Relations of the United States Senate Subcommittee on African Affairs, Hearing on "*UN Peacekeeping in Africa: The Western Sahara and Somalia*", 1 de Octubre de 1992.

CHOPRA, J., "Statement regarding the issue of the Western Sahara before the Fourth Committee of the United Nations General Assembly, 19 october 1992", *Internet: http://heiwww.unige.ch/arso/Chopra-92.htm*.

CHOPRA, J., *An agenda for Western Sahara*, Intervención ante la *International Asociation of Lawyers for Western Sahara*. Barcelona, Noviembre de 1996. *Internet: http://www.arso.org//Chopra2-96.htm*.

CHOWDHURI, R., "The status and norms of self-determination in contemporary international law", *N.I.L.R.* (1977): 72-84.

COLA ALBERICH, J., "España y el Sahara Occidental: Antecedentes de una descolonización", *R.P.I.*, n° 154 Nov.-Dic. (1977): 9-52.

COLA ALBERICH, J., "Las Islas Canarias y los Acuerdos de la OUA", *R.P.I.*, n° 156, Marzo/Abril (1978): 45-66.

COLA ALBERICH, J., "Diario de acontecimientos referentes a España", *R.P.I.*, n° 156, marzo-abril (1978): 280 et seq.

COLIN, J.P. "Réflexions sur l'avenir du Sahara Occidental", *Revue Française d'études Politiques Africaines*, vol. 13, n° 152-153 (1978): 80-92.

CORDERO TORRES, J.M., "Marruecos y el Sahara Español", *R.P.I.*, n° 122, julio/agosto (1972): 233-234.

CORELL, H., "The Legality of Exploring and Exploiting Natural Resources in Western Sahara", in *Conference on Multilateralism and International Law with Western Sahara as a Case Study: Pretoria, South Africa, 4 and 5 December 2008, ed.* by Neville Botha, Michèle Olivier, and Delarey van Tonder, Pretoria: VerLoren van Themaat Centre, University of South Africa (2010): 231-247.

DAILLIER, P., "Commentaire à l'article 96", in *La Charte des Nations Unies*, (Dir. COT, J-P. et PELLET, A.), Ed. Economica / Bruylant, Paris / Bruxelles (1985): 1283-1294.

DAMIS, J., "The Western Sahara conflict: myths and realities", *Middle East Journal*, n° 37 (1983): 167-179.

DAMIS, J., "Morocco and the Western Sahara", *Current History*, 89 (546), Apr. (1990): 165-168 and 184-186.

DAMIS, J., "The UN settlement plan for the Western Sahara: problems and prospects", *Middle East Policy*, 1, n. 2 (1992): 36-46.

DAOUDI, R., "*Commentaire à l'article 35*", in *La Charte des Nations Unies*, (Dir. COT, J-P. et PELLET, A.), Ed. Economica / Bruylant, Paris / Bruxelles (1985): 587-601.

DAVANTURE, S., "Les limites de l'application du droit sur les ressources naturelles: Le cas des territoires palestiniens et du Sahara Occidental", PhD diss., Université du Québec à Montréal (2006).

DAVID, E., "L'exercice de la compétence universelle en Belgique dans le cas du Sahara Occidental", *Revue Belge de Droit International* 43 (2010): 36–42.

DE YTURRIAGA BARBERAN, J.A., "Tribunal Internacional de Justicia. Asunto del Camerún Septentrional (Camerún c. Reino Unido). Sentencia de 2 de diciembre de 1963", *R.E.D.I.*, Vol. XVII, núm. 3, julio-septiembre (1964).

DEL PINO, D., "España y el Sahara", *Leviatán*, n° 21 (1985): 45-55.

DELANEY, T.A. "Article 2.7 of the UN Charter: hindrance to the self-determination of Western Sahara and Eritrea?", *E.I.L.R.*, vol. 4, 2 (1990): 413-454.

DESSENS, P., "Le litige du Sahara Occidental", *Maghreb*, vol. 71 (1976): 29-46.

DESSENS, A., "Le problème du Sahara Occidental", *Maghreb* (1979): 73-86.

DEZCALLAR MAZARREDO, R., "España y el Sahara Occidental", *Revista Española de Defensa*, abril, (1988): 36 and seq.

DIEGO AGUIRRE, J.R., "Los orígenes del Frente POLISARIO. Incidentes en El Aaiún en Junio de 1970", *Historia 16*, n° 137 (1987): 73-82.

DIEGO AGUIRRE, J.R., "Ifni, la ultima guerra colonial española. Historia del Desconocido conflicto de 1957-58 en el Africa Occidental", *Historia 16*, n° 15 (167) (1990): 12-37.

DIEGO AGUIRRE, J. R., "La guerra del Sahara", *Historia 16*, n° 16 (188) (1991): 12-32.

DIEGO AGUIRRE, J.R., "La verdad sobre la entrega del Sahara", *Historia 16*, n° 15 (177) (1991): 12-28.

DIEGO AGUIRRE, J.R., "El conflicto del Sahara Occidental desde una perspectiva histórica", en la obra colectiva *Procesos de cambio y retos pendientes: Este de Europa, China y Sahara Occidental*, Centro Pignatelli (ed.), Zaragoza (1991): 149-178.

DÍEZ-HOCHLEITNER, J., "Les relations hispano-britanniques au sujet de Gibraltar: etat actuel", *A.F.D.I.*, vol. XXXV (1989): 167-187.

DREYER, R., "The United Nations and Namibia: an overview (1946-1990)", *International Geneva Yearbook*, vol. V (1991): 26-38.

DUGARD, J., "The revocation of the mandate for South-West Africa", *A.J.I.L.*, vol. LXII (1968): 78-97.

DUGARD, J., "Walvis Bay and International Law", *The South African Law Journal*, vol. 108, n.1 (1991): 82-92.

DUNBAR, Ch., "Saharan Stasis: Status and Future Prospects of the Western Sahara Conflict", *Middle East Journal* 54 (2000): 522–545.

DUPUY, R.J., "L'Avis Consultatif de la Cour Internationale de Justice", in *Hassan II presénte la Marche Verte* (dir. by Bardonnet, Basri, Dupuy, J.R., Laroui and vVdel, Paris (1990): 117-127.

DURCH, W.J., "Building on sand: UN peacekeeping in the Western Sahara", *International Security*, n° 17, Spring (1993): 151-171.

DUTHEIL DE LA ROCHERE, J., "Les procédures de règlement des différends frontaliers", Societé Française pour la Droit International, Colloque de Poitiers, *La Frontière*, Ed. Pedone, Paris (1980): 112-150.

ECHEVERRIA JESUS, C., "La profundización de relaciones entre España y los países del Magreb", *Estudios Africanos*, 4 (7) (1989): 9-20.

ELIAS, T.O., "The role of the ICJ in Africa", *African Journal of International and Comparative Law*, vol. 1, n° 1, Mar. (1989): 1-12.

EMERSON, R., "Self-determination", *A.J.I.L.* (1971): 459-475.

ERASMUS, G., "Namibian independence and the release of political prisoners", *S.A.Y.I.L.*, 1988-1989, vol. 14, 1988-1989, pp. 137-143.

ESPADA RAMOS, M.L., "La legalidad de las luchas de liberación nacional", *Anuario de Estudios Sociales y Jurídicos*, t. V (1976): 119-175.

ETIENNE, J., "L'accord de pêche CE-Maroc: Quels remèdes juridictionnels européens à quelle illicéité internationale?", *Revue Belge de Droit International* 43 (2010): 77–107.

FAWCETT, "The rôle of the United Nations in the Protection of Human Rights: Is it Misconceived?", in *International Protection of Human Rights*, Eide and Schou, eds., Uppsala, 1968.

FERENCZ, B.B., "Defining Aggression: Where it stands and wher it's going", *A.J.I.L.* (1972): 491-508.

FERNAUD, P., "La dimensión africana de Canarias", *Cuenta y Razón*, setiembre, n° 24 (1986): 81-91.

FITZGERALD, B.F., "*Horta v. Commonwealth*: the validity of the Timor Gap Treaty and its domestic implementation", *I. & C. L. Q.*, Vol. 44, July (1995): 643-649.

FLORY, M., "La notion du territoire Arabe et son application au problème du Sahara", *A.F.D.I.*, 3, (1957): 73-91.

FLORY, M., "L´Avis de la Cour Internationale de Justice sur le Sahara Occidental", *A.F.D.I.*, XXI (1975): 253-277.

FOUGEROUSE, M., "Que font les Marocains au Sahara?", *Jeune Afrique*, n° 34, supplement n° 1722, January (1994): 352-353

FRANCISCI, "La controversia per il Sahara Occidentale (1956-1975)", *Politica Internazionale,* 9 (1978): 61 et seq.

FRANCK, T.M., "The Stealing of the Sahara", *A.J.I.L.*, October, vol. 70, n. 4 (1976): 694-721.

FRANCK, T.M., *Hearing before the Subcommittees on International Organizations and on Africa of the Committee on international elations House of Representatives,* 12 de octubre de 1977, U.S. Government printing Office, Washington (1977): 18-21.

FRANCK, T.M., "The emerging right to democratic governance", *A.J.I.L.*, vol. 86-1 (1992): 46-91.

GARCIA ABAD, A., "El Sahara Español. Perspectivas económicas: los fosfatos", *Memoria de la Escuela Diplomática*, Madrid, 1971.

GARCIA FIGUERAS, T., *"La Acción Africana de España en torno al 98 (1860-1912)"*, Madrid, CSIC, vol. II (1966): 19-28.

GARCÍA VARELA, R., "Reconocimiento de la nacionalidad española a un nativo de la antigua colonia del Sahara Español", *La Ley*, n° 4683 (1998): 15-16.

GILBERT, K., "Aboriginal sovereign position: summary and definitions", Extract from Gilbert, K., Aboriginal Sovereignty: Justice, the Law and Land (1987), *Social Alternatives*, vol.13, no.1, April (1994): 13-15.

GODEAU, R., "Eldorado sous perfusion", in "Que font les Marocains au Sahara?", *Jeune Afrique*, n° 34, suplement n° 1722, Janvier (1994): 38-41.

GOFFINET, T., "Development and fisheries management: the case of Northwest Africa", *Ocean and Coastal Management*, vol. 17, 2 (1992): 105-136.

GOLDSTEIN, E., "Human Rights in Western Sahara and in the Tindouf Refugee Camps: A Commentary", *Revue Belge de Droit International* 43 (2010): 30–35.

GONZÁLEZ, L.M., "La expulsión del Frente POLISARIO", *Gaceta Sindical*, nº 38 (1985): 44-45.

GONZÁLEZ CAMPOS, J., "Los acuerdos nulos de Madrid", *El País*, 18 de setiembre de 1977.

GONZÁLEZ CAMPOS, J. *El Sahara, un problema pendiente*, Instituto de Estudios Políticos para América Latina y Africa (IEPALA), Madrid, Octubre (1978): 67-69, and *Posible*, nº 142, 29-5 setiembre-octubre (1977).

GONZÁLEZ CAMPOS, J.D., intervención en Jornadas sobre el 4º aniversario de los acuerdos tripartitos de Madrid. ASOCIACION DE AMIGOS DEL SAHARA, *Madrid, 14 de Noviembre de 1975: la traición*, Ed. Sedersa, Madrid, 1980.

GONZÁLEZ MATA, L., "Los fosfatos del Sahara: dos claves para un misterio", *Transición*, vol. 12, 8 (1979): 29-34.

GORDON, I. C., "Australians in Western Sahara", *Australian Defence Force Journal*, n. 104, Jan/Feb (1994): 83-85.

GOULDING, W., "The evolution of United Nations peacekeeping, *International Affairs*, nº 69 (3) (1993): 451-464.

GOY, R., "L'indepéndance de la Namibie", *A.F.D.I.*, vol. XXXVII (1991): 387-405.

GOY, R., "L'indépendance de l'Erythrée", *A.F.D.I..*, vol. XXXIX (1993): 337-354.

GOZALVEZ PEREZ, V., "Descolonización y migraciones desde el África española (1956-1975)", *Investigaciones geográficas*, n. 12 (1994): 45-84.

GRAHL-MADSEN, A., "Decolonization: The Modern Version of a 'Just War'", *G.Y.I.L.*, vol. 22 (1979): 255-273.

GRESH, A., "Sahara occidental: la decolonisation a l'ordre du jour", *Cahier du Communisme*, nº 55 (10) (1979): 90-97.

GRETTON, J., "Western Sahara and the international community", *African Contemporary Record*, 12, (1979/1980): A 103- A 110.

GRETTON, J., "The Western Sahara in the international arena [growth of Third World support for Western Saharan liberation movement (Polisario)]", *World Today (London)*, n. 36 (1980): 343-350.

GRETTON, J., "The war Morocco cannot win: Morocco's fight to retain the phosphate rich former Spanish Sahara is dragging the country into bankruptcy", *Geographical Magazine,* vol. 52, n° 10, July (1980): 665-673.

GRIMAUD, N., "Sahara Occidental: un issue possible?", *Monde Arabe: Maghreb-Machrek,* n. 121, Juillet-Août-Septembre (1988): 89-113.

GROS ESPIELL, H., "En torno a la libre determinación de los pueblos", *A.D.I.,* vol.III (1976): 49-74.

GROS ESPIELL, H., "El caso de las Islas Canarias y el derecho a la libre determinación de los pueblos", *R.E.D.I.,* Vol.XXXI, núms. 1-3 (1978-1979): 13-24.

GROS ESPIELL, H., in *Liberté des elections et observation internationale des elections,* ed. Bruylant, Bruxelles (1994).

GROSS, L., "The International Court of Justice: Consideration of Requirements for Enhancing its Role in the International Legal Order", *A.J.I.L.* (1971): 253-326.

GUNTHER, M.M., "Self-determination or territorial integrity", *World Affaires,* vol. 141 (1979): 203-216.

HARRELL-BOND, B., "The struggle for the Western Sahara: Prelude" (part I), "Contemporary politics" (parte II), "The Sahrawi people" (part III), *American Universities Field Staff* (1981).

HAUGEN, H. M., "The Right to Self-Determination and Natural Resources: The Case of Western Sahara", *Law, Environment and Development Journal,* 3 (2007): 70–81.

HERACLIDES, A., "Secession, Self-Determination and Nonintervention: In quest of a Normative Symbiosis", *Journal of International Affairs,* vol. 45 (1992): 399-420.

HERMAN, L.L., "The legal Status of Namibia and of the United Nations Council for Namibia", *C.Y.I.L.* (1975): 306-322.

HERMAN, L.L., "Western Sahara Advisory Opinion. An analysis of the World Court judgement in the Western Sahara Case", *Saskatchewan Law Revue,* vol. 41 (1976): 133-142.

HERRERO DE MIÑON, M., "La configuración del territorio nacional en la doctrina reciente del Consejo de Estado español", *Estudios de Derecho Administrativo (Libro jubilar del Consejo de Estado),* Madrid (1972): 357-427.

HODGES, T., "Western Sahara: the balance shifts to Polisario [interview with Hakim Ibrahim; on the military situation in Spanish Sahara, where the Polisario front guerrillas are fighting on two fronts, with Morocco and with Mauritania]", *New African Development (London)*, n° 11 (1977): 1060-1063.

HODGES, T., "Les developpements du conflit saharien", *Marches Tropicaux et Mediterranéens*, n° 35 (1979): 3438-3439.

HODGES, T., "La question du Sahara occidental: guerre et diplomatie", *Marches Tropicaux et Mediterranéens*, n° 36, 1980, pp. 356-357.

HODGES, T., "Western Sahara: U.S. arms and the desert war [implications of the sale of United States arms to Morocco]", *Africa Report,* n° 25 (1980): 42-47.

HODGES, T., "Western Sahara: the endless war [problems arising from Morocco's attempt to crush the region's guerrilla movement; includes interviews with Moroccan, guerrilla and United States officials]", *Africa Report*, n° 27 (1982): 4-23.

HODGES, T., "The origins of Saharawi nationalism", *Third World Quarterly*; n° 5 (1983): 28-57.

HODGES, T., "Western Sahara: an obstacle to Maghribi unity", *Africa Contemporary Record*, vol. 16 (1983/84): A 90-A 107.

HODGES, T., "The Western Sahara file [developments in the conflict between Morocco and the Polisario Front over the region]", *Third World Quarterly*, n° 6, January (1984): 74-116.

HODGES, T., "The origin of the Saharawi nationalism", in *War and refugees. The Western Sahara Conflict*, LAWLESS, R. & MONAHAN, L. (ed.) London/New York (1987): 31-64.

HOOTS, Ch., "Western Sahara: old conflict, new rules", *Middle East* (London), August (1991): 26-28.

HÖRLER, E., "Forgotten war in the West Sahara", *Swiss Review of World Affairs*, April 1991 pp. 15-19.

HOTTINGER, A., "La lutte pour le Sahara Occidental", *Politique Étrangère*, 45 (1), Mars (1980): 167-180.

IGLESIAS BUIGUEZ, J.L., "La prohibición general del uso de la fuerza y las resoluciones descolonizadoras de la Asamblea General de las Naciones Unidas", *R.E.D.I.*, vol. XXIX, núm. 1-2 (1971): 173-206.

ISOART, P., "Réflexions sur les liens juridiques unissant le Royaume du Maroc et le Sahara Occidental", *Revue Juridique Politique et Economique du Maroc* (1978): 11-47.

ISOART, P., "La Marche Verte, un procédé nouveau de décolonisation", in *Hassan II presénte la Marche Verte*, dirigida por BARDONNET, BASRI, DUPUY, J.R., LAROUI y VEDEL, Paris (1990): 129-154.

JANIS, M.W., "The International Court of Justice: Advisory opinion on The Western Sahara", *H.I.L.J.*, 17, summer (1976): 609-621.

JOFFE, G., "The conflict in the Western Sahara", in the collection *Conflict in Africa*, ed. OLIVER FURLEY, Tauris Publishers, London/New York (1995).

JOUANNET, E., "Le principe de l'or monétaire à propos de l'arret de la Cour du 30 juin 1995 dans l'affaire du Timor Oriental", *R.G.D.I.P.* (1996-3): 673-714.

JUSTE RUIZ, J., "Las obligaciones *erga omnes* en Derecho Internacional Público", in *Estudios de Derecho Internacional. Homenaje al profesor MIAJA DE LA MUELA*, tomo I (1979): 219-234.

KAMTO, M., "L'accession de la Namibie à l'indépendance", *R.G.D.I.P.*, t. 94, 3 (1990): 578-634.

KARDOUN, A., "Charte Africaine des droits de l´homme et des peuples", *Etudes Internationales* (Tunisia), 40 (1991): 106-112.

KEBA, M., "Les droits de l'homme et des peuples. Introduction", en BEDJAOUI, M., (Redactor Gral.) *Droit international. Bilan et perspectives*, t. II (1991): 1109-1127.

KOHEN, M.G., "L'*Uti Possidetis* revisité: L'ârret du 11 septembre 1992 dans l'affaire El Salvador/Honduras", en *R.G.D.I.P.*, t. 97 (1993-94): 939-973.

KOURY, S., "Legal Strategies at the United Nations: A Comparative Look at Namibia, Western Sahara and Palestine", In *International Law and the Israeli-Palestinian Conflict: A Rights-Based Approach to Middle East Peace* (Edited by S.M. Akram, M. Dumper, M. Lynk and Scobbie, I.), Routledge, New York, (2011): 147–183.

KRONER, D.H., "The maroccanization of the Western Sahara", *Swiss Review of World Affaires*, 34 (9), Decembre (1984): 10-12.

KWAKWA, E., "The Namibian conflict: a discussion of the ius ad bellum and the ius in bello", *New York Journal of International & Comparative Law*, vol. 9, núm. 2/3 (1988): 195-236.

LAGHMANI, S., "L´OUA: La crise consécutive à l´admission de la RASD", *Etudes Internationales* (Tunisia), VII/122-XXIX/100 (1982).

LAING, E.A., "The Norm of Self-Determination, 1941-1991", *California Western International Law Journal*, vol. 22, n. 2 (1992): 209-308.

LANDIS, E.S., "Namibia: a transatlantic view", *South African Journal of Human Rights*, vol. 3, núm. 3 (1987): 347-364.

LAPIDOTH, R. y CALVO-GOLLER, N.K., "Les éléments constitutifs de l'Etat et la déclaration du Conseil National Palestinien du 15 novembre 1988", *R.G.D.I.P.* (1992): 777-809.

LAZARUS, "Le statut des mouvements de libération nationale à l'Organisation des Nations Unies", *A.F.D.I.* (1974): 173-214.

LE BORGNE, C., "Sahara Occidental: miracle ou mirage?", *L´Afrique eta l´Asie modernes*, n°159, Hiver (1988-1989): 23-35.

LEVY, G.J., "Advisory opinion on the Western Sahara", *Brooklyn Journal of International Law*, vol. 2 (1976): 289-307.

LEWIS, W.H., "Morocco and the Western Sahara", *Current History*, n° 84, May (1985): 213-216.

LIPPERT, A., "The Western Sahara: an emerging State in Northwest Africa?", in *Hearing before the Subcommittees on International Organizations and on Africa of the Committee on International Relations House of Representatives*, October 12, 1977, U.S. Government printing Office, Washington (1977): 47-61.

LIPPERT, A., "The human costs of War in Western Sahara", *Africa Today*, n° 34, Third Quarter (1987): 47-59.

LOPEZ ARGADOS, A., "Breu judici sobre la historia del Sahara", *L'Avenc*, n° 153 (1991): 28-31.

LOPEZ, B., "El Sahara, España y Marruecos. Historia de un desencuentro", *Política Exterior*, vol. XIII, 70, julio/agosto (1999): 21-26.

LÓPEZ DE LA TORRE, S., "Referéndum en el Sahara Occidental", *Cuenta y Razón*, n° 56-57 (1991): 118-120.

LÓPEZ GARCIA, B., "Elecciones parciales y crisis política en Marruecos. (antecedentes Politicos de los acontecimientos de Casablanca de 20 de junio de 1981)", *Revista de Estudios Políticos*, n° 22 (1981): 7-8.

LÓPEZ GARCIA, B., "Los comunistas marroquíes ante la cuestión del Sahara. Entrevista con Ali Yata, Secretario General del P.P.S. (P.C.N.)", *Materiales*, n° 8 (1978): 147-160.

LÓPEZ BARGADOS, A., "Breu judici sobre la historia del Sahara", *L'Avenc*, n° 153 (1991): 28-31.

LUCHINNI, L., "La Namibie, une construction des Nationes Unies", *A.F.D.I.*, vol. XVI (1970): 355-374.

LYNN, P.D., "Conflict in the Maghreb: The Western Sahara", *Conflict studies. The Institute for the study of conflict.*, n° 127, February (1981): 3-25.

MADDY-WEITZMAN, B., "Conflict and conflict management in the Western Sahara: is the endgame near?", *Middle East Journal*, n° 45, Autumn (1991): 594-607.

MARCELLI, F., "La condizione giuridica internazionale del Fronte Polisario", *Rivista di Diritto Internazionale*, 72, 2 (1989): 282-310.

MAREN, M., "From the Moroccan-controlled Western Sahara: while the search for a negotiated solution to the war in the Western Sahara continues, Morocco is investing vast amounts of money and effort to make its occupation of the territory a fait accompli", *Africa Report*, n° 29 (1984): 32-35.

MARIÑO MENÉNDEZ, F.M., "El conflicto del Sahara Occidental desde una perspectiva histórica", in *Procesos de cambio y retos pendientes: Este de Europa, China y Sahara Occidental*, Centro Pignatelli (ed.), Zaragoza (1991): 179-188.

MARIÑO MENÉNDEZ, F.M., "El Derecho Internacional y la actual situación del Sáhara Occidental", *Africa-América Latina, Cuadernos*, n° 6 (1991): 47-54.

MARIÑO MENÉNDEZ, F.M., "Responsabilidad e irresponsabilidad de los Estados y Derecho Internacional", in *Hacia un nuevo orden internacional y Europeo* (Libro homenaje al profesor M.DÍEZ DE VELASCO), Tecnos, Madrid (1993): 473-488.

MARIÑO MENÉNDEZ, F.M., "Naciones Unidas y el Derecho de Autodeterminación", in *Balance y Perspectivas de Naciones Unidas en el Cincuentenario de su creación* (ed. F.MARIÑO, BOE), Madrid (1996): 77-110.

MARKS, J., "Western Sahara: Africa's forgotten war", *Africa Report*, n° 32 (1987): 16-19.

MARQUINA BARRIO, A., "El conflicto del Sáhara y la cooperación global del Gobierno español con Argelia y Marruecos", *Revista de Estudios Internacionales*, vol. 4, n. 4 (1983): 755-773.

MARQUINA BARRIO, A., "El Tratado libio-marroquí, repercusiones e incidencia en la política exterior española", *Revista de Estudios Internacionales*, vol.6, n° 1 (1985): 125-136.

MARQUINA, A., ECHEVERRIA, C., "La politique de l'Espagne au Maghreb", *Monde Arabe: Maghreb-Machrek*, n° 137, Juil/Sept. (1992): 43-55.

MARTIN, L., "Sahara: Hassan viola el plan de paz", *Iniciativa Socialista*, 19 (1992): 37-41.

MARTÍNEZ LILLO, P., ARIAS CAREAGA, S., TANARRO ALONSO, C. and WEINGÄRTNER, S., eds., *Universidad y Sahara Occidental: Reflexiones para la solución de un conflicto*, Cuadernos Solidarios 6, Universidad Autónoma de Madrid, Madrid, 2010.

MARTÍNEZ LILLO, P., ARIAS CAREAGA, S., TANARRO ALONSO, C. and WEINGÄRTNER, S., eds., *Memoria y tiempo presente del Sahara Occidental: Política, cooperación y cultura*, Cuadernos Solidarios 8, Universidad Autónoma de Madrid, Madrid, 2012.

MARTÍNEZ MILLAN, J.M., "Las pesquerías canario-africanas en el engranaje del africanismo español (1860-1910), *A.W.R.A.Q.*, n.11 (1990): 97-122.

MARTÍNEZ MILLAN, J.M., "La descolonización del Sáhara Occidental", *Espacio, tiempo y forma, Historia Contemporánea*, n° 5, t. 4 (1991):191-199.

MATHY, D., "L'Autodetermination de petits territorires revendiqués par des Etats tiers" (Premiére partie), *R.B.D.I.*, vol. X, 1 (1974): 166-205.

MATHY, D., "L'Autodetermination de petits territorires revendiqués par des Etats tiers" (deuxième partie), *R.B.D.I.*, vol. XI, 1 (1975): 129-160.

McCORQUODALE, R., "Self-Determination: A Human Approach", *I.&C.L.Q.*, vol. 43, 4, October (1994): 857-885.

MENDEZ DE VALDIVIA, M., "Tensiones en el Maghreb", *Affers internacionals*, n. 6 (1985): 55-69.

MERCER, J., "The Sahrawis of Western Sahara", *Minority Rights Group*, Report n° 40, London, February (1979).

MESA GARRIDO, R., "Algunos problemas coloniales del siglo XIX", *R.E.D.I.*, vol. XLIII, 3 (1965): 380-414.

MESA GARRIDO, R., "Las fronteras de la descolonización: reflexiones en torno al conflicto argelino-marroquí", *R.E.D.I.*, 2 (1966): 51-76.

MIAJA DE LA MUELA, A., "La descolonización en la Organización de las Naciones Unidas", in *ONU Año XX (1946-1966)*, Madrid (1966): 306-340.

MIAJA DE LA MUELA, A., "La descolonización y el derecho a la descolonización en la Organización de las Naciones Unidas", *R.E.D.I.*, vol. XXIV, núm.I-2 (1971): 207-240.

MIGUEZ, A., "Le Sahara occidental et la politique maghrébine de l'Espagne", *Politique Etrangère*, n°. 2 (1978): 173-180.

MILANO, E., "The New Fisheries Partnership Agreement between the European Community and the Kingdom of Morocco: Fishing Too South?", *Anuario de Derecho Internacional* 22 (2006): 413-457.

MILUTINOVIC, Z., "In search for solutions", *Review of International Affairs*, 35 (816), 5 April (1984): 20-22.

MONCONDUIT, F., "L'accord du 15 août 1962 entre la République d'Indonésie et le Royaume des Pays-Bas relatif à la Nouvelle-Guinée Occidentale (Irian occidental)", *A.F.D.I* (1962): 491-512.

MONIER, C., "Sahara Occidental. Sixième "mur" de défense marocain: Vers une modification de l´equilibre regional au Maghreb?", *Defense Nationale*, Juillet (1987): 167-168.

MOORSON, R., "El Decreto núm. 1 y la protección de los recursos agrícolas y pesqueros de Namibia", *Simposio regional sobre las medidas internacionales encaminadas a aplicar el Decreto núm. 1 para la protección de los recursos naturales de Namibia*, Naciones Unidas, Ginebra (1984), New York (1985).

MORALES LEZCANO, V., "El africanismo español (1860-1975)", in *España y el Norte de Africa: El Protectorado en Marruecos (1912-1956)*, Madrid, UNED (1986).

MORENO LÓPEZ, M.A., "Sahara Español: una descolonización controvertida", *R.P.I.*, 139, Mayo-Junio (1975): 73-91.

MORILLAS, J., "La República Saharaui independiente: su viabilidad económica", *Africa América Latina Cuadernos*, n° 6 (1991): 35-37.

MORILLAS, J., "El Sahara, la tajada española", *Historia 16*, n° 10 (106) (1985): 75-82.

MORTIMER, R.A., "Maghreb matters", *Foreign Policy*, n° 76, Fall (1989): 160-175.

MORTIMER, R.A., "The Greater Maghreb and the Western Sahara"en la obra colectiva *International dimensions of the Western Sahara Conflict*, Ed. by Zoubir, Yahia H. & Volman, D., Westport (1993): 169-186.

MOYOSORE, T., "The United Nations and Namibia", *Nigerian Forum*, vol. 9, núm. 7/8 (1989): 221-229.

MUNCH, F., "Walvis Bay, un arbitrage peu connu", *Mélanges Morelli, Communicazioni et studi*, t.1, Milán (1975): 607-625.

MUNDY, J., "Neutrality or Complicity? The United States and the 1975 Moroccan Takeover of the Spanish Sahara", *Journal of North African Studies* 11 (2006): 275–306.

MUNDY, J., "The Morocco-Polisario War for Western Sahara, 1975–1991." In *Conflict and Insurgency in the Contemporary Middle East.* Edited by Barry Rubin, Milton Park, Routledge (2009): 209–231.

MURSWIEK, D., "The issue of a Right of Secession-Reconsidered", en la obra colectiva *Modern Law of Self-Determination,* Ed. TOMUSCHAT, C., Martinus Nijhoff Publishers, Dordrecht/Boston/London (1993): 21-40.

NACIONES UNIDAS (Departamento de Asuntos Políticos, Administración Fiduciaria y Descolonización), "Participación de las Naciones Unidas en consultas populares y elecciones", *Descolonización,* n° 19, Diciembre (1983): 2 et seq.

NALDI, G. J., "The OAU and the Saharan Arab Democratic Republic", *Journal of African Law,* vol. 26, (1982): 152-162.

NALDI, G. J., "Peace-keeping attempts by the Organisation of African Unity", *International and Comparative Law Quarterly,* n° 34 (1985): 593-601.

NALDI, G.J., "The Statehood of the Saharan Arab Democratic Republic", *Indian Journal of International Law,* vol. 25 (1985): 448-481.

NAVARRO BATISTA, N., "La práctica comunitaria sobre reconocimiento de Estados: nuevas tendencias", *Revista de Instituciones Europeas,* Madrid (1995): 475-507.

NAYLOR, P.C., "Spain and France and the Decolonization of Western Sahara: Parity and Paradox, 1975-87", *Africa Today,* n° 34, Third Quarter (1987): 7-16.

NDIAYE, B., "Avis de la C.I.J. sur le Sahara Occidental 16 octobre 1975", *Revue Sénégalaise de Droit,* 10 (1976): 31-53.

NISOT, J., "La Namibie et la Court Internationale de Justice: l'avis consultatif du 21 juin 1971", *R.G.D.I.P.* (1971): 940-943.

N'KOLOMBUA, A., "L'ambivalence des relations entre le droit des peuples à disposer d'eux-mêmes et l'intégrité territoriale des Etats en Droit international contemporain", en *Mélanges offerts a Charles Chaumont. Le Droit des peuples à disposer d'eux-mêmes,* Paris (1984): 433-464.

OLIVER LOPEZ-GUARCH, P., "R.A.S.D.: origen y formación de un Estado", *Cuadernos de Historia Contemporánea,* 11 (1989): 127-141.

OLSSON, C., ed. *The Western Sahara Conflict: The Role of Natural Resources in Decolonization*, Current African Issues 33. Uppsala, Sweden: Nordic Africa Institute (2006).

ONU, *La cuestión del Sahara Occidental en las Naciones Unidas*, Departamento de Asuntos Políticos, Administración Fiduciaria, y Descolonización, n° 17, Octubre (1980).

ORTEGA TEROL, J.M., "Una operación de mantenimiento de la paz: la MINURSO", *A.D.I.*, XI (1995): 317-326.

OSTERUD, O., "War termination in the Western Sahara", *Bulletin of Peace Proposals*, vol. 20 (1989): 310-317.

PADRON, N., "El Sahara, compromiso moral y político de Occidente", *Tiempo de Paz*, n. 13 (1989): 77-80.

PANGALANAN, R. and AGUILING, E.H., "The privileged status of National Liberation Mouvements under International Law", *Philippine Law Journal*, t. 58 (1983): 44-65.

PARKER, R..B., "U.S. strategic interests and the war in the Western Sahara", in *International dimensions of the Western Sahara Conflict*, Edited by Zoubir, Yahia H. & Volman, D., Westport (1993): 93-102.

PARTINGTON, E.A., "Walvis Bay: South Africa's Claims to Sovereignity", *Denver Journal of International Law & Policy*, vol. 16, núm. 2/3 (1988): 247-321.

PAYNE, B.A., "The Western Sahara: International Legal Issues" en la obra colectiva *International dimensions of the Western Sahara Conflict*", Edited by Zoubir, Yahia H. & Volman, D., Westport (1993): 127-150.

PAZ SANCHEZ, M., CARMONA CALERO, E., "La colonia de Rio de Oro (Sahara Español) a principios del Siglo XX. Situación general y perspectivas Tebeto", *Anuario del archivo histórico insular de Fuerteventura*, n° 4, (1991): 131-159.

PAZZANITA, A.G., "Legal aspects of membership in the Organization of African Unity: the case of Western Sahara", *Case Western Reserve Journal of International Law*, 17 (1), Winter (1985): 123-158.

PAZZANITA, A.G., "The proposed referendum in the Western Sahara: Background, Developments, and Prospects", en la obra colectiva *International dimensions of the Western Sahara Conflict*, Ed. ZOUBIR, Yahia H., & VOLMAN, D., Westport (1993): 187-226.

PELAEZ MARON, J.M., "Les Malouines: une plaie faussement cicatrisée", *A.F.D.I.*, vol. XL (1994): 194-215.

PENEDO, S.L., "La otra cara de Marruecos", *Derechos Humanos*, (41) (1993): 43-44.

PEREZ RODRIGUEZ, M., "La problemática del Sahara Occidental: aproximación jurídica del conflicto", *I Jornadas de Derecho Internacional: Problemática del Sáhara Occidental*, Ilustre Colegio de Abogados de Las Palmas, VB ediciones, S.L., Las Palmas (1995): 27-29.

PEREZ VERA, E., "La Sentencia del Tribunal Internacional de Justicia sobre el Sudoeste Africano y la XXI Asamblea General de las Naciones Unidas", *R.E.D.I.*, vol. XX, núm. 2, abril-junio (1967): 247-268.

PERSAUD, M., "Namibia and the International Court of justice", *Current History*, Vol. 68 (1975): 220-225.

PETKOVIC, R., "Intégrité territoriale et droit à l'auto-détérmination en Afrique", *Revue de Politique Internationale* (1969): 350-363.

PICONE, P., "Il peace-keeping nel mondo attuale: tra militarizzazione e amministrazione fiduciaria", *Rivista di Diritto Internazionale*, 1 (1996): 5-33.

PIGRAU I SOLE, A., "El proceso de libre determinación de Namibia", en *R.E.D.I.*, vol. XLII, 1 (1990): 43-79.

PIGRAU I SOLE, A., "Culminación del Plan de Naciones Unidas para la independencia de Namibia", *R.E.D.I.*, vol. XLII, 1 (1990): 319-320.

PIMONT, Y., "La Nouvelle Calédonie et le Droit Constitutionnel", *International and Comparative Law Quarterly* (1992): 1687 et seq.

PINHO CAMPINOS, J., "L'actualité de l'*uti possidetis*", Societé Française pour la Droit International, Colloque de Poitiers, *"La Frontière"*, Ed. Pedone, Paris (1980): 95-111.

POMERANCE, M., "The United States and Self-Determination: perspectives on the wilsonian conception", *A.J.I.L.*, vol. 70 (1974): 1-27.

PUENTE EGIDO, J., "Consideraciones sobre la naturaleza y efectos de las Opiniones Consultivas", *Zeitschrift für Ausländisches Offentliches Recht und Völkerrecht, 1971, Band* 31.

QUEL LOPEZ, F.J., "La práctica reciente en materia de reconocimiento de Estados: Problemas en presencia", *Cursos de Derecho Internacional de Vitoria-Gasteiz*, Servicio Editorial de la Universidad del País Vasco, Vitoria-Gasteiz (1992): 39-82.

RAFIQUL I., "The recent self-determination referendum in New Caledonia: terms militating against its validity", *Melanesian Law Journal*, vol. 15 (1987): 136-153.

RAMBAUD, P., "La définition de l'aggression par l'ONU", *R.G.D.I.P.*, vol. II (1976): 835-881.

REISMAN, W.M., "Sovereignity and human rights in contemporary international law", *A.J.I.L.*, 4, (1990): 866-876.

REMIRO BROTONS, A., "Rondó Sahariano", *Meridiano Ceri*, n. 17, Octubre (1997): 3.

RICHARDSON, D.B., "War for Sahara riches: another test for Carter; more is at stake than new arms for Morocco; America's oil supplies and U.S. prestige in the Middle East also hang in the balance", *U.S. News & World Report*, n. 87 (1979): 55-56.

RIEDEL, E.H., "Confrontation in Western Sahara in the Light of the Advisory Opinion of the International Court of Justice of 16 October 1975. A Critical Appraisal", *G.Y.I.L.*, vol. 19 (1976): 405-442.

RIGAUX, F., "Le Décret sur les ressources naturelles de la Namibie adopté le 27 de septembre de 1974 par le Conseil des Nations Unies pour la Namibie", *Revue des Droits de l'Homme*, vol. IX, num. 2-3 (1976): 23-31.

RIGAUX, F., "East Timor and Western Sahara: a comparative view", *International Law and the Question of East Timor*, Catholic Institute for International Relations & International Platform of Jurist for East Timor (1995): 166-173.

RIKHYE, I.I., "The future of Peacekeeping", in *The United Nations and Peacekeeping*, Rikhye, I.J. and Skielsbaek, K. (eds.), Ed. Macmillan, 1990.

RIQUELME CORTADO, R. M., "Ciclo de conferencias organizado por el Departamento de Derecho Internacional sobre el principio de la libre de los pueblos", *Anales de Derecho de la Universidad de Murcia*, vol. 2 (1978): 209-217.

RIQUELME CORTADO, R., "La soberanía permanente del pueblo saharaui sobre sus recursos naturales", *Cursos de Derecho Internacional y Relaciones Internacionales de Vitoria-Gasteiz*, 31 (2011): 387–451.

RIQUELME CORTADO, R., "Derechos humanos y recursos naturales a la sombra de la berma", in *Estudios de Derecho Internacional y Derecho Europeo en homenaje al profesor Manuel Pérez González*. 2 vols. Edited by Jorge Cardona, Jorge Antonio Pueyo, José Luis Rodríguez-Villasante, and José Manuel Sobrino, Valencia, Tirant lo Blanch (2012): 1167–1194.

RIQUELME CORTADO, R., "Marruecos frente a la (des)colonización del Sahara Occidental", *Anuario Mexicano de Derecho Internacional* 13 (2013): 205-265.

ROBINEAULT, B., "Polisario and Western Sahara", *International Perpsectives*, 17 (2) Mars/April (1988): 14-16.

RODRIGUEZ DE VIGURI GIL, L., Intervención en las Jornadas sobre el 4° aniversario de los acuerdos tripartitos de Madrid, ASOCIACION DE AMIGOS DEL SAHARA, *Madrid, 14 de Noviembre de 1975: la traición*, Ed. Sedersa, Madrid (1980).

RONDOT, P., "L'Afrique arabe en 1985: apercu politique, conflits multiples", *Marchés Tropicaux et Mediterraneens*, n. 42 (1986): 108-112.

RONZITTI, N., "Wars of National Liberation. A legal definition", *I.Y.I.L.* (1975): 142-165.

RONZITTI, N., "Resort to force in wars of national liberation", en la obra colectiva *Current Problems of International Law*, A. CASSESE (comp.), Dordrecht (1985): 319-353.

ROOSENS, C., "La question du Sahara Occidental", *Studia Diplomatica*, 32 (1979): 513-533.

ROSENNE, "La participation à la Convention des Nations Unies sur le droit de la mer", in BARDONET et TOMUSCHAT, Martinus Nijhoff Publishers, Dordrecht/Boston/London (1993): 225-252.

ROUSSEAU, Ch., "Révocation du mandat de l'Afrique du Sud sur le Sud-ouest africain par l'Assamblée Générale des Nations Unies (27 octobre 1966)", *R.G.D.I.P.* (1967): 212-256.

RUBINO, P., "Colonialism and the use of force by the States", in *The Current Legal Regulation of the Use of Force*, A.CASSESE (comp.), Dordrecht (1986): 133-145.

RUCZ, C., "Un réferendum au Sahara occidental?", *A.F.D.I.*, vol. XL (1994): 243-259.

RUDDY, F., *Review of United Nations Operations and Peacekeeping*, statement before Subcommittee on the Departments of Commerce, Justice and State, the Judiciary and Related Agencies, January 25 (1995).

RUGGIE, J. G., "Wandering in the void: Charting the United Nations's new strategic role, *Foreign Affairs*, n° 72, Nov./Dec. (1993): 26-31.

RUILOBA SANTANA, E., "Notas sobre un caso de descolonización: El Sahara Español", *A.D.I.*, vol. I (1974): 335-346.

RUILOBA SANTANA, E., "Una nueva categoría en el panorama de la subjetividad internacional: el concepto de pueblo", *Estudios de Derecho Internacional. Homenaje al profesor MIAJA DE LA MUELA*, vol. I. Madrid (1979): 303-336.

RUIZ FABRI, H., "Genèse et disparition de l'Etat à l'epoque contemporaine", *A.F.D.I.*, vol. XXXVIII (1992): 153-178.

RUIZ MIGUEL, C., "La *tercera vía* ante el Derecho constitucional marroquí: una autonomía imposible" (http://sahara_opinions.site.voila.fr).

RUIZ MIGUEL, C., "La propuesta marroquí de autonomía para el Sahara occidental de 2007: una antigua propuesta sin credibilidad", *Revista d'Estudis Autonòmics i Federals*, num. 7, October 2008, p. 268-291.

RUPÉREZ, J., "La política exterior de la transición", *Cuenta y Razón*, n° 41, 12 (1988): 53.

SALAS LARRAZABAL, R., "El Sahara. La solución... Mañana", *Anales de la Real Academia de Ciencias Morales y Políticas*, n° 42 (67) (1990): 175-210.

SÁNCHEZ RODRIGUEZ, L.I., "*Uti possidetis*: la reactualización jurisprudencial de un viejo principio (a propósito de la Sentencia del TIJ (Sala) en el asunto Burkina Fasso/República de Mali)", *R.E.D.I.*, vol. XL, 2 (1988): 121-151.

SÁNCHEZ RODRÍGUEZ, L.I., "Las operaciones de mantenimiento de la paz: aspectos actuales", in *Balance y perspectivas de Naciones Unidas en el Cincuentenario de su creación*, ed. F. MARIÑO, BOE, Madrid (1996): 189-204.

SANTOS, A., "Le basculement vers le sud de la politique de defense de l'Espagne", *Affers Internacionals*, n° 7 (1985): 23-46.

SANTUCCI, J.C., "La question saharienne dans la vie politique marocaine", in *Enjeux Sahariens* (Table ronde du CRESM, nov. 1981), Ed. Centre National de la Recherche Scientifique, Paris (1984): 185-193.

SAYED, B.M., "Europa y el Maghreb en la perspectiva de la República Arabe Saharaui Democrática", *Estudios Africanos. Revista de la Asociacion Española de Africanistas*, 4 (7) (1989): 111-115.

SCHMIDT-JORTZIG, E., "The Constitution of Namibia: An Example of a State Emerging under Close Supervision and World Scrutiny", *G.Y.I.L*, vol. 34 (1991): 413-428.

SCHOENBERG, H.O., "Limits of Self-Determination", *Israel Yearbook of Human Rights*, vol. 6 (1976): 91-103.

SCHRIJVER, N.J., "La situación de Namibia y de sus recursos naturales en el ámbito del Derecho internacional", en *Simposio regional sobre las medidas internacionales encaminadas a aplicar el Decreto núm. 1 para la protección de los recursos naturales de Namibia*. Ginebra, 27 a 31 de agosto de 1984. Naciones Unidas. Nueva York (1985).

SEDDON, D., "Morocco and the Western Sahara", *Review of African Political Economy*, n. 38, April (1978): 24-47.

SEDDON, D., "Polisario and the struggle for the Western Sahara: recent developments, 1987-1989", *Review of African Political Economy*, n° 45/46, (1989): 132-142.

SEDDON, D., "Briefing: Western Sahara Tog-of-War", *Review of African Political Economy*, n° 52 (1991): 110 et seq.

SHAW, M., "The Western Sahara case", *B.Y.I.L.*, 49 (1978): 119-154.

SIMA, B., *The Charter of the United Nations. A commentary*, Oxford University Press, Oxford (1994).

SIMPSON, Ch., "Western Sahara: a land in limbo", *Africa Report*, n° 37 (1992): 68-70.

SMITH, T.K., "Western Sahara: Africa's forgotten war", *Africa Today*, n° 34, Third Quarter (1987): 5-6.

SOLARZ, S.J., "Arms for Morocco? [Conflicting interests of Morocco and Mauritania in the Western Sahara; United States decision to sell arms to Morocco]", *Foreign Affairs*, n°. 58, Winter (1979/1980): 278-299.

SONI, S., "Regimes for Namibia's Independence: A Comparative Study", en *Columbian Journal of Transnational Law*, vol. 29 (1991): 563-607.

SOREL, J.M., MEHDI, R., "L'*uti possidetis* entre la consécration juridique et la practique: essai de réactualization", *A.F.D.I.*, vol. XL (1994): 11-40.

SOROETA LICERAS, J., "La problemática de la nacionalidad de los habitantes de los territorios dependientes y el caso del Sahara Occidental. Análisis de la Sentencia del Tribunal Supremo de 28 de octubre de 1998", *Anuario de Derecho Internacional*, vol. XV (1999): 645-676.

SOROETA LICERAS, J., "El Derecho Internacional y el Derecho interno canadiense, ante el desafío de Quebec", *Cursos de Derechos Humanos de*

Donostia-San Sebastián, vol. I, Servicio de Publicaciones de la Universidad del País Vasco/Euskal Herriko Unibertsitatea, Bilbao (1999): 105-129.

SOROETA LICERAS, J., "La Unión Europea y el conflicto en el Sahara Occidental: Derecho Internacional y realpolitik", en la obra colectiva, GALINSOGA JORDÀ, A., (Dir.) *La vertebración de la Región Mediterránea: un reto para la Unión Europea. Una perspectiva global de la Conferencia de Barcelona de 1995*, Pp. CD-ROM (2002).

SOROETA LICERAS, J., "El plan de Paz del Sahara Occidental, ¿viaje a ninguna parte?", *Revista Electrónica de Estudios Internacionales*, n. 10 (2005): 1-33.

SOROETA LICERAS, J., "Una visión del conflicto palestino: bloqueo histórico, colapso jurídico y fracaso político", *Cursos de Derecho Internacional y Relaciones Internacionales de Vitoria-Gasteiz*, Servicio de Publicaciones de la UPV/EHU (2006): 261-332.

SOROETA LICERAS, J., "La posición de la Unión Europea en el conflicto del Sahara Occidental, una muestra palpable (más) de la primacía de sus intereses económicos y políticos sobre la promoción de la democracia y de los derechos humanos", *Revista de Derecho Comunitario Europeo*, núm. 34, Madrid, September/December (2009): 1-42.

SOROETA LICERAS, J., "La délimitation et l'exploitation des espaces maritimes du Sahara Occidental, un caillou (de plus) dans la chaussure des relations Espagnole-Marocain", in the collection *Protection maritime et violence dans la mer* (Directed by Sobrino Heredia, J.M.), Bruylant, Bruxelles (2011): 131–145.

SOROETA LICERAS, J., "Vigencia del Plan de Paz del Sahara Occidental (1991-2013)", in PALACIOS ROMEO, F. (coord.) *El derecho a la libre determinación del pueblo del Sahara Occidental. Del ius cogens al ius abutendi*, Thompson Reuters Aranzadi, Pamplona (2013): 199-226.

SOROETA LICERAS, J., "La condicionalidad política en los tratados internacionales entre la Unión Europea y los Estados del Mediterráneo Meridional", in *Intereses Públicos, Intereses Privados, su defensa y colisión en el Derecho Internacional* (Dir. Javier Quel López), Thompson Reuters Aranzadi, Pamplona (2013): 171-202.

SOROETA LICERAS, J., "El derecho a la libre determinación de los pueblos en el siglo XXI: entre la realidad y el deseo", *Cursos de Derecho Internacional y Relaciones Internacionales de Vitoria-Gasteiz*, Tecnos, Madrid (2013): 453-504.

SOROETA LICERAS, J., "Las Naciones Unidas, entre la *realpolitik* y el Derecho. Algunas reflexiones en torno al papel del Enviado Especial en los conflictos de Kosovo y del Sahara Occidental, in *El Derecho Internacional en el Mundo Multipolar del Siglo XXI. Obra Homenaje al Profesor Luis Ignacio Sánchez Rodríguez*, ed. Iprolex, Madrid (2013): 585-595.

SOTILLO LORENZO, J.A., "Sahara: la cuenta atrás", *Tiempo de paz*, n. 21 (1991): 122-125.

SOUDAN, F., "Les Americains et le Sahara", *Jeune Afrique*, n° 32 (1992): 16-18.

SOUDAN, F., "Sahara: quand un Americain s'en prend Maroc.", *Jeune Afrique*, n. 35 (1995): 16-18.

STANIC, S., "Morocco and Polisario: developments in the Western Maghreb", *Review of International Affairs*, 37 (868), 5 June (1986): 19-21.

SUR, S., "Les affaires des essais nucléaires", *R.G.D.I.P.*, n° 4 (1975): 3-56.

SUY, E., "The status of observers in International organizations", *Recueil des Cours*, II, t. 160 (1978): 83-179.

TCHIKAYA, R., "Charte Africaine des droits de l´homme et des peuples", *Etudes Internationales* (Tunisie), 40 (1991): 93-96.

THIERRY, H., "Les résolutions des organes internationaux dans la jurisprudence de la Court International de Justice", *Recueil des Cours*, II, t. 167 (1980): 387-446.

THIERRY, H., "Cour Général de Droit International Public", *Recueil des Cours*, III, v. 222 (1990): 9-186.

THORNBERRY, P., "Self-Determination, Minorities, Human Rights: A Review of International Instruments", *I.&C.L.Q.*, vol. 38, October (1989): 867-889.

THORNBERRY, P., "The Democratic or Internal Aspects of Self-Determination with some remarks on federalism", in *Modern Law of Self-Determination*, ed. Ch. TOMUSCHAT, Martinus Nijhoff Publishers, Dordrecht/Boston/London (1993): 101-138.

TIEWUL, S.A., "Relations between the UNO and the OAU in the settlement of secessionist conflicts", *H.I.L.J.*, 16 (1975): 259-302.

TOGORES SANCHEZ, L.E., "El alzamiento y la guerra civil (1936-1939) en las colonias Españolas de Guinea, Sidi Ifni y Sáhara", *Estudios africanos*, 3 (4-5) (1987/1988): 33-47.

TOMAS ORTIZ DE LA TORRE, J. "Sahara Occidental: ¿*Terra Nullius*?. Algunas bases jurídicas de investigación", *Revista General de Legislación y Jurisprudencia*, Junio (1975): 563-605.

TOMAS ORTIZ DE LA TORRE, J., "Recientes aspectos jurídico-internacionales del conflicto del Sahara", *Revista General de Legislación y Jurisprudencia*, n. 126 (1977): 555-590.

TOMUSCHAT, C., "Self-Determination in a Post-Colonial World", en la obra colectiva *Modern Law of Self-Determination*, Ed. TOMUSCHAT, C., Martinus Nijhoff Publishers, Dordrecht/Boston/London (1993): 1-20.

TORRES BERNARDEZ, S., "Territory, Acquisition", *Encyclopediae of Public International Law*, vol. 10, R. Bernhardt (ed.), Amsterdam (1987).

TORRES BERNÁRDEZ, S., "Perspectivas en la contribución de las Naciones Unidas al mantenimiento de la paz y la seguridad internacionales. Comentarios y observaciones sobre la Declaración de los miembros del Consejo de seguridad de 31 de enero de 1992", in *Hacia un nuevo orden internacional y europeo*, Homenaje al Profesor M.DIEZ DE VELASCO, Tecnos, Madrid (1993): 727-769.

TORRES BERNARDEZ, S., "The *Uti Posssidetis Iuris Principle* in Historical Perspective", en la obra colectiva *Völkerrecht zwischen normativem Anspruch und politischer Realität*, Duncker & Humblot, Berlin (1994).

TRONCOSO Y REIGADA, M., "La soberanía española en el Norte de Africa a la vista del Derecho Internacional", *Revista de la Facultad de Derecho de la Universidad Complutense de Madrid*, 74 (1988/1989): 663-724.

TURP, D., "Le droit de sécession en droit international public", *A.C.D.I.*, vol. XX (1982): 24-78.

UMOZURIKE, U.O., "The African Charter on Human people's rights", *A.J.I.L.*, n. 77 (1983): 906-912.

UNITED STATES, House of Representatives, Committee on Foreign Affairs, Report of a Staff Study Mission to Morocco, Algeria, the Western Sahara, and France, august 25- september, 6, 1982, *U.S. Policy Towards the Conflict in the Western Sahara*, Washington (1983).

VALLÉE, Ch., "L´affaire du Sahara Occidental devant la Cour Internationale de Justice", *Maghreb*, 71 (1976): 47-55.

VANCE, R.T.Jr., "Recognition as an Affirmative step in the Decolonization process: The Case of Western Sahara", *Yale Journal of World Public Order*, 7, n° 1, Fall (1980): 45-87.

VELLAS, P., "La diplomatie marocaine dans l´affaire du Sahara", *Politique Étrangère*, 1 (1978): 417-428.

VERDROSS, A., "La compétence nationale dans le cadre de l'ONU", *R.G.D.I.P.*, t. LXIX (1965): 314-325.

VERWEY, W.D., "Decolonization and ius ad Bellum: A Case Study on the Impact of the united Nations General Assembly on International Law", *Liber Amicorum B.V.A., Roling*, Leyden (1977): 121-140.

VIEJOBUENO SONIA, A.M., "Self-determination v. territorial integrity: The Falkland/Malvinas dispute with reference to recent cases in the United Nations", *S.A.Y.I.L.*, Vol. 16 (1990/1991): 312-366.

VIRALLY, M., "Droit International et décolonisation devant les Nations Unies", *A.F.D.I.*, vol. IX (1963): 508-541.

VIRALLY, M., "*Commentaire à l'article* 2.4", in *La Charte des Nations Unies*, (Dir. COT, J-P. et PELLET, A.), Ed. Economica / Bruylant, Paris / Bruxelles (1985): 113-125.

WEEXSTEEN, R., "La question du Sahara Occidental", *Annuaire de l´Afrique du Nord*, 15 (1976): 255-275.

WEEXSTEEN, R., "La question du Sahara Occidental", *Annuaire de l´Afrique du Nord*, 16 (1977): 425-449.

WEEXSTEEN, R., "L´OUA et la question saharienne", *Annuaire de l´Afrique du Nord*, 7 (1978): 213-237.

WEINER, J.B., "The green march in historical perspective [factors leading up to the march of 350,000 Moroccans into disputed areas of the Western Sahara, Nov. 1, 1975; based on conference paper]", *Middle East Journal*, n° 33, Winter (1979): 20-33.

WEINSTEIN, B., "The Western Sahara [policies of various countries towards the area and the effects of the guerrilla war]", *Current History*, n° 78 (1980): 110-114.

WENGER, M., "Reagan stakes Morocco in Sahara struggle", *Middle East Research & Info Project*, n. 12, May (1982): 22-26.

WILLIAMSON, R.S., "The United Nations as peacekeeper", *World Outlook*, Winter (1989): 26-47.

WILSON, C., ZOUBIR, Y., "Western Sahara: a foreign policy success waiting to happen", *Transafrica Forum*, n° 6 (3/4) Spring/Summer (1989): 27-39.

YACKEMTCHOUK, R., "A propos de quelques cas de reconnaissance d'Etat et de Gouvernement en Afrique", *R.B.D.I.*, 2, vol. VI (1970): 504-527.

YACKEMTCHOUK, R., "Les frontières africaines", *R.G.D.I.P.* (1970): 27-68.

YATA, F., "Maroc-France: les non-dits d'une relation ´privilegiee´", *Arabies*, Janvier (1995): 34-35.

ZARTMAN, I.W., "Conflict in the Sahara", SAIS Review (*Prospects for the Middle East* (1981/1982): 167-184.

ZICCARDI CAPALDO, G., "Il parere consultivo della Corte Internazionale di giustizia sul Sahara Occidentale: Un occasione per un riesame della natura e degli effetti della funzione consultiva", *Comunicazioni e Studi*, 15, (1978): 529-564.

ZOUBIR, Y., "Soviet Policy towards the Western Sahara Conflict", *Africa Today*, n° 34, Third Quarter, (1987): 17-32.

ZOUBIR, Y., "Moscow, the Maghreb, and conflict in the Western Sahara" in *International dimensions of the Western Sahara Conflict*, Edited by Zoubir, Yahia H. & Volman, D., Westport (1993): 103-126.

ZOUBIR, Y., PAZZANITA, A.G., "The United Nations' failure in resolving the Western Sahara conflict", *Middle East Journal*, n° 49, Autumn (1995): 614-628.

ZOUREK, J., "La définition de l'aggression et le Droit International. Développements récents de la question", *A.F.D.I.* (1974): 9-30.

ZOUREK, J., "La lutte d'un peuple en vue de faire prévaloir son droit à l'autodétermination constitue-t-elle au regard du Droit international un conflit interne ou un conflit de caractere international?", *Studi in Onore di Manlio Udina*, t. 1, Dott. A. Giuffrè ed., Milano (1975): 896-919.

ZUNES, S., "The United States and Marocco: the Sahara war and regional interests", *Arab Studies Quarterly*, 9 (4), Fall (1987): 422-441.

ZUNES, S., "Nationalism and Non-Alignment: The non-Ideology of the Polisario", *Africa Today*, n° 34, Third Quarter (1987): 33-46.

ZUNES, S., "Participatory democracy in the Sahara: a study of Polisario self-governance", *Scandinavian Journal of Development and Alternatives*, vol. 7 (1988): 141-156.

ZUNES, S., "The United States in the Saharan War: a case of low-intensity intervention", en la obra colectiva *International dimensions of the Western Sahara conflict*, Edited by Zoubir, Yahia H. & Volman, D., Westport (1993): 53-92.